THE RELIGIOUS EXPERIENCE OF
THE ROMAN PEOPLE

THE
RELIGIOUS EXPERIENCE

OF THE

ROMAN PEOPLE

FROM THE EARLIEST TIMES TO THE
AGE OF AUGUSTUS

THE GIFFORD LECTURES FOR 1909-10
DELIVERED IN EDINBURGH UNIVERSITY

BY

W. WARDE FOWLER, M.A.

FELLOW AND LATE SUB-RECTOR OF LINCOLN COLLEGE, OXFORD
HON. D.LITT. UNIVERSITY OF MANCHESTER
AUTHOR OF 'THE ROMAN FESTIVALS OF THE PERIOD OF THE REPUBLIC,' ETC.

" Sanctos ausus recludere fontes "

COOPER SQUARE PUBLISHERS, INC.
NEW YORK   1971

Originally Published 1911
Published 1971 by Cooper Square Publishers, Inc.
59 Fourth Avenue, New York, N. Y. 10003
International Standard Book No. 0-8154-0372-0
Library of Congress Catalog Card No. 71-145870

Printed in the United States of America

PREFACE

LORD GIFFORD in founding his lectureship directed that the lectures should be public and popular, *i.e.* not restricted to members of a University. Accordingly in lecturing I endeavoured to make myself intelligible to a general audience by avoiding much technical discussion and controversial matter, and by keeping to the plan of describing in outline the development and decay of the religion of the Roman City-state. And on the whole I have thought it better to keep to this principle in publishing the lectures ; they are printed for the most part much as they were delivered, and without footnotes, but at the end of each lecture students of the subject will find the notes referred to by the numbers in the text, containing such further information or discussion as has seemed desirable. My model in this method has been the admirable lectures of Prof. Cumont on " les Religions Orientales dans le Paganisme Romain."

I wish to make two remarks about the subject-matter of the lectures. First, the idea running through them is that the primitive religious (or magico-religious) instinct, which was the germ of the religion of the historical Romans, was gradually atrophied by over-elaboration of ritual, but showed itself again in strange forms from the period of the Punic wars onwards. For this religious instinct I have used the Latin word *religio*, as I have explained in the *Transactions of the Third International Congress for the History of Religions*, vol. ii. p. 169 foll.   I am, however, well aware that some scholars take a different view of the original meaning of this famous word, which has been much discussed since I formed my plan of lecturing.   But I do not think that those who differ from me on this point will find that my general argument is seriously affected one way or another by my use of the word.

Secondly, while I have been at work on the lectures, the idea seems to have been slowly gaining ground that the patrician religion of the early City-state, which became so highly formalised, so clean and austere, and eventually so political, was really the religion of an invading race, like that of the Achaeans in Greece, engrafted on the religion of a primitive and less civilised population. I have not definitely adopted this idea ; but I am inclined to think that a good deal of what I have said in the earlier lectures may be found to support it.   Once only, in Lecture XVII., I have used it myself to support a hypothesis there advanced.

I have retained the familiar English spelling of certain divine names, *e.g.* Jupiter (instead of Iuppiter), as less startling to British readers.

I wish to express my very deep obligations to the works of Prof. Wissowa and Dr. J. G. Frazer, and also to Mr. R. R. Marett, who gave me useful personal help in my second and third lectures.   From Prof. Wissowa and Dr. Frazer I have had the misfortune to differ on one or two points ; but " difference of opinion is the salt of life," as a great scholar said to me not long ago.   In reading the proofs I have had much kind and valuable help from my Oxford friends Mr. Cyril Bailey and Mr. A. S. L. Farquharson, who have read certain parts of the work, and

to whose suggestions I am greatly indebted.   The whole
has been read through by my old pupil Mr. Hugh Parr,
now of Clifton College, to whom my best thanks are due
for his timely discovery of many misprints and awkward
expressions.   The loyalty and goodwill of my old Oxford
pupils never seem to fail me.

W. W. F.

KINGHAM, OXON,
　　3rd March 1911.

CONTENTS

LECTURE I

INTRODUCTORY

LECTURE II

ON THE THRESHOLD OF RELIGION : SURVIVALS

xi

CONTENTS xiii

LECTURE VI

THE DIVINE OBJECTS OF WORSHIP

PAGE

LECTURE VII

THE DEITIES OF THE EARLIEST RELIGION :

GENERAL CHARACTERISTICS

LECTURE VIII

RITUAL OF THE IUS DIVINUM

LECTURE XII

THE PONTIFICES AND THE SECULARISATION OF RELIGION

LECTURE XIII

THE AUGURS AND THE ART OF DIVINATION

LECTURE XIV

THE HANNIBALIC WAR

LECTURE XV

AFTER THE HANNIBALIC WAR

LECTURE XVI

GREEK PHILOSOPHY AND ROMAN RELIGION

LECTURE XVII

MYSTICISM—IDEAS OF A FUTURE LIFE

LECTURE XVIII

RELIGIOUS FEELING IN THE POEMS OF VIRGIL

LECTURE XIX

THE AUGUSTAN REVIVAL

LECTURE XX

CONCLUSION

APPENDIX

LECTURE I

INTRODUCTORY

I was invited to prepare these lectures, on Lord Gifford's foundation, as one who has made a special study of the religious ideas and practice of the Roman people. So far as I know, the subject has not been touched upon as yet by any Gifford lecturer. We are in these days interested in every form of religion, from the most rudimentary to the most highly developed; from the ideas of the aborigines of Australia, which have now become the common property of anthropologists, to the ethical and spiritual religions of civilised man. Yet it is remarkable how few students of the history of religion, apart from one or two specialists, have been able to find anything instructive in the religion of the Romans—of the Romans, I mean, as distinguished from that vast collection of races and nationalities which eventually came to be called by the name of Rome. At the Congress for the History of Religions held at Oxford in 1908, out of scores of papers read and offered, not more than one or two even touched on the early religious ideas of the most practical and powerful people that the world has ever known.

This is due, in part at least, to the fact that just when Roman history begins to be of absorbing interest, and fairly well substantiated by evidence, the Roman religion, as religion, has already begun to lose its vitality, its purity, its efficacy. It has become overlaid with foreign rites and ideas, and it has also become a religious monopoly of the

State ; of which the essential characteristic, as Mommsen has well put it, and as we shall see later on, was " the conscious retention of the principles of the popular belief, which were recognised as irrational, for reasons of outward convenience."[1]   It was not unlike the religion of the Jews in the period immediately before the Captivity, and it was never to profit by the refining and chastening influence of such lengthy suffering.   In this later condition it has not been attractive to students of religious history ; and to penetrate farther back into the real religious ideas of the genuine Roman people is a task very far from easy, of which indeed the difficulties only seem to increase as we become more familiar with it.

It must be remarked, too, that as a consequence of this unattractiveness, the accounts given in standard works of the general features of this religion are rather chilling and repellent.   More than fifty years ago, in the first book of his *Roman History*, Mommsen so treated of it—not indeed without some reservation,—and in this matter, as in so many others, his view remained for many years the dominant one.   He looked at this religion, as was natural to him, from the point of view of law ; in religion as such he had no particular interest.   If I am not mistaken, it was for him, except in so far as it is connected with Roman law, the least interesting part of all his far-reaching Roman studies.   More recent writers of credit and ability have followed his lead, and stress has been laid on the legal side of religion at Rome ; it has been described over and over again as merely a system of contracts between gods and worshippers, secured by hard and literal formalism, and without ethical value or any native principle of growth.   Quite recently, for example, so great an authority as Professor Cumont has written of it thus :—

" Il n'a peut être jamais existé aucune religion aussi froide, aussi prosaïque que celle des Romains.   Subordonnée à la politique, elle cherche avant tout, par la stricte exécution de pratiques appropriées, à assurer à l'État la protection des dieux ou à détourner les effets de leur malveillance. Elle a conclu avec les puissances célestes un contrat synallagmatique d'où découlent des obligations réciproques : sacrifices d'une part, faveurs de l'autre. . . . Sa liturgie rappelle par la minutie de ses prescriptions l'ancien droit civil. Cette religion se défie des abandons de l'âme et des élans de la dévotion." And he finishes his description by quoting a few words of the late M. Jean Réville : " The legalism of the Pharisees, in spite of the dryness of their ritualistic minutiae, could make the heart vibrate more than the formalism of the Romans."[2]

Now it is not for me to deny the truth of such statements as this, though I might be disposed to say that it is rather approximate than complete truth as here expressed, does not sum up the whole story, and only holds good for a single epoch of this religious history. But surely, for anyone interested in the history of religion, a religious system of such an unusual kind, with characteristics so well marked, must, one would suppose, be itself an attractive subject. A religion that becomes highly formalised claims attention by this very characteristic. At one time, however far back, it must have accurately expressed the needs and the aspirations of the Roman people in their struggle for existence. It is obviously, as described by the writers I have quoted, a very mature growth, a highly developed system ; and the story, if we could recover it, of the way in which it came to be thus formalised, should be one of the deepest interest for students of the history of religion. Another story, too, that of the gradual discovery of the *inadequacy* of this system, and of the engrafting upon it, or substitution for it, of foreign rites and beliefs, is assuredly not less instructive ; and here, fortunately, our records make the task of telling it an easier one.

Now these two stories, taken together, sum up what we may call the *religious experience of the Roman people* ; and as it is upon these that I wish to concentrate your attention during this and the following course, I have called these lectures by that name. My plan is not to provide an exhaustive account of the details of the Roman worship or of the nature of the Roman gods : that can be found in the works of carefully trained specialists, of whom I shall have something to say presently. More in accordance with the intentions of the Founder of these lectures, I think, will be an attempt to follow out, with such detailed comment as may be necessary, the religious experience of the Romans, as an important part of their history. And this happens to coincide with my own inclination and training ; for I have been all my academic life occupied in learning and teaching Roman history, and the fascination which the study of the Roman religion has long had for me is simply due to this fact. Whatever may be the case with other religions, it is impossible to think of that of the Romans as detached from their history as a whole ; it is an integral part of the life and growth of the people. An adequate knowledge of Roman history, with all its difficulties and doubts, is the only scientific basis for the study of Roman religion, just as an adequate knowledge of Jewish history is the only scientific basis for a study of Jewish religion. The same rule must hold good in a greater or less degree with all other forms of religion of the higher type, and even when we are dealing with the religious ideas of savage peoples it is well to bear it steadfastly in mind. I may be excused for suggesting that in works on comparative religion and morals this principle is not always sufficiently realised, and that the panorama of religious or quasi-religious practice from all parts of the world, and found among peoples of very different stages of development, with which we are now so familiar, needs constant testing by increased knowledge of those peoples in all their relations of life. At any rate, in dealing with Roman evidence the investigator of religious history should also be a student of Roman history generally, for the facts of Roman life, public and private, are all closely concatenated together, and spring with an organic growth from the same root. The branches tend to separate, but the tree is of regular growth, compact in all its parts, and you cannot safely concentrate your attention on one of these parts to the comparative neglect of the rest. Conversely, too, the great story of the rise and decay of the Roman dominion cannot be properly understood without following out the religious history of this people—their religious experience, as I prefer to call it. To take an example of this, let me remind you of two leading facts in Roman history : first, the strength and tenacity of the family as a group under the absolute government of the paterfamilias; secondly, the strength and tenacity of the idea of the State as represented by the *imperium* of its magistrates. How different in these respects are the Romans from the Celts, the Scandinavians, even from the Greeks ! But these two facts are in great measure the result of the religious ideas of the people, and, on the other hand, they themselves react with astonishing force on the fortunes of that religion.

I do not indeed wish to be understood as maintaining that the religion of the Roman was the most important element in his mental or civic development : far from it. I should be the first to concede that the religious element in the Roman mind was not that part of it which has left the deepest impress on history, or contributed much, except in externals, to our modern ideas of the Divine and of worship. It is not, as Roman law was, the one great contribution of the Roman genius to the evolution of humanity. But Roman law and Roman religion sprang from the same root ; they were indeed in origin *one and the same thing*. Religious law was a part of the *ius civile*, and both were originally administered by the same authority, the Rex. Following the course of the two side by side for a few centuries, we come upon an astonishing phenomenon, which I will mention now (it will meet us again) as showing how far more interest can be aroused in our subject if we are fully equipped as Roman historians than if we were to study the religion alone, torn from the living body of the State, and placed on the dissecting-board by itself. As the State grew in population and importance, and came into contact, friendly or hostile, with other peoples, both the religion and the law of the State were called upon to expand, and they did so.   But they did so in different ways ; Roman law expanded *organically* and intensively, absorbing into its own body the experience and practice of other peoples, while Roman religion expanded *mechanically* and extensively, by taking on the deities and worship of others *without any organic change of its own being.*   Just as the English language has been able to absorb words of Latin origin, through its early contact with French, into the very tissue and fibre of its being, while German has for certain reasons never been able to do this, but has adopted them as strangers only, without making them its very own : so Roman law contrived to take into its own being the rules and practices of strangers, while Roman religion, though it eventually admitted the ideas and cults of Greeks and others, did so without taking them by a digestive process into its own system.   Had the law of Rome remained as inelastic as the religion, the Roman people would have advanced as little in civilisation as those races which embraced the faith of Islam, with its law and religion alike impermeable to any change.[3]   Here is a phenomenon that at once attracts attention and suggests questions not easy to answer. Why is it that the Roman religion can never have the same interest and value for mankind as Roman law ?   I hope that we shall find an answer to this question in the course of our studies : at this moment I only propose it as an example of the advantage gained for the study of one department of Roman life and thought by a pretty complete equipment in the knowledge of others.

At the same time we must remember that the religion of the Romans is a highly technical subject, like Roman law, the Roman constitution, and almost everything else Roman ; it calls for special knowledge as well as a sufficient training in Roman institutions generally.   Each of these Roman subjects is like a language with a delicate accidence, which is always presenting the unwary with pitfalls into which they are sure to blunder unless they have a thorough mastery of it.   I could mention a book full of valuable thoughts about the relation to Paganism of the early Christian Church, by a scholar at once learned and sympathetic ;[4] who when he happens to deal for a moment with the old Roman religion, is inaccurate and misleading at every point. He knew, for example, that this religion is built on the foundation of the worship of the family, but he yielded to the temptation to assume that the family in heaven was a counterpart of the family on earth, "as it might be seen in any palace of the Roman nobility." "Jupiter and Juno," he says, "were the lord and lady, and beneath them was an army of officers, attendants, ministers, of every rank and degree." Such a description of the pantheon of his religion would have utterly puzzled a Roman, even in the later days of theological syncretism. Again he says that this religion was strongly moral ; that "the gods gave every man his duty, and expected him to perform it." Here again no Roman of historical times, or indeed of any age, could have allowed this to be his creed. Had it really been so, not only the history of the Roman religion, but that of the Roman state, would have been very different from what it actually was.

The principles then on which I wish to proceed in these lectures are—(1) to keep the subject in continual touch with Roman history and the development of the Roman state ; (2) to exercise all possible care and accuracy in dealing with the technical matters of the religion itself. I may now go on to explain more exactly the plan I propose to follow.

It will greatly assist me in this explanation if I begin by making clear what I understand, for our present purposes, by the word *religion*. There have been many definitions propounded—more in recent years than ever before, owing to the recognition of the study of religion as a department of anthropology. Controversies are going on which call for new definitions, and it is only by slow degrees that we are arriving at any common understanding as to the real essential thing or fact for

which we should reserve this famous word, and other
words closely connected with it, *e.g.* the supernatural.
We are still disputing, for example, as to the relation of
religion to magic, and therefore as to the exact meaning
to be attributed to each of these terms.

Among the many definitions of religion which I have
met with, there is one which seems to me to be particularly helpful for our present purposes; it is contributed by an American investigator. "*Religion is the
effective desire to be in right relation to the Power manifesting itself in the universe.*" [5] Dr. Frazer's definition is
not different in essentials: "By religion I understand a
propitiation or conciliation of powers superior to man
which are believed to direct and control the course of
nature and of human life;" [6] only that here the word is
used of acts of worship rather than of the feeling or
desire that prompts them. The definition of the late
M. Jean Réville, in a chapter on "Religious Experience,"
written near the end of his valuable life, is in my view
nearer the mark, and more comprehensive. "Religion,"
he says, "is essentially a principle of life, the feeling of
a living relation between the human individual and the
powers or power of which the universe is the manifestation. What characterises each religion is its way of
looking upon this relation and its method of applying
it." [7] And a little further on he writes: "It is generally
admitted that this feeling of dependence upon the universe is the root of all religion." But this is not so
succinct as the definition which I quoted first, and it
introduces at least one term, *the individual*, which, for
certain good reasons, I think it will be better for us to
avoid in studying the early Roman religious ideas.

"*Religion is the effective desire to be in right relations
with the Power manifesting itself in the universe.*" This
has the advantage of treating religion as primarily and
essentially a *feeling*, an instinctive desire, and the word
"effective," skilfully introduced, suggests that this feeling
manifests itself in certain actions undertaken in order to

secure a desired end. Again, the phrase " right relations "
seems to me well chosen, and better than the " living
relation " of M. Réville, which if applied to the religions
of antiquity can only be understood in a sacramental
sense, and is not obviously so intended. " Right relation "
will cover all religious feeling, from the most material to
the most spiritual. Think for a moment of the 119th
Psalm, the high-water mark of the religious feeling of
the most religious people of antiquity ; it is a magnificent
declaration of conformity to the will of God, *i.e.* of the
desire to be in right relation to Him, to His statutes,
judgments, laws, commands, testimonies, righteousness.
This is religion in a high state of development ; but our
definition is so skilfully worded as to adapt itself readily
to much earlier and simpler forms. The " Power manifesting itself in the universe " may be taken as including
all the workings of nature, which even now we most
imperfectly understand, and which primitive man so little
understood that he misinterpreted them in a hundred
different ways. The effective desire to be in right relation with these mysterious powers, so that they might
not interfere with his material well-being—with his flocks
and herds, with his crops, too, if he were in the agricultural stage, with his dwelling and his land, or with
his city if he had got so far in social development—this
is what we may call the religious instinct, the origin of
what the Romans called *religio*.[8] The effective desire
to have your own will brought into conformity to the
will of a heavenly Father is a later development of the
same feeling ; to this the genuine Roman never attained,
and the Greek very imperfectly.

If we keep this definition steadily in mind, I think we
shall find it a valuable guide in following out what I call
the religious experience of the Roman people ; and at
the present moment it will help me to explain my plan
in drawing up these lectures. To begin with, in the
prehistoric age of Rome, so far as we can discern from
survivals of a later age, the feeling or desire must have

taken shape, ineffectively indeed, in many quaint acts, some of them magical or quasi-magical, and possibly taken over from an earlier and ruder population among whom the Latins settled.   Many of these continued, doubtless, to exist among the common folk, unauthorised by any constituted power, while some few were absorbed into the religious practice of the State, probably with the speedy loss of their original significance.   Such survivals of ineffective religion are of course to be found in the lowest stratum of the religious ideas of every people, ancient and modern; even among the Israelites,[9] and in the rites of Islam or Christianity.   They form, as it were, *a kind of protoplasm of religious vitality*, from which an organic growth was gradually developed.   But though they are necessarily a matter of investigation as survivals which have a story to tell, they do not carry us very far when we are tracing the religious experience of a people, and in any case the process of investigating them is one of groping in the dark.   I shall deal with these survivals in my next two lectures, and then leave them for good.

I am more immediately concerned with the desire expressed in our definition *when it has become more effective*; and this we find in the Latins when they have attained to a complete settlement on the land, and are well on in the agricultural stage of social development. This stage we can dimly see reflected in the life of the home and farm of later times; we have, I need hardly say, no contemporary evidence of it, though archaeology may yet yield us something.   But the conservatism of rural life is a familiar fact, and comes home to me when I reflect that in my own English village the main features of work and worship remained the same through many centuries, until we were revolutionised by the enclosure of the parish and the coming of the railroad in the middle of the nineteenth century.   The intense conservatism of rural Italy, up to the present day, has always been an acknowledged fact, and admits of easy explanation.   We may be sure that the Latin farmer,

before the City-state was developed, was like his descendants of historical times, the religious head of a family,
whose household deities were *effectively* worshipped by a
regular and orderly procedure, whose dead were cared
for in like manner, and whose land and stock were protected from malignant spirits by a boundary made sacred
by yearly rites of sacrifice and prayer. Doubtless these
wild spirits beyond his boundaries were a constant source
of anxiety to him ; doubtless charms and spells and
other survivals from the earlier stage were in use to keep
them from mischief; but these tend to become exceptions
in an orderly life of agricultural routine which we may
call *religious*. Spirits may accept domicile within the
limits of the farm, and tend, as always in this agricultural
stage, to become fixed to the soil and to take more
definite shape as in some sense deities. This stage—
that of the agricultural family—is the foundation of
Roman civilised life, in religious as in all other aspects,
and it will form the subject of my fourth lecture.

The growing effectiveness of the desire, as seen in
the family and in the agricultural stage, prepares us for
still greater effectiveness in the higher form of civilisation
which we know as that of the City-state. That desire,
let me say once more, is to be in right relations with the
Power manifesting itself in the universe. It is only in
the higher stages of civilisation that this desire can really
become effective ; social organisation, as I shall show,
produces an increased knowledge of the nature of the
Power, and with it a systematisation of the means
deemed necessary to secure the right relations. The
City-state, the peculiar form in which Greek and Italian
social and political life eventually blossomed and fructified,
was admirably fitted to secure this effectiveness. It was,
of course, an intensely *local* system ; and the result was,
first, that the Power is localised in certain spots and propitiated by certain forms of cult within the city wall,
thus bringing the divine into closest touch with the
human population and its interests ; and secondly, that

the concentration of intelligence and will-power within a
small space might, and did at Rome, develop a very
elaborate system for securing the right relations—in other
words, it produced a religious system as highly ritualistic
as that of the Jews.

With the several aspects of this system my fifth and
succeeding lectures will be occupied. I shall deal first
with the religious calendar of the earliest historical form
of the City-state, which most fortunately has come down
to us entire. I shall devote two lectures to the early
Roman ideas of divinity, and the character of their deities
as reflected in the calendar, and as further explained
by Roman and Greek writers of the literary age. Two
other lectures will discuss the ritual of sacrifice and
prayer, with the priests in charge of these ceremonies, and
the ritual of vows and of " purification." In each of these
I shall try to point out wherein the weakness of this
religious system lay—viz. in attempts at effectiveness so
elaborate that they overshot their mark, in a misconception
of the means necessary to secure the right relations, and
in a failure to grow in knowledge of the Power itself.

Lastly, as the City-state advances socially and politi-
cally, in trade and commerce, in alliance and conquest,
we shall find that the ideas of other peoples about the
Power, and their methods of propitiation, begin to be
adopted in addition to the native stock. The first stages
of this revolution will bring us to the conclusion of my
present course; but we shall be then well prepared for
what follows. For later on we shall find the Romans
feeling afresh the desire to be in right relation with the
Power, discovering that their own highly formalised system
is no longer equal to the work demanded of it, and pitiably
mistaking their true course in seeking a remedy. Their
knowledge of the Divine, always narrow and limited,
becomes by degrees blurred and obscured, and their sight
begins to fail them. I hope in due course to explain
this, and to give you some idea of the sadness of their
religious experience before the advent of an age of

philosophy, of theological syncretism, and of the worship of the rulers of the state.

Let us now turn for a few minutes to the special difficulties of our subject.   These are serious enough ; but they have been wonderfully and happily reduced since I began to be interested in the Roman religion some twenty-five years ago.   There were then only two really valuable books which dealt with the whole subject.   Though I could avail myself of many treatises, good and bad, on particular aspects of it, some few of which still survive, the only two comprehensive and illuminating books were Preller's *Römische Mythologie*, and Marquardt's volume on the cult in his *Staatsverwaltung*.   Both of these were then already many years old, but they had just been re-edited by two eminent scholars thoroughly well equipped for the task—Preller's work by H. Jordan, and Marquardt's by Georg Wissowa.   They were written from different points of view ; Preller dealt with the deities and the ideas about them rather than with the cults and the priests concerned with them ; while Marquardt treated the subject as a part of the administration of government, dealing with the worship and the *ius divinum*, and claiming that this was the only safe and true way of arriving at the ideas underlying that law and worship.[10]   Both books are still indispensable for the student ; but Marquardt's is the safer guide, as dealing with facts to the exclusion of fancies.   The two taken together had collected and sifted the evidence so far as it was then available.

The *Corpus Inscriptionum* had not at that time got very far, but its first volume, edited by Mommsen, contained the ancient Fasti, which supply us with the religious calendar of early Rome, and with other matter throwing light upon it.   This first volume was an invaluable help, and formed the basis (in a second edition) of the book I was eventually able to write on the *Roman Festivals of the Period of the Republic*.   At that time, too, in the 'eighties, Roscher's *Lexicon of Greek and Roman Mythology* began to appear, which aimed at summing up all that was then known about the deities of both peoples ; this is not even yet completed, and many of the earlier articles seem now almost antiquated, as propounding theories which have not met with general acceptance.   All these earlier articles are now being superseded by those in the new edition of Pauly's *Real-Encyclopädie,* edited by Wissowa.   Lastly, Wissowa himself in 1902 published a large volume entitled *Die Religion und Kultus der Römer,* which will probably be for many years the best and safest guide for all students of our subject.   Thoroughly trained in the methods of dealing with evidence both literary and archaeological, Wissowa produced a work which, though it has certain limitations, has the great merit of not being likely to lead anyone astray.   More skilfully and success-fully than any of his predecessors, he avoided the chief danger and difficulty that beset all who meddle with Roman religious antiquities, and invariably lead the unwary to their destruction ; he declined to accept as evidence what in nine cases out of ten is no true evidence at all—the statements of ancient authors influenced by Greek ideas and Greek fancy.   He holds in the main to the principle laid down by Marquardt, that we may use, as evidence for their religious ideas, what we are told that the Romans *did* in practising their worship, but must regard with suspicion, and subject to severe criticism, what either they themselves or the Greeks wrote about those religious ideas—that is, about divine beings and their doings.

It is indeed true that the one great difficulty of our subject lies in the nature of the evidence ; and it is one which we can never hope entirely to overcome.   We have always to bear in mind that the Romans produced no literature till the third century B.C. ; and the documentary evidence that survives from an earlier age in the form of inscriptions, or fragments of hymns or of ancient law (such as the calendar of which I spoke just now), is of the most meagre character, and usually most difficult to interpret.   Thus the Roman religion stands alone among the religions of ancient civilisations in that we are almost

entirely without surviving texts of its forms of prayer, of
its hymns or its legends; [11] even in Greece the Homeric
poems, with all the earliest Greek literature and art, make up
to some extent for the want of that documentary evidence
which throws a flood of light on the religions of Babylon,
Egypt, the Hindus, and the Jewish people. We know in
fact as little about the religion of the old Italian popula-
tions as we do about that of our own Teutonic ancestors,
less perhaps than we do about that of the Celtic peoples.
The Romans were a rude and warlike folk, and meddled
neither with literature nor philosophy until they came
into immediate contact with the Greeks ; thus it was that,
unfortunately for our purposes, the literary spirit, when at
last it was born in Italy, was rather Greek than Roman.
When that birth took place Rome had spread her influence
over Italy,—perhaps the greatest work she ever accomplished ; and thus the latest historian of Latin literature
can venture to write that "the greatest time in Roman
history was already past when real historical evidence
becomes available." [12]
We have thus to face two formidable facts : (1)
that the period covered by my earlier lectures must
in honesty be called prehistoric ; and (2) that when
the Romans themselves began to write about it they did
so under the overwhelming influence of Greek culture.
With few exceptions, all that we can learn of the early
Roman religion from Roman or Greek writers comes
to us, not in a pure Roman form, clearly conceived as
all things truly Roman were, but seen dimly through
the mist of the Hellenistic age. The Roman gods, for
example, are made the sport of fancy and the subject
of Hellenistic love-stories, by Greek poets and their
Roman imitators, [13] or are more seriously treated by Graeco-
Roman philosophy after a fashion which would have been
absolutely incomprehensible to the primitive men in whose
minds they first had their being. The process of dis-
entangling the Roman element from the Greek in the
literary evidence is one which can never be satisfactorily

accomplished ; and on the whole it is better, with Wissowa and Marquardt, to hold fast by the facts of the cult, where the distinction between the two is usually obvious, than to flounder about in a slough of what I can only call pseudo-evidence.   If all that English people knew about their Anglo-Saxon forefathers were derived from Norman-French chroniclers, how much should we really know about government or religion in the centuries before the Conquest!   And yet this comparison gives but a faint idea of the treacherous nature of the literary evidence I am speaking of.   It is true indeed that in the last age of the Republic a few Romans began to take something like a scientific interest in their own religious antiquities ; and to Varro, by far the most learned of these, and to Verrius Flaccus, who succeeded him in the Augustan age, we owe directly or indirectly almost all the solid facts on which our knowledge of the Roman worship rests.   But their works have come down to us in a most imperfect and fragmentary state, and what we have of them we owe mainly to the erudition of later grammarians and commentators, and the learning of the early Christian fathers, who drew upon them freely for illustrations of the absurdities of paganism.   And it must be added that when Varro himself deals with the Roman gods and the old ideas about them, he is by no means free from the inevitable influence of Greek thought.

Apart from the literary material and the few surviving fragments of religious law and ritual, there are two other sources of light of which we can now avail ourselves, archaeology and anthropology ; but it must be confessed that as yet their illuminating power is somewhat uncertain. It reminds the scrupulous investigator of those early days of the electric light, when its flickering tremulousness made it often painful to read by, and when, too, it might suddenly go out and leave the reader in darkness.   It is well to remember that both sciences are young, and have much of the self-confidence of youth ; and that Italian archaeology, now fast becoming well organised within

Italy, has also to be co-ordinated with the archaeology of the whole Mediterranean basin, before we can expect from it clear and unmistakable answers to hard questions about race and religion. This work, which cannot possibly be done by an individual without *co-operation*—the secret of sound work which the Germans have long ago discovered —is in course of being carried out, so far as is at present possible, by a syndicate of competent investigators.[14]

In order to indicate the uncertain nature of the light which for a long time to come is all we can expect from Italian archaeology, I have only to remind you that one of the chief questions we have to ask of it is the relation of the mysterious Etruscan people to the other Italian stocks, in respect of language, religion, and art. Whether the Etruscans were the same people whom the Greeks called Pelasgians, as many investigators now hold : whether the earliest Roman city was in any true sense an Etruscan one : these are questions on the answers to which it is not as yet safe to build further hypotheses. In regard to religion, too, we are still very much in the dark. For example, there are many Etruscan works of art in which Roman deities are portrayed, as is certain from the fact that their names accompany the figures ; but it is as yet almost impossible to determine how far we can use these for the interpretation of Roman religious ideas or legends. Many years ago a most attractive hypothesis was raised on the evidence of certain of these works of art, where Hercules and Juno appear together in a manner which strongly suggests that they are meant to represent the male and female principles of human life ; this hypothesis was taken up by early writers in the *Mythological Lexicon*, and relying upon them I adopted it in my *Roman Festivals*,[15] and further applied it to the interpretation of an unsolved problem in the fourth *Eclogue* of Virgil.[16] But since then doubt has been thrown on it by Wissowa, who had formerly accepted it. As being of Etruscan origin, and found in places very distant from each other and from Rome, we have, he says, no good right to use these works

C

of art as evidence for the Roman religion.[17]   The question remains open as to these and many other works of art, but the fact that the man of coolest judgment and most absolute honesty is doubtful, suggests that we had best wait patiently for more certain light.

In Rome itself, where archaeological study is concentrated and admirably staffed, great progress has been made, and much light thrown on the later periods of religious history.   But for the religion of the ancient Roman state, with which we are at present concerned, it must be confessed that very little has been gleaned. The most famous discovery is that recently made in the Forum of an archaic inscription which almost certainly relates to some religious act ; but as yet no scholar has been able to interpret it with anything approaching to certainty.[18]   More recently excavations on the further bank of the Tiber threw a glint of light on the nature of an ancient deity, Furrina, about whom till then we practically knew nothing at all ; but the evidence thus obtained was late and in Greek characters.   We must in fact entertain no great hopes of illumination from excavations, but accept thankfully what little may be vouchsafed to us.   On the other hand, from the gradual development of Italian archaeology as a whole, and, I must here add, from the study of the several old Italian languages, much may be expected in the future.

The other chief contributory science is anthropology, *i.e.* the study of the working of the mind of primitive man, as it is seen in the ideas and practices of uncivilised peoples at the present day, and also as it can be traced in survivals among more civilised races.   For the history of the religion of the Roman City - state its contribution must of necessity be a limited one ; that is a part of Roman history in general, and its material is purely Roman, or perhaps I should say, Graeco-Roman ; and Wissowa in all his work has consistently declined to admit the value of anthropological researches for the elucidation of Roman problems.   Perhaps it is for this very reason that his book is the safest guide we possess for the study of what the Romans did and thought in the matter of religion; but if we wish to try and get to the original significance of those acts and thoughts, it is absolutely impossible in these days to dispense with the works of a long series of anthropologists, many of them fortunately British, who have gradually been collecting and classifying the material which in the long run will fructify in definite results. If we consider the writings of eminent scholars who wrote about Greek and Roman religion and mythology before the appearance of Dr. Tylor's *Primitive Culture*— Klausen, Preuner, Preller, Kuhn, and many others, who worked on the comparative method but with slender material for the use of it—we see at once what an immense advance has been effected by that monumental work, and by the stimulus that it gave to others to follow the same track. Now we have in this country the works of Lang, Robertson Smith, Farnell, Frazer, Hartland, Jevons, and others, while a host of students on the Continent are writing in all languages on anthropological subjects. Some of these I shall quote incidentally in the course of these lectures; at present I will content myself with making one or two suggestions as to the care needed in using the collections and theories of anthropologists, as an aid in Roman religious studies.

First, let us bear in mind that anthropologists are apt to have their favourite theories—conclusions, that is, which are the legitimate result of reasoning inductively on the class of facts which they have more particularly studied. Thus Mannhardt had his theory of the Vegetation-spirit, Robertson Smith that of the sacramental meal, Usener that of the Sondergötter, Dr. Frazer that of divine Kingship; all of which are perfectly sound conclusions based on facts which no one disputes. They have been of the greatest value to anthropological research; but when they are applied to the explanation of Roman practices we should be instantly on our guard, ready indeed to welcome any glint of light that we may get from them, but most carefully critical and even suspicious of their application to other phenomena than those which originally suggested them.   It is in the nature of man as a researcher, when he has found a key, to hasten to apply it to all the doors he can find, and sometimes, it must be said, to use violence in the application ; and though the greatest masters of the science will rarely try to force the lock, they will use so much gentle persuasion as sometimes to make us fancy that they have unfastened it.   All such attempts have their value, but it behoves us to be cautious in accepting them.   The application by Mannhardt of the theory of the Vegetation-spirit to certain Roman problems, *e.g.* to that of the Lupercalia,[19] and the October horse,[20] must be allowed, fascinating as it was, to have failed in the main.   The application by Dr. Frazer of the theory of divine Kingship to the early religious history of Rome, is still *sub judice*, and calls for most careful and discriminating criticism.[21]

Secondly, as I have already said, Roman evidence is peculiarly difficult to handle, except in so far as it deals with the simple facts of worship ; when we use it for traditions, myths, ideas about the nature of divine beings, we need a training not only in the use of evidence in general, but in the use of Roman evidence in particular. Anthropologists, as a rule, have not been through such a training, and they are apt to handle the evidence of Roman writers with a light heart and rather a rough hand.   The result is that bits of evidence are put together, each needing conscientious criticism, to support hypotheses often of the flimsiest kind, which again are used to support further hypotheses, and so on, until the sober inquirer begins to feel his brain reeling and his footing giving way beneath him.   I shall have occasion to notice one or two examples of this uncritical use of evidence later on, and will say no more of it now.   No one can feel more grateful than I do to the many leading anthropologists who have touched in one way or another

on Roman evidence ; but for myself I try never to forget
the words of Columella, with which a great German
scholar began one of his most difficult investigations :
" In universa vita pretiosissimum est intellegere quemque
nescire se quod nesciat." [22]

NOTES TO LECTURE I

1. Mommsen, *Hist. of Rome* (*E. T.*), vol. ii. p. 433.

2. Cumont, *Les Religions orientales dans le paganisme romain*,
p. 36.   Cp. Dill, *Roman Society in the Last Century of the Western
Empire*, p. 63.   Gwatkin, *The Knowledge of God*, vol. ii. p. 133.

3. See some valuable remarks in Lord Cromer's *Modern Egypt*,
vol. ii. p. 135.

4. Since this lecture was written this scholar has passed away,
to the great grief of his many friends ; and I refrain from mentioning
his name.

5. Ira W. Howerth, in *International Journal of Ethics*, 1903,
p. 205.   I owe the reference to R. Karsten, *The Origin of Worship*,
Wasa, 1905, p. 2, note.   Cp. E. Caird, *Gifford Lectures* (" Evolution of Theology in the Greek Philosophers "), vol. i. p. 32.   " That
which underlies all forms of religion, from the highest to the lowest,
is the idea of God as an absolute power or principle."   To this
need only be added the desire to be in right relation to it.   Mr.
Marett's word " supernaturalism" seems to mean the same thing ;
" There arises in the region of human thought a powerful impulse
to objectify, and even to personify, the mysterious or supernatural
something felt ; and in the region of will a corresponding impulse
to render it innocuous, or, better still, propitious, by force of
constraint (*i.e.* magic), communion, or conciliation."   See his
Threshold of Religion, p. 11.   Prof. Haddon, commenting on this
(*Magic and Fetishism*, p. 93), adds that " there are thus produced
the two fundamental factors of religion, the belief in some mysterious
power, and the desire to enter into communication with the power
by means of worship."   Our succinct definition seems thus to be
adequate.

6. *The Golden Bough*, ed. 2, vol. i. p. 62.

7. *Liberal Protestantism*, p. 64.

8. For *religio* as a feeling essentially, see Wissowa, *Religion
und Kultus der Römer*, p. 318 (henceforward to be cited as *R.K.*).
For further development of the meaning of the word in Latin
literature, see the author's paper in *Proceedings of the Congress for
the History of Religions* (Oxford, 1908), vol. ii. p. 169 foll.   A
different view of the original meaning of the word is put forward by

W. Otto in *Archiv für Religionswissenschaft*, vol. xii., 1909, p. 533 (henceforward to be cited as *Archiv* simply).   See also below, p. 459 foll.

9. See, *e.g.*, Frazer in *Anthropological Essays presented to E. B. Tylor*, p. 101 foll.

10. *Staatsverwaltung*, iii. p. 2.   This will henceforward be cited as *Marquardt* simply.   It forms part of the great *Handbuch der römischen Alterthümer* of Mommsen and Marquardt, and is translated into French, but unfortunately not into English.   I may add here that I have only recently become acquainted with what was, at the time it was written, a remarkably good account of the Roman religion, full of insight as well as learning, viz. Döllinger's *The Gentile and the Jew*, Book VII. (vol. ii. of the English translation, 1906).

11. Two fragments of ancient carmina, *i.e.* formulae which are partly spells and partly hymns, survive—those of the Fratres Arvales and the Salii or dancing priests of Mars.   For surviving formulae of prayer see below, p. 185 foll.   Our chief authority on the ritual of prayer and sacrifice comes from Iguvium in Umbria, and is in the Umbrian dialect ; it will be referred to in Bücheler's *Umbrica* (1883), where a Latin translation will be found.   The Umbrian text revised by Prof. Conway forms an important part of that eminent scholar's work on the Italian dialects.

12. F. Leo, in *Die griechische und lateinische Literatur und Sprache*, p. 328.   Cp. Schanz, *Geschichte der röm. Literatur*, vol. i. p. 54 foll.

13. Among Roman poets Ovid is the worst offender, Propertius and Tibullus mislead in a less degree ; but they all make up for it to some extent by preserving for us features of the worship as it existed in their own day.   The confusion that has been caused in Roman religious history by mixing up Greek and Roman evidence is incalculable, and has recently been increased by Pais (*Storia di Roma*, and *Ancient Legends of Roman History*), and by Dr. Frazer in his lectures on the early history of Kingship—writers to whom in some ways we owe valuable hints for the elucidation of Roman problems. See also Soltau, *Die Anfänge der römischen Geschichtsschreibung*, 1909, p. 3.

14. Most welcome to English readers has been Mr. T. E. Peet's recently published volume on *The Stone and Bronze Ages in Italy*, and still more valuable for our purposes will be its sequel, when it appears, on the Iron Age.

15. *Roman Festivals*, p. 142 foll. ; henceforward to be cited as *R.F.*

16. See Virgil's *Messianic Eclogue*, by Mayor, Fowler, and Conway, p. 75 foll.

17. Wissowa, *R.K.* p. 227.

18. An account of this in English, with photographs, will be

found in Pais's *Ancient Legends of Roman History*, p. 21 foll., and notes.

19. Mannhardt, *Mythologische Forschungen*, p. 72 foll.

20. *Ibid.*, p. 156 foll.

21. *Lectures on the Early History of Kingship*, lectures 7-9.

22. Not long after these last sentences were written, a large work appeared by Dr. Binder, a German professor of law, entitled *Die Plebs*, which deals freely with the oldest Roman religion, and well illustrates the difficulties under which we have to work while archaeologists, ethnologists, and philologists are still constantly in disagreement as to almost every important question in the history of early Italian culture. Dr. Binder's main thesis is that the earliest Rome was composed of two distinct communities, each with its own religion, *i.e.* deities, priests, and sacra; the one settled on the Palatine, a pastoral folk of primitive culture, and of pure Latin race; the other settled on the Quirinal, Sabine in origin and language, and of more advanced development in social and religious matters. So far this sounds more or less familiar to us, but when Dr. Binder goes on to identify the Latin folk with the Plebs and the Sabine settlement with the Patricians, and calls in religion to help him with the proof of this, it is necessary to look very carefully into the religious evidence he adduces. So far as I can see, the limitation of the word *patrician* to the Quirinal settlement is very far from being proved by this evidence (see *The Year's Work in Classical Studies*, 1909, p. 69). Yet the hypothesis is an extremely interesting one, and were it generally accepted, would compel us to modify in some important points our ideas of Roman religious history, and also of Roman legal history, with which Dr. Binder is mainly concerned.

LECTURE II

MY subject proper is the religion of an organised State : the religious experience of a comparatively civilised people. But I wish, in the first place, to do what has never yet been done by those who have written on the Roman religion—I wish to take a survey of the. relics, surviving in later Roman practice and belief, of earlier stages of rudimentary religious experience. In these days of anthropological and sociological research, it is possible to do this without great difficulty ; and if I left it undone, our story of the development of religion at Rome would be mutilated at the beginning. Also we should be at a disadvantage in trying to realise the wonderful work done by the early authorities of the State in eliminating from their rule of worship (*ius divinum*) almost all that was magical, barbarous, or, as later Romans would have called it, superstitious. This is a point on which I wish to lay especial stress in the next few lectures, and it entails a somewhat tiresome account of the ideas and practices of which, as I believe, they sought to get rid. These, I may as well say at once, are to be found for the most part surviving, as we might expect, *outside* of the religion of the State ; where they survive within its limits, they will be found to have almost entirely lost their original force and meaning.

Every student of religious history knows that a religious system is a complex growth, far more complex than would appear at first sight ; that it is sure to contain relics of previous eras of human experience, embedded in the social strata as lifeless fossils. These only indeed survive because human nature is intensely conservative, especially in religious matters ; and of this conservative instinct the Romans afford as striking an example as we can readily find. They clung with extraordinary tenacity, all through their history, to old forms ; they seem to have had a kind of superstitious feeling that these dead forms had still a value as such, though all the life was gone out of them. It would be easy to illustrate this curious feature of the Roman mind from the history of its religion ; it never disappeared ; and to this day the Catholic church in Italy retains in a thinly-disguised form many of the religious practices of the Roman people.

Stage after stage must have been passed by the Latins long before our story rightly begins ; how many revolutions of thought they underwent, how much they learnt and took over from earlier inhabitants of the country in which they finally settled, we cannot even guess. As I said in the last lecture, we have no really ancient history of the Romans, as we have, for example, of the Egyptians or Babylonians ; to us it is all darkness, save where a little light has been thrown on the buried strata by archaeology and anthropology. That little light, which may be expected to increase in power, shows survivals here and there of primitive modes of thought ; and these I propose to deal with now in the following order. *Totemism* I shall mention merely to clear it out of the way ; but *taboo* will take us some little time, and so will *magic* in its various forms.

About totemism all I have to say is this. As I write, Dr. Frazer's great work on this subject has just appeared ; it is entirely occupied with totemism among modern savages, true totemic peoples, with the object of getting at the real principles of that curious stratum of human thought, and he leaves to others the discussion of possible survivals of it among Aryans, Semites, and

Egyptians.   He himself is sceptical about all the evidence
that has been adduced to prove its existence in classical
antiquity (see vol. i. p. 86 and vol. iv. p. 13). Under these
circumstances, and seeing that Dr. Frazer has always been
the accepted exponent of totemism in this country since
the epoch-making works appeared of Tylor and Robertson
Smith, it is obviously unnecessary for me either to
attempt to explain what it is, or to examine the attempts
to find survivals of it in ancient Italy.   When it first
became matter of interest to anthropologists it was only
natural that they should be apt to find it everywhere.   Dr.
Jevons, for example, following in the steps of Robertson
Smith, found plenty of totemistic survivals both in Greece
and Italy in writing his valuable *Introduction to the History
of Religion*; but he is now aware that he went too far in
this direction.   Quite recently there has been a run after
the same scent in France ; not long ago a French scholar
published a book on the ensigns of the Roman army,[1]
which originally represented certain animals, and using
Dr. Frazer's early work on totemism with a very imperfect knowledge of the subject, tried to prove that
these were originally totem signs.   Roman names of
families and old Italian tribe-names are still often quoted
as totemistic ; but the Fabii and Caepiones, named after
cultivated plants, and the Picentes and Hirpini, after
woodpecker and wolf, though tempting to the totemist,
have not persuaded Dr. Frazer to accept them as
totemistic, and may be left out of account here ; there
may be many reasons for the adoption of such names
besides the totemistic one.   In the course of the last
Congress of religious history, a sober French scholar,
M. Toutain, made an emphatic protest against the
prevailing tendency in France, of which the leading
representative is M. Salomon Reinach.[2]   Let us pass
on at once to the second primitive mode of thought which
I mentioned just now, and which is not nearly so remote
—speaking anthropologically—from classical times as
totemism.   Totemism belongs to a form of society, that

of tribe or clan, in which family life is unknown in our sense of the word, and it is therefore wholly remote from the life of the ancient Italian stocks, in whose social organisation the family was a leading fact ; but *taboo* seems rather to be a mode of thought common to primitive peoples up to a comparatively advanced stage of development, and has left its traces in all systems of religion, including those of the present day.

By this famous word *taboo*, of Polynesian origin, is to be understood a very important part of what I have called the protoplasm of primitive religion, and one closely allied both to magic and fetishism. For our present purposes we may define it as a mysterious influence believed to exist in objects both animate and inanimate, which makes them *dangerous, infectious, unclean, or holy*, which two last qualities are often almost identical in primitive thought, as Robertson Smith originally taught us.[3] What exactly the savage or semi-civilised mind thought about this influence we hardly yet know ; we have another Polynesian word, *mana*, which expresses conveniently its positive aspect, and may in time help us towards a better understanding of it.[4]   It is in origin pre-animistic, *i.e.* it is not so much believed to emanate from a *spirit* residing in the object, as from some occult miasmatic quality. All human beings in contact with other men or things possessing this quality are believed to suffer in some way, and to communicate the infection which they themselves receive. As Dr. Farnell says in his chapter on the ritual of purification,[5] "The sense-instinct that suggests all this was probably some primeval terror or aversion evoked by certain objects, as we see animals shrink with disgust at the sight or smell of blood. The nerves of savage man are strangely excited by certain stimuli of touch, smell, taste, sight ; the specially exciting object is something that we should call mysterious, weird, or uncanny."

Based on this notion of constant danger from infection, there arose a code of unwritten custom as rigid as that enforced by a careful physician in infectious cases at the present day ; and thus, too, in course of time there was developed the idea of the possibility of *disinfection*, an idea as salutary as the discovery in medical science of effective methods for the disinfection of disease. The code of taboo had an obvious ethical value, as Dr. Jevons pointed out long ago ;[6] like all discipline carried out with a social end in view, it helped men to realise that they were under obligations to the community of which they were a part, and that they would be visited by severe penalties if they neglected these duties. But it inevitably tended to forge a set of fetters binding and cramping the minds of its captives with a countless number of terrors ; life was full of constant anxiety, of that feeling expressed by the later Romans in the word *religio*,[7] which, as we shall see, probably had its origin in this period of primitive superstition. The only remedy is the *discovery of the means of disinfection*, or, as we commonly call it, of *purification* : a discovery which must have been going on for ages, and only finds its completion at Rome in the era of the City-state. We shall return to this part of the subject when we deal with the ritual of purification ; at present we must attend to certain survivals in that ritual which suggest that at one time the ancestors of the Roman people lived under this unwritten code of taboo.

Let us see, in the first place, how human beings were supposed to be affected by this mysterious influence under certain circumstances and at particular periods of their existence. As universally in primitive life, the new-born infant must originally have been taboo ; for every Roman child needed purification or disinfection, boys on the ninth, girls on the eighth day after birth. This day was called the *dies lustricus*, the day of a purificatory rite ; " est lustricus dies," says Macrobius, " *quo infantes lustrantur* et nomen accipiunt."[8] In historical times the naming of the child was doubtless the more practically important part of the ceremony ; though we may note in passing that the mystic value attaching to names, of which there are traces in Roman usage, may have even originally given that part a greater significance than we should naturally attribute to it.[9]   Again, when the child reaches the age of puberty, it is all the world over believed to be in a critical or dangerous condition, needing disinfection; of this idea, so far as I know, the later Romans show hardly a trace, but we may suppose that the ceremony of laying aside the *toga* of childhood, which was accompanied by a sacrifice, was a faint survival of some process of purification.[10]   Once more, after a death the whole family had to be purified with particular care from the contagion of the corpse,[11] which was here as everywhere taboo; a cypress bough was stuck over the door of the house of a noble family to give warning to any passing pontifex that he was not to enter it;[12] and those who followed the funeral cortège were purified by being sprinkled with water and by stepping over fire.[13] *Society had effectually protected itself against the miasma in all these cases by the discovery of the means of disinfection.*

One of the commonest forms of taboo is that on women, who, especially at certain periods, were apparently believed to be " infectious."[14]   Of this belief we have very distinct survivals in Roman ritual, which I must here be content to mention only, leaving details to trained anthropologists to explain.   We find them both in *sacra privata* and *sacra publica*.   Cato has preserved the formula for the propitiation of Mars Silvanus in the private rites of the farm; it is to take place *in silva*, and its object is the protection of the cattle, doubtless those which have been turned out to pasture in the forest, and are therefore in danger from evil beasts and evil spirits.   Now this *res divina* may be performed either by a free man or a slave, *but no woman may be present*, nor see what is going on.[15]   In *sacra publica* women were excluded from the cult of Hercules at the Ara Maxima, and were not allowed to swear by the name of that god; facts which are usually connected with the doubtful identification of Hercules with Genius, or the male principle of life.[16]   More conclusive evidence of taboo in the case of women is the fact that at certain sacrifices they were ordered to withdraw, both *mulieres* and *virgines*, together with other persons to be mentioned directly.[17] Unfortunately we are not told what those sacrifices were ; but it seems clear enough that there had been at one time a scruple (*religio*) about admitting women of any age to certain sacred rites.   If so, it is remarkable how the good sense of the Roman people overcame any serious disabilities which might have been produced by such ideas ; the Roman woman gained for herself a position of dignity, and even of authority, in her household, which had very important results on the formation of the character of the people.[18]   Traces of the old superstition doubtless continued to survive in folklore ; an example, interesting because it seems to illustrate the positive aspect of taboo (*mana*), may be found by the curious in Pliny's *Natural History*, xxviii. 78.

Another widely-spread example of the class of ideas we are discussing is the belief that *strangers* are dangerous. Dr. Frazer tells us that "to guard against the baneful influence exerted voluntarily or involuntarily by strangers is an elementary dictate of savage prudence."   You have to disarm them of their magical powers, to counteract "the baneful influence which is believed to emanate from them."[19] Of this feeling he has collected a great number of convincing illustrations.   We find it also surviving in Roman ritual.   A note, referred to above, which has come down to us from the learned Verrius Flaccus, informs us that at certain sacrifices the lictor proclaimed "*hostis vinctus mulier virgo exesto*," where *hostis* has its old meaning of stranger.[20]   This is, of course, merely the old feeling of taboo surviving in the religious ritual of the City-state, and is also no doubt connected with the belief that the recognised deities of a community could not be approached by any but the members of that community ; but its taproot is probably to be found in the ideas described by Dr. Frazer.

We can illustrate it well from the ritual of another Italian city, Iguvium in Umbria, which, as I mentioned in a note to my last lecture, has come down to us in a very elaborate form.   In the ordinance for the *lustratio populi* of that city the magistrate is directed to expel all members of certain neighbouring communities by a thrice-repeated proclamation.[21]   Such fear of strangers is not even yet extinct in Italy.   Professor von Duhn told me that once when approaching an Italian village in search of inscriptions he was taken for the devil, being unluckily mounted on a black horse and dressed in black, and was met by a priest with a crucifix, who was at last persuaded to " disinfect " him with holy water as a condition of his being admitted to the village.   But the Romans of historical times, in this as in so many other ways, discovered easy methods of overcoming these fears and scruples : we find a good example of this in the organised college of Fetiales, who, on entering as envoys a foreign territory, were fully protected by their sacred herbs, carried by a *verbenarius*, against all hostile contamination.[22]

A remark seems here necessary about the apparent inconsistency between this feeling of anxiety about strangers and the well-known ancient Italian practice of *hospitium*, by which two communities, or two individuals, or an individual and a community, entered into relations which bound them to mutual hospitality and kindness in case of need :[23] a practice so widely spread and so highly developed that it may be considered one of the most valuable civilising agents in the early history of Italy.   There is, however, no real inconsistency here.   In the first place, the stranger who was removed on the occasion of solemn public religious rites may be assumed not to have been in possession of the *ius hospitii* with the Roman state, and in any case it must be doubtful whether that *ius* would give him the right of being present at all sacrificial rites.   Secondly, the researches of Dr. Westermarck have recently, for the first time, made it clear that both the taboo on strangers and the very widely-spread practice of hospitality can ultimately be traced down to the same root. The stranger is dangerous; but for that very reason it is desirable to secure his good-will at once. He may have the evil eye; but if so, it is as well to disarm him by offering him food and drink, and, when he has partaken of these, by entering into communion with him in the act of partaking also yourself. Expediency would obviously suggest some such remedy for the danger of his presence, and this would in course of time, in accordance with the instinct of Romans and Italians, grow into a set of rules sanctioned by law as well as custom—the *ius hospitii*.[24]

Hostis vinctus mulier virgo exesto. We have noticed traces of taboo on women and strangers: what of the *vinctus*? This is, so far as I know, the only proof we have that a man in chains was thought to be religiously dangerous. I am not sure how his expulsion from religious rites is to be explained. It is, however, as well to note that criminals were in primitive societies thought to be uncanny, probably because the commonest of all crimes, if not the only one affecting society as a whole, was the breaking of taboo, which made the individual an outcast.[25] And we may put this together with the fact that in the early City-state such outcasts were probably not kept shut up in a prison, but allowed to wander about secured with chains; this seems a fair inference from the power which the priest of Jupiter (*Flamen Dialis*) possessed of releasing from his chains any prisoner who entered his house, *i.e.* who had taken refuge there as in an asylum.[26] Thus the fettered criminal, who was certainly not a citizen, might find his way to the place where a sacrifice was going on, and have to submit to expulsion together with the strangers. It is, however, also possible that the iron of the chains, if they were of iron, made him doubly dangerous; for, as we shall see directly, iron was taboo, and the chains of the prisoner who took refuge with the Flamen had to be thrown out of the house, no doubt for this reason, by the *impluvium*.[27]

Turning to inanimate objects, which are supposed by

primitive man to be dangerous or taboo, we are met by a fact which will astonish anthropologists, and which I cannot satisfactorily explain.   Blood is everywhere in the savage world regarded with suspicion and anxiety; there is something mysterious about it as containing (so they thought) the life, and its colour and smell are also uncanny ; horses cannot endure it, and there are still strong men who faint at the sight of it.   Yet at Rome, so far as I can discover, there was in historical times hardly a trace left of this anxiety in its original form of taboo ; the religious law had effectually eliminated the various chances that might arouse it.   No student of Roman religious antiquities seems to have noticed this singular fact.   No anthropologist, as far as I know, has observed that among the many taboos to which the Flamen Dialis was subject, blood does not appear. The reason no doubt is that anthropologists are not as a rule Roman historians ; their curiosity is not excited by a fact which must have some explanation in Roman religious history.   From a single passage of Festus (p. 117) we learn that soldiers following the triumphal car carried laurel " ut quasi purgati a caede humana intrarent urbem " ; and this is the only distinct relic of the idea that I can find.   Pliny's *Natural History*, that wonderful thesaurus of odds and ends, affords no help ; the mystic qualities of blood are hardly alluded to there, and the same can be said of Servius' commentary on the *Aeneid*.   The word blood is not to be found in the index to Wissowa's great work, of which the supreme value is its accurate record of the religious law and all the ceremonies of the State.   I am constrained to believe that the priests or priest-kings who developed the *ius divinum* of the Roman City-state deliberately suppressed the superstition, for reasons which it is impossible to conjecture with certainty.   And this guess, which I put forward with hesitation, is indeed in keeping with certain other facts of Roman life.   It is doubtful whether human sacrifice ever existed among this people ; [28] it is certain that the execution of citizens in civil life by beheading was abandoned at a very early period.[29]   The

D

shedding of blood, except when a victim was sacrificed under the rules of sacred law, was carefully avoided ; thus the horror of blood had a social and ethical result of value, instead of remaining a mere *religio* (taboo). It is true that in one or two rites, such as that of the October horse, the blood of a sacrifice seems to have been thought to possess peculiar powers ;[30] but it is at the same time noticeable that this rite is not included in the old calendar, a fact of which a wholly satisfactory explanation has not yet been offered. In the Lupercalia there is a trace of the mystic use of blood in sacrifice, but a very faint one : to this we shall return later on. The two Luperci had their foreheads smeared with the knife bloody from the slaughter of the victims, but the blood was at once wiped off with wool dipped in milk.[31] This rite is of course in the old calendar ; it stands almost alone in its mystical character, and may have been taken over by the Romans from previous inhabitants of the site of Rome. Lastly, in the Terminalia, or boundary-festival of arable land in country districts, the boundary-stone was sprinkled with the blood of the victims, showing that a spirit, or *numen*, was believed to reside in it ;[32] but I cannot find that this practice survived in the public sacrifices of the city. It is found only in the sacrifices (*Graeco ritu*) supervised by the *X Vviri sacris faciundis* in that part of the Ludi Saeculares of Augustus which was concerned with Greek chthonic deities in the Campus Martius.[33]

Yet unquestionably there had been a time when many inanimate objects were supposed to have a mystic or dangerous influence ; this is sufficiently proved by the long list of taboos to which the unfortunate Flamen Dialis was even in historical times subject. He was forbidden to touch a goat, a dog, raw meat, beans, ivy, wheat, leavened bread ; he might not walk under a vine, and his hair and nails might not be cut with an iron knife ; and he might not have any knot or unbroken ring about his person. Dr. Frazer has the merit of being the first to point out the real meaning of this strange list of disabilities, and to explain the mystic or miasmatic origin of some of them.[34] They need not detain us now, as they are survivals only, and survivals of ideas which must have been long extinct before Roman history can be said to begin. Almost the only one among them of which we have other traces is the taboo on iron, which must have been of comparatively late date, as the use of iron in Italy seems only to have begun about the eighth century B.C.[35] This is found also in the ritual of the Arval Brotherhood, the ancient agricultural priesthood revived by Augustus, and better known to us than any other owing to the discovery of its *Acta* in the site of the sacred grove between Rome and Ostia. These Brethren had originally suffered from the taboo on iron ; but in characteristic fashion they had discovered that a piacular or disinfecting sacrifice would sufficiently atone for its use whenever it was necessary to take a pruning-hook within the limits of the grove.[36] We may here also recall the fact that no iron might be used in the building or repairing of the ancient *pons sublicius*, the oldest of all the bridges of the Tiber.[37]

Every one who wishes to get an idea of the nature of taboo in primitive Rome, and of the way in which it was got rid of, should study the disabilities of the Flamen Dialis, and satisfy himself of their absence, with the exception just mentioned, and possibly one or two more, in the ritual of historical Rome. Nothing is more likely to convince him of the way in which Roman civilisation contrived to leave these superstitions as mere fossils, in-capable any longer of doing mischief by cramping the conscience and inducing constant anxiety. If he is dis-posed to ask why such a large number of these fossils should be found attached to the priesthood of Jupiter, I must ask him to let me postpone that question, which would at this moment lead us too far afield.

I may, however, mention here that the Flaminica Dialis, who was not priestess of Juno as is commonly supposed, but assisted her husband in the cult of Jupiter, was also subject to certain taboos. On three occasions in the religious year she might not appear in public with her hair " done up," viz. the moving of the *ancilia* in March, the festival of the Argei in March and May, and during the cleansing of the *penus Vestae* in June. Also she might not wear shoes made from the skin of a beast that had died a natural death, but only from that of a sacrificial victim. There are traces of a *religio* about shoe-leather, I may remark, both in the Roman and in other religious systems. Varro tells us that " in aliquot sacris et sacellis scriptum habemus, Ne quid scorteum adhibeatur: ideo *ne morti-cinum* quid adsit." Leather was taboo in the worship of the almost unknown deity Carmenta. Petronius describes women in the cult of Jupiter Elicius walking barefoot; and we are reminded of the well-known rule which still survives in Mahommedan mosques.[88] The original idea may have been that the skin of an animal not made sacred by sacrifice might destroy the efficacy of the worship contemplated. On the other hand, the skin of a duly sacrificed animal had potency of a useful kind— a fact or belief so widespread as to need no illustration here; but we shall come upon an example of it in my next lecture.

Certain *places* were also affected by the idea of taboo. In the later religious law of the City-state the sites of all temples, *i.e.* all places in which deities had consented to take up their abode, were of course holy; but this is a much more mature development, though it unquestionably had its root in the same idea that we are now discussing. Such sites, as we shall see in a later lecture, were *loca sacra,* and *sacer* is a word of legal ritual, meaning that the place has been made over to the deity by certain formulae, accompanied with favourable auspices, under the authority of the State.[89] But there were other holy places which were not *sacra* but *religiosa*; and the word *religiosum* here might almost be translated " affected by taboo." Wissowa provides us with a list of these places, and this and the quotations he supplies with it are of the utmost value for my present subject.[40]

They comprised, of course, all holy places which the State had not duly consecrated, and therefore some which hardly concern us here, such as shrines belonging to families and gentes, and temple-sites in the provinces of a later age.   More to our purpose at this moment are the spots where thunderbolts were supposed to have fallen. Such spots were encircled with a low wall and called *puteal* from their resemblance to a well, or *bidental* from the sacrifice there of a lamb as a *piaculum* ; the bolt was supposed to be thus buried, and the place became *religiosum*.[41] So, too, all burial-grounds were not *loca sacra* but *loca religiosa*, technically because they were not the property of the state or consecrated by it ; in reality, I venture to say, because the place where a corpse was deposited was of necessity taboo.   Such places were *extra commercium*, and their sanctity might not be violated : "religiosum est," wrote the learned Roman Masurius Sabinus, "quod propter sanctitatem aliquam *remotum et sepositum est* a nobis." [42]   So, too, the great lawyer of Cicero's time, Servius Sulpicius, defines *religio* as "quae propter sanctitatem aliquam remota ac seposita a nobis sit," where he is using *religio* in the sense of a thing or place to which a taboo attaches.[43]   And again, another authority, Aelius Gallus, said that *religiosum* was properly applied to an object in regard to which there were things which a man might not do: "quod si faciat," he goes on, "adversus deorum voluntatem videatur facere." [44]   These last words are in the language of the City-state ; if we would go behind it to that of an earlier age, we should substitute words which would express the feeling or scruple, the *religio*, without reference to any special deity.   Virgil has pictured admirably this feeling as applied to places, in describing the visit of Aeneas to the site of the future Rome under the guidance of his host Evander (*Aen.* viii. 347) :—

> hinc ad Tarpeiam sedem et Capitolia ducit,
> aurea nunc, olim silvestribus horrida dumis.
> *iam tum religio pavidos terrebat agrestis*

> *dira loci* : iam tum silvam saxumque tremebant.
> "hoc nemus, hunc," inquit, "frondoso vertice collem,
> (quis deus, incertum est) habitat deus."

This is a passage on which I shall have to comment again : at present I will content myself with noting how accurately the poet, who of all others best understood the instincts of the less civilised Italians of his own day, has used his knowledge to express the antique feeling that there were places which man must shrink from entering—a feeling far older than the invention of legal *consecratio* by the authorities of a City-state.

Lastly, the principle of taboo, or *religio*, if we use the Latin word, affected certain times as well as places. Just as under the *ius divinum* of the fully-developed State certain spots were made over to the deities for their habitation and rendered inviolable by *consecratio*, so certain days were also appointed as theirs which the human inhabitants might not violate by the transaction of profane business. But I have just pointed out that the consecration of holy places in this legal fashion was a late development of a primitive feeling or *religio* ; exactly the same, if I am not mistaken, was the case with regard to the holy days. These were called *nefasti*, and belong to the life of the State ; but there were others, called *religiosi*, which I believe to have been tabooed days long before the State arose.

When we come to examine the ancient religious calendar, it will be found that I shall not then be called upon to deal with *dies religiosi*, for the very good reason that they are not indicated in that calendar— there is no mark for them as *religiosi*, and some of them are not even *dies nefasti*, as we might naturally have expected.[45] What, then, is the history of them ? We may be able to make a fair guess at this by noting exactly what these days were ; Dr. Wissowa has put them together for us in a very succinct passage.[46] He begins the list with the 18th of Quinctilis (July), on which two great disasters had happened to Roman

armies, the defeats on the Cremera and the Allia ; and
also the 16th, the day after the Ides, because, according
to the legend, the Roman commander had sacrificed on
that day with a view to gaining the favour of the gods
in the battle.   We may regard the story about the 18th
as historical ; but then we are told that *all* days following
on Kalends, Nones, and Ides were likewise made *religiosi*
(or *atri, vitiosi*, which have the same meaning) as being
henceforward deemed unlucky by pronouncement of senate
and pontifices ;[47] thus all *dies postriduani*, as they were
called, were put out of use, or at any rate declared
unlucky, for many purposes, both public and private, *e.g.*
marriages, levies, battles, and sacred rites,[48] simply because
on one occasion disaster had followed the offering of a
sacrifice on the 16th of Quinctilis.   It is difficult to
believe that thirty-six days in the year were thus tabooed,
by a Roman senate and Roman magistrates, in a period
when the practical wisdom of the government was beginning to be a marked characteristic of the State.   Some
people, we are told, went so far as to treat the *fourth
day before* Kalends, Nones, and Ides in the same way ;
but Gellius declares that he could find no tradition about
this except a single passage of Claudius Quadrigarius,
in which he said that the fourth day before the Nones of
Sextilis was that on which the battle of Cannae was
fought.[49]

I am strongly inclined to suggest that the traditional
explanation of the tabooing of these thirty-six, or possibly
seventy-two days was neither more nor less than an
aetiological myth, like hundreds of others which were
invented to account for Roman practices, religious and
other ; and this supposition seems to be confirmed as
we go on with the list of *dies religiosi* as given by
Wissowa.   The three days — Sextilis 24, October 5,
November 8—on which the Manes were believed to
come up from the underworld through the *mundus* (to
which I shall return later on) were *religiosi* ;[50] so were
those when the temple of Vesta remained open (June 7

to 15),[51] those on which the Salii performed their dances in March and October,[52] two days following the *feriae Latinae* (a movable festival),[53] and the days of the Parentalia in February and the Lemuria in May, which were concerned with the cult and the memory of the dead.[54] Now the *religio* or taboo on these days obviously springs either from a feeling of anxiety suggested by very primitive notions of the dead and of departed spirits ; or in the case of the temple of Vesta, by some mystical purification or disinfection preparatory to the ingathering of the crops, which I noticed in my *Roman Festivals* (p. 152 foll.) ; or again in the case of the Salii, by some danger to the crops from evil spirits, etc., which might be averted by their peculiar performances. In fact, all these *dies religiosi* date as such, we may be pretty sure, from a very primitive period before the genesis of the City-state, and were not recognised—for what reason we will not at present attempt to guess— as *religiosi* by the authorities who drew up the Calendar. Some of them appear in that calendar as *dies nefasti*, but not all ; and I am entirely at one with Wissowa, whose knowledge of the Roman religious law is un-paralleled for exactness, in believing that a *religio* affecting a day had nothing whatever to do with its character as *fastus* or *nefastus*.[55]

If all these last-mentioned *dies religiosi* are such because ancient popular feeling attached the *religio* to them, we may infer, I think, that the same was really the case also with the *dies postriduani*. The fact that the authorities of the State had made one or two days *religiosi* as anniversaries of disasters, supplied a handy explanation for a number of other *dies religiosi* of which the true explanation had been entirely lost ; but that there was such a true explanation, resting on very primitive beliefs, I have very little doubt. Lucky and unlucky days are found in the unwritten calendars of primitive peoples in many parts of the world. An old pupil, now a civil servant in the province of Madras, has sent me an elaborate account of the notions of this kind existing in the minds of the Tamil-speaking people of his district of southern India. The Celtic calendar recently discovered at Coligny in France contains a number of mysterious marks, some of which may have had a meaning of this kind.[56] Dr. Jevons has collected some other examples from various parts of the world, *e.g.* Mexico.[57] The old Roman superstition about the luckiness of odd days and the unluckiness of even ones, which appears, as we shall see, in the arrangement of the calendar, was probably at one time a popular Italian notion, not derived, as used to be thought, from Pythagoras and his school.

I therefore conclude that we may add times and seasons to the list of those objects, animate and inanimate, which were affected by the practice of taboo in primitive Rome ; and I hold that the word *religiosus*, as applied both to times and places, exactly expresses the feeling on which that practice is based. The word *religiosus* came to have another meaning (though it retained the old one as well) in historical times, and the Romans could be called *religiosissimi mortalium* in the sense of paying close attention to worship and all its details. But the original meaning of *religio* and *religiosus* may after all have been that nervous anxiety which is a special characteristic of an age of taboo.[58] To discover the best methods of soothing that anxiety, or, in other words, the methods of disinfection, was the work of the organised religious life of family and State which we are going to study. But I must first devote a lecture to another class of primitive survivals.

NOTES TO LECTURE II

1. Renel, *Les Enseignes*, p. 43 foll. For the contrary view, Deubner in *Archiv*, 1910, p. 490.

2. On taboo in general, Jevons, *Introduction to the History of Religion*, ch. vi. ; Robertson Smith, *Religion of the Semites*, p. 142 foll. ; Frazer, *Golden Bough* (ed. 2), i. 343 ; Crawley, *The Mystic Rose*

passim. On the relation of taboo to magic, Marett, *Threshold of Religion*, p. 85 foll.   Lately M. van Gennep in his *Rites de passage* has attempted to classify and explain the various rites resulting from taboo.

3. See the *Transactions of the Congress* (Oxford University Press), vol. i. p. 121 foll.   M. Reinach had alleged that the gens Fabia was originally a totem clan, *Mythes et cultes*, i. p. 47.

4. Marett, *On the Threshold of Religion*, p. 137 foll.   " In *taboo* the mystic thing is not to be lightly approached (negative aspect) ; *qua mana*, it is instinct with mystic power (positive aspect)": so Mr. Marett states the distinction in a private letter.

5. *Evolution of Religion*, p. 94.

6. *Introduction*, ch. viii. ; Westermarck, *Origin and Development of Ethical Ideas*, i. 233 foll.

7. See a paper by the author in the *Transactions of the Congress of the History of Religions*, 1908, ii. 169 foll.

8. Macrobius, *Sat.* i. 16. 36 ; De Marchi, *La Religione nella vita domestica*, i. p. 169 foll.; Samter, *Familienfeste der Griechen und Römer*, p. 62 foll., where the *dies lustricus* is compared with the Greek ἀμφιδρόμια.   Unfortunately the details of the Roman rite are unknown to us, which seems to indicate that the primitive or magical character of it had disappeared.   Van Gennep, *op. cit.* ch. v., reviews and 'classifies our present knowledge of this kind of rite.   See also Crawley, *Mystic Rose*, p. 435 foll.

9. Crawley, *op. cit.* p. 436 ; Frazer, *G.B.* i. 403 foll.   From this point of view Roman names need a closer examination than they have yet received.   See, however, Marquardt, *Privatleben der Römer*, pp. 10 and 81, and Mommsen, *Röm. Forschungen*, i. 1 foll.   Marquardt must be wrong in stating (p. 10) that only the *praenomen* was given on the *dies lustricus* ; children dying before that day usually, as he says on p. 82 note, have no name in inscriptions, and that ceremony must surely have introduced the child to the gens of its parents.   Certainly that introduction had not to wait till the *toga virilis* was taken ; though Tertull. *de Idol.* 16 looks at first a little like it.   The same statement is made in the *Dict. of Antiq.*, *s.v.* "nomen."   Macr. *Sat.* i. 16. 36, and Fest. 120, simply speak of *nomen.*

10. Fowler, *R.F.* p. 56 ; De Marchi, *op. cit.* p. 176.   For the primitive ideas about puberty, Crawley, *Mystic Rose*, ch. xiii.   The idea of the Romans seems to have been simply that the child, who had so far needed special protection from evil influences (of what kind in particular it is impossible to say) by purple-striped toga and amulet (see below, p. 60), was now entering a stage when these were no longer needed.   All notions of taboo seem to have vanished.

11. Marquardt, *Privataltertümer*, p. 337 foll.

12. Serv. *Aen.* ii. 714, and especially iii. 64.   Other references in Marq. *op. cit.* p. 338, note 5, and De Marchi, *La Religione nella*

vita domestica, p. 190.   For similar usages of prohibition see van Gennep, *op. cit.* ch. ii.

13. Festus, p. 3, "itaque funus prosecuti redeuntes ignem supragradiebantur aqua aspersi, quod purgationis genus vocabant suffitionem." For the possibly magic influence of these elements, see Jevons, *op. cit.* p. 70.

14. Frazer, *G.B.* i. 325, iii. 222 foll. ; Jevons, p. 59.

15. Cato, *R.R.* 83, "mulier ad eam rem divinam ne adsit neve videat quomodo fiat."

16. Plutarch, *Quaest. Rom.* 60.   Dogs were also excluded (*ib.* 90); Gellius xi. 6. 2 ; Wissowa, *R.K.* p. 227 ; Fowler, *R.F.* p. 194, where the private and public taboos are compared.

17. Festus, *s.v.* "exesto."   For similar taboos in Greece, Farnell in *Archiv* for 1904, p. 76.

18. Fowler, *Social Life at Rome in the Age of Cicero*, p. 143 foll. Cp. Westermarck, *Origin, etc.*, vol. i. ch. xxvi., especially p. 652 foll.

19. *G.B.* i. 298 foll.

20. Festus, *s.v.* "exesto."

21. Bücheler, *Umbrica*, p. 94 foll.   Cp. Livy v. 50, where it is said that, after the Gauls had left Rome, all the temples, *quod ea hostis possedisset*, were to be restored, to have their bounds laid down afresh (*terminarentur*) and to be disinfected (*expiarentur*). *Digest*, xi. 7. 36, "cum loca capta sunt ab hostibus, omnia desinunt religiosa vel sacra esse, sicut homines liberi in servitutem perveniunt; quod si ab hac calamitate fuerint liberata, quasi quodam postliminio reversa pristino statui restituerentur." Cp. Plutarch, *Aristides*, 20. A friend reminds me that Bishop Berkeley, when in Italy, had his bedroom sprinkled with holy water by his landlady.

22. See Marquardt, p. 420, notes 5 and 6.   The *verbenarius* is mentioned in Serv. *Aen.* xii. 120, and Pliny *N.H.* xxii. 5.   For the disinfecting power of verbena (*myrtea verbena*) see Pliny xv. 119, where it is said to have been used by Romans and Sabines after the rape of the Sabine virgins.

23. See Marquardt, *Privatleben*, p. 192 foll., based on the famous essay of Mommsen in his *Römische Forschungen*, i. 319 foll.   The passages quoted from Livy for the practice in early times (i. 45, v. 50) are not, of course, historical evidence ; but we may fairly argue back from the more explicit evidence of later times, *e.g.* the Senatusconsultum de Asclepiade of 78 B.C. (*C.I. Graec.* 5879).

There is a good example of the feeling in modern Italy in a book called *In the Abruzzi*, by Anne Macdonell, p. 275.   I have experienced it in remote parts of South Wales long ago.   Moritz, the German pastor who travelled on foot in England towards the end of the eighteenth century, noted that even the innkeepers were constantly unwilling to take him in.   His book was reprinted in Cassell's National Library some years ago.

24. See the very interesting chapter in *The Origin and Develop-*

ment of Moral Ideas, vol. i. p. 570 foll., especially p. 590 foll.   Dr. Westermarck aptly points out that hospitality is almost universal among "rude" peoples, and loses its hold as they become more civilised.   M. van Gennep in his recently published work, *Les Rites de Passage*, has attempted to classify the various rites relating to taboo of strangers ; see ch. iii., especially p. 38 foll.

25. Jevons, *Introduction*, p. 70.

26. Gellius x. 15. 8, "vinctum, si aedes eius introierit, solui necessum est."   (In hot countries chains still usually, or in some degree, take the place of bolts and bars, *e.g.* in the Soudan, as I am told by an old pupil now in the Soudan civil service.)   The regular Latin phrase for imprisonment is "in vincula conicere": Pauly-Wissowa, *s.v.* "carcer."

27. Gellius, *l.c.* ; Serv. *Aen.* ii. 57, a curious passage, in which the release of Sinon from his bonds by King Priam is compared with that of the prisoner who enters the flaminia (house of the Flamen Dialis).   That there was something in the iron which interfered with the religious efficacy of the Flamen seems likely ; cp. the rule that he might wear no ring unless it were broken, and have no knot about his dress.   But the latter restriction suggests that binding may have been originally the object of the taboo (cp. Ovid, *Fasti*, v. 432), and that the iron taboo came in with the iron age.   Appel, *de Romanorum precationibus*, p. 82, note 2, seems so to understand it.   Cp. Eurip. *Iph. Taur.* 468, where Orestes and Pylades are unbound before entering the temple.

28. There has been much discussion of this question ; I entirely agree with Wissowa (*R.K.* p. 354, where references are given for the opposite opinion) that there is no evidence for human sacrifice in the old Roman religion or law, except in the rule that a condemned criminal was made over to a deity (*sacer*), which may have been a legal survival of an original form of actual sacrifice.   The alleged sacrifice by Julius Caesar of two mutinous soldiers in the Campus Martius (Dio Cass. xliii. 24) is of the same nature as the sacrifice of captives to Orcus in *Aen.* xi. 81, *i.e.* it is outside of the civil life and religious law ; this is shown in the latter case by the mention of blood in the ritual (*caeso sparsurus sanguine flammas*), and in the former by the beheading of the mutineers.

29. Mommsen, *Strafrecht*, p. 917 foll. ; Livy x. 9 ; Cic. *de Rep.* ii. 31. 65.   All other methods of execution were bloodless.   *Decollatio* remained in use in the army (as in the case just mentioned), but the axe disappeared from the fasces in the city with the abolition of kingship.   As further illustration of the dislike of all bloodshed, cp. the rule of XII. Tables, "mulieres genas ne radunto," *i.e.* at funerals, Cic. *de Legibus*, ii. 59, and Serv. *Aen.* iii. 67 from Varro, and v. 78.   The gladiatorial *ludi* may have been a revival of an old custom akin to human sacrifice of captives in the field.   See *Social Life at Rome in the Age of Cicero*, p. 304, note 3.

We may also note in this connection that there is no distinct trace of the blood-feud in old Roman law ; see *Zum ältesten Strafrecht der Kulturvölker*, p. 38 (questions of comparative law suggested by Mommsen and answered by various specialists). Doubtless it once existed, but vanished at an early date.

30. Fowler, *R.F.* p. 242. The tail of the sacrificed horse was carried to the Regia, where the blood was allowed to drip on the sacred hearth (*participandae rei divinae gratia*), Festus, p. 178.

31. *R.F.* p. 311 foll., from Plutarch, *Rom.* 21.

32. For this practice in many ancient religions, and its substitute, the smearing of the stone with turmeric or other red stain, see Jevons, *Introduction*, p. 139 foll. ; Robertson Smith, *Semites*, p. 415.

33. This is found in Zosimus ii. 1. 5 ; Diels, *Sibyllinische Blätter*, 132, and 73 note. Cp. Virg. *Aen.* viii. 106 ; also a Greek rite.

34. *G.B.* ed. 2, i. 241 foll.

35 The bronze and iron ages, of course, overlap ; see Helbig, *Italiker in der Poebene*, p. 78 foll.

36. Henzen, *Acta Fratr. Arv.* pp. 22 and 128 foll. Other examples are collected by Helbig, *op. cit.* p. 80.

37. Dion. Hal. iii. 45 ; Mommsen in *C.I.L.* i. p. 177. It may be as well to point out that iron, like wheat in the taboos of the Flamen, was considered dangerous, as being a novelty. The old Italian grain was not true wheat but *far*, which continued to be used in religious rites; *R.F.* p. 304, and Marquardt, *Privatleben der Römer*, p. 399 foll.

38. Varro, *L.L.* vii. 84 ; Ovid, *Fasti*, i. 629 ; Petronius, *Sat.* 44. There are many parallels in Greek ritual.

39. See below, p. 146. Mr. Marett suggests to me a comparison with the *rongo* (sacred) of the Melanesians, and *tapu* as used of a place by them, *i.e.* set apart by a human authority ; Codrington, *Melanesians*, p. 77.

40. Wissowa, *R.K.* p. 408 foll. ; cp. 323 and notes.

41. The fullest account of this will be found in Marquardt, p. 262 foll. For the case of a man killed by lightning, see note 4 on p. 263 ; the body was not burnt but buried, and the grave became a *bidental*, and *religiosum*.

42. For the intricate pontifical law of burial-places see Wissowa, p. 409. The quotation from Masurius is in Gellius iv. 9. 8, "M. Sabinus in commentariis quos de indigenis composuit." The word *sanctitas* is here used merely by way of explanation and not in a technical sense ; for which see Marq. p. 145 and references ; but it seems to have had a special use in the cult of the dead. (See below, p. 470.)

43. Quoted by Macrobius, *Sat.* iii. 3. 8. For Sulpicius see *Social Life at Rome in the Age of Cicero*, p. 118 foll.

44. Festus, p. 278. This Aelius lived at the end of the Republican period, and belonged to the school of Sulpicius ; Schanz, *Gesch. der röm. Lit.* i. pt. 2, p. 486.

45. *e.g.* the three days on which the *mundus* was open were all *comitiales*, though at the same time *religiosi*.

46. *R.K.* pp. 376, 377.

47. The authorities for the story are Verrius Flaccus, *ap.* Gell. v. 17, and Macrobius, *Sat.* i. 16. 21.

48. For the extent of the taboo see Gell. iv. 9. 5 ; Macr. i. 16. 18.

49. Gell. v. 17. 3 foll. (*annalium quinto*).

50. Festus, p. 278.

51. *R.F.* p. 151.

52. Wissowa, *R.K.* p. 377, note 6.

53. Cic. *ad Qu. Fratr.* ii. 4. 2.

54. Wissowa, *R.K.* pp. 187, 189.

55. *R.K.* p. 377. Gell. iv. 9. 5 says that the *multitudo imperitorum* confused the *dies religiosi* and *dies nefasti.* The distinction is most clearly seen in the fact that on *dies religiosi* the temples were (or ought to be) shut, and " res divinas facere " was ill-omened (Gell., *ib.*), while on *dies nefasti* the latter was regular, such days being made over to the gods. No wonder that Gellius brands the popular ignorance with such words as *prave* and *perperam.*

56. See Prof. Rhys's paper read before the British Academy, " Notes on the Coligny Calendar," p. 33 and elsewhere.

57. *Introduction*, p. 65 foll.

58. Since writing this sentence I have read the paper by W. Otto on " Religio and Superstitio " in *Archiv für Religionswissen-schaft*, 1909, p. 533 foll. ; in which at p. 544 he hints at a connection of *religio* with the practice of taboo. With some of his conclusions, however, I cannot agree. The same explanation of the origin of *religio, i.e.* in an age of taboo, has also been suggested since my lecture was written by Maximilianus Kobbert, *De verborum " religio atque religiosus " usu apud Romanos*, p. 31 (Königsberg, 1910).

LECTURE III

ON THE THRESHOLD OF RELIGION : MAGIC

TABOO, the traces of which at Rome we examined in the last lecture, is, as we saw, closely allied to magic, even if it be not, as Dr. Frazer thinks, magic in a negative form. We have now to see what traces are to be found of magic in the proper or usual sense of the word—active or positive magic, as we may call it. By this we are to understand the exercise of a mysterious mechanical power by an individual on man, spirit, or deity, to enforce a certain result. In magic there is no propitiation, no prayer. " He who performs a purely magical act," says Dr. Westermarck,[1] " utilises such mechanical power without making any appeal at all to the will of a supernatural being." Religion, on the other hand, is an attitude of regard and dependence ; in a religious stage man feels himself in the hands of a supernatural power with whom he desires to be in right relation.

If we accept this distinction, as I think we may (though one school of anthropologists is hardly disposed to do so), it is plain that magical practices are of a totally different kind from religious practices, as being the result of a different mental attitude towards the supernatural ; they belong to a ruder and more rudimentary idea of the relation of Man to the Power manifesting itself in the universe. True, they have their origin in the same kind of human experience, in the difficulties man meets with in his struggle for existence, and his desire to overcome these ; but unlike religion, magic is a wholly inadequate attempt to overcome them. This inadequacy was long ago well explained by Dr. Jevons.[2]   He showed that man in that early stage of his experience did not understand the true relation of cause and effect ; that, "turned loose as it were among innumerable possible causes (of a given effect), with nothing to guide his choice, the chances against his making the right choice were considerable." As a matter of fact he usually made the wrong one, and is still apt to do so.   There is probably more magic going on behind the scenes even in civilised countries, and more especially both in Greece and Italy, than either men of science or men of religion have any idea of.   In its various forms as they are now classified,[3] e.g. contagious magic, and homoeopathic magic, the exercise of the mysterious will-power, real or imaginary, is to be found all the world over, accompanied usually with a spell or incantation which is believed to enforce and increase that power—a kind of telepathy, which seems to be the psychological basis, so far as there is one, of the whole system. In these rites the virtue resides in some action, which, together with the spell or incantation, enforces the desired result by calling out the will-power, or *mana*, if we adopt the convenient Melanesian word lately brought into use.   Whatever percentage of psychological truth may lie at the root of such performances, it is obvious that they must in the main be wholly inadequate, and must constantly tend to pass into mere quackery and become discredited ; and it was the special function of the religious organisation of early society to eliminate and discredit them.

But it was a long stage in the evolution of society before man arrived at a better knowledge of his relation to the Power manifesting itself in the universe ; before he reached the idea of a god or spirit realisable and nameable, and thus capable of being addressed, placated, worshipped.   When this stage is reached, there supervenes almost always a strong tendency to regulate and systematise

the methods of address, placation, and worship; and
among some peoples, *e.g.* the Romans, for reasons which
it is by no means easy to explain, this tendency is much
stronger than among others. Wherever it has been strong,
wherever these methods of putting oneself in right relation with the Power have been systematised by a central
authority or priesthood, and thus made into religious law,
there, as we might naturally expect, the performances and
performers of magic have been most vigorously dis-
countenanced and outlawed. The interests of religion
and its officials are wholly antagonistic to those of magic
and magicians. In civilised communities and in historical times magic is in the main individualistic, not social;
magical ceremonies for the good of the community seem
to be confined to races in a very early stage of development. The examples on which Dr. Frazer relies
for his theory of the development of the public magician
into a king [4] are of this primitive kind, or are mere survivals of magic in a higher stage of civilisation —
such survivals as there will always be among forms and
ceremonies, of which it is man's nature to be tenacious.
But religion, once firmly established, invariably seeks to
exclude magic; and the priest does his best to discredit the magician, as claiming to exercise mysterious
powers outside the pale of the legally recognised methods
of propitiation and worship. As Dr. Tylor observed
long ago, the more civilised the race, the more apt it is to
associate magic with men of inferior civilisation.[5] In the
Jewish law, though magic was well known to the Jews
and privately practised, there is no recognition of it; the
magical books attributed to Solomon were suppressed,
according to tradition, by the pious king Hezekiah.[6] So
too at Rome, where the outward forms of religion were
also very highly systematised, magic, as it seems to me,
was rigorously excluded from the State ritual, though it
continued in use in private life under certain precautions
taken by the State; in the few genuine examples of it in
the rites belonging to the *ius divinum* (*i.e.* those used and

E

sanctioned for the purposes of the community), it is nothing more than a survival of which the magical meaning was unknown to the writers from whom we hear of it.

A good example of such survivals is the curious ceremony of the *aquaelicium*, without doubt a genuine case of magical "rain-making" —one of the many inadequate and blundering attempts on the part of primitive man to obtain what he needs. Probably it may be classed under the head of "sympathetic magic," but the evidence as to what was done in the ceremony is not quite explicit enough to allow us to do this confidently.[7] It was, of course, not included in the religious calendar, as it would be only occasionally called for, and could not be fixed to a day; but there is clear evidence that it was sanctioned by the State, for the pontifices took part in it, and the magistrates without the *toga praetexta*, and the lictors carrying the fasces reversed.[8] A stone, which lay outside the walls near the Porta Capena, was brought into the city by the pontifices, so far as we can make out the details, and it has been conjectured that it was taken to an altar of Jupiter Elicius on the Aventine hard by, this cult-title of the god of the sky having possibly some relation to the technical name of the ceremony. What was done with the stone we unluckily do not know; but it has been reasonably conjectured that it was a hollow one, and that it was filled with water which was allowed to run over the edge, as a means of inducing the rain-god to suffer the heavens to overflow.[9] It was called *lapis manalis*; and the epithet here can have nothing to do with the Manes, as in the case of another *lapis manalis*, of which I shall have a word to say later on, but must mean "pouring" or "overflowing." One or two other fragments of evidence point in the same direction, and I think we may fairly conclude that the rite was originally one of sympathetic magic—that as the stone overflowed, so the sky would pour down rain. In my *Roman Festivals* I have pointed out a remarkable parallel to this in the collections of the *Golden Bough*; in a Samoan village a stone represented the god of rain, and in a drought his priests carried it in procession and dipped it in a stream.

This parallel I owe to Dr. Frazer's wide knowledge of all such practices among savage peoples. But this ever helpful and friendly guide, in treating of the Jupiter Elicius concerned in this ceremony, has gone beyond the evidence, and attributed to the Romans another kind of magic of which I believe they were quite innocent. He has been led to this by his theory that kings were developed out of successful magicians. In his lectures on the early history of the Kingship [10] he maintains that the Roman kings practised the magical art of bringing down lightning from heaven. " The priestly king Numa passed for an adept in the art of drawing down lightning from the sky. . . . Tullus Hostilius is reported to have met with the same end (as Salmoneus, king of Elis) in an attempt to draw down Jupiter in the form of lightning from the clouds." To support these statements Dr. Frazer quotes Pliny, Livy, Ovid, Plutarch, Arnobius, Aurelius Victor, and Zonaras — truly a formidable list of authorities; but without any attempt to discover where any of these late writers found the stories. Yet he had but to read Aust's admirable article " Jupiter " in the *Mythological Lexicon* [11] to assure himself that legends which cannot be traced farther back than the middle of the second century B.C. cannot seriously be assumed to be genuinely Roman. Pliny happens to mention Calpurnius Piso as his authority; this was the man who is well known in Roman history as the author of the first *lex de repetundis* of the year 149 B.C., a good statesman, but as an annalist much given to indulging a mythological fancy.[12] We happen to know that he wrote with happy confidence about the life and habits of Romulus, and a story about wine-drinking which he attributes to that king is obviously transferred to him from some more historical personage. Romulus would not drink wine one day because he was going to be very busy on the next. Then they said to him, " If we all did so, Romulus, wine would be cheap." "Nay, dear," he replied, "if every one drank as much as he wished ; and that is exactly what I am doing." [13]   I quote the story simply as a good example of the way in which Roman historians could deal with their kings, and of the absolute necessity of acquainting oneself with their methods before building hypotheses upon their statements.   I hardly need to add that another of Dr. Frazer's authorities, Arnobius, informs us that he took the story from the second book of Valerius Antias, a later writer than Piso, whose name is a byword even with the uncritical Livy for shameless exaggeration and mis-statement.[14]

But how did these writers come by such legends, which, as Dr. Frazer shows, are to be found also in Greece and in other parts of the world?   Why should they have wished to make Roman kings into magicians? Rain-making we can understand at Rome,—it had a practical end in view, the procuring of rain for the crops,— but why lightning and thunder, which were so much dreaded that every bit of damage done by a thunder-storm had to be carefully expiated by a religious process? Rome is not in the tropics, where rain and thunder so often come together, and where an attempt to produce rain by magic might naturally include thunder, as in some of Dr. Frazer's examples from tropical lands.   I entirely agree with the latest and most sober investigators of Roman ritual that this kind of magic is quite foreign to Roman ideas and practice ;[15] there is no vestige of it in the Roman cult ; these stories must have come from outside.   And there is every probability that they came from Etruria, where the lore of lightning had become a pseudo-science, a waste of human ingenuity, for the origin of which we must look, as we are now beginning to understand, to Babylonia and the Eastern magic.[16]   The Jupiter Elicius of the Aventine had nothing to do with lightning ; he took his cult-title from the rite of *aquaelicium* ; but as soon as the Romans began to interest themselves in the Etruscan lightning-lore, of which this electrical magic was only a part,[17] they perverted the meaning of the epithet to suit their new studies, and began to attribute to their legendary kings powers which properly belonged to Etruscan or Oriental magicians. The second century B.C., when Piso wrote his *Annals*, is exactly the period when we should naturally expect such studies to come into fashion, and with such perversions of "history" as their consequence.[18]

I go on to note one or two more examples of real magic in the State religion; but they are hard to find. Pliny tells that even in his day people believed that a runaway slave who had not escaped out of the city might be arrested by a spell uttered by the Vestal virgins.[19] I take this to mean that any one who had lost his slave might get the Vestals to use the spell as a means of keeping the runaway within the city. The word for spell is here *precatio, i.e.* a prayer, not *carmen*, which is the usual word for a spell; and Pliny evidently thinks of it as addressed to some god. But no doubt it was originally at least a genuine spell, of the same kind as others used in private life, which we shall notice directly; and it implies a belief in some magical power inherent in the Vestals, of whom we are told that if they accidentally met a criminal being led to punishment they might secure his release.[20] As the spell in this case seems to be telepathic, *i.e.* an exercise of will-power projected from a distance, it may perhaps be paralleled with certain mystical powers exercised by women, especially when their husbands are at war, among some savage peoples;[21] but we have no information about it beyond the passage in Pliny, and further guessing would be useless.

This last is a case of genuine magic, but it is outside the ritual of the State, though exercised by a State priesthood. Within that ritual there is one other very curious case of what must be classed as a magical process, and one that has accidentally become famous. At the Lupercalia on February 15, the two young men called Luperci, or, more strictly, belonging respectively as leaders to the two collegia of Luperci, girt themselves with the skins of the slaughtered victims, which were goats, and then ran round the base of the Palatine hill, striking at all the women who came near them or offered themselves to their blows, with strips of skin cut from the hides of these same victims.   The object was to produce fertility ; on this point our authorities are explicit.[22]   Thus this particular feature of the whole extraordinary ritual of the Lupercalia is unmistakably within the region of magic rather than of religion.   Some potency was believed to work in the act of striking, though apparently without a spoken spell or *carmen*, such as usually accompanies acts of this kind ; and this part of the rite, grotesque though it was, was allowed to survive by the grave religious authorities who drew up the calendar of religious festivals.   It was probably a superstition too deeply rooted in the minds of the people to admit of being excluded ; and, strange to say, it survived, in outward form at least, until Rome had become cosmopolitan and even Christian.   The Lupercalia has always been a puzzle to students of early religion, and as each new theory is advanced, this strange festival is seized on for fresh interpretation ;[23] but for our present purposes it must suffice to point out that we clearly find embedded in it a piece of genuine magic, dating beyond doubt from a very primitive stage of thought.

There is one other very curious performance, occurring each year on the ides of May, which in my view is rather magical than religious, though the ancients themselves looked upon it as a kind of purification : I mean the casting into the Tiber from the *pons sublicius* of twenty-four or twenty-seven straw puppets by the Vestal virgins, in the presence of the magistrates and pontifices.   Recently an attempt has been made by Wissowa to prove that this strange ceremony was not primitive, but simply a case of the substitution of puppets for real human victims as late as the age of the Punic wars.[24]   These puppets were called Argei, which word naturally suggests Greeks ; and Wissowa has contrived to persuade himself not only that a number of Greeks were actually put to death by drowning in an age when everything Greek was beginning to be reverenced at Rome, but (still more extraordinary to an anthropologist) that the primitive device of substitution was had in requisition at that late date in order to carry on the memory of the ghastly deed. And the world of German learning has silently followed their leader, without taking the trouble to test his conclusions by a careful and independent examination of the evidence. It happens that this fascinating puzzle of the Argei was the first curiosity that enticed me into the study of the Roman religion, and for some thirty years I have been familiar with every scrap of evidence bearing on it ; and after going over that evidence once more I can emphatically state my conviction that Wissowa's theory will not hold water for a moment. I shall return to the subject in a later lecture dealing with the religious history of the second Punic war ; at present I merely express a belief that, whatever be the history of the accessories of the rite,—and they are various and puzzling,—the actual immersion of the puppets is the survival of a primitive piece of sympathetic magic, the object being possibly to procure rain. It is, in my opinion, quite impossible to resist the anthropological evidence for this conclusion, though we cannot really be certain about the object ; for this evidence I must refer you to my *Roman Festivals*, and to the references there given.[25]

This rite of the Argei, then, was a case of genuine magic, and exercised by a State priesthood, virgins to whom certain magical powers were supposed to be attached ; it was, I think, a popular performance, like one or two others which are also outside the limit of the Fasti,[26] and was embodied in a more complicated ceremonial long after that calendar had been drawn up. In the ritual authorised by the State, with public objects in view, *i.e.* for the benefit of society as a whole, there is hardly a trace of anything that we can call genuine magic apart from the examples I have just been explaining.   There were, I need not say, many survivals of magical processes of which the true magical intent had long been lost—ancient magical deposits in a social stratum of religion, which I shall notice in their proper place.   This is not peculiar to the religion of the Romans; it is a phenomenon to be found in all religions, even in those of the most highly developed type, and it is one apt to cause some confusion as to the true distinction between magic and religion.[27]   It is easy to find magical processes even in Christian worship, if we have the will to do so ; but if we steadily bear in mind that the true test of magic is not the nature of an act, but the intent or volition which accompanies it, the search will not be an easy one.

The modern French school of sociologists, which now has to be reckoned with in investigating the early history of religion, claims that magic was not originally, as we now see it, a matter of individual skill, but a sociological fact, *i.e.* it was used for the benefit of the community, as religion came to be in a later age.   If this be true, as it very possibly is, we see at once how the dead bones of magical processes might survive, with their original meaning entirely lost, into an age in which higher and more reasonable ideas had been developed about the relation of Man to the Power manifesting itself in the universe.   To take a single example from Rome, divination by the examination of a victim's entrails was originally a magical process, according to the opinion of most modern authorities ;[28] but it ceases to be magic when it is used simply to determine in the State ritual whether in a religious process the victim is perfect and agreeable to the deity.   In fact magical formulae, magical instruments, unless they are used in the true spirit of magic, to compel, not to propitiate a deity, are no longer magic, and may be passed over here.   When we come to discuss the ritual of sacrifice and prayer, of *lustratio*, of vows, of divination, we may find it necessary to recall

what has here been said.   On the whole, we may conclude
that organised religious cult, from its very nature and
object, everywhere excluded magic in the true sense of the
word ; it implies prayer and propitiation, both of which
are absolutely inconsistent with the object and methods of
magic.   Religion is the product of a higher stage of
social development ; it is the expression of a real advance
of human thought ; and in telling the story of the
religious experience of the Roman people we are but
indirectly concerned with those more rude and rudimentary ideas which it displaced.

But in private life, outside of the organised cult of the
State and the family, magic was all through Roman
history abundant, even over-abundant, and in this form I
cannot pass it over entirely.   Though the State authorities seem to have taken pains to exclude it rigidly from
the public rites, and though there is little trace of it in
the religious life of family and gens, yet there is evidence
that it was deeply rooted in the nature of the people,
and that they must have passed through an age in which
it was an important factor in their social life.   This fact,
taken together with its almost complete elimination from
the public religion, throws into relief the persistent efforts
of the State authorities, from the framing of the old
religious calendar to the time of the Augustan revival, to
keep their relations with the Power clear of all that they
believed to be unworthy or injurious.   No better example
can be found of the inherent antagonism between religion
and magic.

Private magic may be divided into two kinds, according as it was used to damage another, or only to benefit
oneself.   In the former case the State interfered to protect the person threatened with damage, and treated this
kind of magic as a crime.   The commonest form of it
was that of the spell, or *carmen*, no doubt often sung, and
accompanied by some action which would bring it under
the head of sympathetic magic ; but the spell alone is
taken cognisance of by the State.   Pliny has preserved

three words from the XII. Tables which tell their own
tale : " qui fruges excantassit." [29]   Servius, commenting on
the line of Virgil's 8th *Eclogue*, " atque satas alio vidi
traducere messes," writes, " magicis quibusdam artibus hoc
fiebat, unde est in XII. Tabb. ' Neve alienam segetem
pellexeris.' "   These last words, with the verb in the second
person, are probably not quoted exactly from the ancient
text,[30] but they help to show us the nature of this hostile
spell.   There must have been a belief that the spirit, or
life, or fructifying power of your neighbour's crops could
be enticed away and transferred to your own.   This is
confirmed by a remark of St. Augustine in the *de Civitate
Dei* ; [31] after quoting the same line from Virgil, he adds,
" eo quod hac pestifera scelerataque doctrina fructus alieni
in alias terras transferri perhibentur, nonne in XII. Tabulis,
id est Romanorum antiquissimis legibus, Cicero com-
memorat esse conscriptum et ei qui hoc fecerit supplicium
constitutum ? "   Given the belief, the temptation can be
well understood if we reflect that the arable land of the
old Romans was divided in sections of a square, and that
each man's allotment would have that of a neighbour on
two sides at least.[32]   If one man's corn were found to be
more flourishing than that of his neighbours, what more
likely than that he should have enticed away the spirit of
their crops ?   The process reminds us, as it reminded
Pliny, of the *evocatio* of the gods of foreign communities,
a rite which belongs to religion and not to magic, though
it doubtless had its origin in the same class of ideas as
the *excantatio*.

In more general terms the old Roman law (*i.e.* originally the *ius divinum*) forbade the use of evil spells, as we
see in another fragment of the Tables, " qui malum carmen
incantassit."   In later times this was usually taken as
referring to libel and slander, but there can be no doubt
that the carmina here alluded to were originally magical,
and became *carmina famosa* in the course of legal interpretation.   Cicero seems to combine the two meanings in
the *de Rep.* (iv. 10. 2) when he says that the Tables made

it a capital offence "si quis occentavisset, sive carmen condidisset quod infamiam faceret flagitiumve alteri" (to bring shame or criminal reproach on another). In the later sense these carmina have a curious history, into which I cannot enter now.[33]   In the earlier sense they existed and flourished without doubt, in spite of the law ; or it may be that, as the words of the Tables were interpreted in the new sense, the old form of offence was tolerated in private.   "We are all afraid," says Pliny, "of being 'nailed' (defigi) by spells and curses" (diris precationibus).[34]   These dirae, and all the various forms of love-charms, defixiones, accompanied by the symbolic actions which are found all the world over, lie outside my present subject, and are so familiar to us all in Roman literature that I do not need to dwell on them.[35]

Nor of the common harmless kind of magic need I say much now.   It survived, of course, alongside of the religion of the family and State, from the earliest times to the latest, as it survives at the present day in all countries civilised and uncivilised ; and being harmless the State took no heed of it.   Some assortment of charms and spells for the cure of diseases will be found in Cato's book on agriculture, and one or two incidentally occur in that of Varro.[36]   They performed the work of insurance against both fire and accident, and even such a man as Julius Caesar was not independent of such arts.   Pliny tells us that after experiencing a carriage accident he used to repeat a certain spell three times as soon as he had taken his seat in a vehicle, and adds significantly, "id quod plerosque nunc facere scimus."[37]   Such carmina were written on the walls of houses to insure them against fire.[38]   Pliny has a large collection of small magical delusions and superstitions, many of which have an interest for anthropologists, in the 28th book of his Natural History.

Another kind of harmless magic, to which the Romans, like all Italians ancient and modern, were peculiarly addicted, is the use of amulets.   Here there is no spell, or

obvious and expressed exercise of will-power on the part
of the individual, but the potent influence, *mana*, or whatever we choose to call it, resides in a material object
which brings good luck, like the cast horse-shoe of our
own times, or protects against hostile will-power, and
especially against the evil eye. This curious and widely-
spread superstition was probably the *raison d'être* of most
of the amulets worn or carried by Romans. A modern
Italian, even if he be a complete sceptic and materialist,
will probably be found to have some amulet about him
against the evil eye, "just to be on the safe side." [39] A
list of amulets, both Greek and Roman, will be found in
the *Dictionary of Antiquities*, and in Pauly-Wissowa, *Real-
Encyclopädie, s.v.* "amulet," and it is not necessary here to
explain the various kinds in use in Italy; but I must
dwell for a moment on one type, which had been taken
up into the life of the family, and in one sense into that
of the State, viz. the *bulla* worn by children, both boys
and girls.

The bulla was a small object, enclosed in historical
times in a capsule, and suspended round the child's neck.
It was popularly believed to have been originally an
Etruscan custom,[40] and borrowed by the Romans, like so
many other ornaments. It is, however, much more probable that the custom was old Italian (as indeed the
"medicine-bag" is world-wide), and that the Etruscan
contribution to it was merely the case or capsule, which
was of gold where the family could afford it—gold itself
being supposed to have some potency as a charm.[41] The
object within the case was, as Pliny tells us, a *res turpicula*
as a rule,[42] and this may remind us that a *fascinum*
was carried in the car of the triumphator as *medicus
invidiae*, to use Pliny's pregnant expression. The
triumphing general needed special protection; he appeared in the guise of Jupiter himself, and was for the
moment lifted above the ordinary rank of humanity.
Some feeling of the same kind must have originally suggested similar means for the protection of children under

the age of puberty.   They also wore the *toga praetexta*,
which, though associated by us with secular magistrates,
had undoubtedly a religious origin.   There are distinct
signs that children were in some sense sacred, and at the
same time that they needed special protection against the
all-abounding evil influences to be met with in daily life.[43]
Thus this particular form of amulet became a recognised
institution of family life, and in due time little more than
a mark of childhood.

Yet another kind of charm must be mentioned here
which was used at certain festivals, though apparently not
at any of those belonging to the authorised calendar.   At
the Compitalia, Paganalia, and *feriae Latinae* we are told
that small images of the human figure, or masks, or simply
round balls (*pilae*), were hung up on trees or doorways,
and left to swing in the wind.[44]   At the Compitalia the
images had a special name, *maniae*, of which the meaning
is lost; but inasmuch as the charms were hung up at
cross-roads on that occasion, where the Lares compitales
of the various properties had their shrine, it was not
difficult to manufacture out of them a goddess, Mania,
mother of the Lares.[45]   The common word for these
figures was *oscilla*, and the fact of their swinging in the
wind suggested a verb *oscillare*, which survives in our own
tongue with the same meaning.   Until lately it used to
be believed that they were substitutes for original human
sacrifices: a view for which there is not a particle of
evidence, though it was originated by Roman scholars.[46]
Modern anthropology has found another explanation,
which is by no means improbable.   Dr. Frazer, in an
appendix to the 2nd volume of the *Golden Bough*, has
collected a number of examples of the practice of swinging
by human beings as a magical rite; they come from many
parts of the world, including ancient Athens, and even
modern Calabria.   He also points out that at the *feriae
Latinae* the swingers seem to have been human beings, if
we accept the evidence of Festus, *s.v.* "oscillantes"; thus
we are left with the possibility that the oscilla were really

imitations of men and women, though not of human sacrificial victims.

Dr. Frazer is obviously hard put to it to explain the original meaning and object of this curious custom. In the Paganalia, as described by Virgil in the second *Georgic*,[47] the object would seem to be the prosperity of the vine-crop.

> coloni
> versibus incomptis ludunt risuque soluto,
> oraque corticibus sumunt horrenda cavatis,
> et te Bacche vocant per carmina laeta, tibique
> oscilla ex alta suspendunt mollia pinu.
> hinc omnis largo pubescit vinea fetu, etc.[48]

But here we must leave a question which is still unsolved. All we can say is that the old idea of substitutes for human sacrifice must be finally given up, and that the *oscilla*, whether or not they were substitutes for human swingers, were probably charms intended to ward off evil influences from the crops. I am not disposed to put any confidence in what Servius tells us, that this was a purification by means of air, just as fire and water were also purifying agents; this looks like the ingenious explanation of a later and a religious age.[49]

So much, then, for magical charms and spells, and the survivals of them in the fully developed Roman religion.[50] It might seem hardly worth while to spend even so much time on them as I have done, and I cannot deny that I am glad now to be able to leave them. My object has simply been to show how little of this kind of practice, which meets us on the threshold of religion, was allowed to survive by the religious authorities of the State; in other words, I wished to make clear that in our inquiries into the nature of the Roman religion it is really religion and not magic that we have to do with.

It is really religion; it is desire, beginning already to be effective, to be in right relation to the Power manifesting itself in the universe. The Romans, as I hope to show in the next lecture, when we can begin to know and feel an interest in them, had not only begun to

recognise this Power in various forms and functions as one
that must be propitiated, because they were dependent on it
for their daily needs, but to regulate and make permanent
the methods of propitiation.   What was the relation
between this simple religion and morality—between ritual
and conduct—is a very difficult question, to which I
shall return later on.   Dr. Westermarck has recently come
to the conclusion that the religion of primitive man has
no true relation to morality, that it is not apt to give a
sanction to good action, or to develop the germs of a
conscience.   But so far as I can discern, the idea of active
duty, and therefore the germ of conscience, must have
been so intimately connected with the religious practice of
the old Latin family that it is to me impossible to think
of the one apart from the other.   Surely it is in that life
that the famous word "*pius*" must have originated, which
throughout Roman history meant the sense of duty
towards family, State, and gods, as every reader of the
Aeneid knows.   That the formalised religion of later times
had become almost entirely divorced from morality there
is indeed no doubt ; but in the earliest times, in the old
Roman family and then in the budding State, the whole
life of the Roman seems to me so inextricably bound up
with his religion that I cannot possibly see how that
religion can have been distinguishable from his simple
idea of duty and discipline.

NOTES TO LECTURE III

1. Westermarck, *Origin etc. of Moral Ideas*, ii. 584.
2. Jevons, *Introduction*, p. 33.
3. A useful summary of the whole subject, embodying the results
and terminology of Tylor, Frazer, and other anthropologists, is Dr.
Haddon's *Magic and Fetishism*, in Messrs. Constable's series, *Religions
Ancient and Modern*.   See also Marett, *On the Threshold of Religion*,
passim.
4. *Lectures on the Early History of the Kingship*, p. 89 foll.   For
an example not mentioned in the text (*devotio*) see below, p. 206 foll.
This may have been originally practised by the Latin kings.   I may

here draw attention to the almost dogmatic conclusions of the modern
French sociological school of research ; *e.g.* M. Huvelin, in *L'Année
sociologique* for 1907, begins by asserting as a fundamental law,
proved by MM. Hubert et Mauss, that magic is just as much a social
fact as religion : " Les uns et les autres sont des produits de l'activité
collective" (*Magie et droit individuel,* p. 1).   But M. Huvelin's paper
is to some extent a modification of this dogma.   He seeks to explain
the fact that magic is both secret and private, not public and social,
in historical times ; and in the domain of law, with which he is
specially concerned, he concludes that "a magical rite is only a
religious rite twisted from its proper social end, and employed to
realise the will or belief of an individual " (p. 46).   This is the only
form in which we shall find magic at Rome, except in so far as a few
of its forms survive in the ritual of religion with their meaning
changed.   In early Roman law, as a quasi-religious body of rules and
practices, there are a few magical survivals which will be found
mentioned by M. Huvelin in this article; but they are of no importance
for our present subject.

5. *Primitive Culture*, vol. i. ch. iv.   See also Jevons, *Introduction,* p. 36 foll.

6. See Schürer, *Jewish People in the Time of Christ* (Eng. trans.),
Division II. vol. iii. p. 151 foll.

7. Fowler, *R.F.* p. 232 ; Wissowa, *R.K.* p. 106.   The most careful
examination of the rite and the evidence for it is that of Aust in
Mythological Lexicon, s.v. "Iuppiter," p. 656 foll.   See also M. H.
Morgan in vol. xxxii. of *Transactions of the American Philological
Association,* p. 104.

8. Tertullian, *de Jejun.* 16.   Petronius, *Sat.* 44, adds that the
matrons went in the procession with bare feet and streaming hair
(cp. Pliny xvii. 266) ; but this seems rather Greek than Roman in
character, and Petronius is plainly thinking of the town (*colonia* he
calls it) in southern Italy where the scene of Trimalchio's supper is
laid ; probably a Greek city by origin, Croton or Cumae.   A translation of this passage will be found in Dill's *Roman Society from
Nero to Marcus Aurelius,* p. 133.   The most useful words in it for
our purpose are " Jovem aquam exorabant."

9. This suggestion was originally made by O. Gilbert, *Röm.
Topographie,* ii. 184.

10. p. 204 foll.

11. p. 657.   The story is mixed up with Greek fables, *e.g.* that
of Proteus, as Wissowa has pointed out, *R.K.* p. 106, note 10.

12. See Schanz, *Gesch. der röm. Literatur,* vol. i. (ed. 3) p. 270
foll.

13. This fragment of Piso is preserved by Gellius, xi. 14. 1.

14. See, *e.g.,* Schanz, *Gesch. der röm. Literatur,* vol. ii.
p. 106.

15. Wissowa,*l.c.* Aust in Roscher's *Lexicon, s.v.*"Iuppiter," p. 657.

16. Cumont, *Religions Orientales dans le paganisme romain*, ch. 5. I shall return to this subject in my second course of lectures.

17. Müller-Deecke, *Etrusker*, ii. ch. vii., especially p. 176 foll.

18. Cp. below, Lecture XV.

19. Pliny, *N.H.* xxviii. 13 : "Vestales nostras hodie credimus nondum egressa urbe mancipia fugitiva retinere in loco precationibus."

20. Plutarch, *Numa*, 10. Virginity would increase the power of the spell ; see Fehrle, *Die kultische Keuschheit im Altertum*, p. 54 foll.

21. See, *e.g.*, Frazer, *G.B.* i. 360 foll.

22. See *R.F.* p. 320, notes 6 and 7.

23. Within the last thirty years or so the Lupercalia has been discussed (apart from writers on classical subjects exclusively) by Mannhardt in his *Mythologische Studien*, p. 72 foll. ; Robertson Smith, *Semites*, p. 459 ; Deubner in *Archiv*, 1910, p. 481 foll. ; and at the moment of writing by E. S. Hartland, *Primitive Paternity*, i. ch. ii. *R.F.* p. 310 foll. See Appendix D.

24. This view was originally stated in Pauly-Wissowa, *s.v.* "Argei." I endeavoured to confute it in the *Classical Review*, 1902, p. 115 foll., and Wissowa replied in *Gesammelte Abhandlungen*, p. 211 foll. Since then my conviction has become stronger that this great scholar is for once wrong. Ennius alluded to the Argei as an institution of Numa, *i.e.* as primitive (frag. 121, Vahlen, from Festus p. 355, and Varro, *L.L.* vii. 44), yet Ennius was a youth at the very time when Wissowa insists that the rite originated. Wissowa makes no attempt to explain this. See below, p. 321 foll.

25. *R.F.* p. 111 foll.

26. *e.g.* the October horse, which also occurred on the Ides ; see *R.F.* p. 241 foll. ; and the festival of Anna Perenna, also on Ides (March 15), *R.F.* p. 50 foll. It is just possible that all the three festivals were originally in the old calendar, and dropped out because the mark of the Ides had to be affixed to the day in the first place. See Wissowa, *Gesammelte Abhandlungen*, p. 164 foll. ; *R.F.* p. 241.

27. Thus Messrs. Hubert et Mauss (*Mélanges d'histoire des religions* Preface, p. xxiv.) maintain that there is no real antinomy between "les faits du système magique et les faits du système religieux." There is in every rite, they insist, a magical as well as a religious element. Yet on the same page we find that they exclude magic from all organised cult, because it is not obligatory, and cannot (if I understand them rightly) be laid down in a code, like religious practice. I think it would have been simpler to consider the magical element in religious rites as surviving, with its original meaning lost, from an earlier stage of thought. M. van Gennep, in his interesting work *Les Rites de passage*, p. 17, goes so far as to call all religious *ceremonies* magical, as distinguished from the *theories* (*e.g.* animism) which constitute religion. This seems to me apt to bring confusion into the discussion ; for all rites are the outward expression of thought, and it is by the thought (or, as he calls it, theories) that we must trace

F

the sociological development of mankind, the rites being used as indexes only. I cannot but think that (as indeed in these days is quite natural) this French school lays too much stress upon the outward acts, and that this tendency has led them to find real living magic where it is present only in a fossil state.

28. *e.g.* Tylor, article " Magic " in *Encycl. Brit.*, and *Primitive Culture*, i. ch. iv. ; Marett, *Threshold of Religion*, 83. See below, p. 180.

29. Pliny, *N.H.* xxviii. 17 and 18. For the singing or murmuring of spells in many countries, see Jevons, *Anthropology and the Classics*, p. 93 foll.

30. Bruns, *Fontes Iuris Romani*, note on this passage.

31. *Civ. Dei*, viii. 19.

32. See, *e.g.*, Wordsworth, *Fragments and Specimens of Early Latin*, p. 446, for an account of simple land measurement which will suffice to illustrate the point made here.

33. The *carmina famosa* sung at a triumph by the soldiers had the same origin, but were used to avert evil from the triumphator. The best exposition of this is in H. A. J. Munro's *Elucidations of Catullus*, p. 76 foll.

34. Pliny, *N.H.* xxviii. 19. For the technical sense of *defigere*, *defixio*, see Jevons in *Anthropology and the Classics*, p. 108 foll.

35. The most familiar examples are Virgil's eighth *Eclogue*, 95 foll. ; Ovid, *Met.* vii. 167, and elsewhere ; *Fasti*, iv. 551 ; Horace, *Epode* v. 72 ; cp. article " Magia " in Daremberg-Saglio ; Falz, *De poet. Rom. doctrina magica*, Giessen, 1903. There is a collection of Roman magical spells in Appel's *De Romanorum precationibus*, p. 43 foll. Many modern Italian examples and survivals will be found in Leland's *Etruscan Roman Remains in Popular Tradition*, pt. ii.

36. Cato, *R.R.* 160 ; Varro, *R.R.* i. 3.

37. Pliny, *N.H.* xxviii. 21.

38. *Ib.* xxviii. 20. The following sections of this book are the *locus classicus* for these popular superstitions.

39. See, *e.g.*, *Italian Home Life*, by Lina Duff Gordon, p. 230 foll.

40. Juvenal v. 164. The idea probably arose, as a passage of Plutarch suggests (*Rom.* 25), from the fact that the triumphator, whose garb was no doubt of Etruscan origin, wore the bulla.

41. Frazer, *G.B.* i. 345, note 2, where we learn that gold was taboo in some Greek worships, *e.g.* at the mysteries of Andania, which sufficiently proves that it possessed potency. Pliny, xxxiii. 84, mentions cases of such potency as medicine, and among them its application to children who have been poisoned.

42. Pliny, *N.H.* xxviii. 39.

43. See an article by the author on the original meaning of the *toga praetexta* in *Classical Review*, vol. x. (1896) p. 317.

44. For the Compitalia, Macrob. i. 7. 34 ; Festus p. 238. For the Paganalia, Probus, *ad Georg.* ii. 385, assuming the *feriae Sementinae*

there mentioned to be the Paganalia (see *R.F.* p. 294). For the *feriae Latinae*, Festus, *s.v.* "oscillantes."

45. Wissowa, *R.K.* p. 193, with whose view I entirely agree. We learn of the imaginary goddess from Varro, *L.L.* ix. 61. Pais, I may remark in passing, is certain that Acca Larentia was the mater Larum ; see his *Lectures on Ancient Legends of Roman History*, p. 60 foll.

46. Wissowa, *R.K.* p. 354, note 5.

47. *Georg.* ii. 380 foll. It is not certain that Virgil is describing the festival generally known as Paganalia, which took place early in January ; but it seems probable from line 382 that he is thinking of some festival of the pagus. The *oscilla* may have been used at more than one.

48. Note that Virgil writes of masks used in rude play-acting, as well as of *oscilla* hung on trees, and conjoins the two as though they had something in common. The evidence of an engraved onyx cup in the Louvre, of which a cut is given in the article "Oscilla" in the *Dict. of Antiquities*, seems to make it probable that masks worn by rustics on these occasions were afterwards hung by them on trees as *oscilla*. Some of these masks on the cup are adorned with horns, which may explain an interesting passage of Apuleius (*Florida*, i. 1) : "neque enim iustius religiosam moram viatori obiecerit aut ara floribus redimita . . . aut quercus cornibus onerata, aut fagus pellibus coronata," etc. See also *Gromatici veteres*, ii. 241.

49. See, however, Dr. Frazer's remarks in *G.B.* ii. p. 454. He thinks that the air might in this way be purged of vagrant spirits or baleful ghosts, as the Malay medicine man swings in front of the patient's house in order to chase away the disease. Cp. *G.B.* ii. 343, where a rather different explanation is attempted of the *maniae* and *pilae*.

50. Magic in the old forms, or many of them, has survived not only into the old Roman religion, but to the present day, in many parts of Italy. "The peasants have recourse to the priests and the saints on great occasions, but they use magic all the time for everything," was said by a woman of the Romagna Toscana to the late C. G. Leland (*Etruscan Roman Remains*, Introduction, p. 9). This enterprising American's remarkable book, though dealing only with a small region of northern Italy, deserves more consideration than it has received. The author may have been uncritical, but beyond doubt he had the gift of extracting secrets from the peasantry. He claims to have proved that "la vecchia religione" contains much that has come down direct from pre-Christian times ; and the appearance of Mr. Lawson's remarkable book on *Modern Greek Folklore and Ancient Greek Religion* may tempt some really qualified investigator to undertake a similar work in Italy before it is too late.

LECTURE IV

THE RELIGION OF THE FAMILY

SOME of the survivals mentioned in the last two lectures seem to carry us back to a condition of culture anterior to the family and to the final settlement on the land. Some attempt has recently been made to discover traces of descent by the mother in early Latium;[1] if this could be proved, it would mean that the Latins were already in Latium before they had fully developed the patriarchal system on which the family is based. However this may be, the first real fact that meets us in the religious experience of the Romans is the attitude towards the supernatural, or "the Power that manifests itself in the Universe," of the family as settled down upon the land. The study of religion in the family, as we know it in historical times, is also that of the earliest organisation of religion, and of the most permanent type of ancient Italian religious thought. Aust, whose book on the Roman religion is the most masterly sketch of the subject as yet published, writes thus of this religion of the family:[2] "Here the limits of religion and superstition vanish . . . and in vain we seek here for the boundary marks of various epochs." By the first of these propositions he means that the State has not here been at work, framing a *ius divinum*, including religion and excluding magic; in the family, magic of all kinds would be admissible alongside of the daily worship of the family deities, and thus the family would represent a kind of half-way house between the age of magic and all such superstitions, and the age of the rigid

68

regulation of worship by the law of a City-state. By the
second proposition he means that the religious experience
of the family is far simpler, and therefore far less liable to
change than that of the State. Greek forms and ideas of
religion, for example, hardly penetrated into its worship:[3]
new deities do not find their way in—the family experience
did not call for them as did that of the State. It may be
said without going beyond the truth that the religion of
the family remained the same in all essentials throughout
Roman history, and the great priesthoods of the State
never interfered with it in any such degree as to affect its
vitality.[4]

But in order to understand the religion of the family,
we must have some idea of what the family originally
was. When a stock or tribe (*populus*) after migration
took possession of a district, it was beyond doubt divided
into clans, *gentes*, which were the oldest kinship divisions
in Italian society. All members of a clan had the same
name, and were believed to descend from a common
ancestor.[5] According to the later juristic way of putting
it, all would be in the *patria potestas* of that ancestor supposing that no deaths had ever occurred in the gens ; and,
indeed, the idea that the gens is immortal in spite of the
deaths of individuals is one which constitutes it as a
permanent entity, and gives it a quasi-religious sanction.
For primitive religion, as has been well said, disbelieves
in death ; most of the lower races believe both in a
qualified immortality and in the non-reality or unnatural-
ness of death.[6] In regard to the kinship of a clan,
death at any rate has no effect : the bond of union never
breaks.

Now a little reflection will show that a clan or gens of
this kind might be maintained intact in a nomadic state,
or during any number of migrations ; it is, in fact, mani-
festly appropriate to such a mobile condition of society,
and expresses its natural need of union ; and when the
final settlement occurs, this body of kin will hold together
in the process, whether or no it has smaller divisions

within it. We may be certain that this was the one
essential kin-division of the Latin stock when it settled in
Latium, and all through Roman history it continues so,
a permanent entity though families may die.[7] Every
Roman lawyer will recognise this fact as true, and I need
not dwell on it now.

It is when the gens has settled upon the land that the
family begins to appear as a fact of importance for our
purpose. Such operations as the building of a permanent
house, the clearing and cultivation of a piece of land, can
best be carried out by a smaller union than the gens, and
this smaller union is ready to hand in the shape of a
section of the gens comprising the living descendants of a
living ancestor, whether of two, three, or even four generations.[8] This union, clearly visible to mortal eye, and
realisable in every-day work, settles together in one
house, tends its own cattle and sheep, cultivates its own
land with the help of such dependants as it owns, slave or
other, and is known by the word *familia*. This famous
word, so far as we know, does not contain the idea of
kinship, at any rate as its leading connotation ; it is
inseparable from the idea of land-settlement,[9] and is
therefore essentially *das Hauswesen*, the house itself,
with the persons living in it, free or servile, and with their
land and other property, all governed and administered
by the paterfamilias, the master of the household, who is
always the oldest living male ancestor. The familia is
thus an economic unit, developed out of the gens, which is
a unit of kin and little more. And thus the religion of the
familia will be a religion of practical utility, of daily work, of
struggle with perils to which the shepherd and the tiller of
the soil are liable; it is not the worship of an idea of kinship
expressed in some dimly conceived common ancestor ; the
familia, as I hope to show, had no common ancestor who
could be the object of worship, except that of the gens
from which it had sprung. The life of the familia was a
realisation of the present and its needs and perils, without
the stimulus to take much thought about the past, or indeed

about the future ; for it, sufficient for the day was the
evil thereof ; for what had been and what was to come it
could look to the gens to which it owed its existence.
But in practical life the gens was not of much avail ; and
instead of it, exactly as we might expect, we find an artificial
union of familiae, a union of which the essential thing is
not the idea of kin, but that of the land occupied, and
known all over Italy by the word *pagus*.[10]   Before I go on
to describe the religion of the family, it is necessary to put
the familia into its proper relation with this territorial
union.

The pagus is the earliest Italian administrative unit of
which we know anything ; a territory, of which the
essential feature was the boundary, not any central
point within the boundary.   In all probability it was
originally the land on which a gens had settled, though
settlement produces changes, and the land of gens and
pagus was not identical in later times.   But within this
boundary line, of which we shall hear something more
presently, how were the component parts, the familiae of
the gens, settled down on the land ?   Of the village community so familiar to us in Teutonic countries, there
is no certain trace in Latium.   *Vicus*, the only word
which might suggest it, is identical with the Greek οἶκος,
a house ; later it is used for houses standing together, or
for a street in a town.   But the vicus in the country has
left no trace of itself as a distinct administrative union
like our village community ; the vico-magistri of the
Roman city were urban officers ; and what is more important, we know of no religious festivals of the vicus, like
those of the pagus, of which there are well-attested records.
The probability then is that the unit within the pagus
was not the village but the homestead, and that these
stood at a distance from each other, as they do in Celtic
countries, not united together in a village, and each housing a family group working its own land and owning its
own cattle.[11]   The question of the amount and the tenure
of the land of this group is a very difficult one, into which

it is not necessary to enter closely here. There can, however, be no doubt that it possessed in its own right a small piece of garden ground (*heredium*), and also an allotment of land in the arable laid out by the settlers in common—*centuriatus ager*; whether the ownership of this was vested in the individual paterfamilias or in the gens as a whole, does not greatly matter for our purposes.[12] Lastly, as it is certain that the familia owned cattle and sheep, we may be sure that it enjoyed the right of common pasture on the land not divided up for tillage.

We see all this through a mist, and a mist that is not likely ever to lift; but yet the outlines of the picture are clear enough to give us the necessary basis for a study of the religion of the familia. The religious points, if I may use the expression—those points, that is, which are the object of special anxiety (*religio*)—lie in the boundaries, both of the pagus as a whole, and of the arable land of the familia, in the house itself and its free inhabitants, and in the family burying-place; and to these three may no doubt be added the spring which supplied the household with water. Boundaries, house, burying-place, spring, —all these are in a special sense sacred, and need constant and regular religious care.

Let us begin with the house, the central point of the economic and religious unit. The earliest Italian house was little more than a wigwam, more or less round, constructed of upright posts connected with wattles, and with a closed roof of straw or branches.[13] This would seem to have been the type of house of the immigrating people who settled on the tops of hills and lived a pastoral life; when they descended into the plains and became a settled agricultural people, they adopted a more roomy and convenient style of building, suitable for storing their grain or other products, and for the maintenance of a fire for cooking these. Whether the rectangular house, with which alone we are here concerned, was developed under Greek or Etruscan influence, or suggested independ-

ently by motives of practical convenience, is matter of
dispute, and must be left to archaeologists to decide.[14]

This is the house in which the Latin family lived
throughout historical times, the house which we know as
the sacred local habitation of divine and human beings.
It consisted in its simplest form, as we all know, of a
single room or hall, the atrium, with a roof open in the
middle and sloping inwards to let the rain fall into a
basin (*compluvium*).   Here the life of the family went on,
and here was the hearth (*focus*), the "natural altar of the
dwelling-room of man," [15] and the seat of Vesta, the spirit
of the fire, whose aid in the cooking of the food was
indispensable in the daily life of the settlers.   This sacred
hearth was the centre of the family worship of later times,
until under Greek influence the arrangement of the
house was modified ; [16] and we may be certain that it was
so in the simple farm life of early Latium.   In front of it
was the table at which the family took their meals, and
on this was placed the salt-cellar (*salinum*), and the
sacred salt - cake, baked even in historical times in
primitive fashion by the daughters of the family, as in all
periods for the State by the Vestal virgins.   After the
first and chief course of the mid-day meal, silence was
enjoined, and an offering of a part of the cake was thrown
on to the fire from a small sacrificial plate or dish
(*patella*).[17]   This alone is enough to prove that Vesta, the
spirit of the fire, was the central point of the whole worship, the spiritual embodiment of the physical welfare of
the family.

Behind the hearth, *i.e.* farther at the back of the *atrium*,
was the *penus*, or storing-place of the household.   *Penus*
was explained by the learned Scaevola [18] as meaning anything that can be eaten or drunk, but not so much that
which is each day set out on the table, as that which is
kept in store for daily consumption ; it is therefore in
origin the food itself, though in later times it became also
the receptacle in which that food was stored.   This store
was inhabited or guarded by spirits, the *di penates*, who

together with Vesta represent the material vitality of the family; these spirits, always conceived and expressed in the plural, form a group in a way which is characteristic of the Latins, and their plurality is perhaps due to the variety and frequent change of the material of the store. The religious character of the store is also well shown by the fact, if such it be, that no impure person was allowed to meddle with it; the duty was especially that of the children of the family,[19] whose purity and religious capability was symbolised throughout Roman history by the purple-striped toga which they wore, and secured also by the amulet, within its capsule the *bulla*, of which I spoke in the last lecture.

Vesta and the Penates represent the spiritual side of the material needs of the household; but there was another divine inhabitant of the house, the Genius of the paterfamilias, who was more immediately concerned with the continuity of the family. Analogy with the world-wide belief in the spiritual double of a man, his "other-soul," compels us to think of this Genius, who accompanied the Latin from the cradle to the grave, as originally a conception of this kind. The Latins had indeed, in common with other races, what we may call the breath-idea of the soul, as we see from the words *animus* and *anima*, and also the shadow-idea, as is proved by the word *umbra* for a departed spirit. But the Genius was one of those guardian spirits, treated by Professor Tylor as a different species of the same genus, which accompany a man all his life and help him through its many changes and chances;[20] and the peculiarity of this Latin guardian is that he was specially helpful in continuing the life of the family. The soul of a man is often conceived as the cause of life, but not often as the pro-creative power itself; and that this latter was the Latin idea is certain, both from the etymology of the word and from the fact that the marriage-bed was called *lectus genialis*. I am inclined to think that this peculiarity of the Latin conception of Genius was the result of the unusually strong idea that the Latins must have had, even when they first passed into Italy, of kinship as determined not by the mother but by the father.[21]   It is possible, I think, that the Genius was a soul of later origin than those I have just mentioned, and developed in the period when the gens arose as the main group of kinsmen real or imaginary.   I would suggest that we may see in it the connecting link between that group and the individual adult males within it; in that case the Genius would be that soul of a man which enables him to fulfil the work of continuing the life of the gens. We can easily imagine how it might eventually come to be his guardian spirit, and to acquire all the other senses with which we are familiar in Roman literature.   With the development of the idea of individuality, the individuality of a man as apart from the kin group, the idea of the individuality of the Genius also became emphasised, until it became possible to think of it as even living on after the death of its companion;[22] in this way, in course of time, the Genius came to exercise a curious influence on the idea of the Manes.   The history of the idea of Genius, and its application to places, cities, etc., is indeed a curious one, and of no small interest in the study of religion; but we must return to the primitive house and its divine inhabitants.   There is one more of these who calls for a word before I pass to the land and the boundaries; we meet him on the threshold as we leave the dwelling.

It is, of course, well known to anthropologists that the door of a house is a dangerous point, because evil spirits or the ghosts of the dead may gain access to the house through it.   Among the innumerable customs which attest this belief there are one or two Roman ones, *e.g.* the practice of making a man, who has returned home after his supposed death in a foreign country, enter the house by the roof instead of the door; for the door must be kept barred against ghosts, and this man may be after all a ghost, or at least he may have evil spirits or miasma

about him.[23]   It was at the doorway that a curious
ceremony took place (to which I shall ask your attention
again) immediately after the birth of a child, in order to
prevent Silvanus, who may stand for the dangerous
spirits of the forest, from entering in and vexing the
baby.[24]   Again, a dead man, as among so many other
peoples, was carried out of the doorway with his feet
foremost, so that he should not find his way back ; and
the old Roman practice of burial by night probably had
the same object.[25]   Exactly the same anxiety (*religio*) is
seen in regard to the gates of a city ; the wall was in
some sense holy (*sanctus*), but the gates, through which
was destined to pass much that might be dangerous,
could not be thus sanctified.   Was there, then, no protecting spirit of these doors and gates ?

St. Augustine, writing with Varro before him, finds
no less than three spirits of the entrance to a house :
Forculus, of the door itself; Limentinus, of the threshold;
and Cardea, of the hinges of the door ; and these Varro
seems to have found in the books of the pontifices.[26]   I
must postpone the question as to what these pontifical
books really represented ; but the passage will at least
serve to show us the popular anxiety about the point of
entrance to a house, and its association with the spirit
world.   Of late sober research has reached the conclusion that the original door-spirit was Janus, whom we
know in Roman history as residing in the symbolic gate
of the Forum, and as the god of beginnings, the first
deity to be invoked in prayer, as Vesta was the last.[27]
But Janus is also wanted for far higher purposes by
some eminent Cambridge scholars ; they have their own
reasons for wanting him as a god of the sky, as a double
of Jupiter, as the mate of Diana, and a deity of the oak.[28]
So, too, he was wanted by the philosophical speculators of
the last century B.C., who tried to interpret their own humble
deities in terms of Greek philosophy and Greek polytheism.
The poets too, who, as Augustine says, found Forculus
and his companions beneath their notice, played strange

tricks with this hoary old god, as any one may read in the
first book of Ovid's *Fasti*. I myself believe that the
main features of the theology (if we may use the word) of
the earliest Rome were derived from the house and the
land as an economic and religious unit, and I am strongly
inclined to see in Janus bifrons of the Forum a developed
form of the spirit of the house-door ; but the question is
a difficult one, and I shall return to it in a lecture on the
deities of early Rome.

So far I have said nothing of the Lar familiaris who
has become a household word as a household deity ; and
yet we are on the point of leaving the house of the old
Latin settler to look for the spirits whom he worships on
his land. The reason is simply that after repeated examination of the evidence available, I find myself forced
to believe that at the period of which I am speaking the
Lar was not one of the divine inhabitants of the house.
When Fustel de Coulanges wrote his brilliant book *La
Cité antique*, which popularised the importance of the
worship of ancestors as a factor in Aryan civilisation, he
found in the Lar, who in historical times was a familiar
figure in the house, the reputed founder of the family ; and
until lately this view has been undisputed. But if my
account of the relation of the family to the gens is correct,
the family would stand in no need of a reputed founder ;
that symbol of the bond of kinship was to be found in the
gens of which the family was an offshoot, a cutting, as it
were, planted on the land. Still more convincing is the
fact that when we first meet with the Lar as an object of
worship he is not in the house but on the land. The
oldest Lar of whom we know anything was one of a
characteristic Roman group of which the individuals
lived in the *compita*, *i.e.* the spots where the land belonging to various households met, and where there were
chapels with as many faces as there were properties,
each face containing an altar to a Lar,—the presiding
spirit of that allotment, or rather perhaps of the whole
of the land of the familia, including that on which the

house stood.[29]   Thus the Lar fills a place in the private worship which would otherwise be vacant, that of the holding and its productive power.   In this sense, too, we find the Lares in the hymn of the Arval Brethren, one of the oldest fragments of Latin we possess ; for the spirits of the land would naturally be invoked in the lustration of the *ager Romanus* by this ancient religious gild.[30]

But how, it may be asked, did the Lar find his way into the house, to become the characteristic deity of the later Roman private worship there ?   I believe that he gained admittance through the slaves of the familia, who had no part in the worship of the dwelling, but were admitted to the Compitalia, or yearly festival of which the Lares of the compita were the central object.   Cato tells us that the vilicus, the head of the familia of slaves, might not "facere rem divinam nisi Compitalibus in compito aut in foco" ;[31] which I take to mean that he might sacrifice for his fellow-slaves to the Lar at the compitum, or to the Lar in the house, if the Lar were already transferred from the compitum to the house.   In the constant absence of the owner, the paterfamilias of Rome's stirring days, the worship of the Lar at the compitum or in the house came to be more and more distinctly the right of the vilicus and his wife as representing the slaves, and thus too the Lar came to be called by the epithet *familiaris*, which plainly indicates that in his cult the slaves were included.   And as it was the old custom that the slaves should sit at the meals of the family on benches below the free members (*subsellia*),[32] what more natural than that they should claim to see there the Lar whom alone of the deities of the farm they were permitted to worship, and that they should bring the Lar or his double from the compitum to the house, in the frequent absence of the master ?[33]

The festival of the Lar was celebrated at the compitum, and known as Compitalia or Laralia ; it took place soon after the winter solstice, on a day fixed by the paterfamilias, in concert, no doubt, with the other heads

of families in the pagus.   Like most rejoicings at this
time of year, it was free and jovial in character, and
the whole familia took part in it, both bond and free.
Each familia sacrificed on its own altar, which was placed
fifteen feet in front of the compitum, so that the worshippers might be on their own land ; but if, as we may
suppose, the whole pagus celebrated this rite on the same
day, there was in this festival, as in others to be mentioned directly, a social value, a means of widening the
outlook of the familia and associating it with the needs of
others in its religious duties.   This is the *religio Larium*
of which Cicero speaks in the second book of his *de
Legibus*, which was " posita in fundi villaeque conspectu,"
and handed down for the benefit both of masters and men
from remote antiquity.[34]

There were other festivals in which all the familiae of
a pagus took part.   Of these we know little, and what
we do know is almost entirely due to the love of the
Augustan poets for the country and its life and customs ;
" Fortunatus et ille deos qui novit agrestes," wrote Virgil,
contrasting himself with the philosopher poet whom he
revered.   Varro, in his list of Roman festivals,[35] just
mentions a festival called Sementivae, associated with
the sowing of the seed, and celebrated by all pagi, if we
interpret him rightly ; but Ovid has given us a charming
picture of what must be this same rite, and places it
clearly in winter, after the autumn sowing [36] :—

> state coronati plenum ad praesaepe iuvenci :
>   cum tepido vestrum vere redibit opus.
> rusticus emeritum palo suspendit aratrum :
>   omne reformidat frigida volnus humus.
> vilice, da requiem terrae, semente peracta :
>   da requiem terram qui coluere viris.
> pagus agat festum : pagum lustrate, coloni,
>   et date paganis annua liba focis.
> placentur frugum matres Tellusque Ceresque,
>   farre suo gravidae visceribusque suis.

Ovid may here be writing of his own home at Sulmo,
and what took place there in the Augustan age ; but we

may read his description into the life of old Latium, for
rustic life is tenacious of old custom, especially where the
economic conditions remain always the same.   We may
do the same with another beautiful picture left us by
Tibullus, also a poet of the country, which I have recently
examined at length in the *Classical Review*.[37]   The
festival he describes has often been identified with Ovid's,
but I am rather disposed to see in it a lustratio of the
ager paganus in the spring, of the same kind as the
famous one in Virgil's first *Georgic*, to be mentioned
directly ; for Tibullus, after describing the scene, which
he introduces with the words "fruges lustramus et agros,"
puts into perfect verse a prayer for the welfare of the
crops and flocks, and looks forward to a time when (if
the prayer succeeds) the land shall be full of corn, and
the peasant shall heap wood upon a bonfire—perhaps
one of the midsummer fires that still survive in the
Abruzzi.   Virgil's lines are no less picturesque ;[38] and
though he does not mention the pagus, he is clearly
thinking of a lustratio in which more than one familia
takes part—

> cuncta tibi Cererem pubes agrestis adoret.

This is a spring festival "extremae sub casum hiemis, iam
vere sereno" ; and I shall return to it when we come to
deal with the processional lustratio of the farm.   Like
the descriptions of Ovid and Tibullus, it is more valuable
to us for the idea it gives us of the spirit of old Italian
agricultural religion than for exact knowledge about
dates and details.   There was, of course, endless variety
in Italy in both these ; and it is waste of time to try and
make the descriptions of the rural poets fit in with the
fixed festivals of the Roman city calendar.

Nor is it quite safe to argue back from that calendar
to the life of the familia and the pagus, except in general
terms.   As we shall see, the calendar is based on the life
and work of an agricultural folk, and we may by all
means guess that its many agricultural rites existed before-

hand in the earlier social life ; but into detail we may not venture. As Varro, however, has mentioned the Saturnalia in the same sentence with the Compitalia, we may guess that that famous jovial festival was a part of the rustic winter rejoicing. And here, too, I may mention another *festa* of that month, of which a glimpse is given us by Horace, another country-loving poet, who specially mentions the pagus as taking part in it. Faunus and Silvanus were deities or spirits of the woodland among which these pagi lay, and in which the farmers ran their cattle in the summer ;[39] by Horace's time Faunus had been more or less tarred with a Greek brush, but in the beautiful little ode I am alluding to he is still a deity of the Italian farmer,[40] who on the Nones of December besought him to be gracious to the cattle now feeding peacefully on the winter pasture :—

> ludit herboso pecus omne campo
> cum tibi Nonae redeunt Decembres :
> festus in *pratis* vacat otioso
> cum bove pagus.

There is one more rite of familia or pagus, or both, of which I must say a word before I return for a while to the house and its inhabitants. One of the most important matters for the pagus, as for the landholding household, was the fixing of the boundaries of their land, whether as against other pagi or households, or as separating that land from unreclaimed forest. This was of course, like all these other operations of the farm, a matter of religious care and anxiety—a matter in which the feeling of anxiety and awe (*religio*) brought with it, to use an expression of Cicero's, both *cura* and *caerimonia*.[41] The *religio terminorum* is known to us in some detail, as it existed in historical times, from the Roman writers on *agrimetatio* ; and with their help the whole subject has been made intelligible by Rudorff in the second volume of the *Gromatici*.[42] We know that many different objects might serve as boundary marks, according to the nature of the land, especially trees and stones ; and in the case of the latter, which would be the usual *termini* in agricultural land at some distance from forest, we have the religious character of the stone and its fixing most instructively brought out. " Fruits of the earth, and the bones, ashes, and blood of a victim were put into a hole in the ground by the landholders whose lands converged at the point, and the stone was rammed down on the top and carefully fixed." [43] This had the practical effect—for all Latin religion has a practical side—of enabling the stone to be identified in the future. But Ovid [44] gives us a picture of the yearly commemorative rite of the same nature, from which we see still better the force of the *religio terminorum.* The boundary-stone is garlanded, and an altar is built ; the fire is carried from the hearth of the homestead by a materfamilias, the priestess of the family ; a young son of the family holds a basket full of fruits of the earth, and a little daughter shakes these into the fire and offers honey-cakes.   Others stand by with wine, or look on in silence, clothed in white.   The victims are lamb and sucking-pig, and the stone is sprinkled with their blood, an act which all the world over shows that an object is holy and tenanted by a spirit. [45]   And the ceremony ends with a feast and hymns in honour of holy Terminus, who in Ovid's time in the rural districts, and long before on the Capitolium of Rome, had risen from the spirit sanctifying the stone to become a deity, closely connected with Jupiter himself, and to give his name to a yearly city festival on February 23.

These festivals on the land were, some of them at least, scenes of revelry, accompanied with dancing and singing, as the poets describe them, the faces of the peasants painted red with minium, [46] according to an old Italian custom which survived in the case of the triumphator of the glorious days of the City-state.   But if we may now return for a moment to the homestead, there were events of great importance to the family which were celebrated there in more serious and sober fashion, with rites that were in part truly religious, yet not without some features that show the prevailing anxiety, rooted in the age of taboo, which we learnt to recognise under the word *religio*. Marriage was a religious ceremony, for we can hardly doubt that the patrician *confarreatio*, in which a cake made of the anciently used grain called *far* was offered to Jupiter, and perhaps partaken of sacramentally by bride and bridegroom, was the oldest form of marriage, and had its origin in an age before the State came into being. We must remember that the house was a sacred place, with religious duties carried on within it, and the abode of household spirits ; and when a bride from another family or gens was to be brought into it, it was essential that such introduction should be carried out in a manner that would not disturb the happy relations of the human and divine inhabitants of the house. It was essential, too, that the children expected of her should be such as should be able to discharge their duties in the household without hurting the feelings of these spirits. Some of the quaint customs of the *deductio* of later times strongly suggest an original anxiety about matters of such vital interest ; the torch, carried by a boy whose parents were both living, was of whitethorn (*Spina alba*), which was a powerful protective against hostile magic, and about which there were curious superstitions.[47]   Arrived at the house, the bride smeared the doorposts with wolf's fat and oil, and wound fillets of wool around them—so dangerous was the moment of entrance, so sacred the doorway ; and finally, she was carried over the threshold, and then, and then only, was received by her husband into communion of fire and water, symbolic of her acceptance as materfamilias both by man and deity.[48]

When the new materfamilias presented her husband with a child, there was another perilous moment ; the infant, if accepted by the father (*sublatus, i.e.* raised from the earth on which it had been placed),[49] did not immediately become a member of the family in the religious sense, and was liable to be vexed by evil or mischievous spirits from the wild woodland, or, as they phrased it in

later days, by Silvanus.   I have already alluded to the
curious bit of mummery which was meant to keep them
off.   Three men at night came to the threshold and struck
it with an axe, a pestle, and a besom, so that " by these
signs of agriculture Silvanus might be prevented from
entering."   The hostile spirits were thus denied entrance
to a dwelling in which friendly spirits of household life and
of settled agricultural pursuits had taken up their abode.
Nothing can better show the anxiety of life in those
primitive times, especially in a country like Italy, full of
forest and mountain, where dwelt mischievous Brownies
who would tease the settler if they could.   But on the ninth
day after the birth (or the eighth in the case of a girl)
the child was " purified " and adopted into the family and
its sacra, and into the gens to which the family belonged,
and received its name—the latter a matter of more importance than we can easily realise.[50]   From this time till
it arrived at the age of puberty it was protected by amulet
and *praetexta* ;   the tender age of childhood being then
passed, and youth and maiden endued with new powers,
the peculiar defensive armour of childhood might be dispensed with.[51]

Lastly, the death of a member of the family was an
occasion of extreme anxiety, which might, however, be
allayed by the exact performance of certain rites (*iusta
facere*).   The funeral ceremonies of the City-state were of
a complicated character, and the details are not all
of them easy to interpret.   But the principle must
have been always the same—that the dead would " walk "
unless they had been deposited with due ceremony in the
bosom of Mother Earth, and that their natural tendency
in " walking " was to find their way back to the house
which had been their home in life.   Whether buried or
burnt, the idea was the same : if burnt, as seems to have
been common Roman practice from very early times,
at least one bone had to be buried as representing the
whole body.   We have seen that certain precautions were
taken to prevent the dead man from finding his way back,

such as carrying him out of the house feet foremost ; and if he were properly buried and the house duly purified afterwards, the process of prevention was fairly complete. His ghost, shade, or double then passed beneath the earth to join the whole body of Manes in the underworld,[52] and could only return at certain fixed times—such at least was the idea expressed in the customs of later ages. But if a paterfamilias or his representative had omitted *iusta facere*, or if the dead man had never been buried at all, carried off by an enemy or some wild beast, he could never have descended to that underworld, and was roaming the earth disconsolately, and with an evil will. The primitive idea of anxiety is well expressed in the Roman festival of the Lemuria in May, when the head of a household could get rid of the ghosts by spitting out black beans[53] from his mouth and saying, " With these I redeem me and mine." Nine times he says this without looking round : then come the ghosts behind him and gather up the beans unseen. After other quaint performances he nine times repeats the formula, " Manes exite paterni," then at last looks round, and the ghosts are gone.[54] This is plainly a survival from the private life of the primitive household, and well illustrates its fears and anxieties ; but the State provided, as we shall see, another and more religious ceremony, put limitations on the mischievous freedom of the ghosts, and ordained the means of expiation for those who had made a slip in the funeral ceremonies, or whose dead had been buried at sea or had died in a far country.

I have thus tried to sketch the life of the early Latin family in its relations with the various manifestations of the Power in the universe. We have seen enough, I think, to conclude that it had a strong desire to be in right relations with that Power, and to understand its will ; but we may doubt whether that desire had as yet become very effective. The circumstances of the life of the Latin farmer were hardly such as to rid him of much of the *religio* that he had inherited from his wilder ancestors, or had found springing up afresh within him as he contended with the soil, the elements, and the hostile beings surrounding him, animal, human, and spiritual. He is living in an age of transition ; he is half-way between the age of magic and a new age of religion and duty.

NOTES TO LECTURE IV

1. Frazer, *Lectures on the Early History of the Kingship*, lect. viii.   Dr. Frazer finds traces of Mutterrecht only in the succession to the kingship of Alba and Rome, of which the evidence is of course purely legendary.   If the legends represent fact in any sense, they point, if I understand him rightly, to a kingship held by a non-Latin race, or, as he calls it, plebeian.   Binder, *Die Plebs*, p. 403 foll., believes that the original Latin population, *i.e.* the plebs of later times, lived under Mutterrecht.

2. Aust, *Religion der Römer*, p. 212.

3. In historical times the household deities were often represented by images of Greek type : *e.g.* the Penates by those of the Dioscuri. Wissowa, *Rel. und Kult.* p. 147, and *Gesammelte Abhandlungen*, p. 95 foll., and 289.   See also De Marchi, *La Religione nella vita privata*, i. p. 41 foll. and p. 90 foll.

4. De Marchi, *op. cit.* i. 13 foll.   In the ordinary and regular religion of the family the State, *i.e.* the pontifices, did not interfere ; but they might do so in matters such as the succession of *sacra*, the care of graves, or the fulfilment of vows undertaken by private persons.   See Cicero, *de Legibus*, ii. 19. 47.

5. Mucius Scaevola, the great lawyer, defined *gentiles* as those "qui eodem nomine sunt, qui ab ingenuis oriundi sunt, quorum maiorum nemo servitutem servivit, qui capite non sunt deminuti," Cic. *Topica*, vi. 29.   This is the practical view of a lawyer of the last century B.C., and does not take account of the *sacra gentilicia*, which had by that time decayed or passed into the care of *sodalitates* : Marquardt, p. 132 foll. ; De Marchi, ii. p. 3 foll.   The notion of descent from a common ancestor is of course ideal, but none the less a factor in the life of the gens ; it crops up, *e.g.*, in Virgil, *Aen.* v. 117, 121, and Servius *ad loc.*

6. Crawley, *The Tree of Life*, p. 47.

7. For the alleged extinction of the gens Potitia, and the legend connected with it, Livy i. 7, Festus 237.

8. See Marquardt, *Privataltertümer*, p. 56, and note 6.

9. There is, I believe, no doubt that the etymological affinities of the word *familia* point to the idea of settlement and not that of kin ; *e.g.* Oscan *Faama*, a house, and Sanscrit *dhâ*, to settle.

10. The exact meaning and origin of the word has been much discussed. It is tempting to connect it with *pax*, *paciscor*, and make it a territory within whose bounds there is *pax*; see Rudorff, *Gromatici veteres*, ii. 239, and Nissen, *Italische Landeskunde*, ii. 8 foll.

11. See Rudorff, *Grom. vet.* ii. 236 foll. ; Mommsen, *Staatsrecht*, iii. 116 foll. ; Kornemann in *Klio*, vol. v. (1905) p. 80 foll. ; Greenidge, *Roman Public Life*, p. 1 foll.

12. Mommsen, *Staatsrecht*, iii. 22 foll. ; Kornemann, *l.c.* ; Roby in *Dict. of Antiquities*, *s.v.* "Agrimetatio," p. 85. The view that there was freehold garden land attached to the homestead gains strength from a statement of Pliny (*N.H.* xix. 50) that the word used in the XII. Tables for villa, which was the word in classical times for the homestead, was *hortus*, a garden, and that this was *heredium*, private property. See Mommsen, *Staatsrecht*, iii. 23. It would indeed be strange if the house had no land immediately attached to it ; we know that in the Anglo-Saxon village community the villani, bordarii and cotagii, had their garden croft attached to their dwellings, apart from such strips as they might hold from the lord of the manor in the open fields. See Vinogradoff, *Villainage in England*, p. 148. For the *centuriatus ager*, Roby *l.c.* We have no direct knowledge of the system in the earliest times, but it is almost certain that it was old-Italian in outline, and not introduced by the Etruscans, as stated, *e.g.*, by Deecke-Müller, *Etrusker*, ii. 128.

13. For Latium this is proved by the sepulchral hut-urns found at Alba and also on the Esquiline. One of these in the Ashmolean Museum at Oxford shows the construction well. See article "Domus" in Pauly-Wissowa, *Real-Encyclopädie* ; Helbig, *Die Italiker in der Poebene*, p. 50 foll. Later there was an opening in the roof.

14. Von Duhn in *Journal of Hellenic Studies*, 1896, p. 125 foll., and article "Domus" in Pauly-Wissowa.

15. This is Aust's admirable expression, *Religion der Römer*, p. 214.

16. See the author's *Social Life at Rome in the Age of Cicero*, p. 242.

17. Serv. *Aen.* i. 270 ; Marquardt, p. 126.

18. *Ap.* Gellium, iv. 1. 17. For the sacredness of food and meals, see below (Lect. VIII. p. 172).

19. See a paper by the author in *Classical Rev.* vol. x. (1896) p. 317, and references there given. Cp. the passage of Servius quoted above (*Aen.* i. 730), where a boy is described as announcing at the daily meal that the gods were propitious. For the purity necessary I may refer to Hor. *Odes*, iii. 23 *ad fin.*, "Immunis aram si tetigit manus," etc.

20. *Primitive Culture*, i. 393.

21. The feminine counterpart of Genius was Juno, of which more

will be said later on.   Each woman had her Juno ; but this "other-soul" has little importance as compared with Genius.

22. See J. B. Carter in Hastings' *Dict. of Religion and Ethics*, i. 462 foll.   For Genius in general, Birt in *Myth. Lex.* s.v. ; Wissowa, *R.K.* p. 154 foll. ; Stewart, *Myths of Plato*, p. 450, for the connexion of souls with ancestry.

23. See the fifth of Plutarch's *Quaestiones Romanae*, and Dr. Jevons' interesting comments in his edition of Phil. Holland's translation, pp. xxii. and xxxv. foll.   Cp. the throwing the fetters of a criminal out by the roof of the Flamen's house.

24. *Civ. Dei*, vi. 9.   These are deities of the Indigitamenta ; see below, p. 84.

25. De Marchi, *La Religione*, etc. i. 188 foll. ; Marquardt, *Privatleben der Römer*, p. 336, "la porte est la limite entre le monde étranger et le monde domestique" (A. van Gennep, *Rites de passage*, p. 26, where other illustrations are given).

26. See below, Lect. XII. p. 281.

27. Wissowa, *R.K.* p. 96 ; Aust, *Rel. der Römer*, p. 117 ; Roscher in *Myth. Lex.* s.v. " Janus "; J. B. Carter, *Religion of Numa*, p. 13.   Cp. Von Domaszewski in *Archiv*, 1907, p. 337.

28. Frazer, *Lectures on the Early History of Kingship*, p. 286 foll. ; A. B. Cook in *Classical Review*, 1904, p. 367 foll.

29. *Gromat. vet.* i. 302, line 20 foll., describes the chapels, but without mentioning the Lares.   Varro (*L.L.* vi. 25) supplies the name : "Compitalia dies attributus Laribus Compitalibus ; ideo ubi viae competunt tum in competis sacrificatur."   Cp. Wissowa, *R.K.* p. 148.   But the nature of the land thus marked off is not clear to me, nor explained (for primitive times) by Wissowa in *Real-Encycl.*, *s.vv.* " Compitum " and " Compitalia."

30. " Enos Lases juvate."   See Henzen, *Acta Fratr. Arv.* p. 26 foll.

31. Cato, *R.R.* 5.   Cp. Dion. Hal. iv. 13. 2.   In Cato 143 the vilica is to put a wreath on the focus on Kalends, Nones and Ides, and to pray to the Lar familiaris pro copia (at the compita ?).

32. Marquardt, *Privatleben*, p. 172.

33. The controversy about the Lar may be read in the *Archiv für Religionswissenschaft*, 1904, p. 42 foll. (Wissowa), and 1907, p. 368 foll. (Samter in reply).   De Marchi (*La Religione*, etc. i. 28 foll.) takes the same view as Samter, who originally stated it in his *Familienfesten*, p. 105 foll., in criticism of Wissowa's view.   See also a note by the author in the *Archiv*, 1906, p. 529.

34. Wissowa, *R.K.* p. 148 ; the details as to the altar occur in *Gromatici vet.* i. 302.   It was on this occasion that *maniae* and *pilae* were hung on the house and compitum ("pro foribus," Macr. i. 7. 35) ; see above, p. 61.   For the *religio Larium*, Cic. *de Legg.* ii. 19 and 27.   That the Compitalia was an old Latin festival is undoubted ; but as we are uncertain about the exact nature of the

earliest form of landholding, we cannot be sure about the nature of the compita in remote antiquity. The passage from the *Gromatici* (Dolabella), quoted above, refers to the *fines templares* of *possessiones*, *i.e.* the boundaries marked by these chapels in estates of later times. See Rudorff in vol. ii. p. 263 ; Wissowa in Pauly-Wissowa, *s.v.* "Compitum."

35. Varro, *L.L.* vi. 26. I have discussed this passage in *R.F.* p. 294 ; it is still not clear to me whether Varro is identifying his Paganicae with the Sementivae, but on the whole I think he uses the latter word of a city rite (*dies a pontificibus dictus*), and the former of the country festivals of the same kind.

36. *Fasti*, i. 663.

37. *Cl. Rev.*, 1908, p. 36 foll.

38. *Georg.* i. 338 foll.

39. See my discussion of Faunus in *R.F.* p. 258 foll. I am still unable to agree with Wissowa in his view of Faunus (*R.K.* p. 172 foll.). I may here mention a passage of the gromatic writer Dolabella (*Gromatici*, i. 302), in which he says that there were three Silvani to each *possessio* or large estate of later times : " S. domesticus, possessioni consecratus : alter agrestis, pastoribus consecratus : tertius orientalis, cui est in confinio lucus positus, a quo inter duo pluresque fines oriuntur." Faunus never became domesticated, but he belongs to the same type as Silvanus. Von Domaszewski, in his recently published *Abhandlungen zur röm. Religion*, p. 61, discredits the passage about the three Silvani, following a paper of Mommsen. But his whole interesting discussion of Silvanus shows well how many different forms that curious semi-deity could take.

40. *Odes*, iii. 18.

41. Cic. *de Inventione*, ii. 161.

42. pp. 236-284.

43. *R.F.* 325, condensed from Siculus Flaccus (*Gromatici*, i. 141).

44. *Fasti*, ii. 641 foll.

45. See, *e.g.*, Jevons, *Introduction*, etc., p. 138 ; Robertson Smith, *Semites*, p. 321.

46. See, *e.g.*, Tibullus ii. 1. 55 ; Virg. *Ecl.* vi. 22, x. 27, and Servius on both these passages. Pliny, *N.H.* xxxiii. 111 ; and cp. below, p. 177. For primitive ideas about the colour red see Jevons, *Introd.* pp. 67 and 138 ; Samter, *Familienfeste*, p. 47 foll. Cp. also the very interesting paper of von Duhn in *Archiv*, 1906, p. 1 foll., esp. p. 20 : " Es soll eben wirklich pulsierendes kraftvolles Leben zum Ausdruck gebracht werden." His conclusions are based on the widespread custom of using red in funerals, coffins, and for colouring the dead man himself : the idea being to give him a chance of new life—which is what he wants—red standing for blood.

47. I am not sure that I am right in calling this whitethorn. For the qualities of the *Spina alba* see Ovid, *Fasti*, vi. 129 and 165, " Sic fatus spinam, quae tristes pellere posset A foribus nexas,

haec erat alba, dedit." In line 165 he calls it *Virga Janalis*. See also Festus, p. 289, and Serv. *ad Ecl.* viii. 29 ; Bücheler, *Umbrica*, p. 136.

48. The details are fully set forth in Marquardt, *Röm. Privat-altertümer*, p. 52 foll. The religious character of *confarreatio* and its antiquity are fully recognised by Westermarck, *History of Human Marriage*, p. 427. Some interesting parallels to the smearing of the doorposts from modern Europe will be found collected in Samter, *Familienfeste*, p. 81 foll. The authority for the wolf's fat was Masurius Sabinus, quoted by Pliny, *N.H.* xxviii. 142 (cp. 157), who adds from the same author, " ideo novas nuptas illo perungere postes solitas, ne quid mali medicamenti inferretur." The real reason was, no doubt, that it was a charm against evil *spirits*, not against poison ; but it is worth while to quote here another passage of Pliny (xx. 101), where he says that a squill hung *in limine ianuae* had the same power, according to Pythagoras. Some may see a reminiscence of totemism in the wolf's fat : in any case the mention of the animal as obtainable is interesting.

49. Dieterich, *Mutter Erde*, p. 6 foll. The idea is that the child comes from mother earth, and will eventually return to her.

50. For Roman names Marquardt, *Privatleben*, p. 7 foll., and Mommsen, *Forschungen*, i. 1 foll., are still the most complete authorities. For the importance of the name among wild and semi-civilised peoples, Frazer, *G.B.* i. 403 foll. ; Tylor, *Primitive Culture*, ii. 430 foll. All these ceremonies of birth, naming, and initiation (puberty) have recently been included by M. van Gennep in what he calls *Rites de passage* (see his book with that title, which appeared after these lectures were prepared, especially chapters v. and vi.). In all these ceremonies he traces more or less successfully a sequence of rites of separation (*i.e.* from a previous condition), of margin, where the ground is, so to speak, neutral, and of " aggregation," when the subject is introduced to a new state or condition of existence. If I understand him rightly, he looks on this as the proper and primitive explanation of all such rites, and denies that they need to be accounted for animistically, *i.e.* by assuming that riddance of evil spirits, or purification of any kind, is the leading idea in them. They are, in fact, quasi-dramatic celebrations of a process of going over from one status to another, and may be found in connection with all the experiences of man in a social state. But the Roman society, of which I am describing the religious aspect, had beyond doubt reached the animistic stage of thought, and was in process of developing it into the theological stage ; hence these ceremonies are marked by sacrifices, as marriage, the *dies lustricus* (see De Marchi, p. 169, and Tertull. *de Idol.* 16) most probably, and puberty (*R.F.* p. 56). I do not fully understand how far van Gennep considers sacrifice as marking a later stage in the development of the ideas of a society on these matters (see his

note in criticism of Oldenburg, p. 78); but I see no good reason to abandon the words purification and lustration, believing that even if he is right in his explanation of the original performances, these ideas had been in course of time engrafted on them.

51. In historical times the *toga pura* was assumed when the parents thought fit; earlier there may have been a fixed day (*R.F.* p. 56, "Liberalia"). In any case there was, of course, no necessary correspondence between "social and physical puberty"; van Gennep, p. 93 foll.

52. Wissowa, *R.K.* p. 191; J. B. Carter in Hastings' *Dict. of Religion and Ethics*, i. 462 foll.; Dieterich, *Mutter Erde*, p. 77. The whole question of the so-called cult of the dead at Rome calls for fresh investigation in the light of ethnological and archaeological research. The recent work of Mr. J. C. Lawson, *Modern Greek Folklore and Ancient Greek Religion*, seems to throw grave doubt on some of the most important conclusions of Rohde's *Psyche*, the work which most writers on the ideas of the Greeks and Romans have been content to follow. Mr. Lawson seems to me to have proved that the object of both burial and cremation (which in both peninsulas are found together) was to secure dissolution for the substance of the body, so that the soul might not be able to inhabit the body again, and the two together return to annoy the living (see especially chapters v. and vi.). But his answer to the inevitable question, why in that case sustenance should be offered to the dead at the grave, is less satisfactory (see pp. 531, 538), and I do not at present see how to co-ordinate it with Roman usage. But I find hardly a trace of the belief that the dead had to be placated like the gods by sacrifice and prayer, except in *Aen.* iii. 63 foll. and v. 73 foll. In the first of these passages Polydorus had not been properly buried, as Servius observes *ad loc.* to explain the nature of the offerings; the second presents far more difficulties than have as yet been fairly faced.

53. For recent researches about beans as tabooed by the Pythagoreans and believed to be the food of ghosts, see Gruppe, *Mythologische Literatur*, p. 370 (Samter and Wünsch). Cp. *R.F.*, p. 110.

54. Ov. *Fasti*, v. 421 foll.; *R.F.* p. 107.

LECTURE V

THE CALENDAR OF NUMA

THE religion of the household had two main characteristics. First, it was a perfectly natural and organic growth, the result of the Roman farmer's effective desire to put himself and his in right relations with the spiritual powers at work for good or ill around him. His conception of these powers I shall deal with more fully in the next lecture; but I have said enough to prove that it was not a degrading one. The spirits of his house and his land and his own Genius were friendly powers, all of them of the greatest importance for his life and his work, and their claims were attended to with regularity and devotion. From Vesta and the Penates, the Lar, the Genius, the Manes, and the spirits of the doorway and the spring, there was nothing to fear if they were carefully propitiated; and as his daily life and comfort depended on this propitiation, they were really divine members of the *familia*, and might become, and perhaps did become, the objects of real affection as well as worship. In this well-regulated practical life of the early agricultural settlers, with its careful attention to the claims of its divine protectors, we may perhaps see the germs of a real religious expression of human life.

Secondly, there was doubtless at the same time constant cause for anxiety. Beyond the house and the land there were unreclaimed spirits of the woodland which might force an entrance into the sacred limits of the house; the ghosts of the dead members were

constantly wishing to return ; the crops might be attacked
by strange diseases, by storms or drought, and man himself
was liable to seasonal disease or sudden pestilence.   The
cattle and sheep might stray into the remote forest and
become the prey of evil beasts, if not of evil spirits.   How
was the farmer to meet all these troubles, caused, as he
supposed, by spirits whose ways he did not understand ?
How were they to be propitiated as they themselves would
wish ?   How were the omens to be interpreted from which
their will might be guessed ?   How were the proper times
and seasons for each religious operation to be discovered ?
If my imagination is not at fault, I seem to see that the
Latin farmer must have had to shift for himself in most
of his dealings with the supernatural powers about him ;
religio, the sense of awe and of dependence, must have
been constantly with him.   But even here we may see, I
think, a possible germ of religious development ; for without this feeling of awe religious forms tend to become
meaningless : lull *religio* to sleep, and the forms cease to
represent effectively man's experience of life.   We have
to see later on how this paralysis of the religious instinct
did actually take place in early Roman history.

For we now have to leave the religion of the household,
and to study that of the earliest form of the City-state.
We have enjoyed a glint of light reflected from later
times on the religion of the early Roman family, and are
about to enjoy another glint—nay, a gleam of real light,
and not merely a reflected one — which the earliest
religious document we possess casts on the religion of the
City-state of Rome.   Between the two there is a long
period of almost complete darkness.   We know hardly
anything as yet, and it is not likely that we shall ever
know anything definite, about the stages of development
which must have been passed before Rome became the
so-called city of the Four Regions, when her history may
be said really to begin.   The pagus hardly helps us here ;
it was not an essential advance on the family, and its
religion was comprehensive, not intensive.   Each pagus,

however, seems to have had within its bounds an *oppidum*, or stronghold on a hill; and such oppida were the seven *montes* of early Rome, which, with the pagi belonging to them, survived in name to the end of the Republic, with some kind of a religious festival uniting them together, about which we have hardly any knowledge.[1]   This looks like a stage in the process of change from farm to city, and it has generally been believed to mark one.   Unfortunately nothing to our purpose can be founded on it. We must be content with the undoubted fact that about the eighth or seventh century B.C. the site of Rome was occupied and strengthened as a bulwark against the Etruscan people who were pressing down from the north upon the valley of the Tiber;[2] we may take it that the old central fortress of Latium, on the Alban hill, was not in the right position for defence, and that it was seen to be absolutely necessary to make a stronghold of the position offered by the hills which abut on the river twenty miles above its mouth—the only real position of defence for the Latin settlements in its rear.   Here an *urbs* was made with *murus* and *pomoerium*, *i.e.* material and spiritual boundaries, taking in a space sufficient to hold the threatened rural population with their flocks and herds, with the river in the front and a common citadel on the Capitoline hill, and including the Palatine, Quirinal, Esquiline, Caelian and Aventine hills, though the last named remained technically outside the pomoerium.[3]

It is to this city that our earliest religious document, the so-called Calendar of Numa, belongs.   That calendar includes the cult of Quirinus on the hill which still bears his name, and that hill was an integral part of the city as just described.   On the other hand, it tells us nothing of the great cult of the *trias* on the Capitoline—Jupiter, Juno, Minerva—which by universal tradition was instituted much later by the second Tarquinius, *i.e.* under an Etruscan dynasty; nor does Diana appear in it, the goddess who was brought from Latium and settled on the Aventine before the end of the kingly period.   We have, then, a

terminus ex quo for the date of the calendar in the inclusion in the city of the Quirinal hill, and a *terminus
ad quem* in the foundation of the Diana temple on the
Aventine.[4]   We cannot date these events precisely ; but
it is sufficient for our purpose if it be taken as proved
that the Fasti belong to the fully developed city, and yet
were drawn up before that conquest by the Etruscans
which we may regard as a certainty, and which is
marked by the foundations of Etruscan masonry which
served to support the great Capitoline temple.   And this
is also borne out by the undoubted fact that the calendar
itself shows no trace of Etruscan influence.   But I must
now go on to explain exactly what this calendar is.

The *Fasti anni Romani* exist chiefly on stone as inscriptions, and date from the Early Empire, between 31 B.C. and
A.D. 51.   They give us, in fact, the calendar as revised by
Caesar ; but no one now doubts that Mommsen was right in
detecting in these inscriptions the skeleton of the original
calendar which the Romans ascribed to Numa.[5]   This is
distinguished from later additions by the large capital
letters in which it is written or inscribed in all the fragments we possess ; it gives us the days of the month with
their religious characteristics as affecting state business,
the names of the religious festivals which concern the
whole state, and the Kalends, Nones, and Ides in each
month.   Excluding these last, we have the names, in a
shortened form, of forty-five festivals ; and these festivals,
thus placed by an absolutely certain record in their right
place in each month and in the year, must be the foundation of all scientific study of the religious practice of the
Roman state, taken together with certain additions in
smaller capitals, and with such information about them as
we can obtain from literary sources.[6]

The smaller capitals give us such entries as *feriae
Iovi, feriae Saturno, i.e.* the name of a deity to whom
a festival was sacred, the foundation days of temples,
generally with the name of the deity in the dative and
the position of the temple in the city, and certain *ludi*

and memorial days, which belong to a much later age than the original festivals.   But the names of those which are inscribed in large letters bear witness beyond all question to their own antiquity ; for among them there is not one which has anything to do, so far as we know, with a non-Roman deity, and we know that foreign deities began to arrive in Rome before the end of the kingly period.   Here, then, we have genuine information about the oldest religious doings of the City-state, in what indeed is, as Mommsen said, the most ancient source of our knowledge about Roman antiquity generally.

The first point we notice in studying this calendar (putting aside for the present the question as to the agency by which it was drawn up) is this : it exactly reflects a transition from the life of a rural population engaged in agriculture, to the highly-organised political and military life of a City-state.   In other words, the State, whose religious needs and experience it reflects, was one whose economic basis was agriculture, whose life included legal and political business, and whose activity in the season of arms was war.

This last characteristic is discernible chiefly, if not entirely, in the months of March and October ; and the former of these bears the name of the great deity, who, whatever may have been his origin or the earliest con-ception of him, was throughout Roman history the god of war.   All through March up to the 23rd the Salii, the war-like priests of Mars, were active, dancing and singing those hymns of which an obscure fragment has come down to us, and clashing and brandishing the sacred spears and shields of the god (*ancilia*).[7]   On the 19th these ancilia were lustrated—a process to which I shall recur in another lecture ;   and on the 23rd we find in the calendar the festival Tubilustrium, which suggests the lustration of the trumpets of the host before it took the field.   On the 14th of March,[8] and also on the 27th of February, we find Equirria in the calendar, which must be understood as lustrations of the horses of the host, accom-

panied with races. If we may take the ancilia as symbol-
ising the arms of the host, we see in the festivals of this
month a complete religious process preparing the material
of war for the perils inevitably to be met with beyond
the *ager Romanus,* whether from human or spiritual
enemies ; and that the warriors themselves were subjected
to a process of the same kind we know from the
historical evidence of later times.[9]   Now in October,
when the season of arms was over, we find indications
of a parallel process, which Wissowa was the first to
point out clearly, but without fully recognising its
religious import.[10]   It was not so much thanksgiving
(*Dankfest*) after a campaign that was necessary on the
return of the army, as purification (or disinfection) from
the taint of bloodshed, and from contact with strange
beings human and spiritual.[11]   On October 15, the Ides,
there was a horse-race in the Campus Martius, with a
sacrifice of the winning horse to Mars with peculiar
primitive ritual ; this, however, for some reason which I
shall presently try to discover, was not embodied in the
calendar under any special name.   On the 19th, however,
we find the entry ARMILUSTRIUM, which tells its own tale.
The Salii, too, were active again in these days of October,
and on the day of the Armilustrium, as it would seem,
put their shields away (*condere*) in their *sacrarium*
until the March following.   As Wissowa says, the ritual
of the Salii is thus a symbolic copy of the procedure of
war.[12]   From these indications in the calendar, helped
out by information drawn from the later entries and from
literary evidence, we see quite plainly that we are dealing
with the religion of a state which for half the year is
liable to be engaged in war.   Rome was, in fact, a frontier
fortress on the Tiber against Etruscan enemies ; she is
destined henceforward to be continually in arms, and she
has already expressed this great fact in her religious
calendar.

The legal and political significance of the calendar con-
sists in the division of the days of the year into two great

H

groups, *dies fasti* and *nefasti* : the former are those on
which it is *fas*, *i.e.* religiously permissible, to transact civil
business, the latter those on which it would be *nefas* to
do so, *i.e.* sacrilege, because they are given over to the
gods.   We need not, indeed, assume that these marks F
and N descend in every case from the very earliest times
into the pre-Julian calendar, or that the few days which
have other marks stood originally as we find them ;
but of the primitive character of the main division we
can have no doubt.   In the calendar as we have it 109
days belong to the divine, 235 to the human inhabitants
of the city.   All but two of the former are days of odd
numbers in the month, and it is reasonable to suppose
that these two exceptions were later alterations.   The
belief that odd numbers are lucky is a very widely-spread
superstition, and we do not need to have recourse to
Pythagoras to explain it ; in this rule, as in others, *e.g.*
their taboo on eating beans, the Pythagoreans were only
following a native prejudice of southern Italy.   " The
idea of luck in odd numbers," says Mr. Crooke,[18] writing
of the Hindus, " is universal."   Thus the simpler odd
numbers, three, five, seven, and nine, all recur constantly
in .folklore ; and the result is visible in this calendar.
Where a festival occupies more than one day in a
month, there is an interval between the two of one or
three days, making the whole number three or five.
Thus Carmentalia occur on 11th and 15th January, and
the Lemuria in May are on the 9th, 11th, and 13th ; the
Lucaria in July on 19th and 21st.   In some months, too,
e.g. August and December, perhaps also July and
February, there seem to be traces of an arrangement
by which festivals which probably had some connection
with each other are thus arranged ; *e.g.* in August six
festivals, all concerned in some way with the fruits of
the earth and the harvest, occur on the 17th, 19th, 21st,
23rd, 25th, and 27th.   It has recently been suggested [14]
that these are arranged round one central festival, which
gives a kind of colouring to the others, as the Volcanalia

in August, the Saturnalia in December. But the reasons
von Domaszewski gives for the arrangement, and the
further speculation that where it does not occur we may
find traces of an older system, as yet unaffected by the
so-called Pythagorean prejudice, do not seem to me
satisfactory. We may be content with the general
principle as I have stated it, and note that while religious
duties *must* be performed on days of odd number, civil
duties were not so restricted : the days belonging to the
gods, which were, so to speak, taboo days, were more
important than those belonging to men. There are, as
I have said, but two days marked in the large letters
as festivals, which are on days of even number, 24th
February and 14th March, the Regifugium and the
second Equirria ; and about these we know so little that
it is almost useless to speculate as to the reason for their
exception from the rule. Two others, 24th March and
24th May, were partly the property of the gods and
partly of men, and are marked QRCF (*quando rex
comitiavit fas*) ; but the sense in which they partially
belonged to the gods is not the same as in the case of
sacrificial festivals.

   This calendar thus shows obvious signs of both military
and political development ; in other words, its witness to
the religious experience of the Romans proves that they
had successfully adjusted the forms and seasons of their
worship to the processes of government at home and of
military service in the field. But the most conspicuous
feature in it is the testimony it bears to the agricultural
habits of the people—to the fact that agriculture and not
trade, of which there is hardly a trace, was the economic
basis of their life. At the time when it was drawn up,
the Romans must have been able to subsist upon the
ager Romanus, though, as we shall see later on, it was
probably not long before they began commercial relations
with other peoples ; for their food, which was almost
entirely vegetarian, and their clothing, which was entirely
of wool and leather,[15] they depended on their crops,

flocks, and herds ; and the perils to which these were liable remain for the State, as for the farming household, the main subject of the propitiation of the gods, the main object of their endeavours to keep themselves in right relation with the Power manifest in the universe.

We can trace the series of agricultural operations in the calendar without much difficulty all through the year. The Roman year, we must remember, began with March, and March, as we have seen, had under the military necessities of the State become peculiarly appropriated to the religious preparation of the burgher host for war- like activity. But the festivals of April, when crops were growing, cattle bringing forth young or seeking summer pasture, all have direct reference to the work of agriculture.[16]   At the Fordicidia, on the 15th, pregnant cows were sacrificed to the Earth-goddess, and their unborn calves burnt, apparently with the object of pro- curing the fertility of the corn ; and the Cerealia on the 19th, to judge by the name, must have had an object of the same kind, though the supersession of Ceres by the Greek Demeter had obscured this in historical times. The Parilia on the 19th, recently illuminated by Dr. Frazer,[17] was a lustration of the cattle and sheep before they left their winter pasture to encounter the dangers of wilder hill or woodland, and may be compared with the lustratio of the host before a campaign.   On the 23rd the Vinalia tells its own tale, and shows that the cultivation of the vine was already a part of the agricultural work. On the 25th the spirit of the red mildew, Robigus, was the object of propitiation, at the time when the ear was beginning to be formed in the corn, and was particularly liable to attack from this pest.

The religious precautions thus taken in April were not renewed in May ; but at the end of that month of ripen- ing the whole of the *ager Romanus* was lustrated by the Fratres Arvales.   This important rite, for some reason which we cannot be sure of, was a movable feast, left to the discretion of the brethren, and therefore does not

appear in the calendar. In June the sacred character of
the new crops, now approaching their harvest, becomes
apparent ; the *penus Vestae*, the symbolic receptacle of the
grain-store of the State, after remaining open from the 7th
to the 15th, was closed on that day for the rest of the
year, after being carefully cleansed : the refuse was religiously deposited in a particular spot. Thus all was
made ready for the reception of the new grain, which, as
is now well known, has a sacred character among primitive
peoples, and must be stored and eaten with precaution.[18]
This was the chief religious work of June ; in July, the
month when the harvest was actually going on, the
festivals are too obscure to delay us ; they seem to have
some reference to water, rain, storms, but it is not clear
to me whether the object was to avert stormy weather
during the cutting of the crops, or, on the other hand, to
avert a drought in the hottest time of the year. The
true harvest festivals begin in August ; the Consualia on
21st and Opiconsiva on 25th both seem to suggest the
operation of storing up (*condere*) the grain, and between
them we find the Volcanalia, of which the object was
perhaps to propitiate the fire-spirit at a time when the
heat of the sun might be dangerous to the freshly-gathered
crops.

After the crops were once harvested, ploughing and
sowing chiefly occupied the farming community until
December ; and as these operations were not accompanied
by the same perils which beset the agriculturist in spring
and summer, they have left no trace in the calendar.
Special religious action was not necessary on their behalf.
It is not till the autumn sowing was over, and the workers
could rest from their labours, that we find another set of
festivals, of which the centre-point is the Saturnalia on the
17th, Saturnus being the deity, I think, both of the operation of sowing and of the sown seed, now reposing in the
bosom of mother earth.[19] A second Consualia on the
15th, and the Opalia on the 19th, like the corresponding
August festivals, seem to be concerned with the housed

grain harvested in the previous August; I am disposed
to think that in all three we should see not only the
natural rejoicing after the labours of the autumn, but the
opening of the granaries and, perhaps, the first eating of
the grain.   For on the Saturnalia there was a sacrifice at
Saturnus' altar, followed by a feast, which was afterwards
Graecised, but doubtless originally represented the primitive feasting of the farm, in which the whole familia took
part.   This brings us practically to the end of the agricultural year as represented in the calendar; for spring
sowing was exceptional, the joyful feasts of pagus and
compitum are not to be found in our document, and the
month of February is specially occupied with the care
and cult of the dead (*Manes*).

At this point I wish to notice one or two results of
the adoption of a religious calendar such as I have been
describing, which are more to the purpose of these lectures
than some of the details I have had to point out.   First,
let us remember that agricultural operations necessarily
vary in date according to the season, and that most of
the rural festivals of ancient Italy were not fixed to a
particular day, but were *feriae conceptivae*, settled perhaps
according to the decision of some meeting of heads of
families or officers of a pagus.   That this was so we may
conjecture from the fact that those which survived into
historical times, *e.g.* Compitalia and Paganalia, and were
celebrated in the city, though not as *sacra pro populo*,[20]
were of varying date.   But all the festivals of the calendar
were necessarily fixed, and the days on which they were
held were made over to the gods.   Now by being thus
fixed they would soon begin to get out of relation to
agricultural life; just as, if the harvest festivals of our
churches were fixed to one day throughout the country,
the meaning of the religious service would sooner or later
begin to lose something of its force.   And how much the
more would this be so if the calendar itself, from ignorance or mismanagement, began to get out of relation with
the true season, as in course of time was frequently the

case ? When once under such circumstances the meaning
of a religious rite is lost, where is its psychological efficacy?
In the life of the old Latin farmer, as we saw, his religion
was a reality, an organic growth, coincident at every point
with the perils he encountered in his daily toil ; here, in
the City-state, it must from the beginning have had a
tendency to become an unreality, and it ended by becoming one entirely. Some of the old rites may have attached
new meanings to themselves ; it is possible, for example,
that beneath the military rites of March there was an
original agricultural significance ; the Saturnalia became
a merry mid-winter festival for a town population. But
a great number wholly lost meaning, and were so forgotten or neglected in course of time that even learned
men like Varro do not seem to have been able to explain
them. The only practical question about them for the
later Romans was whether their days were *dies fasti* or
nefasti or *comitiales*,—what work might or might not be
done on them.

Another point, closely connected with the last, and
tending in the same direction, is that such a calendar as
this implies rigidity and routine in religious duties. A
well-ordered city life under a strong government must, of
course, be subject to routine ; law, religious or civil, written
or unwritten, forces the individual into certain stereo-
typed ways of life, subjects him to a certain amount of
wholesome discipline. The value of such routine to an
undisciplined people has been well pointed out by Bishop
Stubbs, in writing of the effect of the rule of the Norman
and Angevin kings on the English people,[21] where it was
also a religious as well as a legal discipline that was at
work. In neither case was it the ignorant and superstitious routine of savage life, which of late years we have
had to substitute for old fancies about the freedom of the
savage ; it is the willing obedience of civilised man for
his own benefit. But if it means a routine of religious
rites which are beginning to lose their meaning ; if the
relation between them and man's life and work is lost ;

and lastly, if, as was probably the case, the Fasti were not published, but remained in the hands of a priesthood or an aristocracy,[22]—then there is serious loss as well as gain.   You begin sooner or later to cease to feel your dependence on the divine beings around you for your daily bread, to get out of right relation with the Power manifesting itself in the universe.

But, in the third place, we must believe that at first, and indeed perhaps for ages, this very routine had an important psychological result in producing increased comfort, convenience, and confidence in the Roman's relations with the divine inhabitants of his city.   A certain number of deities have taken up their abode within the walls of the city, and are as much its inhabitants, its citizens, as the human beings who live there ; and all the relations between the divine and human citizens are regulated now by law, by a *ius divinum*, of which the calendar is a very important part.   *Religio*, the old feeling of doubt and scruple, arising from want of knowledge in the individual, is still there ; it is, in fact, the feeling which has given rise to all this organisation and routine, the *cura* and *caerimonia*, as Cicero phrases it.   But it must be already losing its strength, its life ; it was, so to speak, a constitutional weakness, and the *ius divinum* is already beginning to act on it as a tonic.   Doubt has passed into fixed usage, tradition has given place to organisation. Time, place, procedure in all religious matters, are guaranteed by those skilled in the *ius divinum* ; they know what to do as the festival of each deity comes round, and at the right time and place they do it with scrupulous attention to every detail.   Thus the organisation of which the calendar is our best example would have as its first result the destruction of fear and doubt in the mind of the ordinary Roman ; it would tend to kill, or at least to put to sleep, the *religio* which was the original motive cause of this very organisation.   As the State in our own day has a tendency to relieve families of such duties as the care and education of children, so the State at Rome

relieved the family of constant anxiety about matters in
which they were ever in danger from the spirit-world.
The State and its authorities have taken the whole re-
sponsibility of adjusting the relations of the human and
divine citizens.[23]

Entirely in keeping with this psychological result of
the calendar is the fact, to which I have already alluded,
that it supplies us with hardly any evidence of the existence of magic, or of those " beastly devices of the heathen"
which may roughly be included under that word ; to use
the language of Mr. Lang, we find none of those " distress-
ing vestiges of savagery and barbarism which meet us in
the society of ancient Greece."   It is true enough that we
do not know much about what was done at the various
festivals of the calendar, but what we do know, with one
or two exceptions, suggests an idea of worship as clean
and rational as that of the Homeric poems, which stands
in such striking contrast to that reflected in later Greek
literature.[24]   When we do read of any kind of grossness
in worship or the accompanying festivities, it is almost
always in the case of some rite which is *not* among those
in the Fasti.   Such was the old festival of Anna Perenna
in March, where the plebs in Ovid's time spent the day
in revelry and drinking, and prayed for as many years of
life as they could drink cups of wine.   Such again was
that of the October horse, when after a chariot-race in
the Campus the near horse of the winning team was
sacrificed, and his tail carried in hot haste to the Regia,
where the blood was allowed to drip on the sacred
hearth ; while the head was the object of a fight between
the men of the Via Sacra and those of the Subura.[25]   We
may perhaps include in the list the ritual of the Argei, if
it was indeed, as I believe, of great antiquity ;[26] on May
15, as we have seen, twenty-seven puppets of reeds or
straw were thrown into the Tiber from the *pons sublicius*,
possibly with the object of procuring rain for the growing
crops.   Let us also note that *dies religiosi* were not
marked in the Fasti, *i.e.* days on which some uncomfort-

able feeling prevailed, such as the three days on which the *mundus* was open to allow the Manes to come up from their shadowy abode below the earth ; with the character of such days as "uncanny" the calendar has simply nothing to do. It is a document of religious law, not of *superstitio*, a word which in Roman usage almost invariably means what is outside that religious law, outside the *ius divinum* ; and it is a document of *religio* only so far as it is meant to organise and carry out the *cura* and *caerimonia*, the natural results of that feeling which the Romans called *religio*. It stands on exactly the same footing as the Law of the Israelites, which supplied them in full detail with the *cura* and *caerimonia*, and rigidly excluded all foreign and barbarous rites and superstitions.

I do not, of course, mean to say that the State did not recognise or allow the festivals which are not marked in the calendar ; the pontifices and Vestals were present at the ceremony of the Argei, and the Regia was the scene of a part of that of the October horse. But those who drew up the calendar as the fundamental charter of the *ius divinum* must have had their reasons for the selection of forty-five days as made over to the deities who were specially concerned with the State's welfare. And on these days, so far as we know, there was a regular ordered routine of sacrifice and prayer, with but little trace of the barbarous or grotesque. The ritual of the Lupercalia is almost a solitary exception. The Luperci had their foreheads smeared with the blood of the victims, which were goats, and then this was wiped off with wool dipped in milk ; after this they were obliged to laugh, probably as a sign that the god (whoever he was) was in them, or that they were identified with him.[27]   They then girt themselves with the skins of the victims and ran round the ancient pomoerium, striking at any women they met with strips of the same victims in order to produce fertility. This was perhaps a rite taken over from aboriginal

settlers on the Palatine, and so intimately connected with
that hill that it could not be omitted from the calendar.
The ritual of the three days of Lemuria in May, when
ghosts were expelled from the house, as Ovid describes
the process, by means of beans,[28] seems also to have
been a reminiscence of ideas about the dead more
primitive than those which took effect in the more
cheerful Parentalia of February : here again we may
perhaps see a concession to the popular tradition and
prejudice of a primitive population.   On the other hand,
the revelry of the Saturnalia in December, of which Dr.
Frazer has made so much in the second edition of the
Golden Bough,[29] is nothing more than the licence of the
population of a great cosmopolitan city, an out-growth,
under Greek influence, from the rude winter rejoicings
of the farmer and his *familia* ; and for his conjecture
that a human victim was sacrificed on this occasion in
ancient Rome there is simply no evidence whatever.
There is, indeed, not a trace of human sacrifice at Rome
so long as the *ius divinum* was the supreme religious
law of the State ; in the whole Roman literature of the
Republic hardly anything of the kind is alluded to ;[30]
it is only when we come to an age when the taste for
bloodshed was encouraged by the shows of the amphitheatre, and when the blood-loving religions of the East
were pressing in, that we hear of human sacrifice, and
then only from Christian writers, who would naturally
seize on anything that came to hand to hold up paganism
to derision, without inquiring into the truth or the history
of the alleged practice.[31]

Thus we may take it as highly probable that those
who drew up the calendar had the deliberate intention
of excluding from the State ritual, as far as was possible,
everything in the nature of barbarism and magic.   For
the religious purposes of a people occupied in agriculture
and war, and already beginning to develop some idea
of law and order, there was no need of any religious
rites except such as would serve, in decency and order,

to propitiate the deities concerned with the fertilisation
of man, beast, and crop, and with the safety and efficacy
of the host in its struggle with the enemies of the city.
The Roman people grew up, in their city life as in the
life of the family, in self-restraint, dignity, and good order,
confident in the course of *cura* and *caerimonia*, itself decent
and stately, if soulless, which the religious authorities
had drawn up for them.

We should naturally like to know something about
those authorities, who thus placed the religion of the State
on a comparatively high level of ritualistic decency, if not
of theological subtlety. The Romans themselves attributed
the work to a priest-king, Numa Pompilius, and probably
their instinct was a right one.   Names matter little in such
matters ; but there is surely something in the universal
Roman tradition of a great religious legislator, something
too, it may be, in the tradition that he was a Sabine,
a representative of the community on the Quirinal which
had been embodied in the Roman city before the calendar
was drawn up, and of the sturdy, serious stock of central
Italy, which retained its *virtus* longer than any other
Italian people.[32]   We are quite in the dark as to all
this, unless we can put any kind of confidence in the
traditional belief of the Romans themselves.   But there
is one point on which I should like to make a suggestion—a new one so far as I know.   Numa was said
to have been the first Flamen Dialis ; but that is
absolutely impossible, for the ancient taboos on that
priesthood would have made it impossible for him to
become supreme legislator.   Evidently this Flamen,
who could hardly leave his own house, might never
leave the city, and was at every turn hedged in by
restrictions on his activity, was a survival of those
magician-kings who make rain and do other useful
things, but would lose their power if they were exposed
to certain contingencies ; the number of possible contingencies increases till the unfortunate owner of the
powers becomes powerless by virtue of the care so

painfully taken of him.[83]   The priest of Jupiter and
his taboos carry us back, beyond a doubt, into the
far-away dim history of primitive Latium.   By the
time the eternal city was founded on the Tiber, he
must have been already practically obsolete.   My suggestion is that he is the representative in the Roman
religious system of another and more primitive system
which existed in Latium, probably at Alba, where Jupiter
was worshipped on the mountain from time immemorial.
When the strength of Latium was concentrated at the
best strategical point on the Tiber, the priest of Jupiter
was transferred to the new city, because he was too
"precious" to be left behind, though even then a relic
of antiquity.   There he became what he was throughout
Roman history, a practically useless personage, about
whom certain sacred traditions had gathered, but placed
in complete subjection to the new legal and religious
king, and afterwards to the Pontifex maximus.[84]

If there be any truth in this—and I believe it to
be a legitimate inference from the legal position of
this Flamen, and his permanent state of taboo—then
I think we may see a great religious change in the era
of the "calendar of Numa."   Inspired with new ideas
of the duty and destiny of the new city of the four
regions, a priest-king, doubtless with the help and advice
of a council, according to the true Roman fashion, put
an end for ever to the reign of the old magician-kingship,
but preserved the magician-king as a being still capable
of wonder-working in the eyes of the people.   As religious
law displaced magic in the State ritual, so the new kings,
with their collegia of legal priests, pontifices and augurs,
neutralised and gradually destroyed the prestige of the
effete survivor of an age of barbarism.

NOTES TO LECTURE V.

1. Kornemann, *op. cit.* p. 87 ; Wissowa, *Gesammelte Abhandlungen,*
p. 230 foll. ; Mommsen, *Staatsrecht,* iii. p. 790, note 1.   For the festival

of the Septimontium, Varro, *L.L.* vi. 24 ; Plutarch, *Quaest. Rom.* 69 ; Fowler, *R.F.* p. 265 foll.   This festival does not appear in the calendar, as not being "feriae populi, sed montanorum modo" (Varro, *l.c.*).   There are some interesting remarks on the relation between agricultural life and the origin of towns in von Jhering's *Evolution of the Aryan* (Eng. trans.), p. 86 foll., with special reference to Rome.

2. Von Duhn in *J.H.S.* xvi. 126 foll.   The latest research (Korte in Pauly-Wissowa, *s.v.* "Etrusker," p. 747) concludes that the arrival of the Etruscans on the west coast of Italy cannot be safely put earlier than the eighth century.

3. Hülsen - Jordan, *Rom. Topogr.* iii. 153.   In a brief but masterly paper in the publications of the *American School at Rome*, 1908, p. 173 foll., J. B. Carter deals with the whole problem of the pomoerium and the pre-Servian city.

4. Wissowa, *R.K.* p. 27.

5. In *C.I.L.* i.[2], p. 297 foll.   See *R.F.* p. 14 foll.

6. See the Fasti in *R.F.* p. 21 foll. ; or in Wissowa, *R.K.*, at end of the book.

7. *R.F.* p. 38 foll.   Marindin's article "Salii," *Dict. of Antiqq.*, is very useful and sensible.   There is little doubt that the dress and armour of the Salii represented that of the primitive Latin warrior, calculated to frighten away evil spirits as well as enemies, and that their dances in procession had some object of this kind.   It is noticeable that there were two gilds or collegia of them belonging to the Palatine and Quirinal cities respectively ; and they are also found at Tibur, Alba, Lanuvium, and other Latin cities.

8. Or 15th (Ides), according to the conjecture of Wissowa ; see *R.F.* p. 44 and *R.K.* p. 131.   It is almost incredible that this should originally have been on a day of even number, contrary to the universal rule of the Fasti.

9. See below, p. 212 foll., for further consideration of this so-called purification.

10. *R.K.* p. 131.

11. See below, p. 217.

12. *R.K.* p. 131.

13. *Popular Religion and Folklore of India*, ii. 51.   For the sacredness of the number three and its multiples, see Diels, *Sibyllinische Blätter*, p. 40 foll. ; but he limits it too much to chthonic religious ritual.   See also H. Usener, "Dreizahl," in *Rheinis. hes Museum*, vol. 58, pp. 1 foll., 161 foll., and 321 foll.   There is a summary of the results of these papers in Gruppe's *Mythologische Literatur*, 1898-1905, p. 360 foll.   I may also refer to my friend Prof. Goudy's very interesting *Trichotomy in Roman Law* (Oxford, 1910), p. 8 foll.

14. By von Domaszewski in *Archiv* for 1907, p. 333 foll.   The learned author's reasoning is often based on mere hypotheses as

to the meaning of the festivals or the gods concerned in them, and his ideas as to the agricultural features of the months July, August, December seem to me doubtful ; but the paper is one that all students of the calendar must reckon with.

15. Marquardt, *Privatleben*, pp. 459 and 569 foll.

16. For the festivals mentioned in the following paragraphs see *R.F.*, *s.v.*, and Wissowa, *R.K.*, section 63.

17. "St. George and the Parilia," in *Revue des études ethnographiques et sociologiques* for Jan. 1908. I owe my knowledge of this admirable study to the kindness of its author.

18. Frazer, *G.B.* ii. 318 foll.

19. Varro, *L.L.* v. 64, says, "Ab *satu* dictus Saturnus." And in Augustine (*Civ. Dei*, vi. 8) he is quoted as holding the opinion "quod pertineat Saturnus ad semina, quae in terram de qua oriuntur iterum recidunt." He was probably the *numen* of the seed-sowing (Saeturnus), and as his festival comes after the end of sowing, we may presume that he was the *numen* of the sown as well as of the unsown seed. In the article " Saturnus " in Roscher's *Lexicon*, which has appeared since the above note was written, Wissowa provisionally accepts Varro's etymology.

20. Festus, p. 245a, "Publica sacra quae publico sumptu pro populo fiunt, quaeque pro montibus, pagis, curiis, sacellis." See article " Sacra " in *Dict. of Antiqq.* ii. 577.

21. "Routine is the only safeguard of a people under a perfect autocracy" (*Select Charters*, Introduction, p. 19).

22. The annalists believed that the publication first took place in the year 304 B.C. : Livy ix. 46. Mommsen (*Chronologie*, p. 31) thought it possible that it had already been done by the Decemvirs in one of the two last of the XII. Tables, but again withdrawn. The object of keeping the Fasti secret was, of course, to control the times available for legal and political business.

23. This paragraph is abridged from a passage in the author's paper in the *Hibbert Journal* for 1907, p. 848.

24. See *Anthropology and the Classics* (Oxford, 1908), p. 44.

25. *R.F.* p. 241 foll.

26. Wissowa holds that it dates from the third century B.C. : Pauly-Wissowa, *Real-Encycl.*, *s.v.* "Argei." I endeavoured to refute this view in the *Classical Review* for 1902, p. 115 foll., and Dr. Wissowa criticised my criticism in his *Gesammelte Abhandlungen*, p. 222. It is dealt with at length in *R.F.* p. 111 foll. See below, p. 321 foll.

27. This is not exactly the view expressed in *R.F.* p. 315 foll., where I was inclined to adopt that of Mannhardt that the laughing symbolised the return to life after sacrificial death. I am now disposed to think of it as parallel with the ecstasy of the Pythoness and other inspired priests, or the shivering and convulsive movements which denote that a human being is "possessed" by a god

or spirit.   See Jevons, *Introduction*, p. 174.   Mannhardt's view seems, however, to gain support from Pausanias' description of the ordeal he underwent himself at the cave of Trophonius, after which he could laugh again : Paus. ix. 39.   See also Miss Harrison, *Prolegomena to the Study of Greek Religion*, p. 580.   Deubner in *Archiv*, 1910, p. 501.

28. *R.F.* p. 109 ; Ov. *Fasti*, v. 421 foll.   Ovid's account is of a private rite in the house, as elsewhere he tells us of things done by private persons on festival days.   We do not know whether there was any public ritual for these days.   For further discussion of the contrast between the two festivals of the dead, see below, Lect. XVII. p. 393.

29. *G.B.* iii. 138 foll.   The attempt to connect the so-called Saturnalia of the army of the Danube in the third century A.D. with the early practice of Roman Saturnalia seems to me to fail entirely, even after reading Prof. Cumont's paper in the *Revue de philologie*, 1897, p. 133 foll.   I should imagine that Cumont would now admit that the Saturn who was sacrificed on the Danube as described in the *Martyrdom of St. Dasius* must have been of Oriental origin, and that the soldiers concerned were in no sense Roman or Italian. For the hellenisation of the Saturnalia, see Wissowa in Roscher's *Lexicon*, *s.v.* " Saturnus," p. 432.   Wissowa, I may note, does not believe in the accuracy of the account of the " Martyrdom."

30. Nothing, that is, in the regular ritual of the Roman State— except in so far as the killing of a criminal who was *sacer* to a god can be so regarded ; and the only instance of any kind that can be quoted is that of the two pairs of Gaulish and Greek men and women who in the stress of the second Punic war and afterwards were buried alive, as it was said, in the Forum Boarium.   Wissowa, *R.K.* p. 355 and notes.   I shall return to this in Lecture XIV.

31. The earliest mention of the slaying of a victim (*bestiarius*) to Jupiter is in Minucius Felix, *Octav.* 22 and 30, *i.e.* towards the end of the second century A.D. or even later.   Cp. Tertull. *Apol.* 9, Lactantius i. 21.   I do not go so far as to say with Wissowa (p. 109, note 3) that this story is " ganz gewiss apokryph," but I take it as simply a case of degeneracy under the influence of the amphitheatre and of Orientalism.

32. For Numa see Schwegler, *Rom. Gesch.* i. 551 foll.

33. See Dr. Frazer's most recent account of this subject, in his *Lectures on the Early History of the Kingship*, chaps. iii.-v.   Prof. Ridgeway's idea that the Flamen Dialis was really a Numan institution is of course simply impossible, and the arguments he founds on it fall to the ground.   Ovid, probably reflecting Varro, speaks of the Flamen Dialis as belonging to the Pelasgian religion, which at least means that he was aware of the extreme antiquity of the office ; *Fasti*, ii. 281.   Dr. Döllinger (*The Gentile and the Jew*, vol. ii. p. 72) with his usual insight was inclined to see in

this Flamen the "ruins of an older system of ceremonial ordinances."

34. He was *sui iuris* (Gaius i. 130), as soon as he was chosen or taken (*captus*) by the Pontifex maximus; but he was subject to the authority of the P.M., like all the other flamines and the Vestals.   See Wissowa, *R.K.* p. 438 ; Tac. *Ann.* iv. 16.

LECTURE VI

THE DIVINE OBJECTS OF WORSHIP

WE must now turn our attention to what is the most difficult part of our subject, the ideas of the early Romans about "the Power manifesting itself in the universe." In my first lecture I indicated in outline what the difficulties are which beset us all through our studies; they are in no part of it so insurmountable as in this. Material fails us, because there was no contemporary literature; because the Romans were not a thinking people, and probably thought very little about the divine beings whom they propitiated; and again, because comparative religion, as it is called, is of scant value in such a study. We have to try and get rid of our own ideas about God or gods, to keep our minds free of Greek ideas and mythology, and, in fact, to abstain from bringing the ideas of any other peoples to bear upon the question until we are pretty sure that we have some sort of understanding of those Roman ideas with which we are tempted to compare them. The first duty of the student of any system of religion is to study that religion in and by itself. As M. S. Reinach observed in an address at the Congress for the History of Religions at Oxford, it is time that we began to attend to differences as well as similarities; and this can only be done by the conscientious use of such materials as are available for the study of each particular religion.

The only materials available in the case of the earliest Rome are (1) the calendar which I was explaining in the last lecture, which gives us the names of the festivals of the religious year ; (2) the names of the deities concerned in these festivals, so far as we know them from later additions to the calendar, from Roman literature, and from evidence, chiefly epigraphical, of the names of deities among kindred Italian peoples ; (3) the fragments of information, now most carefully collected and sifted, about what the Romans did in the worship of their deities. The names and order of the festivals, the names of the deities themselves, the cult, or detail of worship, including priesthoods and holy places,—these are the only real materials we possess, and our only safe guides. To trust to legends is fatal, because such legends as there were in Italy were never written down until the Greeks turned their attention to them, colouring them with their own fancy and with reminiscences of their own mythology. For example, no sane investigator would now make use of the famous story told by Ovid and Plutarch about Numa's interview with Jupiter, and the astute way in which he deceived the god, as an illustration of the Roman's ideas of the divine ; we know that it can be traced back to the greatest liar among all Roman annalists,[1] that it was in part derived from a Greek story, and in part invented to explain a certain piece of ritual, the *procuratio fulminis*. Even what was done in the cult must be handled with knowledge and discretion. Dr. Frazer has a theory that the Roman kings personated Jupiter, and uses as evidence of this the fact that in the triumph the triumphator was dressed after the fashion of the statue of the god in the Capitoline temple, with his face reddened with *minium* : forgetting that the temple, its cult and its statue, all date from the very end of the period of the kingship, and were the work of an Etruscan monarch, almost beyond doubt. There may be truth in his theory, but this is not the way to prove it ; this is not the way to arrive at a true understanding of Roman religious ideas.

What did the old Romans know about the nature of the objects of their worship ? All religion is in its development a process of gaining such knowledge : if it

makes no progress it is doomed. It is because the Jews
made such wonderful progress in this path, in spite of
formalism and backsliding, that they were chosen to produce a Teacher whose life and doctrine revealed the will and
the nature of His Father for the eternal benefit of mankind.   The fear of the Lord is imperfect knowledge, it is
but the beginning of wisdom ; but it could become, in a
Jew like St. Paul, the perfect knowledge of His will.   It
may seem absurd to think of two such religions as the
Jewish and the Roman side by side ; but the absurdity
vanishes when we begin to understand the humble beginnings of the Jewish religion as scientific research has
already laid it bare.   Knowledge of the Power manifesting
itself in the universe is open to all peoples alike, and some
few have made much progress in it beside the Jews.   The
Romans were not among these, at any rate in all the
later stages of their history ; but we have to ask how far
they got in the process, and later on again to ask also
why they could go no farther.[2]

We have seen how one great forward step in the
attainment of this knowledge was made in the religion of
the household, when the house had become a kind of
temple, being the dwelling of divine as well as human
beings, and when the cultivated land had been separated
by a sacred boundary from the mountain or forest beyond,
with their wild and unknown spiritual inhabitants.   We
met, however, with nothing in the house or on the land
that we can properly call a god, if we may use that word
for the moment in the sense of a personality as well as a
name, and a personality perfectly distinct from the object
in which it resides.   Vesta seems to be the fire, Penates
the store, or at least spirits undistinguishable from the
substance composing the store.   But inasmuch as the
farmer knew how to serve these spirits and address them,
looking upon them as friends and co-habitants of his own
dwelling, we may go so far as to guess that they were
somewhat advanced in their career as spirits, and might
possibly develop into powers of a more definite kind, if

not into gods, real *dei* conceived as persons.[8]   In other words—for it is better to keep as far as we can to the subjective or psychological aspect of them—the Roman might realise the Power better by getting to think of his nameless spirits as *dei* at work for his benefit if rightly propitiated.   There are some signs in the calendar and the other sources I mentioned just now that such a process had been going on before the State arose ; and it is certain that the whole field of divine operation had been greatly widened by that time, as we might expect from the enlarged sphere of man's experience and activity.

The deities originally belonging to the city of the four regions, *i.e.* to the city of the calendar of Numa, were known to Roman antiquarians as *di indigetes*, in contra-distinction from the *di novensiles* or imported deities, with which at present we have nothing to do.   On the basis of the calendar, and of the names of the most ancient priesthoods attached to particular cults, the Rex and the Flamines, Wissowa (*R.K.* p. 16) has constructed a list of these *di indigetes* which may be accepted without any further reservation than he himself applies to it.   They are thirty-three in number, but in two cases we have groups instead of individuals, viz. the Lares and the Lemures : the plurality of the Lares (*compitales*) we have already explained, and the Lemures, the ghosts of departed ancestors, we may also for the present leave out of account. Others are too obscure to help us, *e.g.* Carna, Angerona, Furrina, Neptunus, Volturnus,[4] except in so far as their very obscurity, and the neglect into which they and their cults fell in later times, is proof that they were not thought of as lively personal deities.   Then, again, there are others whose names are suggested by certain festivals, Terminus, Fons, Robigus, who seem to be simply sur-vivals from the animistic period—spirits inherent in the boundary-stone, the spring, or the mildew, and incapable of further development in the new conditions of city life. Faunus, the rural semi-deity, perhaps representing a group of such beings, appears in the list as the deity of the Lupercalia ; but this is a point in which I cannot agree with Wissowa and the majority of modern authorities.[5]

We are struck, as we examine the list further, by the adjectival character of many of the names—Neptunus, Portunus, Quirinus, Saturnus, Volcanus, Volturnus : these are not proper names, but clearly express some character or function exercised by the power or *numen* to whom the name is given. Saturnus is the most familiar example ; the word suggests no personality, but rather a sphere of operations (whether we take the name as referring to sowing or to seed maturing in the soil) in which a certain *numen* is helpful. Saturnus, Volcanus, Neptunus were indeed identified later on with Greek gods of a ripe polytheistic system, and have thus become quite familiar to us, far too familiar for a right understanding of early Roman ideas. We might naturally expect that the identification of Saturnus with Kronos, of Neptunus with Poseidon, would give us some clue to the original Roman conception of the *numen* thus Graecised, but it is not so. Neptunus may have had some connection with water, rain, or springs, but we have no real proof of it, and it is impossible to say why Saturnus became Kronos.[6] The only certain result that we can win from the study of these adjectival titles is that they represent a transition between animism and polytheism, a transition exactly expressed by the one word *numen*.

Numen is so important a word in the Roman religion that it is necessary to be perfectly clear as to what was meant by it. It must be formed from *nuere* as *flumen* from *fluere*, with a sense of activity inherent in the verb. As *flumen* is that which actively flows, so *numen* is that which actively does whatever we understand by the word *nuere*; and so far as we can determine, that was a manifestation of will. *Adnuere* is to consent, to give your good will to some act proposed or completed, and is often so used of Jupiter in the *Aeneid*. *Nuere* should therefore express a simple exercise of will-power, and *numen* is the being

exercising it. In time it came to be used for the will of
a god as distinct from himself, as in the fourth
Aeneid (269)—

> ipse deum tibi me claro demittit Olympo
> regnator, caelum ac terras qui numine torquet.

Or in the fourth *Eclogue* (47)—

> concordes stabili fatorum numine Parcae,

where Servius explains it as "potestate, divinatione, ac
maiestate." But beyond doubt this use is a product of
the literary age, and the word originally indicated the
being himself who exercised the will—a sense familiar to
us in the opening lines of the *Aeneid* (" quo numine laeso ")
and in innumerable other passages. Thus von Domaszewski in his collected papers (p. 157) is undoubtedly
right in defining a *numen* as a being with a will—" ein
wollendes Wesen "; though his account of its evolution, and
of the way in which in its turn it may produce a *deus*, may
be open to criticism.

The word thus suggests that the Roman divine beings
were functional spirits with will-power, their functions
being indicated by their adjectival names. Proper names
they had not as a rule, but they are getting cult-titles
under the influence of a priesthood, which titles may in
time perhaps attain to something of the definiteness of
substantival names. This indeed could hardly have been
so in the mind of the ordinary Roman even at a later age ;
and it is quite possible that if an intelligent Greek traveller
of the sixth century B.C. had given an account of the gods
of Rome,[7] he would have said, as Strabo said of an Iberian
people in the time of Augustus, that they were without
gods, or worshipped gods without names. But the name,
even as a cult-title, is of immense importance in the
development of a spirit into a deity, and in most cases, at
any rate at Rome, it was the work of officials, of a state
priesthood, not of the people. To address a deity rightly
was matter of no small difficulty : how were you to

know how he would wish to be addressed ?   Servius tells
us that the pontifices addressed even Jupiter himself thus :
" Iupiter optime maxime, *sive quo alio nomine te appellari
volueris.*"   On the other hand, in the same comment he
tells us that " iure pontificio cautum est, ne suis nominibus
di Romani appellarentur, ne exaugurari possent," *i.e.* lest
they should be enticed away from the city by enemies.
This last statement seems indeed to me to be a doubtful
one,[8] but it will serve to illustrate the nervousness about
divine names, of which there is no doubt whatever.   We
know for certain that those religious lawyers the pontifices
were greatly occupied with the task of drawing up lists of
names by which *numina* should be invoked,—formularising
the ritual of prayer, as we shall see in another lecture ;
and this must have become at one time almost a craze
with them, to judge by the lists of Indigitamenta preserved
in their books, to which Varro had access, and which were
copied from him by St. Augustine.[9]   But after all it
needed the stimulus given by actual contact with a polytheistic system to turn a Roman numen into a full-fledged
personal deity : the pontifices might carry the process
some way, but they never could have completed it themselves without the help of the Greeks.

One deity seems to stand alone in the list—Tellus or
Terra Mater, Mother Earth.[10]   We are coming directly to
the great deity of the heaven, and we might naturally
expect that an agricultural folk would be much concerned
with her who is his counterpart among so many peoples.
She does not give her name to any of the festivals of the
calendar ; but at one of them, the Fordicidia in April, at
a time when the earth is teeming with mysterious power,
and when the festivals are of a peculiarly agricultural
character, she has her own special sacrifice—a pregnant
cow, whose young are torn from her womb, burnt by the
Virgo vestalis maxima, and their ashes used in certain
mystic rites, *e.g.* at the Parilia which followed on the
21st.[11]   She seems to have had her function in human
life as well : but about this we are much in the dark in

spite of Dieterich's attempts to elucidate it in his *Mutter Erde*.[12]   Whether she played a part at the birth of a child we cannot be sure ; but at marriage there is little doubt that she was originally an object of worship, though in later days she gave way before Ceres and Juno.[13]   And as at death the body was laid in her embrace, we are not surprised to find her prominent here also : she was the home of the dead whether buried or burnt, and of the whole mass of the Manes.   We shall presently see how a Roman commander might devote himself and the whole army of the enemy to Tellus and the Manes ; and it is interesting to find that a similar formula of *devotio*, of later date, combines Tellus with Jupiter, the speaker touching the ground when he mentions her name, and holding his hands upwards to heaven when he names the god.[14]   Very curious, too, is the rite of the *porca praecidanea*, which in historical times was offered to Ceres as well as Tellus immediately before harvest ; in case a man had wittingly or unwittingly omitted to pay the proper rites (*iusta facere*) to his own dead, it was his duty to make this offering, lest as a result of the neglect the earth-power should not yield him a good harvest.[15]   Originally, we need hardly doubt, Tellus was alone concerned in this ; but Ceres, who at all times represented rather the ripening and ripened corn than the seed in the bosom of the earth, gradually took her place beside her, and the idea gained ground that the offering was more immediately concerned with the harvest than with the Manes.[16] When Cato wrote his book on agriculture, he included in it the proper formula for this sacrifice, without any indication that Tellus or the Manes had any part in the business.[17] Tellus was not a deity whose life would be vigorous in a busy City-state destined gradually to lose its agricultural outlook ; there the supply of grain, from whatever quarter it might come, was a far more important matter than the process of producing it, and it was natural that Ceres and her April festival should become more popular than Tellus and her Fordicidia, and that the Cerealia should eventually develop into *ludi* of no less than eight days' duration.   Yet Tellus survived in such forms as that of the *devotio* ; and even under the Empire we find her as Terra on sepulchral monuments, *e.g.*—

> ereptam viro et matri mater me Terra recepit,

or

> terra mater rerum quod dedit ipsa teget.

And there is a curious story, noticed by Wissowa and by Dieterich after him, that on the death of Tiberius the plebs shouted not only " Tiberius in Tiberim," but " Terram matrem deosque Manes," in order that his lot might be among the *impii* beneath the earth.[18]

So far we have met with nothing to suggest that the Roman idea of divinity had passed much beyond an advanced type of animism ; we have found little or no trace of personal deities of a polytheistic cast.   There is, however, a fact of importance now to be considered, which has some bearing upon this difficult subject. Some of the *numina* of the calendar had special priests attached to their cults ; *e.g.* among those I have already mentioned, Volcanus, Furrina, Portunus, and Volturnus, to which we may now add Pales, Flora, Carmenta, Pomona, and a wholly unknown deity, Falacer.   These nine all had flamines, a word which is generally derived from *flare*, *i.e.* they were the kindlers of the sacrificial fire.[19]   Sacrificing priests they undoubtedly always were, each limited to the sacrificial rites of a particular cult, unless authorised by religious law to undertake those of some other deity whose name he did not bear, and who was destitute, like Robigus, of a priest of his own.[20]   We have no certain evidence that all these flamines were of high antiquity ; but those attached to deities of the calendar were probably of earlier origin than that document, and as we have no record of the creation of a new flaminium in historical times until the era of Caesar-worship, it is fair to conclude that the others I have mentioned were not younger.

Now what bearing has this fact on the question as to how the early Romans conceived the objects of their worship? There are, of course, so-called priests all the world over, even among the lowest fetishistic and animistic peoples, who exercise power over the various kinds of spirits by potent charms and spells; these should rather be called wizards, medicine-men, magicians, and so on.[21] But the flamines as we know them were not such; they were officials of a State, entrusted with the performance of definite ritualistic duties, more particularly with sacrifice, and therefore, as we may assume from universal Roman practice so far as we know it, also with prayer. If they did not actually slay the victims themselves—and in historical times this was done by an assistant—they superintended the whole process and were responsible for its correct performance.[22] Does the existence of such priests come into relation with the development of the idea of a *deus* out of a numen or a spirit? What is the influence of the sacrificing priest on the divinity whom he serves? This last is a question to which it is not easy to find a ready answer; the history of priesthood, and of the moral and intellectual results of the institution, has yet to be written. Even Dr. Westermarck, in his recently published great work on the development of moral ideas, has little to say of it. It is greatly complicated by the undoubted fact that among many peoples, perhaps to some extent even among the Latins, the earliest real priests had a tendency to personate the deity themselves, to be considered as the deity, or in some sense divine.[23] But in regard to Roman priests we may, I think, go at least as far as this. When a spirit was named and localised as a friendly being at a particular spot within the walls of the city, which is made over to him, and where he has his *ara*; when the ritual performed at this spot is laid down in definite detail, and undertaken by an individual appointed for this purpose by the head of the community with solemn ceremony; then the spirit, hitherto but vaguely conceived, must in course of time become individualised. The priestly if not the popular conception of him is fixed ; there is now no question who he is or how he should be called ; " quis deus incertum est " [24] can no longer be said of him.   Once provided with a flamen and an ordered cult of sacrifice and prayer, I conceive that he had now in him the possibility of turning into a *deus* personally conceived, if he came by the chance.[25]   A few did get the chance ; others did not ; Volcanus, for example, became a god after the model of the Greek Hephaestus, while Volturnus remained a numen and made no further progress, though he was doubtless ready to " take " the Graecising epidemic when it came. I do not say that he or any other numen was the better for the change.   But I must not now pursue the story of this strange double fate of the old Roman deities ; I have perhaps said enough to show that city life, with its priest-hoods and its ordered ritual, had some appreciable effect on the deities who were admitted to it.

Among these deities there were four of whom I have as yet said nothing at all, though they are the most famous of all the divine inhabitants of Rome.   I have mentioned nine flamines ; there were in all twelve, and besides these there was in historical times a priest known as the *rex sacrorum*, the republican successor to some of the religious functions of the civil king.   This rex, and the three *flamines maiores*, so called in contra-distinction to the other nine, were specially attached to the cults of Janus, Jupiter (*Flamen Dialis*), Mars (*Flamen Martialis*), and Quirinus (*Flamen Quirinalis*).   I have kept these deities apart from the others already mentioned, not only because their priests stand apart from the rest, but because they themselves seem from the first to have been more really gods (*dei*) ; Quirinus is the only one who has an adjectival name.   Two of them, Jupiter and Mars, re-mained throughout Roman history of real importance to the State, and in Jupiter there were at least some germs of possible development into a deity capable of influencing

conduct and enforcing morality.   Of Janus this cannot
possibly be said; and as he is historically the least
important of the four, I will begin by saying a few words
about him as a puzzle and a curiosity only.

Janus, ever since he ceased to be an intelligible deity,
has been the sport of speculators; and this happened
long before the Roman religion came to an end.   In the
last century B.C. philosophic writers about the gods got
hold of him, and Varro tells us that some made him out
to be the heaven, others the universe (*mundus*).[26]   Ovid
amused himself with this uncertainty of the philosophers,
and in the first book of his *Fasti* "interviewed" the god,
whose answers are unluckily of little value for us.[27]   At
various times and in different hands Janus has been pronounced a sun-god, a heaven-god, a year-god, a wind-
god; and now a Cambridge school of speculators, to whose
learning I am in many ways indebted, has claimed him
as an oak-god, the mate of Diana, the Jupiter of aboriginal
Latium, and so on.[28]   We have fortunately long left
behind us the age when it was thought necessary to
resolve the Greek and Roman gods into personifications
of natural phenomena, and to try to explain all their
attributes on one principle; but my learned friends at Cambridge have of late been showing a tendency to return to
methods not less dangerous; they hanker, for example, after
etymological evidence, which in the case of deities is almost
sure to be misleading unless it is absolutely certain, and
supported by the history of the name.   This is unluckily
not the case with Janus; his etymology is matter of
dispute,[29] and he is therefore open, and always will be so,
to the inquirer who is hunting a scent, and more concerned to prove a point than to discover what the early
Romans really thought about a god.   In this lecture I am
but humbly trying to do this last, and I may therefore
leave etymology, with the mythology and philosophy of a
later age, and confine myself to such facts of the cult of
Janus as are quite undisputed.   They will admit of being
put together very shortly.

The first and leading fact is that Janus was the first
deity to be addressed in all prayers and invocations ; of
this we have abundant evidence, as also of the corresponding fact that Vesta came last.[30]   Secondly, we know
that he was the object of worship on the Kalends of
January, and probably of every month, and that the
sacrificing priest was in this case the *rex sacrorum*.
Thirdly, we know that he had no temple until the year
260 B.C., but that he was associated with the famous
gateway at the north-east end of the Forum—not a gate
in the wall, but a symbolic entrance to the heart of the
city, as the round temple of Vesta at the opposite end,
with its eternal fire, was symbolic of the common life of
the community.   Fourthly, we know a few cult-titles of
Janus, among them Clusius (or Clusivius), and Patulcius,
in which the connection with gates is obvious ; Junonius,
which may have originated in the fact that Juno also
was worshipped on the Kalends ; Matutinus, which seems
to be a late reference to the dawn as the opening or gate
of the day, and Quirinus, which last is also almost
certainly of late origin.   Clusius and Patulcius are
genuine old titles, if the text of the Salian hymn is
rightly interpreted ; so too is another, Curiatius, for it
was used of the god only as residing in an ancient gateway near the Subura called the *tigillum sororium*.[31]
These are all the most important facts we have to go
upon ; the double head of Janus on the earliest Roman
as is of uncertain origin, and Wissowa seems to have
conclusively shown that this representation was not
admitted to the gate called Janus Geminus until towards
the close of the republican period.[32]   The connection of
the god with the fortress on the hill across the Tiber,
which still bears his name, admits of no quite satisfactory
explanation.

Now if we recall the fact that the entrance to the
house and the entrance to a city were points of great
moment, and the cause of constant anxiety to the early
Italian mind, we may naturally infer that they would be

in the care of some particular numen, and that his
worship would be in the care of the head of the family or
community—in the case of the city, in the care of the
rex, whose duties of this kind were afterwards taken
over by the priest called *rex sacrorum*. The fact that
the word for an entrance was *ianus* confirms this conjecture; Janus was perhaps the spirit guarding the
entrance to the real wall of the earliest city, but when
the city was enlarged in the age from which the calendar
dates, a symbolic gateway was set up where you entered
the forum from the direction of Latium, answering to
the symbolic hearth in the *aedes Vestae*, and this very
naturally took the name of the deity associated with
entrances. Two other *iani* probably existed in the forum,
and the name was later on transferred as a substantive to
similar objects in Roman colonies, while a feminine form,
ianua, came to be used for ordinary house entrances.[33]
Whether there ever was a cult of the god at the real
gateway of a city we do not know; there was none at
the symbolic gateway of Rome, which was in no sense a
temple. But the idea of entrance stuck to the old spirit
of the doorway long after the reconstruction of the city,
and the rex now sacrifices to him on the entrance-day of
each month, and more particularly on the entrance-day
of the month which bears his name and is the beginning
of the natural year after the winter solstice. This is the
best account to be had of the original Janus,[34] a deity, let
it be remembered, of a simple agricultural and warlike
people, without literature or philosophy. But it is not
difficult to see how, when philosophy and literature did at
last come in a second-hand form to this people, they
might well have overlaid with cobwebs of story and
speculation a deity for whom they had no longer any
real use, who was best known to them by the mysterious
double-head on the *as* and the gateway, and for whom
they could find no conclusive parallel among the gods of
Greece.

Next in order of invocation to Janus came Jupiter,

and his priest, the Flamen Dialis, was likewise the second in rank, according to ancient rule, after the *rex sacrorum*.   Unlike Janus, Jupiter (to use the spelling familiar in England) was at all times a great power for the Roman people, and one who could be all the more valued because he was intelligible.   No one doubted then, and no one doubts now, that he was the god of the light and of heaven, *Diovis pater*, or rather perhaps the heaven itself [35] with all its manifestations of rain and thunder, of blessing and damage to the works of man; the common inheritance of the Italian peoples, dwelling and worshipped in their woods and on their hills ; and, as we know now, also the common inheritance of all Aryan stocks, the " European Sky-god," as Mr. A. B. Cook has traced him with learning and ingenuity from the Euxine to Britain.[36]

Jupiter must have had a long and important history in Latium before the era of the Roman City-state ; Dr. Frazer has seen this, and set it forth in his lectures on the early history of the kingship, though basing his conclusions on evidence much of which will not bear a close examination.[37]   The one substantial proof of it lies in the unique and truly extraordinary character of the taboos placed on his flamen, and to some extent on the flamen's wife, by the Roman *ius divinum*.   Even if we suppose that some of these may have been later inventions of an ecclesiastical college like the pontifices (and this is hardly probable), many of them are obviously of remote antiquity, and can only have originated at a time when the magical power of the man responsible for the conduct of Jupiter was so precious that it had to be safeguarded in these many curious ways.   I have already suggested that the scene of the early paramount importance of Jupiter and his flamen, in that age perhaps a king of some kind, was Alba Longa, which by universal tradition was the leading city of Latium before Rome rose to importance, and where the sky-god was worshipped on his holy mountain as the religious centre of Latium from the earliest times.   I have also suggested

that when the new warlike city on the Tiber took the
place of Alba, the worship was transferred thither, but
lost its strength in the process, and that the flamen was
little more than a survival even in the most primitive
period of what we may call for the moment Roman
history.   This can be accounted for by the fact that the
traditions of primitive Rome were connected much more
closely with Mars than with Jupiter.   Not till Etruscan
kings founded the great temple on the Capitol, which was
to endure throughout all later ages of Roman dominion,
did the sky-god become the supreme guardian deity of
his people, under the titles of Optimus Maximus, the best
and greatest of all her deities.

But Jupiter was there ; and we know certain facts of
his cult which give us a pretty clear idea of what the
Romans of the pre-Etruscan period thought about him.
In the calendar all Ides belonged to him, were *feriae
Iovis* ;[88] he seems to be the source of light, whether of
sun or moon, for neither of which the Romans had any
special divinity ; in the hymn of the Salii he is addressed
as Lucetius, the giver or source of light.   The festivals of
the vintage belonged to him, since the production of wine
specially needed the aid of sun and light, and his flamen
was employed in the cult on these occasions.[89]   When
rain was sorely needed, the aid of the sky-god was sought
under the cult-title Elicius, and as Fulgur or Summanus [40]
he was the Power who sent the lightning by day and by
night.   The ideas thus reflected in the Roman cult were
common to all Italian peoples of the same stock ; everywhere we find him worshipped on the summits of hills,
and in woods of oak, ilex, or beech,[41] where nothing but
the trees he loved intervened between the heaven and
the earth.

His oldest cult at Rome was on the Capitoline hill,
but at all times quite distinct from that which became so
famous afterwards ; he was known here as Feretrius, a
cult-title of which the meaning is uncertain,[42] and here, so
far as we can guess, there must have been an ancient oak

K

regarded either as the dwelling of the numen or as the numen himself, upon which Romulus is said to have hung the *spolia opima* taken from the king of the Caeninenses ; [43] here we may see the earliest trace of the triumphal procession that was to be.   Doubtless an *ara* was here from the first, and then followed a tiny temple, only fifteen feet wide as Dionysius describes it from personal knowledge in the time of Augustus,[44] who restored it.   There was no image of the god, but in the temple was kept a *silex*, probably a stone celt believed to have been a thunderbolt ; [45] this stone the Fetiales took with them on their official journeys, and used it in the oath, *per Iovem lapidem*, with which they ratified their treaties.   As the Romans thought of Jupiter, not as a personal deity living in the sky like Zeus, but rather as the heaven itself, so they could think of him as immanent in this stone, *Iuppiter lapis*.   And the use of the flint in treaty-making suggests another aspect of the god, which he retained in one way or another throughout Roman history ; it is his sanction that is called in to the aid of moral and legal obligations, resulting from treaties, oaths, and contracts such as that of marriage.   As Dius Fidius he was invoked in the common Roman oath *medius fidius* ; as Farreus (if this were an old cult-title) he gave his sanction to the solemn contract entered into in the ancient form of marriage by *confarreatio*, where his flamen had to be present, and where in all probability the cake of *far* was eaten as a kind of sacrament by the parties to the covenant.[46]   In much of this it is tempting to see, as we can see nowhere else in the Roman religion, faint traces of a feeling about the heaven-god brought from a remote pastoral life under the open sky, where neither forest nor mountain intervened to shelter man from the great Presence ; [47] and it is also tempting to think that there was here, even for Latins who had learnt to worship Jupiter under the form of stocks and stones in the land of their final settlement, some chance of the development of a deity " making for righteousness."

Third and fourth in the order of invocation came Mars and Quirinus, and the same order held good for their flamines. These two priests may have been subject to some of the taboos which restricted the Flamen Dialis ; [48] they too, that is, may have been to some extent precious, and have been endowed in a lost period of history with magical powers ; but if so, the memory and importance of such disabilities was rapidly forgotten in the City-state, and they were early allowed to fill civil offices, a privilege which the Dialis did not attain till the second century B.C.[49] Of the sacrificial duties of the Martialis we know nothing for certain, and can get no help from him as to the ideas of the early Romans about their great deity Mars.

Mars is in some ways the most interesting of all the Roman deities ; but except as the familiar war-god of Roman history he remains a somewhat doubtful conception. Like Jupiter and Janus he has attained to a real name ; but of that name, which in various forms is still so often on our lips, no convincing account has ever been given. Comparative mythology used to be much occupied with him, and he has been compared with Indra, Apollo, Odin, and others. But as M. Reinach said, it is time to attend more closely to differences ; and Mars seems to stand best by himself, as a genuine Italian religious conception. His name is found all over ancient Italy in various forms—Mavors, Mamers, Marmor, and as Cerfus Martius at Iguvium. His wild and warlike character, his association with the wolf and the spear, seem to suggest the struggle for existence that must have gone on among the tribes that pushed down into a peninsula of rugged mountain and dense forest, abounding with the wolves which are not yet wholly extinct there. Whether or no his antecedents are to be found in other lands, we shall not be far wrong in assuming that the Roman Mars was the product of life and experience in Italy, and Italy only.

There is an excellent general account of him in

Roscher's article in his *Lexicon*, which, like that on Janus, has the advantage of being the result of a second elaborate study, free from the enticements of the comparative method. What we know for certain about his cult at Rome in early times can be very briefly stated. First, we have the striking fact that he is conspicuous, together with the Lares, in the *carmen* which has come down to us as sung by the Arval Brethren in their lustration of the cultivated land of the Roman city :[50] " Neve luerve Marmor sins incurrere in pleores, satur fu fere Mars ! " One is naturally inclined to ask how this wild and war-like spirit can have anything to do with cultivation and crops. But there is no mistake; the connection is confirmed by the fact that he is also the chief object of invocation in the private *lustratio* of the farm, which Cato has pre-served for us.[51]   In each case the victims are the same, the *suovetaurilia* of ox, sheep, and pig, the farmer's most valuable property.   Again, let us remember that the month which bears his name is that not only of the opening of the war season, but of the springing up of vege-tation, and that the dances and singing of the Salii at this time may probably have been meant, like similar per-formances of savage peoples,[52] to frighten away evil demons from the precious cultivated land and its growing produce, and to call on the Power to wake to new life.   The clue to the mystery is perhaps to be found in the cult-title Silvanus which we find in the prayer set down by Cato as proper for the protection of the cattle when they are on their summer pasture (*in silva*): " Marti Silvano in silva interdius in capita singula boum facito." [53]   We know that wealth in early Italy consisted chiefly of sheep and cattle ; we know that these were taken in the warm months, as they still are, into the forest (*saltus*) to feed ;[54] and from this passage of Cato we know that Mars was there.   It is only going one step farther if we conjecture that Mars, like Silvanus, who may have been an offshoot of his own being, was for the early settler never a peaceful inhabitant of the farm or the dwelling, but a spirit of the woodland of great importance for the cattle-owner, and of great importance, too, in all circumambulation of the boundaries which divided the woodland from the cultivated land.[55]

But with conjecture I deal on principle but sparingly. It is time to turn to the Mars of the City-state of Rome ; and it is at once interesting to find that until the age of Augustus, who introduced a new form of Mars-worship, he had no temple within the walls, and even outside only two *fana*, one an altar in his own field the Campus Martius, the other a temple dedicated in 388 B.C. outside the Porta Capena. " He was always worshipped outside the city," says Dr. J. B. Carter in his *Religion of Numa*, " as a god who must be kept at a distance."   Should we not rather say that the god was unwilling to come within those sacred boundaries encircling the works of man ? So stated, we may see in this singular fact a reminiscence of the time when Mars was really the wild spirit of the " outland," where wolves and human enemies might be met with ; he was perhaps in some sense a *hostis*, a stranger, like the many other deities originally strange to Rome who, until the second Punic war, were never allowed to settle within the sacred precincts.[56]   In one sense, however, Mars was actually resident in the very heart of the city.   In a *sacrarium* or chapel of the regia,[57] the ancient dwelling of the king, were kept the spears and shields which the Salii carried in their processions in March and October ; and that the deity was believed to be there too must be inferred from the fact, if it be correctly stated by Servius, that the consul who was about to take the field entered the chapel and shook these spears and shields together, saying, " Mars vigila."   I am, however, rather disposed to think that this practice belongs to a time when Mars was more distinctly recognised as a god of war, and when the weapons of the Salii were thought of rather as symbols of his activity than as objects in which he was immanent.[58]

These are the salient facts in the oldest cult of Mars, and they are entirely in keeping with all we know of the early history and economy of the Roman people—a people economically dependent on agriculture, and especially on cattle-breeding, living in settlements in the midst of a wilder country, and constantly liable to the attacks of enemies who might raid their cattle and destroy their crops.   I do not see in him only a deity of agriculture, or only a god of war ; in my view he is a spirit of the wilder regions, where dwell the wolf and woodpecker which are connected with him in legend : a spirit who dwells on the outskirts of civilisation, and can with profit be propitiated both for help against the enemies beyond, and for the protection of the crops and cattle within, the boundaries of human activity.

Fourth in invocations came Quirinus, and fourth in order of precedence was his flamen.   But of Quirinus I need say little ; there is, on the whole, a consensus of opinion that he was a form of Mars belonging to the community settled on the hill that still bears his name. The most convincing proof of his identity with Mars (though identity is doubtless too strong a word) lies in the well-known fact that there were twelve Salii Collini, *i.e.* belonging to the Collis Quirinalis, occupied with the cult of Quirinus, answering to the twelve Salii Palatini of the cult of Mars.   " Quid de ancilibus vestris," Camillus says in Livy's glowing rhetoric, " Mars Gradive (the particular cult-title of the warlike Mars), tuque Quirine pater ? " [59]   Now the Quirinal was, of course, *within* the walls, and the Romans who identified the two deities noted this point of contrast with the Mars-cult ; for Servius writes, "Quirinus est Mars qui praeest paci et *intra civitatem* colitur, nam belli Mars *extra civitatem* templum habet." In keeping with this is the use of the word Quirites of the Romans in their civil capacity ; but unluckily we are altogether uncertain as to the etymology and history of both Quirites and Quirinus.[60]   And as Quirinus never became, like Mars, an important property of the Roman people, but was speedily obscured and only revived by the legend of late origin which identified him with

Romulus, he is not of importance for my subject, and I may leave him to etymologists and speculators.

There is one other deity of whom I might naturally be expected to say something ; I mean Juno.   But our familiarity with Juno in Roman literature must not be allowed to lead us into believing too rashly that she was one of those great *numina* of the early Roman State with whom I have just been dealing.   She had no special festival in the calendar ;[61] her connection with the Kalends she shared, as we have seen, with Janus.   She had no special priest of her own ; for in spite of all assertions that the flaminica Dialis was attached to her cult, I am convinced that I was right some years ago in maintaining that this is an error, though a natural one.[62]   It cannot be proved that she had any ancient temple in the city ; for the oldest known to us as strictly indigenous, that of Juno Moneta on the arx, was not dedicated till 344 B.C., and we do not know that there was an older altar on the same spot.[63]   Assuredly Rome was not in early times a great centre of the Juno-cult, as were some of the cities in her neighbourhood, *e.g.* Lanuvium, Falerii, and Veii ;[64] and the gradual establishment of her position as a truly Roman goddess may be explained by her appearance in the trias of deities in the Capitoline temple at the end of the regal period, and by the removal to Rome of Juno Regina of Veii still later, after the destruction of that city.

What, then, was Juno originally to the Roman religious mind ?   There is no more difficult question than this in our whole subject ; as we probe carefully in those dark ages she baffles us continually.   Undoubtedly she was a woman's deity, and we may aptly say of her " varium et mutabile semper femina."   The most singular fact we know about her cult is that women used to speak of their Juno as men spoke of their Genius ;[65] and it is not by any means impossible that this may be the clue to the original Italian conception of her.[66]   In that case we should have to explain her appearance as a well-defined goddess in so many Latin towns, as the anthropomorphising result of that penetration of Greek ideas into Latium from the south, of which I shall have something to say later on. Such ideas, when they reached Rome, may have produced the notion that she was the consort of Jupiter, for which I must confess that I can find no sufficient evidence in the early cult of either.[67]   But I must here leave her, for in truth she does not belong to this lecture; and it would need at least one whole lecture to discuss her adequately in all her later aspects.   The latest German discussion of her occupied sixty closely printed pages; and instructive as it was in some ways, arrived at the apparently impossible conclusion that she was a deity of the earth.

Last in the order of invocation, even to the latest days of Rome, came Vesta, "the only female deity among the highest gods of the most ancient State," [68] for Juno can hardly be reckoned among them, and Tellus had no special cult or priesthood of her own.   We have already noticed Vesta as the religious centre of the house, making it into a *home* in a sense almost more vivid than that in which we use the sacred word.   Through all stages of development from house to city this religious centre must have been preserved, and in the Rome of historical times Vesta was still there, inherent in her sacred hearth-fire, which was tended by her six virgin priestesses, and renewed on the Roman New Year's day (March 1) by the primitive method of friction.[69]   The Vestals beyond doubt represented the unmarried daughters of the primitive Latin family, and the *penus Vestae*, a kind of Holy of Holies of the Roman State, recalled the *penus* or storecloset of the agricultural home; this *penus* was cleansed on June 15 for the reception of the firstfruits of the harvest, and then closed until June 7 of the following year.[70]   These and other simple duties of the Vestals, all of them traceable to the old life on the farm, together with their own sex and maidenhood, preserved this beautiful cult throughout Roman history from all contamination. Vesta in her *aedes*, a round dwelling which was never a temple in the technical sense, was represented by no statue, and her title of Mater never suggested to the true Roman worshipper anything but her motherly grace and beneficence.[71] Far more than any other cult, that of Vesta represents the reality and continuity of Roman religious feeling ; and the remains of her latest dwelling, and the statues of her priestesses with no statue of herself among them, may still give the visitor to the Forum some dim idea of the spirit of Roman worship.[72]

NOTES TO LECTURE VI

1. Arnobius (v. 155) fortunately mentions that this story came from the second book of Valerius Antias, whose bad reputation is well known.   It was plainly meant to account for the cult-title of Jupiter Elicius, and the origin of the *procuratio fulminis*, and was invented by Greeks or Graecising Romans at a time (2nd century B.C.) when all reverence for the gods had vanished as completely as in Greece.   Yet Dr. Frazer writes of Numa as "an adept at bringing down lightning from heaven" (*Early History of Kingship*, p. 204).

2. On this subject, the evolution of the knowledge of God, I may refer to Professor Gwatkin's *Gifford Lectures* of 1904-5, published by Messrs. T. & T. Clark, Edinburgh.

3. The meaning of *deus* is well put by Mr. C. Bailey in his sketch of *Roman Religion* (Constable & Co.), p. 12.

4. Guesses can be made about these, but little or nothing is to be learnt from them to help us in this lecture.

5. I adhere to what was said in *R.F.* p. 312 foll.   We do not know, and probably never shall know, the original deity concerned in that festival.   The ritual is wholly unlike that of the *rustica Faunalia* (*R.F.* p. 256 foll.).   I believe that it dates from a time anterior to the formation of real gods—possibly from an aboriginal people who did not know any.   (I am glad to see this view taken in the latest summary of German learning on this subject, *Einleitung in die Altertumswissenschaft*, by Gaercke and Norden, vol. ii. p. 262.) At the moment of printing an interesting discussion of the Lupercalia, by Prof. Deubner, who treats it as a historical growth, in which are embodied ideas and rites of successive ages, has appeared in *Archiv* (1910, p. 481 foll.).   See Appendix B.

6. Wissowa, *R.K.* pp. 170 and 250 foll.

7. Strabo, p. 164.   Cp. Usener, *Götternamen*, p. 277, whose comment is, "Die Götter aller dieser Stämme waren 'namenlos,' weil sie nicht mit Eigennamen sondern durch Eigenschaftsworte

benannt wurden. Für einen griechischen Reisenden vorchristlicher Zeit waren sie nicht fassbar." Arnobius iii. 43, Gellius ii. 28. 2 are good passages for the principle. The latter alludes to the anxiety of *veteres Romani* on this point, "ne alium pro alio nominando falsa religione populum alligarent." Hence the formulae "si deus si dea," or "sive quo alio nomine fas est nominare," Serv. *Aen.* ii. 351; "quisquis es," *Aen.* iv. 576. See also Farnell, *Evolution of Religion,* 184 foll. ; Dieterich, *Eine Mithrasliturgie,* p. 110 foll.

8. Serv. *Aen.* ii. 351. I am inclined to think it is only an inference from the want of substantival names in so many Roman deities; surely, it would be argued, the pontifices must have had some reason for this. It is contradicted by the fact that in such ancient formulae as that of the *devotio* (Livy viii. 9) the great gods are called by their own names, though the army was in the field and in presence of the enemy. There was, however, an old idea that the name of the special tutelary god of the city was never divulged, lest he should become *captivus,* and that the true name of the city itself was unknown ; see Macrob. iii. 9. 2 foll. I believe that these ideas were encouraged by the pontifices, but were not founded on fact.

9. For the Indigitamenta see below, p. 159; *R.F.* p. 341; R. Peter's able article in *Myth. Lex., s.v.* Scholars do not seem to me to have reckoned sufficiently with the tendency of a legal priesthood, devoted to the strict maintenance of religious minutiae, to elaborate and organise the material for god-making which was within their reach. To judge by the elaboration of the ritual at Iguvium, the same tendency must have existed in other kindred Italian communities, both to develop ritualistic priesthoods, and through them to elaborate the ritual. This is, I think, the weak point of Usener's reasoning in his *Götternamen,* and as applied to Roman deities it is the weak point of an interesting article by von Domaszewski, reprinted in his *Abhandlungen zur röm. Religion,* p. 155 foll.

10. The best account of Tellus is in Wissowa, *R.K.* p. 159 foll.

11. *R.F.* p. 71; Ovid, *Fasti,* iv. 631 foll. This was a festival of the populus as a whole, and also of each Curia, like the Fornicalia in February. Both were clearly agricultural in origin, though the Curia as we know it was probably an institution of the city. I must own that I am quite uncertain as to what the thing was which was originally meant by the word Curia ; my friend Dr. J. B. Carter may have something to say on the subject in his book on the Roman religion in the Jastrow series.

12. Dieterich, *Mutter Erde,* pp. 11 and 73 foll.

13. Virg. *Aen.* iv. 166, "prima et Tellus et pronuba Iuno Dant signum"; commenting on which Servius wrote, "quidam sane etiam Tellurem praeesse nuptiis tradunt ; nam et in auspiciis nuptiarum invocatur : cui etiam virgines, vel cum ire ad domum mariti coeperint, vel iam ibi positae, diversis nominibus vel ritu sacrificant." There is little doubt that Tellus is frequently concealed under the names of

Ceres, Dea Dia, etc. For Ceres and Juno in marriage rites, see Marquardt, *Privatleben*, p. 49.

14. See below, p. 206 foll.; Macrob. iii. 9. 11; Deubner in *Archiv*, 1905, p. 66 foll.

15. See De Marchi, *La Religione, etc.*, i. p. 188 and reff. (The reference to Gellius should be iv. 6. 7, not iv. 67.) Like some other operations of the Roman religion, this became a form, and was used as a kind of insurance, whether or no there had been any omission; Wissowa, *R.K.* p. 160.

16. That Ceres represented the *fructus* is shown by the fact that in the XII. Tables the man who raided a field of standing corn at night was made *sacer* to her; Pliny, *N.H.* xviii. 12.

17. Cato, *R.R.* 134. De Marchi, *op. cit.* p. 135. Janus, Jupiter, and Juno are concerned in this rite, Ceres coming last. Varro has preserved the part of Tellus for us: "quod humatus non sit, heredi porca praecidanea suscipienda Telluri et Cereri, aliter familia non pura est" (*ap. Nonium*, p. 163).

18. The verses are quoted by Dieterich, *Mutter Erde*, p. 75, among others from Buecheler's *Anthology of Roman Epitaphs*, Nos. 1544 and 1476. The story is told in Suetonius' *Life of Tib.* c. 75, and again of Gallienus by Aurelius Victor (*Caes.* c. 33).

19. Marquardt, p. 326, who notes that the Romans themselves derived the word from *filum*, a fillet; *e.g.* Varro, *L.L.* v. 84, "quod in Latio capite velato erant semper, ac caput cinctum habebant *filo*." Modern etymologists equate the word with *Brahman*.

20. Thus the Flamen Quirinalis sacrificed at the Robigalia, *R.F.* p. 89, and with the Pontifices and Vestals took part in the Consualia, Marq. 335.

21. We may note here that the most general Latin name for a priest was *sacerdos*, which seems to have excluded all magic, etc.; it means an office sanctioned by the State. On the general question of the origin of priesthood see Jevons, *Introduction, etc.*, ch. xx., with whose explanations, however, I cannot entirely agree. I should prefer to keep the word priest for an official who sacrifices and prays to his god. In this view I am at one with E. Meyer, *Geschichte des Altertums*, i.[2] p. 121 foll. God and priest go together as permanent, regular in function, and entrusted by a community with certain duties.

22. Marquardt, p. 180; Wissowa, *R.K.* p. 427. The popa or victimarius is seen in many artistic representations of sacrifice, *e.g.* Schreiber, *Atlas of Classical Antiquities*, plate xvii. figs. 1 and 3.

23. Jevons, ch. xx.; Frazer, *G.B.* i. 245 foll., and *Lectures on Early History of Kingship*, Lectures ii. and v.

24. Virg. *Aen.* viii. 352.

25. In a valuable paper in his *Gesammelte Abhandlungen* (p. 284) Wissowa says that "personal conception of deity is absolutely strange to the old Roman religion of the *di indigetes*." I believe this to be

essentially true; but my point is that localisation and ritual prepared the way for the reception of Greek ideas of personality. The process had already begun in the religion of the house; but it was not likely there to come in contact with foreign germs. When Janus and Vesta, who were in every house (Wissowa, p. 285), were localised in certain points in a city, they would be far more likely to acquire personality, if such an idea came in their way, than in the worship of the family.

26. Aug. *Civ. Dei*, vii. 28, "quem alii caelum, alii dixerunt esse mundum." Dr. Frazer, citing this passage (*Kingship*, p. 286) in support of his view that Janus was a duplicate of Jupiter, has omitted to notice that some theorisers fancied he was the *universe*, which by itself is enough to betray the delusive nature of this kind of theological speculation. Varro elsewhere gives us a clue to the liability of Janus to be exalted in this unnatural fashion, *L.L.* vii. 27, "divum deo" (in the Salian hymn), if this be taken as referring to Janus, as it may be, comparing Macrob. i. 9. 14. But this is easily explained by the position of Janus in prayers; cp. Cic. *Nat. Deor.* ii. 27. 67, "cum in omnibus rebus vim haberent maximam prima et extrema, principem in sacrificando Ianum esse voluerunt." The phrase "Deorum" or "Divum deus" is indeed remarkable, and unparalleled in Roman worship; but no one acquainted with Roman or Italian ritual will for a moment suspect it of meaning "God of gods" in either a Christian or metaphysical sense. I shall have occasion to notice the peculiar use of the genitive case and of genitival adjectives in worship later on. See below, p. 153 foll.

27. *Fasti*, i. 89 foll.; *R.F.* p. 281 foll.

28. Frazer, *l.c.* (a page of which every line appears to me to be written under a complete misapprehension of the right methods of research into the nature of Roman gods); A. B. Cook, *Classical Review*, vol. xviii. 367 foll.; Professor Ridgeway, *Who were the Romans?* p. 12, where, among other remarkable statements, Janus is confidently said to have been introduced at Rome by the Sabine Numa, and therefore to have been a Sabine deity, an assumption quite irreconcilable with those of Dr. Frazer and Mr. Cook. In striking contrast with such speculations is a sensible paper on Janus in M. Toutain's *Études de mythologie et d'histoire*, p. 195 foll. (Paris, 1909).

29. Dr. Frazer is aware of this; see his *Kingship*, p. 285, note 1. See also Roscher in *Myth. Lex., s.v.* "Janus," p. 45 foll.

30. For the evidence for this and the following facts, see Roscher's article just cited, or Wissowa, *R.K.* p. 91 foll.; cp. *R.F.* p. 280 foll. The cult epithets of Janus are thus explained by von Domaszewski, *Abhandlungen*, p. 223, note 1, "Bei Ianus tritt regelmässig der Begriff des Wesens hinzu, dessen Wirkung er von Anfang an bestimmt, so I. Conseuius der Anfang der in Consus wirkenden Kraft, und in derselbe Weise I. Iunonius, Matutinus," etc. This is reasonable, but it does not suit with I. Patulcius-Clusius, and I cannot accept it with confidence at present.

31. Roscher, *op. cit.* p. 34.

32. Wissowa, *Gesammelte Abhandlungen*, p. 284 foll

33. Festus, p. 185.

34. It is due to the good sense and learning of Dr. Roscher; he had previously, when working on the old methods, tried to prove that Janus was a "wind-god" (*Hermes der Windgott*, Leipzig, 1878); but a more searching inquiry into the Roman evidence, when the prepossessions had left him which the comparative method is so likely to produce, brought him to the view I have explained in outline, which has been adopted in the main by Wissowa, Aust, and J. B. Carter, as well as by myself in *R.F.* The last word about so puzzling a deity can of course never be said; but if we indulge in speculations about him we must use the Roman evidence with adequate knowledge of the criticism it needs.

35. This difference between Zeus and Jupiter has been pointed out by Wissowa, *R.K.* p. 100; Jupiter stands for the heaven even in classical Latin literature, as we all know.

36. See his papers in the *Classical Review*, vol. xvii. 270 and xviii. 365 foll., and in *Folklore*, vol. xv. 301; xvi. 260 foll.

37. *Kingship*, p. 196 foll.

38. Macrobius i. 15. 14. In historical times a white victim, *ovis idulis*, was taken to the Capitol by the *via sacra* in procession (Ov. *Fasti*, i. 56. 588). Festus says that some derived the term *via sacra* from this procession (p. 290); and to this Horace may be alluding in *Ode* iii. 30. 8, "dum Capitolium Scandet cum tacita virgine pontifex."

39. *R.F.* pp. 86, 204.

40. *R.F.* p. 160.

41. No doubt Jupiter was specially connected with the oak, as Mr. Cook has shown with great learning in the paper cited above, note 36; but at Rome he had an ancient shrine among beeches, and was known as I. Fagutalis: Varro, *L.L.* v. 152; Paulus 87. For I. Viminalis, see *R.F.* p. 229.

42. See Aust's article "Jupiter" in *Myth. Lex.* p. 673.

43. Aust gives a cut of a coin of the consul Claudius Marcellus (223 B.C.) dedicating *spolia opima* in this little temple, according to the ancient fashion, supposed to be initiated by Romulus, Livy i. 10.

44. Dionys. Hal. ii. 34.

45. *R.F.* p. 230.

46. See De Marchi's careful investigation, *La Religione, etc.*, i. p. 156 foll.; Gaius i. 112. The cult-title should indicate that the god was believed to be immanent in the cake of *far*, rather than that it was offered to him (so I should also take I. Dapalis, though in later times the idea had passed into that of sacrifice, Cato, *R.R.* 132), and if so, the use of the cake was sacramental; cp. the rite at the Latin festival, *R.F.* p. 96.

47. There are distinct traces of a practice of taking oaths in the

open air, *i.e.* under the sky ; of Dius Fidius, unquestionably a form of Jupiter, Varro says (*L.L.* v. 66), "quidam negant sub tecto per hunc deiurare oportere." Cp. Plutarch, *Quaest. Rom.* 28 ; *R.F.* p. 138. For the conception of a single great deity as primitive, see Lang, *The Making of Religion*, ch. xii.; Flinders Petrie, *Religion of Egypt* (in Constable's shilling series), ch. i.; Ross, *The Original Religion of China*, p. 128 foll.; Warneck, *Die Lebenskräfte des Evangeliums*, p. 20 (of the Indian Archipelago). The last reference I owe to Professor Paterson, of Edinburgh University.

48. Serv. *Aen.* viii. 552, "more enim veteri sacrorum neque Martialis flamen neque Quirinalis omnibus caerimoniis tenebantur quibus flamen Dialis, neque diurnis sacrificiis distinebatur." It is, however, possible that under the word *caerimonia* Servius is not here including taboos, but active duties only.

49. See my paper, "The Strange History of a Flamen Dialis," in *Classical Review*, vol. vii. p. 193.

50. Henzen, *Acta Fratr. Arv.* p. 26.

51. Cato, *R.R.* 141 ; Henzen, *op. cit.* p. 48.

52. Frazer, *G.B.* iii. 123, note 3 ; *R.F.* p. 40, for further examples. It may be worth while to point out here that the coupling of all farm animals except goats took place in spring or early summer ; Varro, *R.R.* ii. 2 foll. Isidorus (*Orig.* v. 33), who embodies Varro and Verrius to some extent, derived the name Mars from *mares*, because in the month of March "cuncta animalia ad mares aguntur."

53. I prefer, with De Marchi, to take Silvanus here as a cult-title, though we do not meet with it elsewhere ; see *La Religione, etc.*, p. 130 note ; but Wissowa, who has a prejudice against the view that Mars was connected with agriculture, insists on taking Marti Silvano as a case of asyndeton, *i.e.* as two deities.

54. See, *e.g.*, Varro, *L.L.* v. 36, "quos agros non colebant propter silvas aut id genus, ubi pecus possit pasci, et possidebant, ab usu salvo saltus nominarunt."

55. Cato, *R.R.* 141. Mars is there invoked as able to keep off (*averruncare*) evil influences and to make the crops grow, etc.; he has become in the second century B.C. a powerful deity in the actual processes of husbandry, just as he became in the city a powerful deity of war. But as he was not localised either on the farm or in the city, I prefer to think that he was originally conceived as a Power outside the boundary in each case, but for that very reason all the more to be propitiated by the settlers within it.

56. See below, p. 235.

57. So Wissowa, *R.K.* p. 131. Cp. *R.F.* p. 39, note 4. Deubner in *Archiv*, 1905, p. 75.

58. Servius, commenting on line 3 of *Aen.* viii. (*utque impulit arma*) writes : "nam is qui belli susceperat curam, sacrarium Martis ingressus, primo ancilia commovebat, post hastam simulacri ipsius

dicens, Mars vigila." The mention of a statue shows that this account belongs to a late period. But Varro seems to have stated that there was originally only a spear; see a passage of Clement of Alexandria in the fragments of the *Ant. rer. div.*, Agahd, p. 210, to which Deubner (*l.c.*) adds Arnobius vi. 11. Deubner calls this spear a fetish, which is not the right word if the deity were immanent in it in the sense suggested by "Mars vigila." See above, p. 116. If Servius correctly reports the practice, it must be compared with the clashing of shields and spears by the Salii, which may thus have had a positive as well as negative object.

59. Livy v. 52.

60. Mr. A. B. Cook (*Classical Review*, 1904, p. 368) has tried to connect both names with the Greek word πρῖνος, and Professor Conway, quoted by him, is inclined to lend the weight of his great authority to the conjecture. Thus Quirinus would be an oak-god, and Quirites oak-spearmen. We must, however, remember that Mr. Cook is, so to speak, on an oak scent, and his keenness as a hunter leads him sometimes astray. One is a little perplexed to understand why Jupiter, Janus, Mars, and Quirinus should all be oak-gods (and all in origin identical as such !). On the other hand, it is fair to note that the original spear was probably of wood, with the point hardened in the fire, like the *hasta praeusta* of the Fetiales: Festus, p. 101. If *quiris* has really anything to do with oaks, it would be more natural to explain the two words as springing from an old place-name, Quirium, as Niebuhr did long ago, and to derive that again from the oaks among which it may have stood. But I am content to take *quiris* as simply a spear, as Buecheler did; see Deubner, *op. cit.* p. 76. Since the above was written, the article " Quirinus " by Wissowa in the *Myth. Lex.* has appeared. Naturally it does not add anything to our knowledge; but Wissowa holds to the opinion that the most probable derivation of the name Quirinus is from Quirium, possibly the name of the settlement on the Quirinal; and compares *Q. pater* (*e.g.* Livy v. 52. 7) with the *Reatinus pater* of *C.I.L.* ix. 4676.

61. The Nonae Caprotinae (July 7), the day when women sacrificed to Juno Caprotina under a wild fig-tree in the Campus Martius, is not known to us except from Varro. See *R.F.* p. 178, where (note 8) is a suggestion that the festival had to do with the *caprificatio*, or method of ripening the figs, which Dr. Frazer has expanded in his *Lectures on Kingship*, p. 270, believing the process to be that of fertilisation.

62. *Classical Review*, vol. ix. p. 474 foll. The same view has recently been taken independently by W. Otto in *Philologus*, 1905, pp. 215 foll., 221. It is perfectly clear that the monthly sacrifice to Juno was the duty of the wife of the *rex sacrorum*; a pontifex minor is also mentioned (Macrob. i. 15. 19).

63. Wissowa, *R.K.* p. 116.

64. *Ib.* p. 114.

65. See Ihm's article "Iunones" in *Myth. Lex.* vol. ii. 615; Pliny, *N.H.* ii. 16.

66. Dr. J. B. Carter tells me that he has abandoned this explanation of the evolution of Juno. On the other hand, von Domaszewski seems in some measure to accept it (*Abhandlungen*, p. 169 foll.), when he says that "similar functions, when exercised by different *numina*, can eventually produce a god. *Auf diese Weise ist Iuno geworden.*" He means that the creative power is called Juno in a woman, or in a people (Iuno Populonia), or in the curiae (Iuno Curitis), and that an independent deity, Juno *par excellence*, emerges from all these. But so far I cannot follow him.

67. There is no real evidence from purely Roman sources of this fancied conjugal or other relation, if we exclude that of the alleged cult of Juno by the Flaminica Dialis. This has been well seen and expressed by W. Otto, *l.c.* p. 215 foll.; see also *Classical Review* as quoted above. As we shall see in the next lecture, Dr. Frazer is much concerned to show that Jupiter and Juno are actually a married pair, and consequently he will have nothing to do with my opinion on this point : *Early History of Kingship,* p. 214 foll., and *Adonis, Attis, Osiris,* ed. 2, p. 410, note 1.

68. Wissowa, *R.K.* p. 141.

69. Festus, p. 106 ; Macrob. i. 12. 6.

70. I have discussed the Vestalia and the nature of Vesta and her cult in *R.F.* p. 145 foll. See also Marquardt, p. 336 foll., and Wissowa, *R.K.* p. 141 foll.

71. Ovid, *Fasti,* vi. 296, says that he had been stupid enough to believe that there was a statue in the *aedes Vestae,* but found out his mistake :—

> esse diu stultus Vestae simulacra putavi ;
> mox didici curvo nulla subesse tholo.

The passage is interesting as showing how natural it was for a Roman of the Graeco-Roman period to suppose that his deities must be capable of taking iconic form. For anthropomorphic representations of Vesta in other places and at Pompeii, see Wissowa, *Gesammelte Abhandlungen,* p. 67 foll.

72. See Lanciani, *Ruins and Excavations of Ancient Rome,* p. 223 foll. The statues of the *virgines vestales maximae,* discovered in the Atrium Vestae, all belong to the period of the Empire. They are now in the museum of the Baths of Diocletian.

LECTURE VII

THE DEITIES OF THE EARLIEST RELIGION: GENERAL CHARACTERISTICS

In the last lecture we interrogated the calendar as to the deities whose festivals are recorded in it, with the aid of what we know of the most ancient priesthoods attached to particular cults. The result may be stated thus: we found a number ot impersonal *numina*, with names of adjectival form, such as Saturnus, Vertumnus, and so on; others with substantival names, Tellus, Robigus, Terminus; the former apparently functional deities, concerned in the operations of nature or man, and the latter spirits immanent in objects—Mother Earth herself, a stone, the mildew, or (like Janus and Vesta) the entrance and the hearth-fire of human dwellings or cities. Lastly, we found from the evidence, chiefly of the priesthoods, that certain more important divinities stand out from the crowd of spirits, Janus, Jupiter, Mars, Quirinus, and Vesta; and we found some reason to think that these, and possibly a few of the others, by becoming the objects of priestly *cura* and *caerimonia* at particular spots in the city, were not unlikely to become also in some sense personal deities, to acquire a quasi-human personality, if they came by the chance. In the present lecture I must go rather more closely into such evidence as we possess bearing on the mental conception which these early Romans had formed of the divine beings whom they had admitted within their city.

And, first, we must be quite clear that in those early ages there was nothing in Rome which we can call a temple, as we understand the word ; nor was there any such representation of a deity as we can call an image or *eidolon*. The deities were settled in particular spots of ground, which were made *loca sacra*, *i.e.* handed over to the deity by the process of *consecratio* authorised by the *ius divinum*.[1] It was matter of no moment what might be erected on this bit of ground ; there might be a rude house like that of Vesta, round in shape like the oldest Italian huts ; there might be a gateway like that of Janus ; or the spot might be a grove, or a clearing within it (*lucus*), as in the case of Robigus or the Dea Dia of the Arval Brethren. All such places might be called by the general name *fanum* ; and as a rule no doubt each *fanum* contained a *sacellum*, *i.e.* a small enclosure without a roof, containing a little altar (*ara*). These "altars" may at first have been nothing more than temporary erections of turf and sods ; permanent stone altars were probably a later development. Servius tells us that in later times it was the custom to place a sod (*caespes*) on the top of such a stone altar, which must be one of the many survivals in cult of the usages of a simpler age.[2]

With such spots as these we cannot associate anything in the nature of an image of the deity established there ; and we have every reason to believe that no such thing was known at Rome until the Etruscan temple of the Capitoline trias was built near the end of the regal period. Varro expressly declared that the Romans remained for more than 170 years without any images of their gods, and added that those who first introduced such images " civitatibus suis et metum dempsisse et errorem addidisse."[3] What he had in his mind is clear ; he had indeed no direct knowledge of those early times, but he is thinking of a definite traditional date in the kingly period—the last year of the reign of Tarquinius Priscus, who, according to Varro's own account, built the temple on the Capitol and placed in it a statue of Jupiter.[4] That was the oldest image of which he knew anything ; and, as Wissowa has remarked, his belief is entirely corroborated

by the fact that in every single case in which the image of
a god has any part in his cult, it is always either this
Capitoline Jupiter or some deity of later introduction and
non-Roman origin.   It is also borne out by another significant and interesting fact—that the next image to be
introduced, that of Diana in the temple on the Aventine,
was a copy of the ξόανον of Artemis at Massilia, itself a
copy of the famous one at Ephesus.[5]   Let us note that
these two earliest statues were placed in roofed temples
which were the dwelling-places of gods in an entirely new
sense ; so far no Roman deity of the city had been so
housed, because he could not be thought of in terms of
human life, as visible in human form and needing shelter.
But this later and foreign notion of divinity so completely
took possession of the minds of the Romans of the cosmopolitan city that Varro is the only writer who has preserved
the tradition of the older way of thinking.   In the religion
of the family Ovid indeed has charmingly expressed it,
perhaps on the authority of some lost passage of Varro[6] :—

> ante focos olim scamnis considere longis
> mos erat, et mensae credere adesse deos.

Tibullus in one passage has mentioned what seems to be
some rude attempt to give outward shape and form to an
ancient pastoral deity[7] :—

> lacte madens illic suberat Pan ilicis umbrae
> et facta agresti lignea falce Pales.

And Propertius hints at a like representation of Vertumnus,
the garden deity.   But without some corroborative evidence it is hardly safe to take these as genuine examples
of early iconic worship.
    Thus we may take it as certain that even the greater
deities of the calendar, Janus, Jupiter, Mars, Quirinus, and
Vesta, were not thought of as existing in any sense in
human form, nor as personal beings having any human
characteristics.   The early Romans were destitute of
mythological fancy, and as they had never had their
deities presented to them in visible form, could hardly

have invented such stories about them as sprang up in a most abundant crop when Greek literature and Greek art had changed their mental view of divinity. Roman legends were occupied with practical matters, with kings and the foundation of cities; and even among these it is hardly possible to detect those which may be really Roman, for they are hidden away, like rude ancient frescoes, under the elaborate decorations of the Greek artists, who seized upon everything that came to hand, including the old deities themselves, to amuse themselves and win the admiration of their dull pupils at Rome. He who would appreciate the difficulty of getting at the original rude drawings must be well acquainted with the decorative activity of the Alexandrian age.

Thus we might well presume *a priori* that the old Roman gods were not conceived as married pairs, nor as having children; and this is indeed the conclusion at which we have arrived after half a century or more of most careful and conscientious investigation by a series of German scholars. But quite recently in this country the contrary view has been put forward by an author of no less weight than Dr. Frazer; and another eminent Cambridge scholar, Mr. A. B. Cook, evidently inclines to the same view. I should in any case be reluctant to engage in controversy with two valued personal friends; but it is just possible that in what follows I may be able to throw some faint light on the evolution of the idea of marriage among divine beings; and on the strength of this I am content for the moment to be controversial. Dr. Frazer's arguments, with strictures on my opinions, will be found in an appendix to his book on *Adonis, Attis, Osiris*, 2nd edition.

In pure animism the spirits are nameless; when their residence and functions are more clearly recognised they acquire names, and these names are naturally masculine or feminine among peoples whose language is not genderless, as was the case with the Sumerians of Babylonia.[8] This would seem to be the first step on the path to a

personal conception of divinity.   But there are signs that
the Romans had not got very far on this path when we
begin to know anything about their religion.   I have
already alluded to the formula " Sive deus sive dea," which
occurs in the ritual of the Fratres Arvales, in the formula
given by Cato for making a new clearing, and elsewhere ;[9]
and indeed there seems to have been always some uncertainty about the sex of one or two well-known deities,
such as Pales and Pomonus or Pomona.[10]   It is not,
therefore, *a priori* probable that the process of personalisation (if I may coin the word) should have proceeded, at
the period we are treating of, so far as to ascribe to these
named deities of both sexes the characteristics of human
beings in social life and intercourse.   Yet Varro, as Dr.
Frazer points out, is quoted by St. Augustine as saying
that his ancestors (that is, as Augustine adds), " veteres
Romanos," believed in the marriage of gods and in their
procreative power.[11]   If Varro wrote " maiores meos," as
he seems to have done, of whom was he really thinking ?
Was Augustine's comment based on the rest of Varro's
text, or was he jumping to a conclusion which would
naturally serve his own purpose ?   Varro, of course, was
not a Roman, but from Reate in the Sabine country.
But even if he were thinking of Rome, how far back
would his knowledge extend ?   The Romans had known
Greek married gods for three or four centuries before his
time, and he may quite well be thinking of these.   Of
the *di indigetes* of an earlier period he could hardly know
more than we do ourselves ; his only sources of information were the facts of the cult and the books of the pontifices.   The facts of the cult, so far as he and others have
recorded them, suggest no pairing of deities, no " sacred
marriage." [12]   The pontifical books, which contained rules
and formulae for the proper invocation of deities by their
right names, do indeed seem to have suggested a certain
conjunction of male and female divine names ; and it is
just possible that this is what Varro had in his mind
when he wrote the passage seized upon by Augustine.

I will proceed at once to examine this evidence, as it is incidentally of great interest in the history of Italian religion ; and Dr. Frazer will probably allow that his conclusion must stand or fall by it.

The evidence to which I allude is preserved in the 13th book of the *Noctes Atticae* of Aulus Gellius (ch. xxiii.), and extracted from " libri sacerdotum populi Romani," as " comprecationes deorum immortalium " ; these also occur, he says, in *plerisque antiquis orationibus, i.e.* in the invocations to the gods made by the orator at the beginning or end of his speech.[18]   Among these Gellius found the following conjunctions of divine names : Lua Saturni, Salacia Neptuni, Hora Quirini, Virites Quirini, Maia Volcani, Herie Iunonis, Moles Martis, and Neriene Martis, or Nerio Martis.   Now among these conjunctions there are three which obviously do not express pairs of deities, married or other, viz. Virites Quirini, Moles Martis, and Herie Iunonis ; the first two of which plainly mean the strength or force of Quirinus and Mars, and the third conjoins two female names.   The question is whether the others are to be understood as giving us the names of the " wives " of Saturnus, Neptunus, Quirinus, Volcanus, and Mars.   The fact that these are associated with others which cannot mean anything of the kind is itself against this conclusion ; but I have carefully examined each pair by the light of such stray information about them as we possess, and have failed to find anything to suggest Dr. Frazer's emphatic conclusion that these are married pairs.   I should be tedious if I were to go through the evidence in detail in a lecture like this ; but I will take the pair which Gellius himself discusses, and on which Dr. Frazer chiefly relies, Neriene or Nerio Martis : it is the pair about which we know most, and in every way is the most interesting of the set.[14]

After giving the list of names, Gellius goes on to express his own opinion that *Nerio Martis* means (like *Moles Martis*) the *virtus* or *fortitudo* of Mars, *Nerio* being a Sabine word meaning strength or courage ;[15] and a little further he sums up his view thus: "Nerio igitur Martis vis et potentia et maiestas quaedam esse Martis demonstratur." This seems to fit in very comfortably with what can be guessed of the meaning of two of the other pairs, Virites Quirini and Maia Volcani: Maia was explained by another Roman scholar as equivalent to Maiestas.[16]

But Gellius goes on to quote three passages from old Latin authors in which Nerio (or Neria) appears positively as the wife of Mars; and again concludes that there was also a tradition that these two were *coniuges*. Of these passages we luckily have the context of one, for it occurs in the *Truculentus* of Plautus: turning this out (line 515) we find that a rough soldier, arriving at Athens, salutes his sweetheart with the words "Mars peregre adveniens salutat Nerienen uxorem suam"— words which Plautus must have adapted from his Greek original in such a way as to make them intelligible to a Roman audience. Gellius says that he had often heard a learned friend blame Plautus for thus putting a false notion about Mars (that he had a wife) into the mouth of his soldier—"nimis comice"—merely to produce a comic effect. But, he adds, there was some justification for it; for if you read the third book of the annals of Gellius (a namesake who lived in the second century B.C.) you will find that he puts into the mouth of Hersilia, pleading for peace before Ti. Tatius, words which actually make Nerio the wife of Mars: "De tui, inquit, coniugis consilio, Martem scilicet significans." Little, I fear, can be said to the credit of this Gellius;[17] he lived in an age when annalists were many and inventive, and long after the Romans had grown accustomed to Greek ideas of the gods; but we may take this passage as evidence of what may have been in his day a popular idea of Mars and his consort. Lastly, Aulus Gellius quotes a brace of lines from one Licinius Imbrex, an old comic writer of the same century, who, in a *fabula palliata* called Neaera, wrote:—

nolo ego Neaeram te vocent, aut Nerienem,
cum quidem Marti es in connubium data.

The real question is whether these passages from comic
writers and an annalist of no reputation combine to prove
that there was an ancient popular idea of Mars as a
married god ; as to the priestly view of the matter they
can, of course, prove nothing.   It seems to me that Dr.
Frazer is entitled to argue that in the second century B.C.
such a popular idea existed,[18] which the Roman state
religion did not recognise, and which Aulus Gellius, as
we have seen, could not agree with.   I do not, however,
think him entitled to go farther, and to infer that this was
an idea of divinity native to Italy or of very old standing.
Is it not much simpler to suppose, with a cool-headed
scholar whom Dr. Frazer is willing to follow when it suits
his turn, that pairs or conjunctions of this kind, the true
meaning of which I hope to explain directly, were easily
mistaken by the vulgar mind for married god and goddess?[19]   In those degenerate days of the Roman religion,
after the war with Hannibal, to which these writers
belong—and all are later than Ennius, the first to make
mischief by ridiculing the gods—nothing could be easier
than to take advantage of what looked like married life
to invent comic passages to please a Roman audience,
now consisting largely of semi-educated men who had
lost faith in their own religion, and of a crowd of smaller
people of mixed descent and nationality.   Such passages,
in fact, cannot safely be used as evidence of religious
ideas, apart from the tendencies of the age in which they
were written.   Had there really been religious beliefs,
rooted in the old Roman mind, about the wedded life
of gods and goddesses, it would even then have been
dangerous to use them mockingly in comedy.   And once
more, had there been such genuinely Roman ideas, why,
in an age that made for anthropomorphism, did they not
find their way into the Roman Pantheon,—why did they
survive only in literary allusions, to the bewilderment of
scholars like Aulus Gellius?

The real explanation of these curious conjunctions of masculine and feminine names is, I think, not very hard to come by. Let us remember, in the first place, that they were found in the books of the priests, and that they belonged to forms of prayer—*comprecationes deorum immortalium*; in other words, they do not represent popular ideas of the deities, but ritualistic forms of invocation. As such they may indeed no doubt be regarded as expressing, or as growing out of, a popular way of thinking of the Power manifesting itself in the universe ; but they are themselves none the less, like those strange lists of divine names called *Indigitamenta*, with which I shall deal directly, the creations of an active professional priesthood, working upon the principle that every deity must be addressed in precisely the correct way and no other, and accounting the name of the deity, as indicating his or her exact function, the most vitally important thing in the whole invocation. I have already pointed out how difficult the early Latin must have found it to discover how to address the *numina* at work around him, and I shall return to the subject in another lecture ; at present all I want to insist upon is that the priests of the City-state relieved him of this anxiety, and indeed must have carried the work so far as to develop a kind of science of divine nomenclature. Every one who has studied the history of religions knows well how strong the tendency is, when once invocation has become ritualised, for the names and titles of the objects of worship to abound and multiply. The Roman Church of to-day still shows this tendency in its elaborate invocation of the Virgin.

With the old Romans the common method of elaboration lay in the invention of cult-titles, of which the different kinds have been distinguished and explained by Dr. J. B. Carter in his treatise " de Deorum Romanorum cognominibus." [20] Most of them are suggestive of function or character, as, *e.g.*, Janus Patulcius Clusivius, or Jupiter Lucetius, Ops Opifera ; sometimes they doubled the idea, as in Aius Locutius, or Anna Perenna, or Fors

Fortuna; and in one or two cases they seem to have combined two deities together in rather puzzling conjunctions, which usually, however, admit of some possible explanation, as Janus Junonius, or Ops Consiva (*i.e.* Ops belonging to Consus).[21]   In the Iguvian ritual, which is the highly-elaborated work of a priesthood as active as the Roman, we find combinations of not less than four names:[22] Cerfe Martie, Praestita Cerfia Cerfi Martii, Tursa Cerfia Cerfi Martii, which may perhaps be rendered " Spirit of Mars, protecting (female) spirit of the (male) spirit of Mars, fear-inspiring (female) spirit of the (male) spirit of Mars."

Such strange multiple combinations as these suggest that expressions like Moles Martis or Virites Quirini are only another form of the usual cult-title, expressing adoration of the power of the deity addressed; and it is only reasonable to explain the others of the same group on the same principle.   As we have seen, Roman scholars themselves explained Nerio Martis as equivalent to Virtus Martis; Herie Iunonis probably means something of the same kind; the others are not so easily explained, and guesswork about them is unprofitable.   But I hope I have said enough to show that there is absolutely no good ground for supposing that these combinations of names in nominative and genitive indicate a relationship of any kind except a qualitative one.   Abstract qualities, let us note, are usually feminine in Latin, and I think it is not improbable that abstractions such as Fides and Salus, which were deified at a very early period at Rome, may have reached divinity by attachment to some god from whom they subsequently became again separated.[23]   And lastly, we can trace the same tendency to combine names and ideas together far down the course of Roman history; witness the combination of Genius with cities, legions, gods, etc., as well as with the individual man, and again such expressions as Pietas Legionis, by analogy with which von Domaszewski, wrongly as I think, would explain those we have been discussing.[24]

Before leaving this complicated and cloudy system of divine nomenclature, it is as well to ask the question once more, even if we cannot answer it, whether if left to itself it might have developed into a polytheistic system of personal deities.   I will give my own opinion for what it is worth.   I do not think that such a result could have been reached without the magic touch of the Greek poet and artist, or the arrival of Greek deities and their images in Latium.   Professor Sayce, in his Gifford lectures on the religion of Babylonia, has shown how the non-Semitic Sumerians knew only of spirits and demons until the Semite arrived in the Persian Gulf with his personal gods of both sexes;[25] and I gather that he does not suppose that without such immigration the Sumerian ideas of divinity could have become personalised.   The question is not exactly the same at Rome; for there the spirit world had passed into the hands of an organised priesthood occupied with ritual, and especially with its terminological aspect; and the chance of personalisation, if it were there at all, lay in the importance of the functional name.   But the question is after all beside the mark; we shall see what happened when the Greeks arrived. We may be content at present to note the fact that they found the functional terminology sufficiently advanced to take advantage of it, and to revolutionise the whole Roman conception of the divine.

Dr. Frazer gives me an opportunity of adverting to another point bearing on the question we are discussing,— the way in which the old Roman thought of his deities. " It is difficult," he says,[26] "to deny that the epithets Pater and Mater, which the Romans bestow on so many of their gods, do really imply paternity and maternity; if this implication be admitted, the inference appears to be inevitable that these divine beings were supposed to exercise sexual functions, etc."   In a footnote he adds a number of formidable-looking references, meant, I suppose, to prove this point.   I have closely examined these passages; what they do prove is simply that many deities

were called Pater and Mater.   Not one even suggests that
paternity and maternity were in such cases to be understood literally and, so to speak, physically.   The two
that come nearest to what he is looking for are those
from Varro and Lactantius.   Varro says [27] that Ops was
called Mater because she was identical with Terra, who
was, of course, Terra Mater : " Haec enim—

'terris gentes omnes peperit et resumit denuo,

quae dat cibaria,' ut ait Ennius." [28]   It is clear, then, that
neither Varro nor Ennius understood this title of Ops and
Terra in Dr. Frazer's sense of the word.   The quotation
from the early Christian father Lactantius, which contains three well-known lines of Lucilius, might possibly
deceive those who neglect to turn it out and read the context ; there we find at once that not even Lactantius
could attribute to these epithets the meaning which Dr.
Frazer wishes to put on them.   He would have been as
glad to do so as Dr. Frazer himself, though for a very
different reason ; but what he actually wrote is this :—

"Omnem Deum qui ab homine colitur, necesse est
inter solennes ritus et precationes patrem nuncupari, non
tantum honoris gratia, verum etiam rationis ; quod et
antiquior est homine, et quod vitam, salutem, victum
praestat, ut pater.   Itaque ut Iuppiter a precantibus pater
vocatur, etc." [29]

Dr. Frazer's quotation begins with this last sentence ;
it is a pity that he did not read the context.   If he had
read it, his candour would have compelled him to confess
that not even a Christian father, with a keen sense of
what was ridiculous or degrading in the pagan religion,
understood the fatherhood of the gods as he wishes to
understand it.

But I am wasting time in pressing this point.   Dr.
Frazer would hardly have used such an argument if he
had not been hard put to it.   The figurative use of human
relationships is surely a common practice, when addressing
their deities, of all peoples who have reached the stage

of family life.   As another distinguished anthropologist says : "The very want of an object tends to supply an object through the imagination ; and this will be either the vital energy inherent in things, or the reflex of the human father, who once satisfied his needs (*i.e.* of the worshipper).   So, in Aryan religions, the supreme god is father, Ζεὺς πατήρ, Diespiter, Marspiter.   Ahura-Mazda is a father. . . . Another analogy shows the relationship of brother and friend, as in the case of Mithra." [80]   The Romans themselves were familiar from the first with such figurative use of relationship, as was natural to a people in whom the family instinct was so strong ; we have but to think of the *pater patratus* of the Fetiales,[81] of the Fratres Arvales, or the Fratres Attiedii of Iguvium.   What exactly they understood by Pater and Mater when applied to deities is not so easy to determine : we have not the necessary data.   They were never applied, I believe, to imported deities, *di novensiles* ; always to *di indigetes*, those on whom the original Roman stock looked as their fellow-citizens and guardians.   And we shall not be far wrong if we conclude that in general they imply the dependence of the human citizen upon his divine protector, and thus bring the usage into line with that of other Aryan peoples.   Behind this feeling of dependence there may have been the idea, handed down from remote ages, that Father Sky and Mother Earth were in a sense the parents of all living things ; but there is nothing in the Roman religion to suggest that the two were thought of as personally uniting in marriage or a sexual act.

I will sum up this part of the discussion by translating an admirable passage in Aust's book on the Roman religion, with which I am in cordial agreement [82]:—

"The deities of Rome were deities of the cult only. They had no human form ; they had not the human heart with its virtues and vices.   They had no intercourse with each other, and no common or permanent residence ; they enjoyed no nectar and ambrosia . . . they had no children, no parental relation. They were indeed both male and female, and a male and female deity are often in close relations with each other; but this is not a relation of marriage, and rests only on a similarity in the sphere of their operations. . . . These deities never become independent existences; they remain cold, colourless conceptions, *numina* as the Romans called them, that is supernatural beings whose existence only betrays itself in the exercise of certain powers."

They were, indeed, cold and colourless conceptions as compared with the Greek gods of Olympus, whose warmth and colour is really that of human life, of human passions; but the one remarkable and interesting thing about these Roman and Italian numina is the life and force for good or evil which is the very essence of their being. The puzzling combinations we have just been studying are quite enough to illustrate this character. Moles, Virites, Nerio, and perhaps others too, seem to mean the strength or force inherent in the numen; Cerfius, or Cerus, as the Latins called it, Liber, Genius, all are best interpreted as meaning a functional or creative force. Jupiter is the sky or heaven itself, with all its manifestations of activity; Tellus is Mother Earth, full of active productive power. At the bottom of these cold and colourless conceptions there is thus a real idea of power, not supernatural but rather natural power, which may both hurt and benefit man, and which he must attempt to enlist on his side. This enlistment was the task of the Roman priesthood and the Roman government, and so effectually was it carried out that the divine beings lost their vitality in the process.

We shall be better able to follow out this curious fate of the Roman deities in later lectures; here I wish to note one other aspect of the Roman idea of divinity, which will help to explain what I have just been saying about the life and force inherent in these numina.

In most cursory accounts of the Roman religion it has been the practice to lay particular stress upon an immense

number of "gods," as they used to be called, each of
which is supposed to have presided over some particular
act or suffering of the Roman from the cradle to the
grave—from Cunina, the "goddess" of his cradle, to
Libitina who looked after his interment.   I have as yet
said nothing about all these.   I will now briefly explain
why I have not done so, and why I hesitate to include
them, at any rate in the uncompromising form in which
they are usually presented, among the genuine religious
conceptions of the earliest period.   Later on I shall have
further opportunity of discussing them; at the end of
this lecture I can only sum up the results of recent
research into this curious cloud of so-called deities.

   We know of them mainly, but not entirely, from
Tertullian, and the *de Civitate Dei* of St. Augustine.[33]
These scholarly theologians, wishing to show up the
absurdity of the heathen religions, found a mine of
material in the great work of Varro on the Roman religious
antiquities; and though they found him by no means so
elegant a writer as Cicero, they studied him with pains,
and have incidentally added immensely to our knowledge
both of Varro himself and of the Roman religion.   St.
Augustine tells us that it was in the last three books of
his work that Varro treated of the Roman deities, and
that he divided them under the heads of *di certi, di incerti*,
and *di selecti*.   In the first of these he dealt chiefly with
those with which we are now concerned: they were *certi*
because their names expressed their supposed activity
quite clearly.[34]   We know for certain that Varro found
these names in the books of the pontifices, and that they
were there called Indigitamenta:[35] a word which has been
variously interpreted, and has been the subject of much
learned disputation.   I believe with Wissowa that it means
" forms of invocation," *i.e.* the correct names by which gods
should be addressed.

   Thus these lists of names come down to us at third
hand: Varro took them from the pontifical books, and
the Christian fathers took them from Varro.   It is obvious

that this being the case they need very careful critical examination ; and till recently they were accepted in full without hesitation, and without reflection on such questions as, *e.g.*, whether they are psychologically probable, or whether they can be paralleled from the religious experience of other peoples. Some preliminary critical attempts were made about fifty years ago in this direction,[36] but the first thoroughgoing examination of the subject was published by R. Peter in the article " Indigitamenta " in Roscher's *Mythological Lexicon*. This most industrious scholar, though his interpretation of the word Indigitamenta is probably erroneous,[37] was the first to reach the definite conclusion that the lists are not really primitive, and do not, as we have them, represent primitive religious thought. It was after a very careful study of this article, which is long enough to fill a small volume, that I wrote in my *Roman Festivals* of the Indigitamenta as " based on "—not actually representing, I might have added— " old ideas of divine agency, now systematised by something like scientific terminology and ordered classification by skilled legal theologians " ; and as " an artificial priestly exaggeration of a primitive tendency to see a world of nameless spirits surrounding and influencing all human life." [38]

I was not then specially concerned with the Indigitamenta, and only alluded to them in passing. But before my book was published there had already appeared a most interesting work on the names of deities (*Götternamen*) by H. Usener, a brilliant investigator, which drew fresh attention to the subject. Usener found in mediaeval records of the religion of the heathen Lithuanians what seemed to be a remarkable parallel with this old Roman theology, and he also compared these records with certain facts in what we may call the pre-Olympian religious ideas of the Greeks.   " The conclusion which he draws," writes Dr. Farnell [39]—and I cannot state it better—" is that the Indo-Germanic peoples, on the way to the higher polytheism, passed through an earlier stage when the objects of cult were beings whom he designated by the newly - coined words 'Augenblickgötter' and 'Sondergötter'" (gods of momentary or limited function).   He went further than this, and claimed that the anthropomorphic gods of Greece and Italy, of the Indo-Iranians, Persians, and Slavs, were developed out of these spirits presiding over special functions and particular moments of human life ; but with this latter part of his theory I am not now concerned.   What we want to know now is whether in writing thus of the Roman Indigitamenta Usener was using a record which really represents an early stage of religious thought in Italy ; and I may add that we should be glad to know whether his Lithuanian records are also to be unhesitatingly relied on.[40]   As regards Greece, Dr. Farnell has criticised his theories with considerable effect.

The most recent contribution to the discussion of the Roman part of the subject is that of Wissowa, who in 1904 published a paper on "True and False Sondergötter at Rome" ; [41] this is a piece of most valuable and weighty criticism, but extremely difficult to follow and digest.   I here give only the main results of it.   Wissowa takes two genuine examples of Sondergötter which have come down to us from other sources, and more directly than those mentioned above : the first from Fabius Pictor, the oldest Roman historian,[42] and the other from the Acta Fratrum Arvalium.[43]   Fabius   said   that   the   flamen (Cerealis ?), when sacrificing to Tellus and Ceres, also invoked the following deities : Vervactor, for the first ploughing, as Wissowa interprets it ; Redarator, for the second ploughing ; Imporcitor, for the harrowing ; Insitor, for the sowing ; Oberator, for the top-dressing ; Occator, Sarritor, Subrincator, Messor, Convector, Conditor, Promitor, for subsequent operations up to the harvest and actual distribution of the corn for food.   Secondly, in the Acta of the Arval Brethren we find, on the occasion of a *piaculum* caused by the growth of a fig-tree on the roof of the temple of Dea Dia, at the end of a long list of

M

deities invoked, and before the names of the *divi* of the
Imperial families, the names of three Sondergötter,
Adolenda Commolenda Deferunda, and on another occasion, Adolenda and Coinquenda ; these seem beyond
doubt to refer to the process of getting the obnoxious
tree down from the roof, of breaking it up, and burning it.

In both these examples, which have come down to us
more directly than the lists in the Fathers, Wissowa sees
assistant or subordinate deities (if such they can be called)
grouped around a central idea, that of the main object
of sacrifice in each case ; [44] these are the result of the *cura*
and *caerimonia* supervised and over-elaborated by pontifical law and ritual. It is, I may add on my own account,
most unlikely, and psychologically almost impossible, that
any individual farmer should have troubled himself to
remember and enumerate by name twelve deities
representing the various stages of an agricultural process ;
and Cato, in fact, says nothing of such ritual. It was the
flamen of the City-state, who, when sacrificing to Tellus
and Ceres before harvest,[45] pictured, or recalled to mind,
the various processes of a year of what we may call high
farming rather than primitive, under the names of deities
plainly invented out of the words which express those
processes—words which themselves are certainly not all
antique. And in the second example, which dates from
the second century A.D., we see that the process of
destroying the intruding fig-tree is represented in ritual
in exactly the same curious way : the names of the deities,
Deferunda and the rest, being invented for the occasion
out of the words which express the several acts of the process of destruction. These Arval Brethren of the second
century inherited the traditions of their predecessors of an
earlier age, and carried out the work of amplification in
their invocations by pedantically imitating the pontifices
of five or six centuries earlier. They held, in a way which
to us is ludicrous, to the old notion that you should try
and cover as much ground as possible in worship, and to
cover it in detail, so that no chance might be missed of

securing the object for which you were taking so much trouble.

Now to return to Varro and his lists of names. What is Dr. Wissowa's conclusion about these, after examining the two examples of Sondergötter which have not come down to us through so much book-learning as the rest?

Varro's *di certi*, he says[46]—and I think there is no doubt that he is right—included the name of every deity, great or small, of which he could feel sure that he knew something, as he found it in the books of the pontifices ; and the part of those books in which he found these names, known as Indigitamenta, probably contained formulae of invocation, *precationum carmina*,[47] of the same kind as the *comprecationes deorum immortalium* from which Gellius quoted the pairs of male and female deities which we discussed above. Varro arranged all these names in groups of principal and subordinate or assistant deities, the latter amplifying in detail the meaning and scope of the former, as we have just seen ; and of this grouping some traces are still visible in the accounts of Augustine and Tertullian. But the good Fathers tumbled the whole collection about sadly in their search for material for their mockery, having no historical or scientific object in view ; with the result that it now resembles the bits of glass in a kaleidoscope, and can no longer be re-arranged on the original Varronian plan. The difficulty is increased by the etymologies and explanations which they offer of the divine names, which, as a rule, are even more absurd than the divinities themselves.[48]

But, in the last place, the question must be asked whether these Sondergötter of the real kind, such, for example, as those twelve agricultural ones invoked by the flamen at the Cereale sacrum, had their origin in any sense in popular usage or belief. At the end of his paper Wissowa emphatically says that he does not believe it. For myself, I would only modify this conclusion so far as this : they must, I think, have been the theological, or perhaps rather the ritualistic outcome, of a psychological tendency rooted in the popular mind. I have already noticed that curious bit of folklore in which three spirits of cultivation were invoked with a kind of acted parable at the birth of a child ; [49] and I cannot regard this custom as a piece of pontifical ritualism, though the names may have been invented by the priests to suit the practice. The old Roman seems to have had a tendency to ascribe what for want of a better word we may call divinity, not only to animate and inanimate objects, but to actions and abstractions ; this, I take it, is an advanced stage of animism, peculiar, it would seem, to a highly practical agricultural people, and it is this stage which is reflected in the ritualistic work of the priests. They turned dim and nameless powers into definite and prehensible deities with names, and arranged them in groups so as to fall in with the life of the city as well as the farm. What was the result of all this ingenuity, or whether it had any popular result at all, is a question hardly admitting of solution. What is really interesting in the matter, if my view is the right one, is the curious way in which the early Roman seems to have looked upon all life and force and action, human or other, as in some sense associated with, and the result of, divine or spiritual agency.

NOTES TO LECTURE VII

1. For *loca sacra* and *consecratio* see Marquardt, p. 148 foll. ; Wissowa, *R.K.* p. 400.

2. Serv. *ad Aen.* xii. 119, " Romani moris fuerat cespitem arae super imponere, et ita sacrificare." Cp. some valuable remarks of Henzen, *Acta Fratr. Arv.* p. 23. The altar of the Fratres was in front of their grove ; they used also a movable one (*foculus*) of silver, but *cespiti ornatus* (*ib.* p. 21) : this was for the preliminary offering of wine and incense (Wissowa, *R.K.* p. 351).

3. In Aug. *Civ. Dei*, iv. 31 ; Agahd's edition of the fragments of Varro's *Ant. rer. div.* p. 164.

4. Aug. *Civ. Dei*, iv. 23 ; Agahd, p. 159. See Wissowa, *Gesammelte Abhandlungen*, p. 280 foll.

5. Strabo iv. 180.

6. *Fasti*, vi. 305.

7. Tibull. ii. 5. 27.   The lines of Propertius are iv. (v.) 2. 59, " Stipes acernus eram, properanti falce dolatus, Ante Numam grata pauper in urbe deus." The question is whether these are genuine examples of the natural evolution of a " stock or stone " into something in the nature of an anthropomorphic image of a deity, or whether they are the result of the introduction of Greek statues acting on the popular mind in rustic parts of Italy. The passages, so far as I know, stand alone, and we have no means of deciding whether the anthropomorphic tendency was native or foreign. Vortumnus was, however, undoubtedly of Etruscan origin ; Wissowa, *R.K.* p. 233. The subject of iconic development of this kind is well summarised in E. Gardner's little volume on *Religion and Art in Ancient Greece*, ch. i.

8. See Sayce, *Gifford Lectures on the Religions of Egypt and Babylonia*, p. 302. An interesting paper on the evolution of *dei* at Rome out of functional *numina* will be found in von Domaszewski's *Abhandlungen zur röm. Religion*, p. 155 foll., based on Usener's theory of Sondergötter. It is ingenious and imaginative, but in my view does not square with the facts as far as we know them. His stages are : (1) momentary function of *numina*, *e.g.* lightning ; (2) elevation of this into a permanent power or function ; (3) consequent limitation of the numen to a special well-marked function ; (4) elevation of the numen to a *deus*, conceived in the likeness of man, and male or female, because man cannot think of power otherwise than on the analogy of male or female creative energy. Lastly, when the *deus* is complete, the functions of the former numen become attributes or qualities, traces of which we find in the pairs of deities in Gellius, xiii. 23, which are discussed later on in this lecture. Some of these, of course, eventually became separate deities—Salacia, Maia, Lua. As I cannot accept the view that the earliest Roman idea of the supernatural is to be found in *comprecationes* of a comparatively late period, *i.e.* in the so-called Indigitamenta, this charmingly symmetrical account has no charm for me beyond its symmetry.

9. Henzen, *Acta Fratr. Arv.* pp. 144, 146 ; Cato, *R.R.* 139 ; *C.I.L.* vi. 110 and 111.   Other references are given by Wissowa, *R.K.* p. 33, note 2.

10. For Pales, *R.F.* p. 80 note ; for Pomona, Wissowa, *R.K.* p. 165.

11. The passage runs thus (Aug. *C.D.* iv. 32) : " Dicit enim (Varro) de generationibus deorum magis ad poetas quam ad physicos fuisse populos inclinatos, et ideo et sexum et generationes deorum maiores suos (id est veteres credidisse Romanos) et eorum constituisse coniugia." There is an amusing passage in Lactantius, i. 17 (*de Falsa Religione*), which Dr. Frazer might read with advantage. It begins, " Si duo sunt sexus deorum, sequitur concubitus." Then he goes on mockingly to argue that the gods

must have houses, cities, lands which they plough and sow, which proves them mortal.   Finally he takes the whole series of inferences backwards, finishing with "si domibus carent, ergo et concubitu.   Si concubitus ab his abest, et sexus igitur foemineus," etc.   All this, he means, can be inferred from the fact that gods are of both sexes ; but that they have *concubitus* can no more be inferred from his argument than that they plough and sow.

12. Dr. Frazer conjectures a sacred marriage of Jupiter and Juno under the forms of Janus and Diana, in *Kingship*, p. 214 ; but he is well aware that it is pure guesswork.   There was, indeed, at Falerii such a marriage of Juno with an unknown deity (Ovid, *Amores*, iii. 13), of which, however, we do not know the history. Falerii was one of those cities, like Praeneste, where Etruscan, Greek, and Latin influences met.   The "Orci nuptiae" on which Frazer lays stress was simply the Greek marriage of Pluto and Proserpine : "Orci coniux Proserpina," Aug. *C.D.* vii. 23 and 28, Agahd, p. 152.   Wissowa shows this conclusively, *R.K.* p. 246. Orcus was Graecised as Plutus, but was himself totally without personality.

13. Dr. Frazer wrongly translates this as "ancient prayers" (p. 411), adding "the highest possible authority on the subject." *Oratio* is never used in this sense until Christian times : the word is always *precatio*.   All scholars are agreed that what is meant is invocations to deities in old speeches, such as occur once or twice in Cicero (*e.g.* at the end of the *Verrines*) ; cp. Livy xxix. 15.   As the recording of speeches cannot be assumed to have begun before the third century B.C., this does not carry us very far back.   That century is also the age in which the pontifices were probably most active in drawing up *comprecationes* ; see below, p. 285 foll.

14. See Appendix B at end of volume.

15. Cp. Ovid, *Fasti*, iii. 850, "*forti* sacrificare deae." In *R.F.* p. 60 foll., I have criticised the attempts, ancient and modern, to make this Nerio the subject of myths.

16. Macrob. i. 12. 18.   This word Maiestas shows the doubtful nature of these feminine names, and probably betrays the real meaning of Maia.   I may mention here that Bellona instead of Nerio is ascribed as wife to Mars by Seneca ap. Aug. *C.D.* vi. 10 ; also Venus to Volcanus instead of Maia.   Neither have any connection, so far as we know, with the gods to whom Seneca ascribes them as wives : Venus-Vulcan is, of course, Greek.   Both Augustine and Dr. Frazer might with advantage have abstained from citing Seneca on such a point : as a Spaniard by birth he was not likely to know much about technical questions of Roman ritual.

17. See Schanz, *Gesch. der röm. Literatur*, i. 274.

18. In the Graeco-Roman age Mars seems to have been rather a favourite subject of myth-making ; see Usener's article on Italian myths in *Rhein. Mus.* vol. xxx. ; Roscher in *Myth. Lex.* for works

of Graeco-Etruscan art in which he appears in certain mythical scenes.

19. H. Jordan, quoted in *R.F.* p. 61 note. I relegate to an appendix what needs to be said about the other pairs of deities mentioned by Gellius.

20. Leipzig, 1898, p. 7 foll.

21. Wissowa, *R.K.* p. 168. Carter, *op. cit.* p. 21.

22. See Buecheler, *Umbrica*, pp. 22 and 98.

23. So Fides is usually explained, as originally belonging to Jupiter (Wissowa, *R.K.* p. 103 foll.) ; but a different view is taken by Harold L. Axtell in his work on the *Deification of Abstract Ideas at Rome* (Chicago, 1907), p. 20.

24. In the Festschrift f. O. Hirschfeld, p. 243 foll.

25. *Religion of the Babylonians*, introductory chapter.

26. *Op. cit.* p. 412.

27. *L.L.* v. 64.

28. This fragment is No. 503 in Baehrens, *Fragm. Poet. Rom.*

29. Lactantius, *Div. inst.* iv. 3.

30. Crawley, *The Tree of Life*, p. 256 ; Farnell, *Evolution of Religion*, p. 180 ; von Domaszewski, *Abhandlungen*, p. 166, " Man ruft sie an im Gebete als pater und mater zum Zeichen der Unterwerfung unter ihren Willen, wie der Sohn dem Gebote des paterfamilias sich fügt. Der sittlich strenge Gehorsam, der das Familienleben der Römer beherrscht, die pietas, ist der Sinn der römischen religio." Cp. also Appel, *de Rom. precationibus*, pp. 102-3, who thinks that they regarded the gods " velut patriarchas sive patres familias." He quotes Preller-Jordan i. 55 and Dieterich, *Eine Mithrasliturgie*, p. 142 sq. So too with mater—" velut mater familias."

31. The expression seems to mean " a father made for the purpose of the embassy." Wissowa, *R.K.* p. 477, note 3.

32. p. 19. This was written, it may be noted, several years after Aust had thoroughly investigated the cult of Jupiter for his article in the *Mythological Lexicon* ; in which cult, if anywhere, one may be tempted to see evidence of a personal conception of deities. As Dr. Frazer has referred to the cult of Jupiter at Praeneste, to which I referred him as evidence of a possibly personal conception of the god in that Latin city, I may say here that I adhere to what I said about this in *R.F.* p. 226 foll. ; no piece of antique cult has occupied my attention more than this, and I have tried to lay open every source of confirmation or criticism. Wissowa has expressed himself in almost exactly the same terms in *R.K.* p. 209 : we arrived at our conclusions independently.

33. Tertullian, *ad Nationes* 11, and *de Anima*, 37 foll. ; Aug. *de Civ. Dei*, iv. *passim*, and especially ch. xi. ; R. Peter compiled a complete list (*Myth. Lex.*, *s.v.* " Indigitamenta," p. 143) from these and other sources.

34. Aug. *C.D.* vii. 17. That this was what Varro meant by *di certi* was first affirmed by Wissowa in a note to his edition of Marquardt, p. 9; it has been generally accepted as the true account. A full discussion will be found in Agahd's edition of the fragments of Varro's work, p. 126 foll.; cf. Peter's article quoted above, and Wissowa, *R.K.* pp. 61 and 65. A somewhat different view is given in Domaszewski's article in *Archiv* for 1907, p. 1 foll., suggested by Usener's *Götternamen.*

35. The evidence for this will be found in Marquardt's note 4 on p. 9. I have no doubt that Wissowa is right in explaining Indigitamenta as "Gebetsformeln," formulae of invocation; in which the most important matter, we may add, would be the name of the deity. See his *Gesammelte Abhandlungen*, p. 177 foll. The Indigitamenta contained, as one section, the invocations of *di certi.*

36. Chiefly by Ambrosch in his *Religionsbücher der Römer.* Peter's article contains a useful account of the whole progress of research on this subject.

37. *Lex.* p. 137; it was that of his master Reifferscheid. Cp. Wissowa, *op. cit.* (*Ges. Abhandl.* p. 306 foll.).

38. *R.F.* pp. 191, 341.

39. "The place of the Sondergötter in Greek Polytheism," printed in *Anthropological Essays addressed to E. B. Tylor*, p. 81. Usener's discussion of the Roman and Lithuanian Sondergötter is in his *Götternamen*, p. 73 foll.

40. Wissowa writes (*Ges. Abhandl.* p. 320 note) that he has reason to believe that a great number of the Lithuanian Sondergötter only became such through the treatment of the subject by the mediaeval writers on whom Usener relied!

41. *Ges. Abhandl.* p. 304 foll.

42. Servius (Interpol.) *ad Georg.* i. 21.

43. Henzen, *Acta Fratr. Arv.* p. 147; *C.I.L.* vi. 2099 and 2107.

44. *Op. cit.* p. 323 foll.; for *famuli* and *anculi divi*, Henzen, *op. cit.* p. 145.

45. See above, p. 121.

46. p. 312; cp. 320, where he further asserts his belief that Varro is responsible himself for the creation of a great number of these Sondergötter, owing to his extreme desire to fix and define the function of every deity in relation to human life; just as the mediaeval writers Laskowski and Pretorius may have created many Lithuanian Sondergötter. As I am not quite clear on this point, I have not mentioned it in the text.

47. *Op. cit.* p. 314, note 1. See above, note 33.

48. *e.g.* Vaticanus, "qui infantum vagitibus praesidet"; *Rusina* from *rus*; *Consus* from *consilium*, etc.

49. See above, p. 84.

LECTURE VIII

RITUAL OF THE *IUS DIVINUM*

I HAVE already frequently mentioned the *ius divinum*, the law governing the relations between the divine and human inhabitants of the city, as the *ius civile* governed the relations between citizen and citizen.[1] When we examined the calendar of Numa, we were in fact examining a part of this law ; we began with this our studies of the religion of the Roman city-state, because it is the earliest document we possess which illuminates the dark ages of city life, so far as religion is concerned. The study of the calendar naturally led us on to consider the evidence it yields, taken together with other sources of information, as to the nature of the deities for whose worship it fixes times and seasons, or, more accurately, the amount of knowledge to which the Romans had attained about their divine beings. But we must now return to the *ius divinum*, and study it in another aspect, for which the calendar itself does not suffice as evidence.

Perhaps the simplest way of explaining this *ius* is to describe it as laying down the rules for the maintenance of right relations between the citizens and their deities ; as ordaining what things are to be done or avoided in order to keep up a continual *pax*, or quasi-legal covenant, between these two parties. The two words *ius* and *pax*, we may note, are continually meeting us in Roman religious documents. In a prayer sanctioned by the pontifices for use at the making of a new clearing, we read : " Si deus, si dea sit cuius illud sacrum est, *ut tibi*

ius siet porco piaculo facere illiusce sacri coercendi ergo," [2]
i.e. " O unknown deity, whether god or goddess, whose
property this wood is, let it be legally proper to sacrifice
to thee this pig as an expiatory offering, for the sake of
cutting down trees in this wood of thine." " Pacem
deorum exposcere " (or " petere ") is a standing formula, as
all readers of Virgil know ; [3] and it occurs in many other
authors and religious documents.   When Livy wants to
express the horror of the old patrician families at the
idea of plebeians being consuls—men who had no knowledge of the *ius divinum* and no right to have any—he
makes Appius Claudius exclaim, " Nunc nos, tanquam
iam nihil pace deorum opus sit, omnes caerimonias
polluimus." [4]   How can we maintain our right relations
with the gods, if plebeians have the care of them ?

Thus it is not going too far to describe the whole
Roman religion of the city-state as a *Rechtsverkehr*,[5]
a legal process going on continually.   When a *colonia*
was founded, *i.e.* a military outpost which was to be a
copy in all respects of the Roman State, it was absolutely
essential that its *ius divinum* should be laid down ; it
must have a religious charter as well as a civil one.
Even at the very end of the life of the Republic, when
Caesar founded a colony in Spain, he ordained that,
within ten days of its first magistrates taking office, they
should consult the Senate " quos et quot dies festos esse
et quae sacra fieri publice placeat et quos ea sacra facere
placeat," *i.e.* as to the calendar, the ritual, and the priesthood.[6]   The Romans, of course, assumed that Numa, their
priest-king, had done the same thing for Rome ; Livy
describes him as ordaining a pontifex to whom he entrusted the care of all these matters, with written rules to
follow.[7]   This was the imaginary religious charter of the
Roman State.   Without it the citizen, or rather his
official representative, would not know with the necessary
accuracy the details of the *cura* and *caerimonia* ; without
it, too, the deities could not be expected to perform their
part of advancing the interests of the State, and indeed,

as I think we shall find, could not be expected to retain the strength and vitality which they needed for the work. Support was needed on each side ; the State needed the help of the gods, and the gods needed the help of the State's care and worship.

The ways and means towards the maintenance of this *pax* were as follows. First, the deities must be duly placated, and their powers kept in full vigour, by the ritual of sacrifice and prayer, performed at the proper times and places by authorised persons skilled in the knowledge of that ritual. Secondly, there must be an exact fulfilment of all vows or solemn promises made to the deities by the State or its magistrates, or by such private persons as might have made similar engagements. Thirdly, the city, its land and its people, must be preserved from all evil or hostile influences, whether spiritual or material or both, by the process broadly known as *lustratio*, which we commonly translate *purification*. Lastly, strict attention must be paid to all outward signs of the will of the gods, as shown by omens and portents of various kinds. This last method of securing the *pax* became specially prominent much later in Roman history, and I prefer to postpone detailed discussion of it for the present ; but the other three we will now examine, with the help of evidence mainly derived from facts of cult, not from the fancies of mythologists.

First, then, I take sacrifice, dealing only with the general principles of sacrificial rites, so far as we can discern them in the numerous details which have come down to us. The word *sacrificium*, let us note, in its widest sense, may cover any religious act in which something is made *sacrum, i.e.* (in its legal sense) the property of a deity ;[8] I am not now concerned to conjecture what exactly may have been the meaning of this immortal word before it was embodied in the *ius divinum*. "Sacrificium" is limited in practical use by the Romans themselves to offerings, animal or cereal, made on the spot where the deity had taken up his residence, or at some place on the boundary of land or city (*e.g.* the gate) which was under his protection, or (in later times at least) at a temporary altar erected during a campaign.   Thus it was as much a sacrificium when the paterfamilias threw at each meal a portion of the food into the fire, the residence of Vesta, as when the consul offered a victim to Mars on the eve of a battle.

Sacrifices have generally been divided into the three classes of (1) honorific, where the offering is believed to be in some sense a gift to the deity ; (2) piacular, or sin-offerings, where the victim was usually burnt whole, no part being retained for eating (though this was not the case at Rome); (3) sacramental sacrifices, where the worshippers enter into communion with the deity by partaking of the sacred offering together with him.[9]   The two former are constant and typical in the Roman religion ; but traces of the sacramental type, which Robertson Smith believed to be the oldest, are also found, and it will clear the ground if I refer to them at once.   By far the most interesting example is that of the Latin festival on the Alban mount, where the flesh of the victim, a white heifer that had never felt the yoke, was partaken of by the deputies of all the cities of the Latin league, great importance being attached to the due distribution.[10]   Here the Latin race "yearly acknowledges its common kinship of blood, and seals it by partaking in the common meal of a sacred victim," thus entering into communion with Jupiter, the ancient god of the race, and with each other, by participation in the flesh of the sacred animal.   "This common meal is perhaps a survival from the age when cattle were sacred animals, and were never slain or eaten except on the solemn annual occasions when the clan or race renewed its kinship and its mutual obligations by a solemn sacrament."   It is tempting to compare with this great sacrament the *epulum Iovis* on the Ides of September, the dedication-day of the Capitoline temple of Jupiter, Juno, and Minerva, which three deities seem to have been present in visible form to share the meal with the

magistrates and senate.[11]   But we have not yet arrived
at the age when this temple was built, and we have no
evidence enabling us to carry the rite back in any form
to the pre-Etruscan period.   There are, however, faint
indications that the old Italians believed the deities to be
in some sense present at their meals, though not in visible
form ; and at one festival, the Fornacalia, which was a
concern not of the State as a whole, but of the thirty
curiae into which it was divided,[12] there seems to be no
doubt that a common meal took place in which the gods
were believed to have a part, or at any rate to be present
though invisible.   Yet the *ius divinum* of the Roman
State assuredly did not encourage this kind of sacrament ;
for in the regular round of State festivals, in which we
cannot include even the *feriae Latinae*, the sacrifices, so
far as we are informed, were all honorific or piacular.   If
I am not mistaken, the idea of participation by the
people in solemn sacred rites was discouraged by the
Roman priesthood ; in the *ius divinum* the line drawn
between *sacrum* and *profanum* was clear ; scenes of
gluttony or revelry, like the Greek hecatombs, were
eliminated from the *sacra publica*, as I have already
pointed out.   Not till the advent of the Sibylline books
and the *Graecus ritus* did the people take an active part
in the State religion ; their duty was merely to abstain
from disturbance during the performance of sacred rites.
" Feriis iurgia amovento " is the only reference in Cicero's
imaginary sketch of the *ius divinum* to the conduct of
the citizen on festival days.[13]   Within the family, the
curia, the gens, there might be direct and active participation in daily or yearly ceremonies, but it was an essential
principle of the life of the city-state that its business,
religious as well as civil, should be carried out for the
citizens by officials specially appointed.

In the typical and organised worship of the State, *i.e.*
sacrifice honorific and piacular, sanctioned by the *ius
divinum*, the utmost care was taken that the whole procedure should be in every sense acceptable to the deity ;

that nothing *profanum* should cross the threshold of the divine; hence it was quiet, orderly, dignified. The feeling that communication with the deity invoked was impossible save under such conditions was very strong in the Roman mind, stronger perhaps than with any other people whose religious practice is known to us; and the sense of obligation and duty, *pietas*, as they called it, was thus very early developed, and of infinite value to the State in its youth. This is entirely in keeping with what we have learnt in the last two lectures of the ideas of the Romans about the nature of their deities, and throws additional light on those ideas. They did not as yet know too much about the divine beings and their powers and wishes; familiarity had not yet bred contempt; *religio*, as we saw, was still strong among them—the feeling of awe that is likely to diminish or disappear when you have your god before you in the form of an idol. It is a principle of human nature that where knowledge is imperfect, care must be taken to be on the safe side; this is true of all practical undertakings, and as the religion of the Romans was that of a practical people with a practical end in view, it was particularly true of them.

First then, in order that the worship might be entirely acceptable to the deity invoked, it was essential that the person who conducted it should be also acceptable. At the head of the whole system was the rex, who was priest as well as king. We do not know, of course, exactly how the rex was appointed; but in the case of the typical priest-king Numa, Livy has described his *inauguratio* in terms of the *ius divinum* of later times for the appointment of priests, and we may take it as fairly certain that the same principle held good from the earliest times.[14] After being summoned (so the story ran) from the Sabine city of Cures by the Senate, he consulted the gods about his own fitness. He was then conducted by the augur to the arx on the Capitol, and sat down on a stone facing the south. The augur took his seat on his left hand (the lucky side) with veiled head, holding the *lituus* [15] of his office in his right hand, with which, after a prayer, he marked out the *regiones* from east to west, the north being to the left, the south to the right, and silently noted some object in the extreme distance of the *ager Romanus*, as the farthest point where the appearance of an omen might be accepted. Then, passing the *lituus* to his left hand, he laid his right on the head of Numa, and uttered this prayer : " Father Jupiter, if it be thy will (*fas*) that this Numa Pompilius, on whose head my hand is laid, be king of Rome, I pray thee give us clear token within the limits which I have marked out." Then he said aloud what auspicia he sought for (*i.e.* whether of birds, lightning, or what) ; and when they appeared, Numa descended as rex from the citadel. This process was called *inauguratio* ; it is attested for the confirmation of the election of the three flamines maiores, the rex, and the augurs, in historical times,[16] whatever was the method of that election, and without it the priest was not believed to be acceptable to the gods. It is not mentioned by Roman writers in connection with the Pontifices or the Vestals ; if this be not merely from dearth of evidence, it is not easy to account for, unless the reason were that neither body was specially concerned with sacrifice. But the principle is perfectly clear—that the person who is to represent the community in worship must be one of whom the *numina* openly express approval.

A priest, *sacerdos*, is thus a person set apart by special ritual for the service of the *sacra populi Romani*. The rex no doubt himself made the selection and supervised the inauguratio of the other priests at whose head he was. When the kingship came to an end, his powers of this kind passed to the pontifex maximus ; and it may be as well to add at once that his sacrificial powers, though they were in a special sense inherited by a priest who took his title, the *rex sacrorum*, passed with the civil power to all magistrates *cum imperio*, who wore the *toga praetexta* symbolic of priestly function, and had the right of presiding at sacrificial rites both at home and in the field.

Thus magistrate and priest, though quite distinct under the Republic from the point of view of public law, have certain characteristics in common as deriving from a common source in the powers of the rex.[17]

But to return to the period of Numa and the calendar: it was not only necessary that the priest should be acceptable to the gods, but that he should be marked off from the rest of the community as being dedicated to their service. As Dr. Jevons says,[18] in all early religions priests are marked off from other worshippers, partly by what they do, and partly by what they may not do; and what he means is (1) that the priest originally was the person who alone could slay a victim; (2) that in consequence of his sacredness he was subject to a great number of restrictions. I have already spoken of these restrictions or priestly taboos in my second lecture; and as I believe that in the period we are now dealing with they were little more than a survival, I shall not return to them now. But of the outward insignia, which marked off the priest as alone entitled to perform the essential act of worship, the sacrifice, and which bring him out of the region of the *profanum* into that of *sacrum*, I must say a few words before going farther.

In historical times the actual slaying of the victim was done by subordinates, *popae, victimarii*, etc.; but there is no doubt whatever that it was originally the work of the priest, for he seems at all times to have used one gesture which is clearly symbolic of it,[19] and there are traces also of a practice of wearing the toga in such a way as to leave the right arm free for the act.[20] That toga, or any other special robe worn by the priest, was always in whole or part red or purple. The purple-edged *toga praetexta* was worn both by priests and magistrates, and by children under age; and I think there is good reason to believe that in all these cases the original idea was the same—that they took part, directly or indirectly, as primary or secondary agents in sacrificial acts. The Salii and the augurs wore the *trabea*, which was of purple or red, or both ; the flamines had a special robe about the colour of which we are not informed, but the Flaminica Dialis wore a purple garment called *rica*, and a red veil called *flammeum*, which was also worn by the bride in the religious ceremony of marriage. Whether we are to see in this prevalence of red or purple any symbolism of the shedding of blood in sacrifice I cannot be sure, but the inference is a tempting one, and has been put forward with confidence by some recent investigators. It is worth noting that the Vestals, who did not sacrifice animals, wore white only.[21] If the red colour has anything to do with blood-shedding, it is probably more than merely symbolic; it may mean that the sacrificing priest partakes of that life and strength which he passes on to the god through the blood, that is the life, of the victim.[22]

The Roman priests had also other insignia, of which the original meaning is less evident. The Flamen Dialis, and probably all the flamines, wore a cap with an olive-twig fastened to the top of it ; this is well shown in the sculptures of the Ara Pacis of Augustus.[23] The flaminicae had a head-dress called *tutulus*, which consisted in part, at least, of a purple fillet or ribbon. The flamines, when actually sacrificing, wore a *galerus*, or hood of some kind made of the skin of a victim, and the Flamen Dialis in particular wore one made of the skin of a white heifer sacrificed to Jupiter.[24] In these various ways all priests were outwardly shown to be holy men, *sacerdotes*, marked off from the *profanum vulgus*. Only for the pontifices we have no information as to a special dress, just as we also have none as to their inauguratio.[25]

Thus there is no question that the priests were chosen and separated from the people in such a way as to meet with the approval of the gods ; and even the acolytes, *camilli* and *camillae*, boys and girls who frequently appear in sacrificial scenes on monuments, wore the *toga praetexta*, and, in order to be acceptable, must be the

N

children of living parents.[26]   This rule has lately been
the subject of a discussion by Dr. Frazer, on which he
has brought to bear, as usual, a great range of learning.
He regards the restriction not so much as a matter
of good omen, *i.e.* of freedom from contamination
by the death of a parent, but as pointing to a notion
that they were " fuller of life and therefore luckier than
orphans." [27]   Whether or no this explanation is the
right one, it is quite consistent, as we shall see directly,
with the general idea of sacrifice at Rome, and the
learning by which it is supported is in any case of interest
and value.

   There is abundant evidence from historical times that
all worshippers, and therefore *a fortiori* all priests, when
sacrificing, had to be personally clean and free from
every kind of taint ; a rule which also held good for the
utensils used in the worship, which in many cases at least
were of primitive make and material, not such as were
in common use.[28]   The need of personal purity is well
expressed by Tibullus in his description of a rural
festival [29]:—

> vos quoque abesse procul iubeo, discedat ab aris
>   cui tulit hesterna gaudia nocte Venus.
> casta placent superis : pura cum veste venite
>   et manibus puris sumite fontis aquam.

   These lines indicate an approach at least to the idea
of mental as well as material purity ; and Cicero in his *ius
divinum* in the *de Legibus* [30] actually reaches that idea :
" caste iubet lex adire ad deos, animo videlicet, in quo
sunt omnia : nec tollit castimoniam corporis," etc.   But
this is the language of a later age, and does not reflect
the notions of the old Roman, but rather those of the
religious philosophy of the Greek.   The personal purity
which the Roman rule required was a survival from a
set of primitive ideas, closely connected with taboo,
which we are only now beginning to understand fully.
They are common to all or almost all peoples who have
made any progress in systematising their sacrificial

worship.   As Dr. Westermarck has recently expressed
it,[81] " they spring from the idea that the contact of a
polluting substance with anything holy is followed by
injurious consequences.   It is supposed to deprive a
deity or holy being of its holiness. . . . So also a sacred
act is believed to lose its sacredness by being performed
by an unclean individual."   And in the next sentence he
goes still farther back in the history of the belief, pointing
out that a polluting substance is itself held to contain
mysterious energy of a baneful kind.   But I must leave
this interesting subject now ; the story of the evolution
of the habit of cleanliness from these ancient ideas will
be found in the thirty-ninth chapter of his *Origin and
Development of Moral Ideas.*

Coming next to the act of sacrifice itself, it is needless
to say that the victim must be as exactly fitted to please
the deity—if that be the right way to express the
obligation—as the priest who sacrificed it.   It must be
of the right kind, sex, age, colour ; it must go willingly
to the slaughter, adorned with fillets and ribbons (*infulae,
vittae*), in order to mark it off from other animals as
holy ; in the case of oxen, we hear also of the gilding
of the horns, but this must have been costly and unusual.[82]
All these details were doubtless laid down in the *ius
divinum*, and in later times, when the deities dwelt in
roofed temples, they were embodied in the *lex* or charter
of each temple.[83]   I do not need to go into them here
minutely ; for my present purpose, the elucidation of the
meaning which the Romans attached to sacrificial worship,
it will be sufficient to point out that all victims, so far
as we know, were domestic animals, and in almost all
cases they were valuable property (*pecunia*), such as
belonged to the stock of the Latin farmer, ox, sheep, pig,
varying according to age and sex.   Goats were used at
the Lupercalia, and a horse was sacrificed to Mars, as we
have seen, on October 15, and at the Robigalia in April
a red dog was offered to the spirit of the mildew.   But
though time forbids me to explain all these rules, a

careful study of the evidence for them is most useful
for any one who wishes to understand the influence of
the *ius divinum* on the mind of the early Roman.   In
the family what rules were needed were matter of
tradition ; deities were few, and offerings limited.   But
in the city-state it was very different ; here even the *di
indigetes* were many, with diverse wishes and likings as
well as functions : how were these to be ascertained and
remembered at the right moment ?   Here, as in all methods
of securing the *pax deorum*, a central supervising authority
was needed, in whose knowledge and wisdom the whole
community had confidence ; and he was found in the rex,
as is clearly shown in the whole traditional account of the
priest-king Numa.   Very naturally tradition also ascribed
to Numa the institution of the pontifices, whom the
historical Romans knew as succeeding the rex in the
supervision of religious law.[34]

If all went well, the victim going willingly and no ill
omen supervening, the actual slaughter followed at the
altar.   During the whole operation silence was enjoined ;
the priests' heads were veiled with the folds of the
toga ;[35] pipers (*tibicines*) continued to play, in order
that no unlucky sound or word might be heard
which would make it necessary to start afresh with
another victim (*instauratio*).   Immediately before the
slaughter the victim was made holier than ever by
sprinkling upon it fragments of sacred cake made of *far*
(*immolatio*), and by pouring on it libations of wine from
a *foculus* or movable altar containing this holy condiment,
together with incense if that were used in the rite.   As
soon as it was dead, the internal organs were examined
to make sure that there was no physical defect or
abnormal growth, for it was, of course, quite as necessary
that the animal should be "purus" within as without ;
this was the only object of the examination, until the
Etruscan art of *extipicina* made its way to Rome.   What
became of the blood we are not told ; I have already
remarked that blood has curiously little part in Roman

ritual and custom.[86]   But the *exta, i.e.* internal organs of
life, were separated from the rest of the carcase, and
carefully cooked in holy vessels, before being laid upon
the altar (*porrectio*), together with certain slices of flesh
called *magmenta*, or increase-offerings, while the rest of
the flesh, which had now lost its holiness, was retained
for the use of the priests.[87]   The time occupied in
the actual slaughter and inspection of the organs was not
long ; but the cooking of these must have been often a
lengthy process.   Ovid tells us how on April 25 he met
the Flamen Quirinalis carrying out the exta of a dog and
a sheep, which had been sacrificed at Rome to Robigus
that morning, in order to lay them on the altar of that
deity at the fifth milestone on the Via Claudia.[88]   Certain
days in the calendar, called *endotercisi*, which were *nèfasti*
in morning and evening, were *fasti* in the middle of the
day, between the slaying of a victim and the placing of
its exta on the altar (*inter hostiam caesam et exta por-
recta*).[89]

I have so far purposely omitted one important detail
—the prayer which, so far as we know, invariably
accompanied the sacrifice.   It is not absolutely certain
at what moment of the rite it was said at Rome ; in
the ritual of Iguvium we find it occurring immediately
before the placing of the exta on the altar ;[40] but as that
ritual is a processional one, concerned with sacrifices at
several spots, the two chief parts of the rite, the slaughter
and the *porrectio*, probably followed closely on one
another.   We may perhaps guess that where these two
parts were separated by a considerable interval, as in the
majority of Roman festivals, the prayer was said by the
priest also at the moment of *porrectio*.   The prayer is
so important a detail as to need separate handling—
important because it helps us to interpret the ideas of
the Romans about their sacrifices, and the attitude in
which they conceived themselves as standing towards
the deities whom they thus approached.   I propose to
occupy the rest of this lecture in considering this most

interesting topic. I wish first to draw attention to a particular feature, or rather expression, which occurs in the authentic wording of certain prayers which we are lucky enough to possess, because I think it throws some light on the meaning which the Romans attached to the sacrifice it accompanied; and secondly, to consider the character of Roman prayers generally, in view of a question now being largely discussed, *i.e.* whether prayer is a development from spell or charm, belonging in its origin to the region of magic.

We have various forms of prayer surviving in Roman literature: some of them are versified by the poets, and therefore give us a general impression of the contents without the actual and genuine wording; we have also two fragments of ancient *carmina* which have the form of prayers, those of the Salii and the Fratres Arvales; and we have certain forms used on special occasions, such as the *evocatio* of the gods of a hostile community, or the formulae of vows (*vota*) which I must postpone to the next lecture. But the only unquestionably genuine old Roman prayers used at sacrifice, taken from the books of the pontifices and preserved word for word, are those which Cato embodied in his treatise on agriculture in the second century B.C., as proper to be used with sacrifice on certain occasions in the agricultural year.[41] It is here that we meet with the phrase, familiar in another form to all Latin scholars, on which I wish to lay stress now. It occurs in all the four forms of prayer which Cato copied down. The first is at the time of the flowering of the pear-trees, on behalf of the oxen: "Iuppiter dapalis, quod tibi fieri oportet in domo familia mea culignam vini dapi eius rei [42] ergo, *macte hac illace dape polucenda esto.*" And again, when the wine is offered: "Iuppiter dapalis, *macte istace dape polucenda esto. Macte vino inferio esto.*" So in the piacular sacrifice when a clearing is made, the unknown deity is addressed in the last words of the prayer thus: "harum rerum ergo *macte hoc porco piaculo immolando esto.*" We find this *macte esto* again in the prayer for the ceremony of lustratio, at the end of the formula : "*macte hisce suovetaurilibus lactentibus immolandis esto.*" In the rite of the *porca praecidanea*, to which I have already referred, the instruction for the invocation of Jupiter runs : "*Fertum* (*i.e.* a kind of cake) *Iovi obmoveto et mactato sic, Iuppiter, te hoc ferto* obmovendo bonas preces precor, uti sies volens propitius mihi liberisque meis domo familiaeque meae *mactus hoc ferto.*" Janus gets another kind of cake (*strues*) and a wine-offering, and is addressed in the same way. Then we read, "Iovi fertum obmoveto *mactatoque item,* ut prius feceris."

What is the real meaning of this phrase *macte esto,* which must surely have been in universal use at sacrifices, not only at private rites like those of Cato, since it came to be used in common speech of congratulation or felici-tation, e.g. *macte virtute esto* ?[43] Servius in commenting on Virgil has made it sufficiently clear. He explains it as *magis aucte,* and connects it with *magmentum,* increase-offering, *quasi magis augmentum,* and adds that when the victims had been slain and their exta placed on the altar, they were said to be *mactatae.* So, too, in another comment he seems to connect the word with the victim rather than with the deity. But he is quite clear as to the meaning of the word, as signifying an increase or addition of some kind; and though his etymology is wrong, we may be sure that he was right in this respect, for it is beyond doubt built on a base, *mac* or *mag,* which produced *magnus, maius, maiestas,* and so on. " Macte nova virtute puer " means "Be thou increased, strengthened in *virtus* " ; a fragment of Lucilius (quoted by Servius) brings this out well, "*Macte inquam virtute simulque his viribus esto,*" and another from Ennius, " Livius inde redit magno *mactatus* triumpho."[44] We might almost translate it in these passages by " glorified " ; but it most certainly includes the meaning of " strengthened " or " increased in might."

Now in the formulae of Cato we have seen that it is

applied to the deity and not to the victim ; this naturally
did not occur to Servius, whose mind was occupied rather
with Virgil and the literary use of the word than with the
original use and meaning of the language of prayer.   Undoubtedly he has made a mistake here, which Cato's piety
has enabled us to detect.   It was, in fact, the deity whose
strength was to be increased by the offerings ; so much
at least seems to me to be beyond doubt.   There is,
indeed, no certain trace in the ritual, or in Roman literature, that the gods were supposed to consume the exta,
or the cakes and wine offered them ; that primitive
notion must have been excluded from the *ius divinum*.
But instead of it we find the more spiritual idea that by
placing on the altar the organs of the life of the victim,
with ancient forms of sacred cake and offerings of wine,
the vitality of the deity, his power to help his worshippers, to make the corn grow and the cattle bring forth
young, to aid the State against enemies, or what not, was
really increased in this semi-mystic way.   Let us remember that the Roman numina were powers constantly at
work in their own sphere ; they are the various manifestations of the one Power as conceived in immediate relation
to man and his wants ; they are sometimes addressed in
prayer, as we have seen, by additional titles which suggest
their strength and vitality : Virites Quirini, Nerio Martis,
Moles Martis, Maia or Maiestas Volcani.   What, then,
could be more natural than that the Roman should call upon
his divine fellow-citizen to accept that which, according
to ancient tradition and practice, will keep up his strength,
and at the same time increase his glory and his goodwill
towards his worshippers ?   This is, then, the idea which I
believe to have been at the root of Roman sacrificial
ritual, and it seems to confirm the dynamic theory of
sacrifice recently propounded by some French anthropologists, *i.e.* that a mystic current of *religious force*
passed through the victim, from priest to deity, and
perhaps back again.[45]   I believe that we have here a
transitional idea of the virtue of sacrifice—an idea that

bridges over the gulf between the crude notion that the gods actually partake of the offering, and the later more spiritual view that the offering is an honorary gift " to the glory of God." It seems also to be found in the Vedic religion. Dr. Farnell writes : " In the Vedic ritual we find a pure and spiritual form of prayer ; yet a certain spell-power may attach even to the highest types, for we find not infrequently the conception that not only the power of the worshipper, but the power of the deity also is nourished and strengthened by prayer, and the prayer itself is usually accompanied by a potent act (such as that of sacrifice). " May our prayers increase Agni ": " The prayers fill thee with power and strengthen thee, like great rivers the Sindhu." [46]

I must now turn to the form and manner of Roman prayers, in order to gain further light on the question as to the mental attitude of the worshipper towards the deity invoked. Of late years there has been a strong tendency to find the origin of prayer in spell ; or, in other words, to discover a bridge between that mental attitude which believes that a deity can be forced into a certain course of action by magical formulae, and the humble attitude of the petitioner in prayer, which assumes that the power of the deity altogether transcends that of his worshipper. The evidence of Roman prayers is, I think, of considerable value in dealing with this question ; but it needs to be carefully studied and handled. The general impression conveyed by those who have written on the subject is that Roman prayers were dull, dry formulae, which were believed to have a constraining influence on the deity simply as formulae, if they were repeated with perfect precision the right number of times. Dr. Westermarck, for example, has no shadow of a doubt about this ; quoting Renan, he says that " in the Roman, as in the majority of the old Italian cults, prayer is a magic formula, producing its effect by its own inherent quality." And again, he writes that the Romans were much more addicted to magic than to religion ; " they wanted to compel the gods rather than to be compelled by them. Their *religio* was probably near akin to the Greek κατάδεσμος, which meant not only an ordinary tie, but also a magic tie or knot or a bewitching thereby."[47]   I need not stop to point out the misconception of the word *religio* which suggested the whole of this passage ; the supposed derivation from *ligare* was quite enough to suggest magic to those who are on the trail of it.[48]   Let us go on to examine the prayers themselves ; I think we shall find that though there is much truth in the common view of them, it is not quite the whole truth.

The oldest Roman prayers we possess are usually called hymns, because the Latin word for them was *carmen*, viz. the *Carmen Saliare*, which is too obscure and fragmentary to be of use to us, and the *Carmen* of the Arval Brethren, which is preserved on stone and is quite intelligible.[49]   The word *carmen*, let us notice, was used by the old Romans for any kind of metrical formula, whether hymn, prayer, or spell.   Pliny, when writing of magic and incantations, plainly includes prayer among them ;[50] and Dr. Jevons has recently pointed out that singing, and especially singing in a low voice or muttered tones, is a characteristic of magic not only in Greece and Rome, but in many parts of the world at the present day.[51] The evidence of the word is thus strongly in favour of the view that these ancient *carmina* of Roman worship were really spells ; and the *Carmen Arvalium* itself does not contradict it.   After an elaborate sacrificial ceremonial the priests, using a written copy of the *carmen* (*libellis acceptis*), danced in triple rhythm (*tripodaverunt*) while they sang it ; it consisted of six clauses, each repeated three times.   "*Enos Lases iuvate !   Neve luerve Marmar sins incurrere in pleores !   Satur fu fere Mars, limen sali, sta berber !   Semunes alternei advocapit cunctos !   Enos Marmar iuvato !   Triumpe !*"   With the precise inter-pretation of these words I am not now concerned ; but they obviously contain invocations to the Lares and Mars, which may be either petitions or commands, and which perhaps are really on the borderland between the two; and as thrice repeated, and accompanied with dancing and gesticulation, they seem certainly to belong rather to the region of magic than of religion proper.

It is interesting to compare with this *carmen* the prayers of the guild of brethren (*Attiedii*) at Iguvium; these are the best preserved of all old Italian prayers, and though not Roman, are the product of the same race. In the lustratio of the *arx* (*Ocris Fisius*) of Iguvium we find three several deities invoked, with elaborate sacrificial ritual, at three gates, and a long prayer addressed to each deity, thrice repeated, as in the *Carmen Arvale*. It is to be said under the breath (*tacitus precator totum*, vi. A. 55), which was a common practice also at Rome, and is believed to be characteristic of the magical spell;[52] and except in the case of the first prayer, which is addressed to the chief deity Jupiter Grabovius, it is accompanied by some kind of dancing or rhythmical movement (*tripodatio*).[53] Thus in outward form this ritual seems to show but little advance on the Roman prayer of the Arvales, and indeed it may in substance go back to a time as remote as that in which the latter had its origin. But when we examine the matter of the prayer, we find that it is cast in the language of petition beyond all doubt—if it be rightly interpreted, as we may believe it is :—

"Te invocavi invoco divum Grabovium pro arce Fisia, pro urbe Iguvina, pro arcis nomine, pro urbis nomine : *volens sis, propitius sis* arci Fisiae, urbi Iguvinae, arcis nomini, urbis nomini. Sancte, te invocavi invoco divum Grabovium. Sancti fiducia te invocavi invoco divum Grabovium. Dive Grabovie te hoc bove opimo piaculo pro arce Fisia, etc. Dive Grabovi, illius anni quiquomque in arce Fisia ignis ortus est, in urbe Iguvina ritus debiti omissi sunt, pro nihilo ducito. Dive Grabovi, quicquid tui sacrificii vitiatum est, peccatum est, peremptum est, fraudatum est, demptum est, tui sacrificii visum invisum vitium est, dive Grabovi, quicquid ius sit, hoc bove opimo piaculo piando. . . . Dive Grabovi, piato arcem Fisiam, piato urbem Iguvinam. Dive Grabovi, piato arcis Fisiae, urbis Iguvinae, nomen, magistratus, ritus, viros, pecora, fundos, fruges : piato, *esto volens propitius pace tua* arci Fisiae, etc. Dive Grabovi, salvam servato arcem Fisiam salvam servato urbem Iguvinam. . . . Dive Grabovi, te hoc bove opimo piaculo pro arce Fisia, pro urbe Iguvina, pro arcis nomine, pro urbis nomine, Dive Grabovi, te invocavi." [54]

That in this prayer, and the others which accompany it, exactness of wording was believed to be essential, as in the ritual which preceded it exactness of performance, there is no doubt ; for at the end of the whole document (vi. B. 48) we find that if there had been any slip in the ritual, the Brethren had to go back to the first gate and begin all over again.   There is plainly present the idea, surviving from an age of magic, that the deities had strong feelings about the right way of invocation, and would not respond to the performance unless those feelings were understood and appealed to ; that they would miss something and decline to do their part.   Yet are we justified in going on to assume that they were bound, as by a solemn contract, to perform their part, if there were no slip in the ritual ?   I confess it is difficult for me to take this further step, in view of the language of the prayers, which is so clearly that of petition, nay, of humble petition. We are not dealing here with *vota*, to which I shall come in the next lecture, and in which there is a kind of legal contract between the man and the god—the former undertaking to do something pleasing to the deity, if the latter shall have faithfully performed what is asked of him. These *vota*, so abundant in historical times, are really responsible for the idea that Roman prayer is simply a binding formula—a magical spell, let us say, which in the hands of a city priesthood has become a quasi-legal formula.   But these prayers are not *vota* ; they do not contain any language which betrays the notion of binding the deity.   They seem to me to mark a process of transition between the age of spell and magic and the age

of prayer and religion; they retain some of the outward characteristics of spell, but internally, *i.e.* in the
spirit in which they were intended, they have the real
characteristics of prayer.[55]   The numina to whom
they were addressed were powerful spirits, unknown,
unfamiliar, until their wishes were discovered by the
organised priesthood which handed down these forms of
petition.

To return to Rome, and to the prayers in Cato's book,
to which I referred just now when discussing the word
macte.   Attempts have been made to prove that these
were originally written in metre;[56] and this is quite possible.
If so, it only means that they retained the outward form
of the primitive spell; it must not lead us on to fancy
that the sacrifice which accompanied the prayer was a
magical act, or that the whole process was believed to
compel the deity.   No doubt there was believed to be
efficacy in the exact repetition, as is shown by the
directions for piacular sacrifices in case of error of any
kind.[57]   But the language is the language of prayer, not
of compulsion, nor even of bargaining : " Eius rei ergo
te hoc porco piaculo immolando bonas preces precor, ut sies
volens propitius mihi, domo familiaeque meis." [58]   " Mars
pater, te precor quaesoque uti sies volens propitius mihi,
domo," etc.[59]   No amount of vain repetition or scruple
can deprive this language of its natural meaning.   The
god is powerful in his own sphere of action, and man has
no control over him ; man is fully recognised as liable to
misfortune unless the god helps him ; but he can worship
in full assurance of faith that his prayer will be answered,
if it be such as the authorities of the State have laid down
as the right wording, and if the ritual accompanying it is
equally in order.   The faith is, indeed, thus founded upon
man's devices rather than the god's good-will as such ; it
is a belief in the State and its authorities and *ius divinum*,
which is conceived, not indeed as constraining the deity,
but as calling upon him (*invocare*) to perform his part, in
formulae which he cannot well neglect, simply because it

would be unreasonable to do so, contrary to his nature as a deity of the Roman State and its *ager*.

It is obvious in all this sacrificial ritual that the officiating person or persons were expected to observe the traditional forms with the utmost care and exactness. Any slip or omission was, in fact, a *piaculum*, or *sacrum commissum*—terms of the *ius divinum* which seem to suggest, if I may use the expression, the obverse side of holiness. It is now well known that cleanness and uncleanness, holiness and its opposite, can be expressed in religious vocabulary by the same terms, for in both cases there is something beyond the ordinary, something dangerous, uncanny; thus we are not surprised to find that such words as I have just mentioned can be used to express some kind of impurity caused by a breach of ritual as well as that ritual itself. If we accept the latest theory of sacrifice, *i.e.* the dynamic theory, as it is called, we explain this intense nervousness about a ritualistic flaw as occasioned by the consciousness of a breach in the current of "religious force" (the expression is that of Messrs. Hubert and Mauss[60]), which must pass in regular sequence from the sacrificer through the victim to the deity, or vice versa. If this is the true explanation—and at present it may be said to hold the field—then the extreme exactness of the Roman ritual was a survival from an age when this strange feeling was a reality ; but no more than a survival, for, so far as I can discover, the Roman idea was rather that the deity to whom the ritual was addressed was in some way offended by the omission.[61] The dynamic notion is lost, if it ever were there, and its place has been taken by one that we may perhaps call theological. But however that may be, the culprit was regarded as in a state of sin or impurity, "un être sacré," and had to get rid of this sin or impurity by another sacrifice before the whole ritual could be started afresh (*instaurare*).

According to the "dynamic" theory of sacrifice, we might naturally expect that the victim, as being destined to carry away the unholiness (or whatever we choose to call it) of the culprit, would be burnt whole, not offered to the deity in the form of exta, or eaten by the sacrificers.[62]   But this does not seem to have been the case in the Roman practice; in all the examples of *piacula* of which we have details, the exta are laid on the altar as in the typical sacrifice.[63]   The inference seems to be that the theological idea of sacrifice had established itself completely ever since the formation of the *ius divinum*; the victim is not a scapegoat in any sense, but really an expiatory offering; and not only does the sacrificer yield up something of value, but he offers it to increase the strength of the deity as well as to appease his anger.

A curious point may be noticed in the last place. The practical Roman mind seems to have invented a kind of sacrificial insurance, by which a piacular sacrifice might be offered beforehand to atone for any omission in the ritual which was to follow.   Thus the Fratres Arvales, if they had to take an iron implement into their sacred grove, offered a piaculum before as well as after this breach of religious rule.[64]   Again, the *porca praecidanea*, which I have already mentioned as offered before harvest, was an example of the same system of insurance; for the first cutting of the corn was a sacred rite, and one in which it was easy to take a false step.   Writing of this, Gellius says in general terms that *hostiae praecidaneae* are those which are offered the day before *sacrificia solennia*.[65]

The term " piacular sacrifice " (*piaculum*) had a wide range of meaning, apart from the examples here given. With one important form of it I shall deal in the next lecture :[66] others we shall come across later on.

NOTES TO LECTURE VIII

1. See Appendix C.

2. Cato, *R.R.* 139, where the language suggests that as the deity was unknown, the *ius* of the religious act was also uncertain, *i.e.* the ritual was not laid down.   De Marchi translates (*La Religione*

nella vita domestica, i. 132) "sia a te fatto il debito sacrificio," etc.,
which sufficiently expresses the anxiety of the situation.   Keil reads
here "ut tibi ius *est*," and gives no variant in his critical note ; but
the words just below, "uti id recte factum siet," seem to me to
suggest the subjunctive.   In any case there is no doubt about
ius.   In *Tab. Iguv.* vi. A. 28 (*Umbrica,* p. 58) Buecheler translates
the Umbrian *persei mersei* by "quicquid ius sit," and compares this
passage of Cato, together with Gellius i. 12. 14, where the phrase is
used of the duties of a Vestal under the *ius divinum* in the formula
used by the Pontifex Maximus, *cum virginem capiat* : "Sacerdotem
Vestalem, quae sacra faciat, quae ius siet sacerdotem Vestalem facere
pro pop. Rom." etc.

3. *e.g. Aen.* iv. 56, x. 31 ("si sine pace tua atque invito numine,"
etc.).   Cp. *Tab. Iguv.* vi. 30, 33, etc. (*Umbrica,* p. 59), "esto volens
propitiusque pace tua arci Fisiae."

4. Livy vi. 41 *ad fin.*

5. Wissowa, *R.K.* p. 318, and p. 319 for the illustrations that
follow.   Cp. Cicero, *Part. Or.* xxii. 78, where *religio* is explained as
"iustitia erga deos."

6. *Lex Coloniae Genetivae,* cap. 64 ; *C.I.L.* ii., supplement No.
5439.

7. Livy i. 20. 5.

8. This follows from the definition in Festus, p. 321, and in
Macrobius iii.3. 2.   This last is quoted from Trebatius *de religionibus* : "sacrum est quicquid est quod deorum habetur."   In common
use *sacrificium* seems to be reserved for animal sacrifice, but the verb
sacrificare is not so limited.   Festus, p. 319 : "mustum quod Libero
sacrificabant pro vineis . . . sicut praemetium de spicis, quas primum
messuissent, sacrificabant Cereri."   It has been suggested to me by
Mr. Marett that the termination of the word *sacrificium* may have
reference to the use of *facere* for animal sacrifice, as in Greek ῥέζειν,
ἔρδειν, δρᾶν ; but on the whole I doubt this.   *Facere* and *fieri* are in
that sense, I think, euphemisms, occasioned by the mystic character
of the act (examples are collected in Brissonius *de formulis,* p. 9).
Rem divinam facere seems to be the general expression, as in Cato,
R.R. 83 ; or the particular victim is in the ablative, *e.g. agna Iovi
facit* (Flamen Dialis) in Varro, *L.L.* vi. 16 ; cp. Virg. *Ecl.* iii. 77.

9. This classification, originally due to R. Smith, article "Sacrifice" in *Encycl. Brit.,* ed. 10, has lately been criticised by Hubert et
Mauss, in *Mélanges d'histoire des religions,* p. 9 foll. ; but it is
sufficiently complete for our purposes.   At the same time it is well to
be aware that no classification of the various forms of sacrifice can
be complete at present ; that which these authors prefer, *i.e.* constant
and occasional sacrifices, is, however, a useful one.

10. *R.F.* p. 95 foll.   Cp. Robertson Smith, *Rel. of Semites,*
Lect. VIII.

11. *R.F.* p. 217 foll.

12. *R.F.* p. 302 foll.   Meals in connection with sacrifice are also
found at the Parilia (*R.F.* p. 81, and Ovid, *Fasti*, iv. 743 foll.) and
Terminalia (Ovid, *Fasti*, ii. 657) ; but in both cases Ovid seems to be
describing rustic rites ; nor is it certain that the meal was really
sacramental.   What does seem proved is that the old Latins and
other Italians believed the deities of the house to be present at their
meals—

> ante focos olim scamnis considere longis
> mos erat et mensae credere adesse deos (*Fasti*, vi. 307),

and thus the idea was maintained that in some sense all meals had a
sacred character, *i.e.* all in which the members of a *familia* (see
above, p. 78), or of *gens* or *curia*, met together.   Cp. R. Smith, *op. cit.*
p. 261 foll.   We may remember that the Penates were the spirits of
the food itself, not merely of the place in which it was stored; it had
therefore a sacred character, which is also shown by the sanctification
of the firstfruits (*R.F.* pp. 151, 195).   (The *cenae collegiorum*,
dinners of collegia of priests, were in no sense sacrificial meals ; see
Marquardt, p. 231, note 7 ; Henzen, *Acta Fratr. Arv.* pp. 13, 39, 40.)

13. Cic. *de Legibus*, ii. 8. 19.

14. Livy i. 18.   For constitutional difficulties in this passage, see,
e.g., Greenidge, *Roman Public Life*, p. 50.

15. For this and the augurs generally, see Lecture XII.

16. The passages are collected by Wissowa, *R.K.* p. 420, note 3.
There is no doubt about the inauguratio of the three great flamines and
the rex sacrorum, who were all specially concerned with sacrifice, and
of the augurs, who would obviously need it in order to perform the
same ceremony for others—as a bishop needs consecration for the
same reason.   As regards the pontifices, Dionysius (ii. 73. 3) clearly
thought it was needed for them, and we might a priori assume that
one who might become a pontifex maximus would need it; but
Wissowa discounts Dionysius' opinion, and I am unwilling to differ
from him on a point of the *ius divinum*, of which he is our best
exponent.   If he is right, it may be that the three *flamines maiores*,
who were reckoned in strict religious sense as above the pontifices,
including their head (Festus, p. 185), needed "holiness" more than
any pontifex, and so with the augurs.   The insignia of the pontifices,
as well as many historical facts, show that the pontifices were competent
to perform sacrifice in a general sense (Marq. p. 248 foll.) ; but it is
possible that they never had the right, like the flamines, actually to
slay the victim.   I do not feel sure that the *securis* was really one of
their symbols, though Horace seems to say so in *Ode* iii. 23. 12.   The
whole question needs further investigation.   It may be found that
the essential distinction between the pontifices and magistrates *cum
imperio* on the one hand, and the flamines on the other, is to be
sought in the ideas of holiness connected with the shedding of
blood in sacrifice.   The flamen is permanently holy, having charge
of constant sacrifices; *e.g.* the Dialis had duties every day.   He

O

is the duly sanctified guide for all rites within his own religious range.

17. Wissowa, *R.K.* pp. 339, 410 foll.

18. The whole subject of the preparation of the sacrificer for his work, and of the steps by which he becomes separated from the pro·fane, is well treated by Hubert et Mauss, *Mélanges d'histoire des religions*, p. 23 foll.   The reference to Dr. Jevons is *Introduction*, ch. xx. p. 270 foll.

19. Serv. *Aen.* xii. 173; Virgil wrote "dant fruges manibus salsas, et tempora ferro Summa notant pecudum"; to which Servius adds that the symbolic movement was a (pretended) cut from head to tail of the victim.   Wissowa, *R.K.* p. 352.

20. Pauly-Wissowa, *Real-Encycl.*, *s.v.* "cinctus Gabinus."

21. Marquardt, p. 340.   The Vestals were never, so far as we know, directly concerned in animal sacrifice.

22. See below, p. 190.   For the colour of the garments, and the explanation referred to, see Samter, *Familienfeste*, p. 40 foll. ; Diels, *Sibyllinische Blätter*, p. 70; and cp. von Duhn's paper, "Rot und Tot" in *Archiv*, 1906, p. 1 foll.   That red colouring was used in various ways in sacred and quasi-sacred rites there is no doubt (see above, p. 89, note 46); but whether it can be always connected with bloodshed is by no means so certain (Rohde, *Psyche*, i. 226).   In the case of women it is at least hard to understand.   The idea of consecration through blood, which is very rare in Roman literature, comes out curiously in the words which Livy puts into the mouth of Virginius after the slaughter of his daughter (iii. 48): "Te Appi tuumque caput sanguine hoc consecro" (*i.e.* to a deity not mentioned). The sentence to which this note refers was written before the appearance of Messrs. Hubert et Mauss' essay on sacrifice (*Mélanges d'histoire des religions*, pp. 1-122).   The theory there developed, that the victim is the intermediary in all cases between the sacrificer and the deity, and that the *force religieuse* passes from one to the other in one direction or another, does not essentially differ from the words in the text; but the French savants would, I imagine, prefer to look on the insignia in a general sense as bringing the person wearing them within the region of the *sacrum*, the force of which would react on him still more strongly after the destruction of the victim (see p. 28 foll.).

23. See, *e.g.*, *Roman Sculpture* by Mrs. Strong, Plates xi. and xv.

24. For this and other insignia see Marquardt, p. 222 foll.   The question is under discussion whether some of these insignia are not old Italian forms of dress (see Gruppe, *Mythologische Literatur*, 1898-1905, p. 343).   For the wearing of the skin of a victim, which meets us also at the Lupercalia (*R.F.* p. 311), see Robertson Smith, *Semites*, p. 416 foll. ; Jevons, *Introduction*, p. 252 foll. ; Frazer, *G.B.* iii. 136 foll.

25. They, of course, wore the *praetexta* when performing religious

acts. Cp. the Fratres Arvales, who laid aside the *praetexta* after sacrificing. Henzen, *Acta Fr. Arv.* pp. 11, 21, and 28.

26. Serv. *Aen.* xi. 543. The *camillae* assisted the *flaminicae*, Marquardt, p. 227. This is one of the most beautiful features of the stately Roman ritual, and has been handed on to the Roman Church. It was, of course, derived from the worship of the household (see above, p. 74).

27. *Adonis, Attis, Osiris*, p. 413 foll. Dr. Frazer is criticising Dr. Farnell, who had touched on the subject in the *Hibbert Journal* for 1907, p. 689, and had taken the more obvious view that death in a family disqualified for actions requiring extreme holiness.

28. The passages are collected in Marquardt, p. 174 foll. ; we may notice in particular Livy xlv. 5. 4, where, though only the washing of hands is referred to, we have the important statement that " omnis praefatio sacrorum," *i.e.* the preliminary exhortation of the priest, enjoined *purae manus*. Livy must be using the language of Roman ritual, though he is not speaking here of a Roman rite. For the material of sacred utensils see Henzen, *Acta Fratr. Arv.* p. 30.

29. Tibullus ii. 1. 11.

30. Cic. *de Legibus*, ii. 10. 24.

31. Westermarck, *Origin and Development of Moral Ideas*, ii. 352 foll. ; consult the index for further allusions to the subject. Cp. Farnell, *Evolution of Religion*, Lecture III. [Fehrle, *Die kultische Keuschheit im Altertum* (Giessen, 1910), has reached me too late for use in this chapter.]

32. Full details, with the most important references quoted in full, are in Marquardt, p. 172 foll. ; but some of the latter are applicable only to the Graeco-Roman period.

33. So we may gather from the Lex Furfensis of 58 B.C. (*C.I.L.* ix. 3513), and that of the Ara Augusti at Narbo of A.D. 12 (*C.I.L.* xii. 4333).

34. The real origin of the pontifices and their name is unknown to us. If they took their name from the bridging of the Tiber, as Varro held (*L.L.* v. 83) and as the majority of scholars believe (see O. Gilbert, *Rom. Topographie*, ii. 220, note), the difficulty remains that they are found in such a city as Praeneste, where there was no river to be bridged, and where they could not well have been merely an offshoot from the Roman college ; see Wissowa, *R.K.* p. 432, note. Nor can we explain how they came to be set in charge of the *ius divinum* ; and where there are no data conjecture is useless.

35. The covering of the head (*operto capite*, as opposed to *aperto capite* of the *Graecus ritus*) is usually explained as meant to shut out all sounds belonging to the world of the *profanum* ; and the playing of the tibicines is interpreted in the same way. Hubert et Mauss explain the covered head differently : " le rituel romain prescrivit généralement l'usage du voile, signe de séparation et partant de consécration " (p. 28). Miss Harrison, *Prolegomena to*

the Study of Greek Religion, p. 522, also holds that it is the outward sign of consecration ; cp. S. Reinach, *Cultes, mythes, et religions*, i. 300 foll.   The fact, noted by Miss Harrison, that in Festus's account of the *ver sacrum* (p. 379, ed. Müller) the children expelled were veiled, seems to point to the idea of dedication—unless, indeed, *velabant* here means that they blindfolded them.

36. The wine was poured over the altar as well as on the victim, which suggests a substitution for blood ; Arnobius vii. 29 and 30 ; Dion. Hal. vii. 72.   I cannot find that any one of the many utensils used in sacrifice were for pouring out blood.   Blood was, however, poured on the stone at the Terminalia (*R.F.* pp. 325-326); but the rite here described by Ovid seems to be a rural one, outside the *ius divinum*.   In the sacrifice of victims to Hecate in Virg. *Aen.* vi. 243 foll., which cannot be *ritus Romanus*, the warm blood is collected in *paterae* ; but nothing is said of what was done with it, nor does Servius help.   Cp. *Aen.* viii. 106.   In Lucretius v. 1202, " aras sanguine multo spargere quadrupedum," the context shows that the ritual alluded to is not old Roman.   In Livy's description of the " occulti paratus sacri " of the Samnites (ix. 41), we find " *respersae fando nefandoque sanguine arae*, et dira exsecratio ac furiale carmen." Livy seems to think of this blood-sprinkling, whether the blood be human or animal, as unusual and horrible.   Ancient, no doubt, is the practice, recorded in the *Acta Fratr. Arv.* (see Henzen, pp. 21 and 23), of using the blood in a religious feast, in the process of cooking: " porcilias piaculares epulati sunt et sanguem."   (There is a mention of the pouring of blood in an inscription from Lusitania in *C.I.L.* ii. 2395.)   For the use of wine as a substitute for blood, see the recently published work of Karl Kircher, " Die sakrale Bedeuting des Weines," in *Religionsgeschichtliche Versuche, etc.*, p. 82 foll., where, however, the subject is not worked out.

37. According to Lübbert (*Commentarii pontificales*, p. 121 foll.) *magmentum* is the same as *augmentum*, which word is also found (Varro, *L.L.* v. 112).   Festus, p. 126, " magmentum magis aug-mentum " ; Serv. *Aen.* iv. 57, to which passage I shall return. For the equivalent in the Vedic ritual of the cooking and offering of the exta, see Hubert et Mauss, *op. cit.* p. 60 foll.

38. *R.F.* p. 89.

39. *ib.* p. 10.

40. Buecheler, *Umbrica*, pp. 60, 69, etc.   Of course the prayer might be said while other operations were going on.   For the con-stant connection of prayer and sacrifice, see Pliny, *N.H.* xxviii. 10, " quippe victimam caedi sine precatione non videtur referre aut deos rite consuli."   If Macrobius is right (iii. 2. 7 foll.) in asserting that the prayer must be said while the priest's hand touches the altar, one may guess that this was done at the same time that the exta were laid on it.   Ovid saw the priest at the Robigalia offer the exta and say the prayer at the same time (*Fasti*, iv. 905 foll.), but does

not mention the hand touching the altar.   For this see Serv. *Aen.* vi.
124 ; Horace, *Ode* iii. 23. 17, and Dr. Postgate on this passage in
Classical Review for March 1910.

41. Cato, *R.R.* 132, 134, 139, and 141.   That these formulae
were taken from the books of the pontifices is almost certain, not
only from the internal evidence of the prayers themselves, but
because Servius (Interpol.) on *Aen.* ix. 641 quotes the words :
"macte hoc vino inferio esto," which occur in 132, introducing them
thus : "et in pontificalibus sacrificantes dicebant deo. . . ."

42. The verb is omitted here for some ritualistic reason, as in
the Iguvian prayers (*Umbrica*, p. 55).

43. Virg. *Aen.* ix. 641, "macte nova virtute puer, sic itur ad
astra," etc., and many other passages.   The verb *mactare* acquired
a general sense of sacrificial slaying, as did also *immolare*, though
neither had originally any direct reference to slaughter.   The best
account I find of the word is in H. Nettleship's *Contributions to
Latin Lexicography*, p. 520.   He takes *mactus* as the participle of
a lost verb *maco* or *mago*, to make great, increase, equivalent to
augeo, which is also a word of semi-religious meaning, as Augustus
knew.   Nettleship quotes Cicero *in Vatinium*, 14, "puerorum extis
deos manes mactare."

44. Baehrens, *Fragm. Poet. Lat.* 180 ; Lusilius fragm. 143 ;
Nonius, 341, 28 has "versibus."

45. It may possibly be objected that some of the deities were
powerful for evil as well as good, *e.g.* Robigus, the spirit of the red
mildew, and that the power of such a deity was not to be encouraged
or increased.   But all such deities (and I cannot mention another
besides Robigus) were of course conceived as able to restrain their
own harmful function ; they were not invoked to go away and leave
the ager Romanus in peace, but to limit their activity in the land
where they had been settled for worship.   We have no prayer to
Robigus (or Robigo, feminine, as Ovid has it) except that which
Ovid somewhat fancifully versified after hearing the Flamen
Quirinalis say it (*Fasti*, iv. 911 foll.), in which of course the word
macte does not occur.   As the victim was a dog, an uneatable one,
it is possible that the ritual was not quite the usual one.   But the
language of the prayer is interesting and brings out my point :

> aspera Robigo, parcas Cerialibus herbis.
>   vis tua non levis est ; . . .
> parce precor, scabrasque manus a messibus aufer
>   neve noce cultis : posse nocere sat est.

It concludes by praying Robigo to direct her strength and attention
to other objects, *gladios et tela nocentia* ; but this is the poet's
fancy.

46. *Evolution of Religion*, p. 212, quoting *Vedic Hymns*, pt. ii
pp. 259 and 391.

47. *Origin and Development of Moral Ideas*, vol. ii. p. 585 foll. ; cp. 657.   See also Farnell, *Evolution of Religion*, p. 195.

48. See above, p. 9.   *Religio* in the sense of an obligation to perform certain ritualistic acts is in my view a secondary and later use of the word. See *Transactions of the Congress of Historical Religion for 1908*, vol. ii. p. 169 foll.

49. Henzen, *Acta Fratr. Arv.* p. 26 foll. ; *C.I.L.* vi. 2104, 32 foll. ; Buecheler und Riese, *Carmina Lat.*, epigr. pars ii., no. 1. All surviving Roman prayers are collected in Appel's *De Romanorum precationibus*, Giessen, 1909.

50. Pliny, *N.H.* xxviii. 10 foll.

51. In *Anthropology and the Classics*, p. 94.

52. Cp. Tibullus ii. 1. 84, "vos celebrem cantate deum pecorique vocate, Voce palam pecori, clam sibi quisque vocet." This murmuring was certainly characteristic of Roman magic ; see Jevons, p. 99, and especially the reference to a Lex Cornelia, which condemned those "qui susurris magicis homines occiderunt" (Justinian, *Inst.* iv. 18. 5).

53. On the nature of this *tripodatio* see Henzen, *op. cit.* p. 33. Buecheler, *Umbrica*, p. 69, gives the Umbrian verb a different meaning, though he translates it *tripodato*.

54. Buecheler, *Umbrica*, pp. 13 and 52.

55. Wissowa, *R.K.*, 333, inclines to the belief that prayer had a legal binding force upon the deity ; but he does not cite any text which confirms this view, and is arguing on general grounds.   I gather from the language of Aust (*Religion der Römer*, p. 30) that he thinks there was a germ which might have developed into a more truly religious attitude towards the gods, if it had not been killed by priestly routine and quasi-legal formulae.   With this opinion I am strongly inclined to agree.   Cp. the story of Scipio Aemilianus audaciously altering and elevating the formula dictated by the priest in the censor's lustratio (Val. Max. iv. 1. 10), to which I shall return in the proper place.

56. Westphal, quoted by De Marchi, *La Religione, etc.*, i. p. 133, note.

57. See, *e.g.*, ch. 141 *ad fin*.   The prayer in the Acta of the Ludi Saeculares to the Moirae is an imitation of old prayers.   See below, p. 442.

58. *ib.* ch. 139.

59. *ib.* ch. 141.

60. Hubert et Mauss, *Mélanges d'histoire des religions*, p. 74.

61. So Cato, *R.R.* 141, "si minus in omnes litabit, sic verba concipito ; Mars pater, quod tibi illuc porco neque satisfactum est, te hoc porco piaculo." (The word for the slaughter is here euphemistically omitted ; De Marchi, p. 134.)

62. Hubert et Mauss, *op. cit.* p. 55 foll. ; Leviticus vi.   I doubt whether the theory of the learned authors will hold good generally on this point

63. Marquardt, p. 185, asserted the contrary, but cited no evidence except Serv. *Aen.* vi. 253, which does not prove the practice of the holocaust to be really Roman.   Wissowa's exactness is well illustrated in his detection of this error ; see *R.K.* p. 352, note 6. Henzen, *Acta Fratr. Arv.* p. 135, leaves no doubt on the question possible.

64. Henzen, *Acta Fratr. Arv.* p. 131.   See above, p. 35. Festus, p. 218.

65. Gellius iv. 6. 7.

66. *i.e.* lustratio.   That this was a form of piaculum is clear from the use of the word *pihaklu* of the victim in the lustratio of the arx of Iguvium, *e.g.* Buecheler, *Umbrica,* index, 5, v.

LECTURE IX

In the last lecture we found that the magical element in the Roman ritual is exaggerated by recent writers. But it has also long been the practice to describe that ritual as a system of bargaining with the gods : as partaking of the nature of a legal contract. " The old Roman worship was businesslike and utilitarian. The gods were partners in a contract with their worshippers, and the ritual was characterised by the hard formalism of the legal system of Rome. The worshipper performed his part to the letter with the scrupulous exactness required in pleadings before the praetor."[1] This is an excellent statement of a view very generally held, especially since Mommsen, whose training in Roman law made him apt to dwell on the legal aspects of Roman life, wrote the famous chapter in the first volume of his history. I now wish to examine this view briefly.

No doubt it was suggested by the necessary familiarity of the Roman historian with *vota publica*, the vows so frequently made on behalf of the State by its magistrates, in terms supplied by the pontifices, and dictated by them to the magistrate undertaking the duty. Some few of these formulae have survived, and it may certainly be said of them that they are analogous to legal formulae, and express the quasi-contractual nature of the process. Such legalised religious contracts seem to be peculiar to Rome ; they are curiously characteristic of the Roman genius for formularisation, which in course of time had most important effects in the domain of civil law. But the vow as such is, of course, by no means peculiar to Rome ; it is familiar in Greek history, and is found in an elementary form among savages at the present day.[2] But at Rome both in public and private life it is far more frequent and striking than elsewhere. This is a phenomenon that calls for careful study ; and we must beware that we are not misled by quasi-legal developments into missing the real significance of it from the point of view of morality and religion.

The *vota privata*, which include vows and offerings made to deities by private individuals, had never been adequately examined till De Marchi wrote his book on the private religion of the Romans ; nor could they have been so examined until the *Corpus Inscriptionum* was fairly well advanced. There the material is extraordinarily abundant, but it is, of course, almost entirely of comparatively late date, and the great majority of votive inscriptions belong to the period of the Empire. Yet it is quite legitimate to argue from this to an origin of this form of worship in the earliest times, and we have enough early evidence to justify the inference. Among the oldest Latin inscriptions are some found on objects such as cups or vases, showing that the latter were votive offerings to a deity : thus we have *Saeturni poculum, Kerri poculum*, and other similar ones which will be found at the beginning of the first volume of the *Corpus*.[3] They give only the name of the deity as a rule, and do not tell us why the object was offered to him ; but they must have been thank-offerings for some supposed blessing. In one case, not indeed at Rome, but not far away at Praeneste, we have proof of this ; for a mother makes a dedication to Fortuna *nationu cratia*, which plainly expresses gratitude for good luck in childbirth ;[4] and this inscription is one of the oldest we possess. Nor do they tell us whether there was a previous vow or promise of which the offering is the fulfilment. But in the majority of inscriptions of late date the familiar letters V.S.L.M. (*votum solvit lubens merito*) betray the nature of the transaction, and it is not unreasonable to guess that there was usually a previous undertaking of some kind, to be carried out if the deity were gracious.

But these private *vota* were not, strictly speaking, legal transactions, supposed to bind both parties in a contract, as we shall see was to some extent the case with the *vota publica*. They could not have needed the aid of a pontifex, or a solemn *voti nuncupatio*, *i.e.* statement of the promise; they were rather, as De Marchi asserts,[5] spontaneous expressions of what we may call religious feeling; and it may be that he is right in maintaining that throughout Roman history they remained as expressions of the religious sense and of the better feeling of the lower classes. The practice implies three conceptions: (1) of the deity as really powerful for good and evil; (2) of the gift, a work of supererogation, as likely to please him; (3) of the grateful act and feeling as good in themselves. Surely there must have been in this practice a germ of moral development; I am surprised that Dr. Westermarck has not mentioned in his chapter on gratitude the extraordinary abundance of Roman votive offerings and inscriptions. Doubtless there lies at the root of it the idea of *Do ut des*, or rather of *Dabo ut des*; doubtless also it could be turned to evil purposes in the form of *devotio*, when promises were made to a deity on condition that he killed or injured an enemy; but in the ordinary and common example it is impossible to deny that the final act, the performance of the vow, must have been accompanied by a feeling of gratitude. The merest recognition of a supposed blessing is of value in moral development.

But it is in the *vota publica* that we undoubtedly find something in the nature of a bargain—covenant would be a more graceful word—with a deity in the name of the State. Even here, however, the impression is rather produced by the use of legal terms and the formularisation of the process, than by any assumed attitude of contempt towards, or even of equality with, the deity concerned. There is no trace in early Roman religious history of any

tendency to abuse or degrade the divine beings if they
did not perform their part, such as is well known in
China,[6] or even, strange to say, occasionally met with in
the southern Italy of to-day ; the attitude towards the
deity in cult (though not invariably in the later Graeco-
Roman literature) was ever respectful, as it was towards
the magistrates of the State.   The farthest the Romans
ever went in condemning their gods was when misfortune
persuaded them that they were become indifferent or useless ; then they began to neglect them, and to turn to
other gods, as we shall see in subsequent lectures.

The public *vota* were of two kinds : the ordinary, or
regularly recurring, and the extraordinary, which were
occasioned by some particular event.   Of the ordinary,
the most familiar is that undertaken by the consul, and no
doubt in some form by the Rex in the days of the kingship,
for the benefit of the State on the first day of the official
year.   Accompanied by the Senate and a crowd of people,
the consuls went up to the Capitoline temple, and performed the sacrifice which had been vowed by their predecessors of a year before ; after which they undertook a new
votum, "*pro reipublicae salute.*"[7]   We have not the
formula of this vow, and cannot tell what resemblance it
bore to a bargain ; but the ceremony itself must have been
most impressive, and calculated to remind all who were
present of the greatness and goodwill of the supreme
deity who watched over the interests of the State.   So
too at the *lustrum* of the censors, which took place in the
Campus Martius every five years, it is almost certain that
the *votum* of the predecessors in office was fulfilled by a
sacrifice, and a new one undertaken.   Here again we are
without the formula, but that there was one we know from
a very interesting passage of Valerius Maximus.   He tells
us that Scipio Aemilianus, when as censor he was conducting this sacrifice, and the *scriba* (on behalf of the pontifex?)
was dictating to him the *solemne precationis carmen ex
publicis tabulis*, in which the immortal gods were besought
to make the prosperity of the Roman State " better and

greater," had the audacity to interrupt him, saying that
the condition of the State was sufficiently good and great :
" itaque precor ut eas (res) perpetuo incolumes servent."
This change, Valerius says, was accepted, and the formula
altered accordingly in the *tabulae*.[8]   This story, which is
probably genuine and is quite characteristic of Scipio,
must convince an impartial mind that in this votive ceremony there was enough truth and dignity to suggest a
real advance in religious thought, so far at least as the
State was concerned.

The extraordinary *vota* were innumerable.   They were
occasioned by dangers or misfortunes of various kinds, the
magistrate undertaking to dedicate something to the god
concerned if the State should have come safely through
the peril.   Many temples had their origin in this practice ;[9]
we meet also with *ludi*, special sacrifices, or a tithe of the
booty taken in war.   In two or three cases Livy has
copied the formula from the *tabulae* of the pontifices ;
thus before the war with Antiochus in 191 B.C., the
consul recited the following words after the pontifex
maximus : " Si duellum quod cum Antiocho rege sumi
populus iussit, id ex sententia senatus populique Romani
confectum erit ; tum tibi Iuppiter populus Romanus ludos
magnos dies decem continuos faciet . . . quisquis magistratus eos ludos quando ubique faxit, hi ludi recte facti,
donaque data recte sunto."[10]   This document dates from
the days of the decay of the Roman religion, and is, of
course, modernised by Livy ; but it may give an idea of
what is meant by writers who speak of an element of
bargain or covenant in these *vota*.   Still more elaborate,
and probably more antique, is the famous formula of the
vow of the *ver sacrum* in the darkest hour of the war with
Hannibal.[11]   This very curious rite, which proves beyond
question the devotion of the Italian stocks to the principle
of the *votum*, consisted of a promise to dedicate to Mars
or Jupiter all the valuable products of a single spring,
including the male children born at that time ; to this the
Romans had recourse for the last time in 217 B.C., and

Livy has fortunately preserved the words of the vow. These, with the exception of the dedication of the children, which is judiciously omitted, probably stand much as they had come down from a remote antiquity. The *votum* is put in the form of a *rogatio* to the people, without whose sanction it could not be put in force; are they willing to dedicate to Jupiter all the young of oxen, sheep, or pigs born in the spring five years after date, if the State shall have been preserved during those years from all its enemies? The curious feature of the document is, not that it binds the deity to any course of action, but that it secures the individual Roman against his anger in case of any chance slip in his part of the process, and the people against any evil consequences arising from such a slip or from misdoing on the part of an individual. " Si quis clepsit, ne populo scelus esto neve cui cleptum erit : si atro die faxit insciens, probe factum esto." [12] Of this formula a recent writer of great learning and ability has written thus : " The well-known liturgical archive containing Rome's address to Jupiter in the critical days of the Hannibalic war is a wary and cleverly drawn legal document, intended to bind the god as well as the State." [13] He is no exception to the rule that those who have not habitually occupied themselves with the Roman religion are liable to misinterpret its details. This is not an address to Jupiter, nor is there any sign in it that the god was considered as bound to perform his part as in a contract ; the covenant is a one-sided one, the people undertaking an act of self-renunciation if the god be gracious to them, and thereby going far to assure themselves that he will so be gracious. And the legal cast of the language, which seems so apt to mislead the unwary,[14] is only to be found in the clauses which guarantee the people against the contingency of the whole vow being ruined by the inadvertence or the rascality of an individual ; surely a very natural and inevitable *caveat*, where for once the whole people, and not only their priests or magistrates, were concerned in the transaction.

A curious form of the *votum*, which, however, I can only mention in passing, is that addressed to the gods of a hostile city, with a view to induce them to desert their temples and take up their abode at Rome ; this is the process called *evocatio*, which was successfully applied at the siege of Veii, when Juno Regina consented to betray her city.[15] Macrobius, commenting on Virgil's lines (*Aen.* ii. 351),

> excessere omnes adytis arisque relictis
> di quibus imperium hoc steterat,

has preserved the *carmen* used at the siege of Carthage.[16] It is cast in the language of prayer : " Si deus si dea est cui populus civitasque Carthaginiensis est in tutela . . . precor venerorque veniamque a vobis peto ut vos populum civitatemque Carthaginiensem deseratis," etc. ; but it ends with a vow to build temples and establish *ludi* in honour of these deities if they should comply with the petition. It is worth noting here that it was, of course, impossible to make a bargain with strange or hostile gods, or in any way to force their hand ; the promise is entirely one-sided ; and I am inclined to think that in dealing with his own gods the mental attitude of the Roman was much the same, though his faith in them was undoubtedly greater.

This is the proper place to mention another very curious rite, closely allied to the *votum*, but differing from it in one or two important points, which is almost peculiar to the Romans and most characteristic of them ; I mean the *devotio* of himself on the field of battle by a magistrate *cum imperio*.[17] The famous example, familiar to us all, is that of Decius Mus at the battle of Vesuvius in the great Latin war [18] (340 B.C.) : the same story is told of his son in a war with Gauls and Samnites, and of his grandson in the war with Pyrrhus.[19] The historical difficulties of these accounts do not concern us now ; by common consent of scholars the method and formula of the *devotio* are authentic, and the rite must have had its origin in remote antiquity.

The story runs[20] that Decius, at whose preliminary sacrifice before the battle with the Latins the liver of the victim had been found imperfect, while that of his colleague was normal, perceived that his wing of the army was giving way.   He therefore resolved to sacrifice himself by *devotio*, and called on the pontifex maximus, who was present, to dictate for him the correct formula.   He was directed to put on the toga praetexta, to wear it with the cinctus Gabinus, to veil his head with it, to touch his chin with his hand under the folds of the robe, and to stand upon a spear.   He then repeated after the pontifex the following formula : "Iane, Iuppiter, Mars pater, Quirine, Bellona, Lares, divi Novensiles, di Indigetes, divi quorum est potestas nostrorum hostiumque, diique Manes, vos precor, veneror, veniam peto feroque, uti populo Romano Quiritium vim victoriamque prosperetis, hostesque populi Romani Quiritium terrore formidine morteque adficiatis.   Sicut verbis nuncupavi, ita pro re publica Quiritium, exercitu legionibus auxiliis populi Romani Quiritium, legiones auxiliaque hostium *mecum* deis Manibus Tellurique devoveo" (Livy ix. 9).   He then mounted his horse and rode into the midst of the enemy to meet his death.   The Latins were seized with panic and the Romans were victorious.

Here the vow is made and fulfilled almost at the same moment,—*the fulfilment takes place before the gods have done their part.*   Here too the offering made is the life of a human being which brings the act within the domain of sacrifice.   Its sacrificial nature is obvious in all the details.[21]   The dress is that of the sacrificing priest or magistrate ;[22] Decius was therefore priest and victim at the same time, and the two characters seem to be combined in the symbolic touching of the chin, which has been rightly explained,[23] I think, as analogous to the laying on of hands in the consecratio of the Rex, as we saw it in the case of Numa, and perhaps to the *immolatio* of a victim by sprinkling the *mola salsa* on its head ; where the object of consecration is made holy by contact with holy things.[24]   The standing on the spear is difficult to explain ; it may have been a symbolic dedication to Mars, whose spear or spears, as we have seen, were kept in the Regia.[25]

The formula contains certain points of great interest. Firstly, it is not only the Roman gods of all sorts and conditions who are invoked, but those of the enemy also, or, in vague language, those who have power over both Romans and Latins.[26]   Secondly, it begins with a prayer combined with a curse upon the enemy : in which respect it resembles the prayer at the *lustratio populi* at Iguvium [27] (which I shall mention again directly) and to a later type of *devotio* used at the siege of Carthage and preserved by Macrobius.[28]   Thirdly, in spite of this religious aspect of the formula, it ends with what can only be called a magical spell.   By the act of self-sacrifice, which is the potent element in the spell, Decius exercises magical power over the legions of the enemy, and devotes them with himself to death,—to the Manes and Mother Earth.[29]

The story suggests to me that the rite had been at one time well known ; the pontifex maximus was ready with the instructions and formula.   It was a survival from an age of magic, but the priests have given it a religious turn, and the language of the first part is quite as much that of prayer as is the language of the collect to be said in time of war which still disfigures the Anglican prayer-book.[30]   What is still more remarkable is that it has not only a religious but an ethical character.   The idea of service to the State is here seen at its highest point.   The sacrifice is a vicarious one.[31]   Livy significantly adds that a private soldier might be chosen by the commander to represent him, and that if this man were not killed by the enemy an image seven feet long must be buried in the earth and a piacular sacrifice offered.[32]   Later on it would seem that instead of sacrificing himself, the consul might implore the gods to accept the hostile army or city as his substitutes : " eos

vicarios pro me fide magistratuque meo pro populi
Romani exercitibus do devoveo, ut me exercitumque
nostrum . . . bene salvos siritis esse." [33] The idea here,
and indeed in the *devotio* of Decius, bears some analogy
to that which lies at the root of the old Roman practice,
of making a criminal *sacer* to the deity chiefly concerned
in his crime ; when this was done, any man might kill
him, and he was practically a victim offered as *vicarius*
for the Roman people, who had been contaminated by
his deed.[34]

But I must now pass on the last kind of ritual to be
explained in these lectures, and far the most impressive
of all, that of *lustratio*, or the purification, as it is
commonly called, of land, city, human beings, or even
inanimate objects, by means of a solemn procession
accompanied with sacrifice.

So important a part did these processional rites play
in the public life of the Roman people,—so characteristic
are they too of the old Roman habit of thought and
action, that they have given a wonderful word to the
Latin language. *Lustrare* has many meanings ; but
the one which is immediately derived from the rites I
speak of, that of slow processional movement, is the
most beautiful and impressive of them all. When
Aeneas first sees Dido in all her stately beauty, he
says : [35]

> in freta dum fluvii current, *dum montibus umbrae*
> *lustrabunt convexa*, polus dum sidera pascet,
> semper honos nomenque tuum laudesque manebunt,
> quae me cunque vocant terrae.

" So long as the cloud-shadows move slowly over the
hollows of the hills." Here in Scotland you must have
all seen this procession of the shadows, as I have watched
it when fishing in Wales ; let us always associate it with
the magic of a poet of nature as well as with the religious
processions of his people.

Lustrare, lustratio, are words which, as I think, belong

P

to an age of religion, that is, according to our formula of effective desire to be in right relation with the Power manifesting itself in the Universe.   In other processes which are usually called purificatory, magic seems to survive : the word *februum*, from which comes the name of our second month, meant an object with magical potency, such as water, fire, sulphur, laurel, wool, or the strips of the victims sacrificed at the Lupercalia, and the verb *februare* meant to get rid of certain unwholesome or miasmatic influences by means of these objects.[36]   What was the really primitive idea attached to these words need not concern us now ; but Varro, and Ovid following him, explicitly explain them as meaning *purifying* agents and processes,[37] from which we may infer that they had a magical power to produce certain desired conditions, or to protect from evil influences, like charms and amulets.   But *lustrare* and *lustratio* seem to belong to an age when the thing to be driven or kept away is rather spiritual mischief, and when the means used are sacrifices and prayers, with processional movement.

What is the original meaning of the word *lustrare*? It seems to be a strong form of *luere* ; and *luere* is explained by Varro as equivalent to *solvere*.[38]   The word *lustrum*, he says, *i.e.* the solemn five-yearly ceremony in the Campus Martius, is derived from *luere* in the sense of *solvere*, to pay ; because every fifth year the contract-moneys for the collection of taxes and for public undertakings were paid into the treasury through the censors. Servius,[39] doubtless following him, explains such expressions as *peccata luere*, *supplicium luere*, on the same principle— in the sense of payment, just as we speak of paying the penalty.   We might thus be tempted to fancy that the root-idea of *lustrare* is to perform a duty and so get rid of it, as we do in paying for anything we buy ; but this would be to misapprehend the original meaning of the word as completely as Varro did when he explained *luere* by reference to the payments of contractors.   Varro

and Servius do, however, suggest the right clue; they
see that the idea lurking in the word is that of getting
rid of something, but they understand that something
in the light, not of primitive man's intelligence, but of
the duty of man in a civilised State.   What exactly it
was that was to be got rid of is a more difficult question;
but all that we have so far learnt about the early religious
ideas of the Romans strongly suggests that they were in
what we may call an advanced *animistic* stage of religious
ideas, and that whatever may have been the notion of
their primitive ancestors, they themselves, in these rites
as we know them, saw the means of getting rid of and
so keeping away hostile spirits.   A French sociologist,
M. van Gennep, whose book *Les Rites de passage* I have
read with great interest, has kindly written me a long
letter in which he insists that this animistic interpretation of
lustratio is really superfluous, and that the idea of separation alone, *i.e.* of separation between sacred and profane,
without any reference to spirits or *dei*, is a fully sufficient
explanation.   So no doubt it may be among many savage
peoples; but he would probably allow that as a people
advances from one stage of superstition to another,
while it retains in outline the scheme of its rites, it will
apply new meanings to them in keeping with the changes
in its mental attitude.   This is one of the most interesting
processes with which modern research has been occupied;
we are now familiar with the adoption of pre-Christian
ceremonies, with a complete change of meaning, in the
ritual of the Christian Church.   These very processions
of *lustratio*, which had already been once metamorphosed
in an animistic period, were seized upon by the Roman
Church with characteristic adroitness, adapted to its ritual,
and given a new meaning; and the Catholic priest still
leads his flock round the fields with the prayers of the
Litania maior in Rogation week, begging a blessing on
the flocks and herds, and deprecating the anger of the
Almighty.[40]

But let us now pass briefly in review the more important

of these rites of lustration and compare them with each other; we shall find the essential features the same in all of them.

The first permanent difficulty of new settlers in Latium was to mark off their cultivated land from the forest or waste land beyond it, and so, as M. van Gennep would phrase it,[41] to make a margin of separation between the sacred and the profane, within which the sacred processes of domestic life and husbandry might go forward, undisturbed by dangers—human, spiritual, or what not—coming from the profane world without. The boundary was marked out in some material way, perhaps by stones (*cippi*) or posts, placed at intervals;[42] and thus "a fixed piece of ground is appropriated by a particular social group, so that if any stranger penetrated it he would be committing a sacrilege as complete as he would if he trespassed in a sacred grove or a temple." This boundary-line was made sacred itself by the passage round it (*lustratio*) at some fixed time of the year, usually in May, when crops were ripening and especially liable to be attacked by hostile influences, of a procession occupied with sacrifice and prayer. The two main features of the rite, as formulated by Cato in his treatise on agriculture, are—1, the procession of the victims, ox, sheep, and pig (*suovetaurilia*), the farmer's most valuable property; 2, the prayer to Mars pater, after libations to Janus and Jupiter, asking for his kindly protection of the whole *familia* of the farm, together with the crops of all kinds and the cattle within the boundary-line.[43] We are not expressly told that this procession followed the boundary throughout, but the analogy of other lustrations forbids us to doubt it; and thus the rite served the practical purpose of keeping it clear in the memory,—a matter of the utmost importance, especially for the practical Roman. In Cato's formula the farmer's object is to ward off disease, calamity, dearth, and infertility; and it is Mars who is invoked, *i.e.* a great god who has long ago emerged from the crowd of impersonal spirits; but we may safely believe that the primitive farmer used other language, addressing the spirits of disease and dearth themselves; and we may guess, if we will, that again before that there was no invocation or sacrifice at all, but that the object was only to mark the boundary between land civilised and sacred and land uncivilised and profane.

As we have seen, the farms and homesteads of the early Latins were grouped together in associations called *pagi*; and we can hardly doubt that these were subjected to the same process of *lustratio* as the farms themselves. We have no explicit account of a circumambulation in this case, but we have in the later poets several charming allusions to a *lustratio pagi*, and it is of a rite of this kind that Virgil must have been thinking when he wrote the beautiful passage in the first Georgic beginning " In primis venerare deos ";[44] and the lines

> terque novas circum felix eat hostia fruges,
> omnis quam chorus et socii comitentur ovantes, etc.,

clearly imply a procession with the object of keeping away harmful influences from the crops at a critical time. And when the city-state came into being we may be equally sure that its *ager*, so long at least as it was small enough to admit of such a processional ritual, was lustrated in the same way. In historical times this *ager* had become too extensive, and there is no procession to be found among the duties of the Fratres Arvales as we know them when they were revived by Augustus; but we have not, of course, the whole of the " acta " of the Brethren, and even if we had, it would not be likely that we should find any trace of a practice which must have been dropped in course of time as the Roman territory increased. Let us go on to the beginnings of the city, where we shall find the same principle and practice applied in striking fashion.

As it was necessary to protect the homestead and its land by a sacred boundary, so the city had to be clearly

marked off from all that was outside of it. Its walls
were sacred, or, strictly speaking, a certain imaginary
line outside of them called the *pomoerium* was sacred.
This is well shown in the traditional method of founding
a city even in historical times, *e.g.* a *colonia*, as described
by Varro, Servius, and Plutarch.[45]   A white ox and a
white cow were harnessed to a plough, of which the
share must be made of bronze—a rule which shows at
once the antiquity and the religious character of the
rite, for iron, as we saw, was taboo in most religious
ceremonies.   A rectangular furrow was drawn where the
walls of the city were to be ; the earth was turned
inwards to mark the future line of the wall, and the
furrow represented the future *pomoerium*.   When the
plough came to the place where there was to be a gate,
it was lifted over it, and the ploughing resumed beyond
it.   This probably meant, as Plutarch expressed it, that
the walls (or rather the *pomoerium*), were sacred while the
gates were profane ; had the gates been holy, scruple
would necessarily have been felt about the passage in
and out of them of things profane.   Thus the *pomoerium*
was a boundary line between the sacred and the profane,
like that of the farm ; but in historical times it acquired
a more definite religious meaning, for within it there
could only dwell those deities who belonged to the city
and its inhabitants, *i.e.* the *di indigetes*, and who were
recognised as its divine inhabitants.[46] And only within its
limits could the *auspicia* of the city be taken.

We should naturally expect that this sacred boundary
would have its holiness secured or revived by an annual
lustratio like that of the farm and *pagus* ; and so no
doubt it was.   But the memory of this survives only in
the word *amburbium*, which, on the analogy of *ambarvalia*,
must mean a rite of this processional kind.   Luckily
we have definite knowledge of the real *lustratio* of a
city in those ritualistic inscriptions of Iguvium which I
have more than once referred to.[47]   It is the *lustratio*
of the *arx*, the citadel of Iguvium, which we may guess

to have been the original *oppidum* or germ of the
historical city.   The details are complex, and show clear
traces of priestly organisation ; but the main features
stand out unmistakably.   A procession goes round the
arx (*ocris Fisia*), with the *suovetaurilia*—ox, sheep, and
pig—as in the Latin *lustratio* ; at each gate it stops,
while sacrifice and prayer are offered on behalf of the
citadel, the city, and the whole people of Iguvium.
There were three gates, and each of them is the scene
of sacrifice and prayer, because they are the weak points
in the wall, and they need to be strengthened by annual
religious operations ; such at least is the most obvious
explanation.   Whether the Fratres Attiedii would have
been able to explain it thus we may doubt ; neither in
the sacrificial ritual nor in the prayers, as recorded in
the inscription, do we find any clear trace of a distinction
between the sacred and the profane, or of the idea of a
hostile spiritual world outside the sacred boundary.   So
far as we can judge from the prayers, the object is really
a religious one, to implore the deities of the city to
preserve it and all within it.   The language of these
prayers hardly differs from that in which a Christian
Church of to-day asks for a blessing on a community.[48]

So far I have been speaking of the permanent separation of land or city by a sacred boundary line from the
profane world without.   But human beings *en masse*
might be subjected to the same process—an army, for
example, at the opening of the season of war ; and so,
too, might its appurtenances—horses, arms, and trumpets.
In the account of the census and *lustrum* in the Campus
Martius given by Dionysius of Halicarnassus, who passed
some years in Rome in the time of Augustus, we find
the *suovetaurilia* driven three times round the assembled
host and sacrificed to Mars.   This was doubtless the
early form of the political census, which had a military
meaning and origin.   But we have a more exact and
reliable account of a similar rite in the Iguvian documents, which contain instructions for the *lustratio* of the

people apparently before a campaign.[49]   So far as we can gather from the Umbrian text, the male population was assembled in a particular spot in its military divisions, and round this host a procession went three times ; at the end of each circuit there was sacrifice and prayer to Mars and two female associates of his power, the object of which, as we can read in the words of the prayer, was to bless the people of Iguvium and to curse its enemies, who were to be confounded and frightened and paralysed.

Here religion of a rude sort has been superimposed on the originally magical ceremonial.   For the idea must have been that by drawing a "magic circle" around the host, which might have to march against enemies living far beyond the pale of the *ager Romanus* (or Iguvinus), where hostile magical influences might be brought to bear against them, they were in some mysterious way marked off, rendered "holy," and so protected against the wiles of the enemy.   A later and animistic age would think of them as needing protection against hostile spirits, of whose ways and freaks they were of course entirely ignorant.   Of these primitive ideas about the danger of entering hostile territory and of leaving your own, Dr. Frazer has collected some examples in his *Golden Bough* (i. 304 foll.), both from savage tribes and from Greek usage.   A single parallel from the pen of a Roman historian, which Dr. Frazer has not mentioned, may suffice us here.   Livy tells us that the method in Macedonia was to march the whole host in spring between the severed limbs of a dog : [50] the principle is here the same as in Italy, but the method differs slightly.   In each case some mysterious influence is brought to bear on the whole army without exception ; but in the one case a line is drawn round it, in the other it passes through the parts of an object which must have been supposed to be endowed with magical power.

And once more, in spring before the season of arms, all the belongings of the host were subjected

to some process of the same kind.   I have alluded
to this in my lecture on the calendar, and need not
now reproduce the evidence of the Equirria at the end of
February and on March 14, or of the Quinquatrus on
March 19, when the *lustratio* took place of the shields
(*ancilia*) of the Salii, the war-priests of Mars, and the
Tubilustrium on March 23, which tells its own tale.[51]
But I may recall the fact that the calendar supplies us
also with evidence that on the return of the host to
their own territory all these lustrations had to be
repeated in order to rid men, horses, arms, and trumpets
of such evil contagion as they might have contracted
during their absence.   It may be that one special object
of lustration after the return of an army was to rid it,
with all belonging to it, of the taint of bloodshed, just
as the Jewish warriors and their captives were purified
before re-entering the camp.[52]   But in the Roman pontifical
law this idea is hardly discernible, and the only trace I
can find of it is a statement of Festus that the soldiers
who followed the general's car in a triumph wore laurel
wreaths " ut quasi purgati a caede humana intrarent
urbem." [53]   I may add here that the passage of a
triumphing army through the Porta triumphalis, which
was probably an isolated arch in the Campus Martius
just outside the city wall,[54] most likely had as its original
meaning the separation of the host from the profane
world in which it had been moving ; and the triumphal
arches of later times, which were within the city, were
thus developed architecturally from an origin which belongs
to the region of magic.[55]   To the same class of ideas, if
I am not much mistaken, belongs the familiar Italian
practice of compelling a surrendered army to pass under
the yoke.   As Livy explains this when he first mentions
it, it was symbolical of subjection : " ut exprimatur
confessio subactam domitamque esse gentem " ;[56] and
this was no doubt the idea in the minds of the historical
Romans.   But it may well have been that it had its
root in a process which was supposed to deprive the

conquered enemy of all dangerous contagion—to separate them from their own land and people before they came into peaceful contact with their conquerors.

A last word before I leave this part of my subject. Though it is interesting to try to get at the root-idea of these processes of *lustratio*, we must remember that in the Rome of history they had lost not only such magical meaning as they ever had, but also much of the religious meaning which in course of time was super-imposed upon it. The sacrifices and the prayers remained, but the latter were muttered and unheard by the people. And except in the country districts these ceremonies were more and more absorbed, as time went on, into the social, military, and political life of the community, as *e.g.* the lustration of the host became a political census ; or they tended to disappear altogether, like the *ambarvalia* and perhaps the *amburbium*. They grew up in the religious experience of the Romans, beginning with its very earliest and quasi-magical forms ; but they came at last to represent that experience no longer, and when we meet with them in historical times it is impossible to ascribe to them any real influence on life and conduct. *Lustratio* never in pagan Italy developed an ethical meaning as *catharsis* did in Greece.[57] But meaningless as they were, the stately processions remained, and could be watched with pride by the patriotic Roman all through the period of the Empire, until the Roman Church adapted them to its own ritual and gave them, as we saw, a new meaning. As the cloud-shadows still move slowly over the hollows of the Apennines, so does the procession of the patron saint pass still through the streets of many an Italian city.[58]

NOTES TO LECTURE IX

1. Dill, *Roman Society in the Last Century of the Western Empire*, p. 63.

2. See Westermarck, *Origin and Development of Moral Ideas*, ii. 615 foll.

3. *C.I.L.* i. Nos. 43 foll.

4. *C.I.L.* xiv. 2863.   See *R.F.* p. 224, and Wissowa, *R.K.* p. 209.

5. *Op. cit.* vol. i. p. 252 ; cp. 271.

6. See Sir Alfred Lyall's *Asiatic Studies*, Series I. ch. vi.   No one would call the vow of Aeneas, in *Aen.* vi. 69, a bargain with Apollo and the Sibyl.

7. Marquardt, p. 266 ; Mommsen, *Staatsrecht*, i.² 594 foll.   The ceremony is best described by Ovid, *Ex Ponto*, iv. 9. 5 foll.   He is addressing the consul of the year from his place of exile :

> at cum Tarpeias esses deductus in arces,
>   dum caderet iussu victima sacra tuo,
> me quoque secreto grates sibi magnus agentem
>   audisset media qui sedet aede deus.
>   (ll. 28 foll.)

8. Valerius Maximus iv. 1. 10.

9. A list of these is given in Aust, *De aedibus sacris populi Romani* (Marpurg, 1889).   A valuable work, which will be of service to us later on.

10. Livy xxxvi. 2. 3.

11. *Ib.* xxii. 10.

12. *Ib.* sec. 6.   The meaning is that if any one has stolen an animal which was intended to be dedicated, no blame attaches to the person so robbed ; and that if a man performs his dedication on a day of ill omen unwittingly, it will hold good none the less.

13. Farnell, *Evolution of Religion*, p. 195.

14. The fact that words like *reus* and *damnatus* were applied respectively to persons who had made a vow and to those who had performed it, *i.e.* as being liable like a defendant, and then released from that position by a verdict or sentence (see Wissowa, *R.K.* p. 320), is of course significant of the idea of the transaction in the mind of the Roman, who, as Macrobius says (iii. 2. 6) *se numinibus obligat*, as an accused person is *obligatus* to the authorities of the State (Mommsen, *Strafrecht*, 189 foll.).   It is the natural tendency of the Roman mind to give all transactions a legal sanction ; but it does not thence follow that the original idea was really thought of as a contract, and we have only to reflect that the final act was a thank-offering to see the difference between the civil and the religious process.

15. Livy v. 21.

16. Macr. iii. 9, 6.   He says that he found it in the fifth book of *Res reconditae* by one Sammonicus Serenus, and that the latter had himself found it " in cuiusdam Furii vetustissimo libro."

17. On this subject see article " Devotio " in Pauly-Wissowa.

18. Livy viii. 10, "licere consuli dictatori praetori. . . ." Cp. Cic. *de Nat. deorum*, ii. 10, " at vero apud maiores tanta religionis vis fuit, ut quidam imperatores etiam se ipsos dis immortalibus capite velato certis verbis pro republica devoverent."

19. See Münzer's article "Decii" in Pauly-Wissowa, *Real-Encycl.* ; Soltau, *Die Anfänge der röm. Geschichtschreibung*, p. 48 foll.

20. Livy viii. 9 foll. ; Dio Cassius, fragment, xxxv. 6 ; Ennius, *Ann.* vi. 147, Baehrens. The latter fragment is the oldest reference to the event which we possess, and just sufficient to confirm Livy's account : "Divi hoc audite parumper, ut pro Romano populo prognariter armis certando prudens animum de corpore mitto."

21. It is worth remarking that the sacrificial aspect struck St. Augustine. In *Civ. Dei*, v. 18, he writes : "Si se occidendos certis verbis quodam modo consecrantes Decii devoverunt, ut illis cadentibus et iram deorum sanguine suo placantibus Romanus liberaretur exercitus," and goes on to compare the Decii with Christian martyrs. I am indebted for this reference to Mayor's note on Cicero, *de Nat. deor.* ii. 3. 10.

22. See above, p. 176 ; Wissowa, *R.K.* p. 352, note 1.

23. By Deubner in *Archiv*, 1905, p. 69 foll. This touching of the chin seems to be an example of that personal contact which makes a man or thing holy ; see, *e.g.*, Westermarck, *op. cit.* i. 586. Decius makes himself holy for the sacrifice (as victim) by touching (as priest) the only part of his person which was exposed. For the magic touch of the hand see O. Weinrich, *Antike Heiligungswünder*, p. 63 foll., and Macrobius iii. 2. 7, for the touching of the altar by a sacrificing priest.

24. See above, p. 180.

25. This is Deubner's explanation, which he elaborates at length by examples of the worship of the spear or sword among various peoples.

26. This is peculiar to the formula in Livy viii. 9. Is it possible that it may have some reference to the fact that the Romans were fighting their own kin, the Latins ?

27. Buecheler, *Umbrica*, pp. 22 and 102 : "hastatos inhastatos completo timore tremore, fuga formidine, nive nimbo, fragore furore, senio servitio," where, however, the translator from the Umbrian is assisted by the Latin formulae we are discussing.

28. Macrobius iii. 9. 10, "exercitum quem ego me sentio dicere fuga formidine terrore compleatis," etc. This is of comparatively late origin, as it is addressed to Dis pater, who only became a Roman deity in 249 B.C. (Wissowa, *R.K.* p. 257). The interesting feature in this *devotio*, used at the siege at Carthage, is that it is not himself whom the commander devotes—the common sense of the Romans had got beyond that—but the enemy as substitutes for himself. "Eos vicarios pro me fide magistratuque meo pro populo Romano exercitibus do devoveo, ut me meamque fidem imperiumque legiones exercitumque nostrum bene ˙salvos siritis esse." Thus the enemy is made the victim, and this is˙why the only gods invoked are the Di Inferi, Dis pater, Veiovis, Manes, while in the older formula it is the gods of Romans and Latins. Pacuvius in a praetextata called *Decius* wrote : "Lue patrium hostili fusum sanguen sanguine" (Ribbeck, p. 280). This is the language Ennius used before him of the sacrifice

of Iphigenia: "ut hostium eliciatur sanguis sanguine," where, however, the word *eliciatur* shows that it is magic.   The curious thing in this last passage is that the parallel passage in the Euripidean *Iph. in Aul.* (1486) does not suggest magic.   Is the idea Italian?   The curse (for such it really is) is to be witnessed by Tellus and Iuppiter, and the celebrant points down and up respectively in invoking them, as also in the *devotio* of Curtis in the Forum (Livy vii. 6), which was an abnormal *procuratio prodigii.*

29. Cp. the language used by Livy of the second Decius (x. 29): "prae se agere formidinem ac fugam . . . contacturum funebribus diris signa tela arma hostium."   For spells or curses of this kind see Westermarck i. 563 : a curse is conveyable by speech, especially if spoken by a magistrate or priest.   "Among the Maoris the anathema of the priest is regarded as a thunderbolt that an enemy cannot escape."   See also Robertson Smith, *Semites*, p. 434, for the Jewish ban, by which impious sinners, or enemies of the city and its God, were devoted to destruction.   He remarks that the Hebrew verb to ban is sometimes rendered "consecrate" : Micah iv. 13 ; Deut. xiii. 16 ; and Joshua vi. 26 (Jericho), which exactly answers to the consecratio of Carthage.   For curses conveyable by sacrifices, as in all the cases I have mentioned, see Westermarck ii. 618 foll. 624, and the same author's paper on conditional curses in Morocco, in *Anthropological Essays*, addressed to E. B. Tylor, p. 360.

30. "Abate their pride, assuage their malice, and confound their devices."   I well remember hearing this read in church throughout the Crimean war.

31. "Pro republica Quiritium," in the formula quoted above.

32. Livy viii. 10 *ad fin.*

33. See above, note 28.

34. See Marquardt, p. 276 and notes ; Mommsen, *Strafrecht*, 900 foll.   The subject has generally been treated from the legal point of view rather than the religious ; but from the religious point of view it has generally been assumed that the sacrifice was to appease the god.   So no doubt it was ; but I venture also to conjecture that the victim was *vicarius* for the contamination of the community.   On the subject generally Westermarck's two chapters on human sacrifice and blood-revenge (xix. and xx. in vol. i.) are extremely well worth reading.

35. *Aen.* i. 607 foll.   Cp. *Aen.* iii. 429—

> praestat Trinacrii metas lustrare Pachyni
> cessantem, longos et circumflectere cursus,

where the slow movement and circuitous course of a lustratio must have been in Virgil's mind.   The movement round an object for lustral purposes is seen in *Aen.* vi. 229, "idem ter socios pura circumtulit unda," where Servius explains *circumtulit* by *purgavit.*   As early as Livius Andronicus (second century B.C.) we find "classem lustratur" of fishes swimming round a fleet (Ribb. *Trag. Fragmenta*, p. 1).

36. Marquardt, p. 324, for the *februa* of the Luperci, *R.F.* p. 320 foll., and the explanations there given.   More will be found alluded to in Van Gennep, *Les Rites de passage*, p. 249.   To my mind none are quite convincing.   The Romans believed that blows with these *februa* (strips of the victim's skin) made women fertile ; they were therefore clearly magical implements, but beyond this we do not seem to get.   (See also Deubner in *Archiv*, 1910, p. 495 foll.)

37. Varro, *L.L.* vi. 13, "Februum Sabini purgamentum, et id in sacris nostris verbum." Cp. Varro, *ap. Nonium*, p. 114 ; Ovid, *Fasti*, ii. 19 foll., where he calls *februa piamina, purgamenta*, in the language of the *ius divinum*.

38. *L.L.* vi. 11.

39. Servius, *ad Aen.* x. 32 ; xi. 842 ; cp. i. 136.

40. See *R.F.* p. 127, for the same rite in the Church of England (Brand, *Popular Antiquities*, p 292).

41. *Les Rites de passage*, ch. ii.

42. For boundary marks in historical times see *Gromatici auctores*, vol. ii. p. 250 foll. (Rudorff).

43. If the cattle were in the woodland beyond the settlement, as they would be in summer, they could not be protected in this way : like an army going into the country of *hostes* (see above, p. 216) they were treated in another way, which we may connect with the ritual of the Parilia, as Dr. Frazer has beautifully shown in his paper on St. George and the Parilia (*Revue des études ethnographiques et sociologiques*, 1908, p. 1 foll.).

44. *Georg.* i. 338 foll.

45. Varro, *L.L.* v. 143 ; Servius, *Aen.* v. 755 (from Cato) ; Plutarch, *Romulus*, xi.

46. See above, p. 117.

47. Buecheler, *Umbrica*, pp. 12 foll. and 42 foll.

48. The deities of the city were invoked to preserve the name, the magistrates, rites, men, cattle, land, and crops : a list in which the name is the only item that carries us back to pre-Christian times.

49. Buecheler, *Umbrica*, pp. 21 and 84 foll.

50. Livy xl. 6 init.

51. See above, p. 96.

52. Numbers xxxi. 19.

53. Festus, p. 117.

54. See Hülsen-Jordan, *Röm. Topographie*, vol. iii. p. 495 ; Von Domaszewski, *Abhandlungen*, p. 217 foll.

55. Suggested by Van Gennep, *Les Rites de passage*, p. 28.

56. Livy iii. 28. 11.

57. Farnell, *Evolution of Religion*, p. 132 foll.

58. The account of *lustratio* given in this lecture is adapted from the author's chapter on the same subject in *Anthropology and the Classics*, Oxford University Press, 1908.

LECTURE X

I SAID in my first lecture that the whole story of Roman religious experience falls into two parts : first, that of the formularisation of rules and methods for getting effectively into right relations with the Power manifesting itself in the universe ; secondly, that of the gradual discovery of the inadequacy of these, and of the engrafting on the State religion of Rome of an ever-increasing number of foreign rites and deities. The first of these stories has been occupying us so far, and before I leave it for what will be practically an introduction to succeeding lectures, it will be as well for me to sum up the results at which we have already arrived.

I began with what I called the protoplasm of religion, the primitive ideas and practices which form the psychological basis of the whole growth. The feeling of awe and anxiety about that which is mysterious and unknown, the feeling which the Romans called *religio*, seems to have manifested itself in Italy, as elsewhere, in those various ways which I discussed in my second and third lectures, in the various forms of magic, negative and positive. We find unmistakable evidence of the existence of those strict rules of conduct called taboos, which fetter the mind and body of primitive man, which probably arise from an ineffective desire to put himself in right relations with forces he does not understand, and which have their value as a social discipline. Again, we find surviving in historical Rome numerous forms of active or positive magic, by which it was thought possible to compel or overcome those powers, so as to use them for your own benefit and against your enemies. But I was careful to point out that on the whole little of all this evidence of the early existence of magic at Rome is to be found in the public religion of the Roman State, and that the natural inference from this is that at one time or another there must have been a very powerful influence at work in cutting away these obsolete root-leaves of the plant that was to be, and in making of that plant a neat, well-defined growth.

I went on to deal with the first stage in the working of this influence, which we found reflected in the religion of the family as we know it in historical times. The family, settled on the land, with its homestead and its regular routine of agricultural process, developed a more effective desire to get into right relation with the Power manifesting itself in the universe. Anxiety is greatly lessened both in the house and on the land, because within those limits there is a " peace " (or covenant) between the divine and human inhabitants who have taken up their residence there. The supernatural powers, conceived now (whatever they may have been before) as spirits, are friendly if rightly propitiated, and much advance has been made in the methods of propitiation ; magic and religion are still doubtless mixed up together in these, but the tendency seems to be to get gradually rid of the more inadequate and blundering methods. In fact, man's knowledge of the Divine has greatly advanced ; spirits have some slight tendency to become deities, and magic is in part at least superseded by an orderly round of sacrifice and prayer, which is performed daily within the house, and within the boundary of the land at certain seasons of the year. This stage of settlement and routine was the first great revolution in the religious experience of the Romans, and supplied the basis of their national character.

The second revolution which we can clearly discern, and far the most important as a factor in Roman history, is that of the organisation of the religion of the city-state of Rome. Doubtless there were stages intermediate between the two, but they are entirely lost to us. We had to concentrate our attention on the city of the four regions—the first city we really know—and to examine the one document which has survived from it, the so-called calendar of Numa. In my fifth lecture I explained the nature of that calendar, and noted how it reflects the life of a people at once agricultural and military, and how it must presuppose the existence of a highly organised legal priesthood, or of some powerful genius for political as well as religious legislation. The tradition of a great priest-king is not wholly to be despised, for it expresses the feeling of the Romans that religious law and order were indispensable parts of their whole political and social life. During the rest of these lectures I have been trying to interrogate this religious calendar, with such help as could be gained from any other sources, on two points : (1) the conception, or, if we can venture to use the word, the knowledge, which the Romans of that early city-state had of the Divine ; (2) the chief forms and methods of their worship. We saw that they did not think of the divine beings as existing in human form with human weaknesses, but as invisible and intangible functional powers, *numina*. Each had its special limited sphere of action ; and some were now localised within the *pomoerium*, or just outside it within the *ager Romanus*, and worshipped under a particular name. I suggested that this very settlement had probably some influence in preparing them for assuming a more definite and personal character, should the chance be given them. In regard to the forms of cult with which they were propitiated, I found in the ritual of sacrifice and prayer a genuine advance towards a really religious attitude to the deity, the sacrifices being meant to increase his power to benefit the community, and the prayers to diminish such inclination as he might have to damage it ; but that there are in these certain survivals of the age of magic, which are, however, only formal, and

Q

have lost their original significance.   I found some curious examples of such survivals in the rite of *devotio*, and in vows generally a somewhat lower type of method in dealing with the supernatural.   But, on the other hand, the forms of *lustratio*, at the bottom of which seems to lie the idea of getting rid of evil spirits and influences, present very beautiful examples of what we may really call religious ceremony.

There was, then, in this highly-organised religion of the city-state, in some ways at least, a great advance.   But in spite of this gain, it had serious drawbacks.   Most prominent among these was the fact that it was the religion of the State as a whole, and not of the individual or the family.   Religion, I think we may safely say, had placed a certain consecration upon the simple life of the family, which was, in fact, the life of the individual ; for the essence of religion in all stages of civilisation lies in the feeling of the individual that his own life, his bodily and mental welfare, is dependent on the Divine as he and his regard it.   But to what extent can it be said that religion so consecrated the life of the State as to enable each individual in his family group to feel that consecration more vividly ?   That would have constituted a real advance in religious development ; that was the result, if I am not mistaken, of the religion of the Jewish State, which with all the force of a powerful hierarchical authority addressed its precepts to the mind and will of the individual.   But at Rome, though the earliest traces and traditions of law show a certain consecration of morality, inasmuch as the criminal is made over as a kind of propitiatory sacrifice to the deity whom he has offended, yet in the ordinary course of life, so far as I can discern, the individual was left very much where he was, before the State arose, in his relation to the Divine.

In no other ancient State that we know of did the citizen so entirely resign the regulation of all his dealings with the State's gods to the constituted authorities set over him.   His obligatory part in the religious ritual of the

State was simply *nil*, and all his religious duty on days of religious importance was to abstain from civil business, to make no disturbance.   Within the household he used his own simple ritual, the morning prayer, the libation to the household deities at meals ; and it is exactly here that we see a *pietas*, a sense of duty consecrated by religion, which seems to have had a real ethical value, and reminds us of modern piety.   But in all his relations with the gods *qua* citizen, he resigned himself to the trained and trusted priesthoods, who knew the secrets of ritual and all that was comprised in the *ius divinum* ; and by passive obedience to these authorities he gradually began to deaden the sense of *religio* that was in him. And this tendency was increased by the mere fact of life in a city, which as time went on became more and more the rule ; for, as I pointed out, the round of religious festivals no longer exactly expressed the needs and the work of that agricultural life in which it had its origin.

It would be an interesting inquiry, if the material for an answer were available, to try and discover how this gradual absorption of religion (or rather religious duties) by the State and its authorities affected the morality of the individual Roman.   It has often been maintained of late that religion and morality have nothing in common ; and even Dr. Westermarck,[1] who, unlike most anthropologists, treats the whole subject from a psychological point of view, seems inclined to come to this conclusion. For myself, I am rather disposed to agree with another eminent anthropologist,[2] that religion and morality are really elemental instincts of human nature, primarily undistinguishable from each other ; and if that be so, then the over-elaboration of either the moral or religious law, or of the two combined, will tend to weaken the binding force of both.   If, as at Rome, the citizen is made perfectly comfortable in his relations with the Power manifesting itself in the universe, owing to the complete mastery of the *ius divinum* by the State and its officials, there will assuredly be a tendency to paralyse the elemental religious impulse, and with it, if I am not mistaken, the elemental sense of right and wrong. For in the life of a state with such a legalised religious system as this, so long at least as it thrives and escapes serious disaster, there will be few or none of those moments of peril and anxiety in which "man is brought face to face with the eternal realities of existence,"[3] and when he becomes awakened to a new sense of religion and duty. In the life of the family, the critical moments of birth, puberty, marriage, and death regularly recur, and keep up the instinct, because man is then brought face to face with these eternal facts; there is no need of extraordinary perils, such as tempests or pestilences, to keep the instinct alive. But in the life of the State as such there were no such continually recurring reminders; even the old agricultural perils were out of sight of the ordinary citizen. Thus the farthest we can go in ascribing a moral influence to the State religion is in giving it credit for helping to maintain that sense of law and order which served to keep the life of the family sound and wholesome. That it did to some extent perform this service I have already pointed out;[4] and it is a remarkable fact that the decay of the State religion was coincident, in the last two centuries B.C., with the decay of the family life and virtues. But on the whole, as we shall see, the *ius divinum* had rather the effect of hypnotising the religious and moral instinct than of keeping it awake. It needed new perils for the State as a whole to re-create that feeling which is the root of the growth of conscience; and when the craving did at last come upon the Roman, which in times of doubt and peril has come upon individuals and communities in all ages, for support and comfort from the Unseen, it had to be satisfied by giving him new gods to worship in new ways—aliens with whom he had nothing in common, who had no home in his patriotic feeling, no place in his religious experience.[5]

I wish to conclude this first part of my subject by giving some account of the first beginning of this introduction of new deities, *di novensiles* as they were called,[6] into the old Roman religious world.   Those, however, of whom I shall speak here were not introduced as the result of disaster or distress, but were simply the inevitable consequence of the growing importance of the city on the Tiber—of the beginnings of her commercial and political relations with her neighbours, and also of her own development in the arts of civilisation.   The religious system with which I have so far been dealing was the exclusive property, we must remember, of those *gentes*, with the families composing them, which formed the original human material of the State, and were known as *patrician*.   If we had no other reason for being sure of this, the fact that all State priesthoods were originally limited to patrician families would be sufficient to prove it ;[7] even down to the latest times the *rex sacrorum*, the three *flamines maiores*, and the *Salii* were necessarily of patrician birth—a fact which had much to do with their tendency to disappear in the last age of the Republic.

But in the course of the period within which the Numan calendar was drawn up, this community of patrician burghers began to suffer certain changes.   A population of "outsiders," as in so many Greek cities, had gained admittance to the site of Rome, though not into its political and religious organism.[8]   So solid a city, in such an important position, was sure to attract such settlers, whether from the Latins dwelling about it, or from the Etruscans on the north, or the Greek cities along the coast southwards and in Sicily.   The Latins were, of course, of the same stock as the Romans, and already in some loose political relation to them ; and as each Latin city was open, like Rome, to Greek and Etruscan influences, we should probably see in Latium an indirect channel of communication between those peoples and Rome, to be reckoned in addition to the direct and obvious one.   As Dr. J. B. Carter has well said,[9] "the Latins, becoming rapidly inferior to Rome, were enabled to do her at least this service, that of absorbing the foreign influences which came, and in certain cases of Latinising them, and thus transmitting them to Rome in a more or less assimilated condition." As Dr. Carter has been the first to explain the arrival of these new religious influences to English readers, I shall in what follows closely follow his footsteps. They indicate and also reflect a change from agricultural economy and habits to a society interested in trade and travel : I say interested, because we cannot be quite sure how far the old Romans engaged in such pursuits themselves, as well as admitting from outside those who did, with their worships. They indicate also the growth of an industrial population, organised in gilds, as in the Middle Ages ; here beyond doubt the workers were mainly of native birth. Lastly, they indicate an advance in military efficiency and, as a result of this military progress, some change in the relation of Rome to her fellow-communities of Latium.

Perhaps the first of these new deities to arrive was the famous Hercules Victor or Invictus of the *ara maxima* in the Forum Boarium, who continued for centuries to accept the tithes of the booty of generals and the profits of successful merchants. Virgil in the eighth *Aeneid* [10] makes Evander show his guest this altar and the celebration of its festival, and tell him the tale of Cacus and the oxen and the cave on the Aventine hard by ; the poet, like every one else until the last few years, believed the cult to be primeval and Roman. But one of the many gains for the history of Roman religion which have recently been secured—even since the publication of my *Roman Festivals*—is the certainty that the Italian Hercules is really the Greek Heracles acclimatised in the sister peninsula, and that the cult of the *ara maxima*, though that altar was inside the sacred boundary of the *pomoerium*, was not native in Rome. [11] It seems, however, almost certain that it did not come direct from any part of Hellas, though its position, close to the Tiber and its landing-place, might naturally lead us to think so. It is almost impossible to believe that Heracles would have been allowed inside the *pomoerium*, had he been introduced by foreigners in the strict sense of the word. No doubt much has yet to be learnt about Hercules in Italy; but recent painstaking researches have made it possible for us to acquiesce in the belief that this Hercules of the *ara* came from a Latin city,—from that Tibur which by tradition was of Greek origin—"Tibur Argeo positum colono,"—and which, like its neighbour Praeneste, was curiously receptive of foreign influence.[12] It is believed that the Greek traders from Campania and Magna Graecia made their way northwards through Latium, and thus eventually reached Rome with the deity whom they seem to have always carried with them. He was, in the words of Dr. Carter,[13] a deity of whom, by the contagion of commerce, the Romans already felt a great need, a god of great power from whom came success in the practical undertakings of life; and it was quite natural that his shrine should be in the busy cattle-market of the city, if we remember that the wealth of the early Romans, *pecunia* as they called it, mainly consisted in sheep and oxen. As Heracles in various forms was to be met with all over the Mediterranean coasts, it would indeed be strange if he were not found in the growing city commanding the central water-way of Italy; and his appearance there may be said to have put Rome in touch with the Mediterranean business of that day. There he was destined to remain, with all the honour of an oldest cult, though other cults of the same god came in later, and were established quite close to him; and though never a State deity of much importance, he exercised a wholesome influence in matters of trade, as the god who sanctioned your oath, and who accepted the tithe of your gain which you had vowed at the outset of an enterprise.[14]

In the same period, though the traditional date of their temple is later, came the Twin Brethren, Castor and Pollux, and found their way, like Hercules, into the city within the *pomoerium*. The famous temple of Castor (before whom his brother gradually gave way) was at

the end of the Forum under the Palatine, close to the
fountain of Juturna, where the Twins watered their horses
after the battle of Lake Regillus; and there the beautiful
remains of the latest reconstruction of it still stand.[15] This
position alone should make us feel confident that the cult
did not come direct from Greek sources; and it had its
origin, perhaps, in the period when Rome was in close
relation with Latin cities, which themselves had been
gradually absorbing the cults and products of the Greeks
of Campania.   There is a strong probability that it came
from Tusculum, with which the legend of the Regillus
battle is closely connected, and where the cult had beyond
doubt taken strong root.[16]   Like the Hercules of the *ara
maxima*, the Twins were no doubt brought by the course
of trade, which was continually pushing up from the south;
for they too were favourites of the merchant adventurer,
and throughout Hellas were the special protectors of the
seafarer.   Their connection with horses is well known, and
not as yet satisfactorily explained in its Roman aspect;
but Dr. J. B. Carter thinks that they first became prominent
in Greece when the Homeric use of chariots was abandoned
for a primitive kind of cavalry, and that " the Castor-cult
moved steadily northward (from Magna Graecia), carried,
as it were, on horseback," and that when it reached Rome
it became connected with the reorganisation of the cavalry.
This seems to be almost pure guess-work, and, attractive
as it is, I fear we cannot put much faith in it.[17]   The
position in the Forum, and the well-known connection of
both twins with oaths,[18] seem to me rather to suggest a
more natural origin in trade.   I would suggest that the
equine character of the cult in Latium was secondary, and
that the connection of the temple and cult with the Roman
cavalry was a natural result, but not a primary feature, of
its introduction.   I should be inclined to look on it as coming in with the building of the temple, which was probably
of later origin than the original introduction of the cult.

Some time after the calendar was drawn up, a deity
was established on the Aventine, *i.e.* not within the

pomoerium, whose arrival marks a development in the organisation of handicraft. We cannot indeed *prove* that the settlement of Minerva on the Aventine took place so early, but we have strong grounds for the conclusion.[19] This temple was in historical times the religious centre of trade-gilds; and these gilds were by universal Roman tradition ascribed to Numa as founder, which simply means that they were among the oldest institutions of the City-state. As Minerva does not appear in the calendar, had no *flamen*, and therefore must have been altogether outside the original patrician religious system, the natural inference is that the temple was founded, like the shrines of Hercules and the Twin Brethren, towards the end of the period we are dealing with, and was from the first the centre of the gilds. Of those mentioned by Plutarch in his life of Numa (ch. 17), we know that the following gilds belonged to Minerva: *tibicines*, *fabri* (carpenters?), *fullones*, *sutores*; and it is a reasonable guess that the others, *coriarii*, *fabri aerarii*, and *aurifices*, were also under her protection. These trades, as Waltzing remarks in his great work on Roman gilds,[20] are all in keeping with the rudimentary civilisation of primitive Rome; they are those which were first carried on outside of the family. Workers in iron are not among them; bronze is still the common metal.

Now of course we must not go so far as to assume that none of these trades existed before the cult of Minerva came to Rome; but from her close association with them all through Roman history, and from the fact that the Romans were originally an agricultural folk, as the calendar shows, with a simple economy and simple needs, it is legitimate to connect the arrival of the goddess with the growth of town life and the demand for articles once made in rude fashion chiefly on the farms, and with a period of improvement in manufacture, and the use of better materials and better methods. Whence, then, did these improvements come? This is only another way of asking the question, Whence did Minerva come?

By the common consent of investigators she came from the semi-Latin town of Falerii in southern Etruria, where these arts were practised by Etruscans, or those who had learnt of Etruscans.[21] Her name is Italian, not Etruscan;[22] she was an old Italian deity taken over by the invading Etruscans from the peoples whose land they occupied. But while in the hands of Etruscans she had adopted Greek characteristics, especially those of Athene, the patroness of arts and crafts. She soon, indeed, appeared with some of the character of Athene Polias, as we shall see at the end of this lecture; but her real importance, far down into the period of the Empire, was in the temple on the Aventine, and in connection with the crafts. The dedication day of the temple was March 19, which was known, as we learn on the best authority, also as *artificum dies*.[23]

There was another famous temple on the Aventine which by universal consent is attributed to the same period as that of Minerva. Diana does not appear in the calendar, and had no *flamen*; Roman tradition ascribed her arrival to Servius Tullius, and we shall not be far wrong if we place it at or towards the end of the age of the kingship. The temple was celebrated as containing an ancient statue of Diana, the oldest or almost the oldest representation of a deity in human form known at Rome, which was a copy of a rude image of Artemis at Massilia, of the type of the famous ξόανον of the Ephesian Artemis.[24] It also contained a *lex templi* in Greek characters, and a treaty or charter of a federation of Latin cities with Rome as their head, which was seen by Dionysius of Halicarnassus when in Rome in the time of Augustus.[25]

The explanation of the arrival of Diana is simple. The *dies natalis* of the temple is the same as that of the famous shrine of the same goddess at Aricia—the Ides of August.[26] Aricia was at this time the centre of a league of cities including Tusculum and Tibur, with both of which, as we have just seen, Rome was closely connected at this time; a league which is generally supposed to have superseded that of Alba, marking some revolution in Latium con-

sequent on the fall of Alba.[27]   Diana was a wood-spirit, a
tree-spirit, as Dr. Frazer has taught us, with some relation
to the moon and to the life of women ; of late she has
become familiar to every one, not as she was known later,
in the disguise of Artemis, but as the deity of that shrine—
"pinguis et placabilis ara Dianae"—of which the priest
was the Rex Nemorensis : he who "slew the slayer and
shall himself be slain."[28]   But in those days it was only
the fact that she was the chief local deity of Aricia, the
leading city of the new league, which brought her suddenly
into notice.   When the strategic position of Rome gave
her in turn the lead in Latium, Diana passed on from
Aricia to the Tiber, entered on a new life, and eventually
took over the attributes of Artemis, with whom she had
much in common.   The Diana whom we know in Roman
literature is really Artemis ; but Diana of the Aventine,
when she first arrived there, was the wood-spirit of Aricia,
and her temple was an outward sign of Rome's new position in Latium : it was built by the chiefs of the Latin
cities in conjunction with Rome, and is described by Varro
as "commune Latinorum Dianae templum."[29]   It was
appropriately placed on the only Roman hill which
was then still covered with wood, and was outside the
pomoerium.

There was one other goddess, a Latin one, who was
traditionally associated with this period, and especially
with king Servius Tullius—Fortuna, or Fors Fortuna ;
she does not appear in the calendar, had no *flamen*, and
must have been introduced from outside.   But it was long
before Fortuna became of any real importance in Rome,
and I shall leave her out of account here.   She had two
homes of renown in Latium, at Antium and Praeneste, and
was in each connected with a kind of oracle, which seems
to have been specially resorted to by women before and
after childbirth.   She was also very probably a deity of
other kinds of fertility ; and in course of time she took on
the characteristics of the Greek Tyche, and became a
favourite deity of good luck.[30]

Let us pause for one moment to reflect on the character of these new deities of whom I have been speaking : Hercules, Castor, Minerva, Diana. It must be confessed that, as compared with the great deities of the calendar, they are uninteresting; with the exception, perhaps, of Hercules, they do not seem to have any real *religious* significance. They are local deities brought in from outside, and have no root in the mind of the Roman people as we have so far been studying it. They seem to indicate the growth of a population in which the true old Roman religious instinct was absent; they represent commerce, business, handicraft, or politics, pursuits in which the old Roman and Latin farmers were not directly interested ; they were suffered to be in Rome because the new population and the new interests must of necessity have their own worships, but they were not taken into the heart and mind of the people. So at least it seems to us, after we have been examining the development of the native religious plant from its root upwards. But we must remember that of that new population, its life and its needs, we know hardly anything, and it would not be safe to assume that the conception of Minerva had no influence on the conscience of the artisan, or that of Hercules no power of binding the trader to honest dealing and respect for his oath. As for Diana, though, as Dr. Carter says, she had been introduced "as part of a diplomatic game, not because Rome felt any religious need of her," the fact that the Latin treaty was kept in her temple has a certain moral as well as political significance which ought not to be overlooked. It is impossible to put ourselves mentally in the position of the men who brought these cults to Rome, or of the Romans who granted them admittance ; but we shall be on the safe side if we imagine the former at least to have had a conviction that their dealings at Rome would not prosper unless they were carried out with the blessing of their own gods.

But we now come, in the last place, to the foundation of a cult of a very different kind from these, and of far

greater import than any of them in the history of Roman
religious experience. We have seen that the temple of
Diana on the Aventine meant the transference of the
headship of the Latin league from Aricia to Rome. When
Rome took over this headship, and by removing its religious
centre to Rome—or, perhaps more accurately, by offering
Diana of Aricia a new home by the Tiber—removed also
any danger of a new power growing up in Latium outside
her own influence, she seems to have taken another important step in the same direction. Archæological evidence
confirms the tradition that at this time the temple of
Jupiter Latiaris, the real and original god of the league, on
the Alban hill, was rebuilt;[31] and as the remains of its
foundation are of Etruscan workmanship, we may believe
that the work was undertaken at that period of an Etruscan
dominion in Rome which no one now seriously doubts,
and which is marked by the Etruscan name Tarquinius,
and by the old tradition that Servius Tullius was really
an Etruscan bearing the Etruscan name Mastarna.[32]   Now
those in power at Rome at this time, whoever they were,
not content with rebuilding the ancient temple of Jupiter
on the Alban hill, conceived the idea of also building a
great temple at Rome, on the steep rock overlooking the
Forum, to the same deity of the heaven who had long
presided over the Latin league. The tradition was that
this temple was vowed by the first Tarquinius, begun by
the second, and finally dedicated by the first consul
Horatius in the year 509.[33]   It is quite possible that this
tradition indicates the truth in outline—that it was an
Etruscan who conceived the idea of the great work, and
that the foreign domination gave way to a Roman reaction
before the temple was ready for dedication. We cannot
know what exactly was the Etruscan intention as to the
cult; but we know that the temple was built in the Etruscan
style, that its foundations were of Etruscan masonry,[34] and
that the deities inhabiting it were three—a *trias*—a feature
quite foreign to the native Roman religion.[35]   Jupiter,
Juno, and Minerva had each a separate dwelling (*cella*)

within the walls of the temple, which, in order to meet this innovation, was almost as broad as it was long.   Whether this trias was the one originally intended by the Etruscan king or kings it is impossible to say ; but I have great doubts of it.   I confess that I have no ground but proba- bility to go on when I conjecture that a long period elapsed between the beginning of this great undertaking and the final completion, and that in the meantime many things had happened of which we have no record ; that when the temple was finished it was in Roman hands, though retaining its Etruscan characteristics, and especially the combination of three deities ; and that those three deities were essentially Roman in conception.   Roman, too, was the idea that one of the three should be para- mount ; the two goddesses never attained to any special significance, and the temple always remained essentially the dwelling of the great Jupiter, the Father of heaven.[86]

The cult-titles of this Jupiter, Optimus Maximus, the best and greatest, seem to raise him to a position not only far above his colleagues in the temple, but above all other Jupiters in Latium or elsewhere, and presumably above all other deities.   They thus suggest a deliberate attempt to place him in a higher position than even the Jupiter Latiaris of the Mons Albanus, whose temple had been rebuilt in the same period.   The very novelty of such cult-titles betrays both power and genius in their originator ; they are wholly unlike any we have met with so far ; they do not suggest a function or a locality or a connection with some other deity ; they stand absolutely alone in the history of the Roman religion till far on in the Empire.[37]   Here is no *numen* needed at a particular season to bless some agricultural operation ; Jupiter Optimus Maximus seems hardly to be limited by space or season, and is to be always there looking down on his people from his seat on the hill which was hence- forward to be called Capitolinus, because the space which had been prepared there for his reception bore the name of Capitolium, the place of headship.[88]   These titles, Best

and Greatest, call for reflection, for more thought than we
are apt to give them ; one wonders whether they can be
as old as tradition claimed, and in fact at least one recent
writer has been tempted, without sufficient reason, to
date the whole foundation two centuries later than the
Tarquinii.[39]   To me they rather suggest the hypothesis
that the break-up of the Etruscan domination in Rome
was the work of a man or men inspired by a new national
feeling which ascribed the revolution to the great god of
the race, to whose shrine on the same hill the kings had
been used to bring the spoils of their enemies[40] ; and
that they took advantage of the uncompleted Etruscan
temple, with its huge foundations and underground
favissae, to settle there a new Jupiter, better and greater
than any other, to whom his people would be for ever
grateful, and in whom they would for ever put their trust.
All older associations with cults of the Heaven-god were
to be banished from the Capitolium, just as all other
deities were believed to have fled from the spot, save
only Terminus ; the ancient priest of Jupiter, the Flamen
Dialis, had no special connection with this temple and its
cult, which were under the immediate charge of an *aedituus*
only.[41]   Here was the centre of the public worship of the
State as a whole, not only of the old patrician State ; and
no such ancient curiosity as the Flamen Dialis, who, as
I have suggested, was a survival from some older era of
Latin religious history, was to be supreme there.   Here
the Consul of the free Republic was to offer, on entering
office, the victim—the white heifer of the Alban cult—
which his predecessor had vowed, and himself to bind his
successor to a like sacrifice ; and this he did on behalf of
patrician and plebeian alike.   Here the victorious general
was to deposit his spoils, reaching the temple in the
solemn procession of the *triumphus*, and wearing the
ornamenta of the deity himself ; for here, contrary to all
precedent in the worship of Romans, there was an image
of the god wrought in terra cotta and brought from
Etruria.[42]   It is in connection with such solemn events as

these that we may find the origin of those imposing processions which for centuries were to impress the minds of the Roman people, and indeed of their enemies also, with the might and magnificence of their Empire ; for apart from the triumphal processions with which we are all familiar, the scene at the entrance of new consuls on their office must have been most impressive.   They were accompanied by the other magistrates, the Senate, the priests in their robes of office, and by an immense crowd of citizens.   After the ceremony the Senate met *in the temple* to transact the first religious business of the year. Here too the tribal assembly met for the purpose of enrolling the new levies before each season of war, in order that the youths who were to fight the battles of Rome might realise the presence of Rome's great protecting deity.   Even in the most degenerate days of the Roman religion, though Jupiter had suffered from the ridicule of playwrights or the speculations of philosophers, an orator's appeal to the Best and Greatest looking down on the Forum from his seat above it, could not fail to move the hearers; " Ille, ille Iuppiter restitit," cried Cicero in the peril of the Catilinarian conspiracy, "ille Capitolium, ille haec templa, ille cunctam urbem, ille vos omnes salvos esse voluit." [43]

Nor was it only the State as represented by its officials that could and did address itself to the worship of this great god.   It seems probable that the new idea of a single guardian deity, with his two attendant goddesses, for which the Romans were indebted to the genius (whoever he may have been) who released them from the yoke of the Etruscan, opened the cult to the individual in a way which must have been a novelty in the religious life of the people.[44]   The most memorable example of this is in the famous story told of Scipio, the conqueror of Hannibal, which is not likely to be an invention of the annalists.   As Gellius records it, it stands thus : Scipio was wont to ascend to the temple just before daylight, to order the *cella Iovis* to be opened for him, and there to remain alone for a long time, as if taking counsel with the god about the affairs of the State. The dogs, it was said, which guarded the entrance, astonished the temple-keepers by treating him always with respect, while they would attack or bark at others.[45]

The reader may remark, that during the last few minutes I have wandered quite away from the Roman religion which we have so far been trying to understand, and he will be right. I have but just touched on this great cult, which properly belongs to Rome of the Republic, in order to show how great a change must have taken place, how great a revolution must have been consummated, when this temple arose on its Etruscan substructures. We have marked two forward steps in the social and political experience of the Romans : the settlement of the family on the land and the organisation of the City-state with its calendar. Here is a third, the liberation of that State from a foreign dominion, and the development, in matters both internal and external, which subjection and liberation alike brought with them. In regard to religious experience, the first produced the ordered worship of the household, which had a lasting effect on the Roman character ; the second produced the *ius divinum*, the priesthoods and the ritual for the service of the various *numina* which had consented to take up their abode in the city and its precincts. These two taken together changed doubt and anxiety into confidence, stilled the *religio* natural to uncivilised man, and developed the machinery of magic into forms and ceremonies which were more truly religious. Now we note a third great social step forward, which brings with it a new conception and expression of the religious unity of the State ; henceforward, alongside of a multiplicity of cults and of priests attached to them, we have one central worship to which all free citizens may resort, and a trinity of guardian deities, of whom one, Jupiter Best and Greatest, is the one presiding genius of the whole State.

Lastly, there can hardly be a doubt that this new cult

R

marks a more extensive communication with neighbouring peoples than the State had as yet experienced or encouraged. Etruria, Latium, and Greece, all seem to have had a hand in it. Of its relation to the Latins and Etruscans I have already spoken. It only remains for me to note the fact that it was here, in this Capitoline temple, according to unanimous tradition, that those legendary " Sibylline books " were deposited which came from a Greek source, and according to the story, from Cumae.[46] These mysterious books were destined to change the whole character of the religion of the Romans during the next two centuries; and this is why the dedication of the great temple is a convenient halting-place on our journey. I propose to begin the second part of my subject by examining the nature of this change, and then to pass on to others, until we have reached the end of the religious experience of the genuine Roman people.

NOTES TO LECTURE X.

1. *Origin and Development of Moral Ideas*, chapters l.-lii. : " Gods as guardians of morality."

2. Crawley, *The Tree of Life*, in a remarkable chapter on the function of religion (ch. ix.), especially p. 287 foll. " Morality," says Mr. Crawley, " is one of the results of the religious impulse." What he means here by morality is not " that elaborated by abstract thinkers," but the " morality of elemental human nature." " Elemental morality " may be a somewhat obscure term ; but I think it is highly probable that Mr. Crawley is, in part at least, right in ascribing the origin of morality to the religious impulse.

3. Crawley, *op. cit.*, p. 265.

4. Above, pp. 107-8.

5. See the author's article in *Hibbert Journal* for July 1907, p. 894.

6. Wissowa, *R.K.* p. 15 foll.

7. *Ib.* p. 421 : Aust, *Religion der Römer*, p. 47.

8. I am, of course, well aware that quite recently attempts have been made to explain the *plebs* as the original inhabitants of Latium, and the Romans as conquering invaders ; *e.g.* by Prof. Ridgeway in his paper, " Who were the Romans," read to the British Academy, and by Binder in his recently published volume *Die Plebs*.

The theory is a natural one, and not out of harmony with the facts as known ; but it has yet to be further developed and tested, and as those who hold it are not as yet in agreement with each other, and as the evidence which alone can prove it is of a very special character, archaeological and linguistic, I have expressed myself in terms of the older view.

9. *The Religion of Numa*, p. 30.

10. *Aen.* viii. 184 foll. ; the description of the festival is in 280 foll. ; where the interesting points are the priests of the *gentes* appointed to look after the cult (the Potitii only are here mentioned) "pellibus in morem cincti," and the Salii "populeis evincti tempora ramis."

11. Wissowa, *R.K.* p. 219 foll. ; Carter, *Religion of Numa*, p. 31 foll.   The ground had been prepared for the new view by the elaborate articles in Roscher's *Mythological Lexicon*, vol. ii. pp. 2253 foll. and 2901 foll.   Of late a painstaking discussion by J. G. Winter has appeared in the *University of Michigan Studies for* 1910, p. 171 foll. ; he mainly confirms Wissowa's conclusions, but provisionally accepts a suggestion of mine (*R.F.* 197) that the tithe practice of the *ara maxima* may possibly have been of Phoenician origin, and points out that E. Curtius made the same suggestion as long ago as 1845.   On p. 269 he also dwells, very properly, I think, on the part which the Etruscans may have had in the dissemination of the myth and cult of the Greek Heracles. Wissowa, however, stoutly maintains that these are simply Greek and of commercial origin.   It has been Wissowa's special and valuable function to elucidate the Greek origin of many Roman cults and legends ; but I doubt if he has adequately considered the influence of other peoples, and in particular of Phoenicians and Etruscans.   Certainly the Hercules question is not finally settled by his masterly analysis of it in *R.K.* p. 220 foll.   But most of what I said in *R.F.* about the Hercules of the *ara maxima* may now be considered obsolete ; and I may add that my remarks on the supposed connection of Hercules with Genius, Dius Fidius, and Jupiter in the same work, p. 143 foll., have lost much strength since Wissowa's book appeared.   Yet I am not prepared to accept the view which would deny to Hercules on Italian soil all contamination with Italian ideas ; as Willamowitz - Moellendorf puts it (*Herakles*, ed. 2, vol. i. p. 25), "Die Italiker haben dem Körper, den sie übernahmen, den Odem ihrer eigenen Seele eingeblasen : aber wie der Name ist der Gestalt des Hercules hellenischer Import."   There are points in connection with the Roman Hercules, *e.g.* the *nodus herculaneus* of the bride's girdle, which Wissowa does not explain, and which, so far as I can see, can only be explained by assuming that, as might have been expected, the Greek Hercules became to some extent entangled in the web of Italian thought.

12. The cult was Greek in detail; *Graeco ritu*, according to Varro as quoted by Macrobius iii. 6. 17; see also references in Wissowa, *R.K.* 222, note 2. Following R. Peter in the articles in Roscher, I assumed, in *R.F.* p. 194, that this might be a later reconstruction of an originally Italian cult; but for the present it is safer to look on the *Graecus ritus* as primitive, and on the presence of Salii, a genuine Italian institution, as brought from Tibur by the gens Pinaria, of which there is a trace in that city (*C.I.L.* xiv. 3541). There also Salii were engaged in the cult of Hercules Victor, to whom tithes were also offered (*C.I.L.* xiv. 3541). The evidence for the theory that the cult came to Rome from Tibur is summarised by Wissowa, *R.K.* p. 220.

13. *Op. cit.*, p. 37.

14. For the connection of the cult with trade, Wissowa, *R.K.* 225; and the story told in Macrobius iii. 6. 11, from Masurius Sabinus, of a *tibicen* who became a merchant and had an interview with the god in a dream. For the connection with *oaths*, *R.F.* p. 138. I may say before leaving Hercules that though I accept the latest hypotheses provisionally, I am far from believing that the last word has been said on the subject.

15. See, *e.g.*, Lanciani, *Ruins and Excavations of Ancient Rome*, p. 271 foll. The date of the temple is 482 B.C., but it was vowed in 496 after the Regillus battle. The three columns still standing date from 7 B.C.

16. Wissowa, *R.K.* p. 217, who points out that the Dioscuri never appear in *lectisternia* at Rome, as they do at Tusculum, which shows that the latter cult was more directly Greek than that at Rome, and that the Roman authorities admitted it as a Latin cult without the Greek details.

17. Carter, *op. cit.* p. 38. There seemed to be difficulties in the way of his conclusion; the Dioscuri were very strong in the Peloponnese, yet the Spartans neglected the use of cavalry. At any rate the theory needs careful historical testing. See article " Dioscuri " in Pauly - Wissowa, *Real - Encycl.* It would seem natural that when once the cult had been introduced by traders it might become specially attached to the cavalry, owing to the ancient connection of the Twins with horses.

18. Ecastor and Edepol, which were oaths used especially by women, who were not allowed to swear by Hercules, Gell. xi. 6.

19. The reasoning will be found in full in Wissowa, *R.K.* p. 203 foll., and in his article " Minerva " in the *Mythological Lexicon*. See also Carter, *Religion of Numa*, p. 45 foll. For the position of this temple and that of Diana on the Aventine, a suburb which cannot be proved to have been then within any city wall, see Carter in *Proceedings of the American Philosophical Society for* 1909, p. 136 foll.

20. Waltzing, *Étude historique sur les corporations romaines,*

vol. i. pp. 63 and 199. The relation between town life and trades is stated with his usual insight by von Jhering, *Evolution of the Aryan*, p. 93 foll.

21. See Müller-Deecke, *Etrusker*, ii. 47 ; Deecke, *Falisker*, p. 89 foll.

22. Minerva or Menrva is assuredly not Etruscan, though frequently found on Etruscan monuments ; see Deecke, *l.c.* p. 89 foll.

23. Fasti Praenestini in *C.I.L.* i.[2] March 19. "Artificum dies (quod Minervae) aedis in Aventino eo die est (dedicata)." This is one of those additional notes in the Fast. Praen., which are believed to have been the work of Verrius Flaccus : see *Roman Festivals*, p. 12.

24. Wissowa, *Gesammelte Abhandlungen*, p. 288. We know the fact from Strabo's account of Massilia, Bk. iv. p. 180.

25. Dion. Hal. iv. 26. See *R.F.* p. 198.

26. Statius, *Silvae* iii. 1. 60. See Wissowa's article "Diana" in Pauly-Wissowa, *Real-Encycl.*

27. Wissowa, *l.c.* p. 332.

28. *Golden Bough*, i. p. 1 foll. ; *Early History of the Kingship*, Lecture I.

29. Varro, *L.L.* 5. 43 ; Carter, *op. cit.* p. 55.

30. See on Fortuna the exhaustive article by R. Peter in the *Mythological Lexicon* ; Wissowa, *R.K.* 206 foll. ; *R.F.* p. 161 foll., and 223 foll. ; Carter, *op. cit.* p. 50 foll. Dr. Carter seems to me to be too certain of the absence of any idea of luck or chance in the original conception of Fortuna : the word *fors*, so far as we know, never had any other meaning, and the deity Fors must be a personification of an abstraction, like Ops, Fides, and Salus. See Axtell, *Deification of abstract idea in Roman literature*, p. 9, with whom I agree in rejecting the notion of Marquardt and Wissowa that she was a deity of horticulture. He rightly points out that she is not included in the list of agricultural deities in Varro, *R.R.* i. 1. 6.

31. See Aust in his article "Jupiter" in the *Myth. Lex.* p. 689, where the evidence for the contemporaneous origin of the temple on the Alban hill and that on the Capitol is fully stated. In this case excavations have confirmed the Roman tradition, which ascribed the former temple to one or other of the Tarquinii. Jordan, *Röm. Top.* i. pt. 2. p. 9.

32. See the speech of Claudius the emperor, *C.I.L.* xiii. 1668, printed in Furneaux' *Tacitus' Annals*, vol. ii. Gardthausen, *Mastarna*, p. 40 ; Müller-Deecke, *Etrusker*, i. 111. For the Etruscan name Mastarna, see Dennis, *Cities and Cemeteries of Etruria*[8], ii. 506 foll. : Gardthausen gives a cut of the painting found in a tomb at Vulci in which he appears with the name attached. Even the ultra-sceptical Pais does not doubt the fact of an Etruscan domination in Rome ; but he does not believe the Tarquinii and

Mastarna to have been historical personages, and will not date the temples attributed to this age earlier than the fourth century B.C. See his *Ancient Legends of Roman History*, ch. vii. ; *Storia di Roma*, i. 310 foll.   But the names of these kings do not concern us, except so far as they connect Etruria with Roman history in the sixth century.

33. Cic. *Rep*. ii. 24. 44 ; Livy i. 38. and 55 ; Dionys. iii. 69 ; iv. 59. 61.   The whole evidence will be found collected in Jordan, *Topogr*. i. pt. ii. p. 9 foll., and in Aust, *Myth. Lex.*, *s.v.* Jupiter, p. 706 foll.   If the date 509 were seriously impugned Roman chronology would be in confusion, for this is believed to be the earliest date on which we can rely, and on it the subsequent chronology hangs : Mommsen, *Röm. Chronologie*, ed. 2, p. 198.

34. Aust, p. 707 foll. ; Jordan, *op. cit.*, p. 9.

35. *i.e.* the admission of more than one deity into a single building.   The word "trias" is sometimes used of the three old Roman deities, Jupiter, Mars, Quirinus (*e.g.* by Wissowa, *Myth. Lex. s.v.* Quirinus), but this is in a different sense.   On the idea of a trias generally, see Kuhfeldt, *de Capitoliis imperii Romani*, p. 82 foll. ; Cumont, *Religions orientales dans le paganisme romain*, p. 290, note 51.

36. The technical name of the temple was aedes Iovis Opt. Max. : for other indications of Jupiter's supremacy see Aust, p. 720.

37. On Oriental developments of Jupiter Opt. Max. see an interesting paper by Cumont in *Archiv* for 1906, p. 323 foll. (*Iuppiter summus exsuperantissimus*).   A relief in the Berlin Museum has a dedication *I.O.M. summo exsuperantissimo* ; but Prof. Cumont believes the deity to have been really Oriental, introduced by Greek philosophical theologians in the last century B.C., but probably Chaldaean in origin.

38. Jordan, *op. cit.* p. 7 and note.   It is uncertain whether the whole hill had any earlier name.   The Mons Saturnius of Varro, *L.L.* v. 42, with the legend of an oppidum *Saturnia*, and the Mons Tarpeius (*Rhet. ad Herenn.*, iv. 32. 43 ; Pais, *Ancient Legends*, chs. v. and vi.) need not be taken into account.

39. Pais, *Ancient Legends of Roman History*, ch. v.

40. See above, p. 130.

41. This is an inference from the fact that this Flamen is nowhere mentioned as connected with the Capitoline cult.   Macrob. i. 15, 16, speaks of the ovis Idulis as sacrificed on every ides *a flamine*, and this, it is true, took place on the Capitolium (Aust, in *Lex. s.v.* Jupiter, 655), but (1) Festus, 290, mentions sacerdotes, Ovid, *Fasti* i. 588, castus sacerdos only ; and (2) this sacrifice may well, as O. Gilbert conjectured, have originally taken place in the Regia (*Gesch. und Topogr. Roms*, i. 236).   In any case the Flamen was not in any special sense priest of Iup. Opt. Max.

42. The *locus classicus* for this is Pliny, *N.H.* xxxv. 157.   The

artist was said to have been one Volcas of Veii.   Ovid, *Fasti* i.
201, says that the god had in his hand a *fictile fulmen.*   Varro
believed this to be the oldest statue of a god in Rome ; see above,
p. 146, and Wissowa, *Gesammelte Abhandlungen,* p. 280, accepts his
statement as probably correct.

43. Cic. *Catil.* iii. 9. 21.

44. Jordan, *Topogr.* i. 2. pp. 39 and 62, notes.   The most convincing passages quoted by him are Suet. *Aug.* 59, and Serv. *Ecl.* iv.
50 (of boys taking toga virilis who "ad Capitolium eunt ") ; but was
not this to sacrifice to Liber or Iuventas ?   *R.F.* p. 56.

45. Gellius vi. 1. 6, from C. Oppius et Iulius Hyginus.   In his
famous character of Scipio (xxvi. 19) Livy seems to think that Scipio
did this to make people think him superhuman or of divine descent.

46. Ovid, *Fasti,* iv. 158. 257 ; Virg. *Ecl.* iv. 4, *Aen.* vi. 42 ;
Marquardt, 352, note 7, for evidence that the books came to Cumae
from Erythrae.   See also Diels, *Sibyllinische Blätter,* p. 80 foll.

LECTURE XI *

I SAID at the beginning of my first lecture that Roman religious experience can be summed up in two stories. The first of these was the story of the way in which a strong primitive religious instinct, the desire to put yourself in right relation with the Power manifesting itself in the universe, *religio* as the Romans called it, was gradually soothed and satisfied under the formalising influence of the settled life of the agricultural family, and still more so under the organising genius of the early religious rulers of the City-state. This story I tried to tell in the last few lectures. The second story was to be that of the gradual discovery of the inadequacy of this early formalised and organised religion to cope with what we may call new religious experience; that is, with the difficulties and perils met with by the Roman people in their extraordinary advance in the world, and with the new ideas of religion and morals which broke in on them in the course of their contact with other peoples. This story I wish to tell in the present course of lectures. It is a long and complicated one, including the introduction of new rites and ideas of the divine, the anxious attempts of the religious authorities to put off the evil day by stretching to the uttermost the capacity of the old forms, and the final victory of the new ideas as Roman life and thought became gradually hellenised.

I propose to divide the story thus. In the latter part of this first lecture I will deal with the first introduction

* This Lecture was the first of a second and separate course.

of Greek rites into the State worship under the directions
of the so-called Sibylline books.   Then I will turn to the
efforts of the lay priesthoods, pontifices and augurs, to
meet the calls of new experience by formalising the old
religion still more completely in the name of the State,
until it became a mere skeleton of dry bones, without
life and power.   That will bring us to the great turning-
point in Roman history, the war with Hannibal, to the
religious history of which I shall devote my fourth lecture;
and the fifth will pursue the subject into the century
that followed.   In the next lecture I hope to sketch the
influence on Roman religious ideas of the Stoic school of
philosophy, and in the seventh to discuss, so far as I may
be able, the tendency towards mysticism prevalent in the
last period of the life of the Republic.   My eighth lecture
I intend to devote to the noble attempt of Virgil to combine religion, legend, philosophy, and consummate art in
a splendid appeal to the conscience of the Roman of that
day.   Then I turn to the more practical attempt of
Augustus to revive the dying embers of the old religion;
and in my last lecture I shall try to estimate the contribution, such as it was, of the religious experience we have
been discussing, to the early Christian church.

We shall shortly hear so much of petrifaction and
disintegration, that it may be as well, before I actually
begin my story, to convince ourselves that the old religion
was in its peculiar way a real expression of religious feeling, and not merely a set of meaningless conventions and
formulae.   It was the positive belief of the later Romans
that both they and their ancestors were *religiosissimi
mortales*,[1] full to the brim, that is, of religious instinct,
and most scrupulous in fulfilling its claims upon them;
for the word *religio* had come, by the time (and probably
long before the time) when it was used by men of letters,
to mean the fulfilment of ritualistic obligation quite as
much as the anxious feeling which had originally suggested
it.[2]   Cicero, writing in no rhetorical mood, declared that,

as compared with other peoples, the Romans were far superior " in religione, id est cultu." [3]   This is in his work on the nature of the gods ; in an oration he naturally puts it more strongly : " We have overcome all the nations of the world, because we have realised that the world is directed and governed by the will of the gods." [4]   Sallust, Livy, and other Roman prose writers have said much the same thing [5] ; the *Aeneid* as a whole might be adduced as evidence, and in a less degree all the poets of the Augustan age. Foreigners, too, were struck with the strange phenomenon, in an age of philosophic doubt.   Polybius in the second century B.C. declared his opinion that what was reckoned among other peoples as a thing to be blamed, *deisidaimonia*, both in public and private life, was really what was holding together the Roman state. [6]   Even in the wild century that followed, Posidonius could repeat the assertion of Polybius, and in the age of Augustus, Dionysius of Halicarnassus, then resident at Rome, looking back on the early history of Rome, stated his conviction that one needed to know the *pietas* of the Romans in order to understand their wonderful career of conquest. [7]   Aulus Gellius, in a curious passage in which he notes that the Romans had no deity to whose activity they could with certainty ascribe earthquakes, describes them as " in constituendis religionibus atque in dis immortalibus animadvertendis *castissimi cautissimique*,"—a rhetorical but happy conjunction of epithets.   He means that they would order religious rites, though ignorant of the *numen* to whom they were due.

It might be argued that these later writers knew really little or nothing about the primitive Romans, and that these passages only prove that this people had an extraordinary scrupulosity about forms and ceremonies in this as in other departments of action.   But the argument will not hold ; the survival of all this formalism into an age of disintegration really proves beyond a doubt that there must have been a time when these forms really expressed anxieties, fears, convictions, the earliest germs of *conscience*.

May we not take the constant occurrence in literature of such phrases as *dis faventibus, dis iuvantibus* or *volentibus*, as evidence of an idea deeply rooted at one time in the Roman mind, that nothing should be undertaken until the will of the deities concerned had been ascertained and that early form of conscience satisfied? Let us remember that the whole story of the *Aeneid* is one of the bending of the will of the hero, as a type of the ideal Roman, to the ascertainable will of the powers in the universe.

And we have abundant evidence that as a matter of fact the good-will of the divine inhabitants of house and city was asked for whenever any kind of work was undertaken,—even the ordinary routine work of the farm or of government. In the household every morning some offering with prayer was made to the Lar familiaris in historical times, and again before the *cena*, the chief meal of the day.[9] On Kalends, Nones, Ides, and on all *dies festi* a *corona* was placed on the hearth, and prayer was made to the Lar; we know that this was so in the old Roman home, because in the second century B.C. Cato instructs the *vilicus* to discharge these duties on behalf of the absent or non-resident owner.[10] Before the flocks were taken out to summer pasture, and doubtless when they returned, some religious service (so we should call it) was held,[11] just as in the Catholic cantons of Switzerland the blessing of God is asked when the cows first ascend to the alpine pastures, and again when they leave them for the valleys. Before a journey the later Romans prayed for good fortune;[12] in the old times travelling was of course unusual, and when it did occur the traveller was surrounded by so many spiritual as well as material dangers that *special* religious measures must have been taken, as by fetials or armies on entering foreign territory. The survival of the same kind of belief and practice is also seen in private life in the religious commendations of some authors at the outset of their literary work; Varro, for example, at the beginning of his work on agriculture, calls on all the agrarian deities (*iis deis ad venerationem*

advocatis) before he goes on to mention even the biblio-
graphy of his subject.[13]   Livy in the last sentence of his
preface would fain imitate the poets in calling on the
gods to bless and favour his undertaking.   And in all
time of their tribulation, even if not in all time of their
wealth, the pious Romans sought help from the deities
from whom help might be expected ; if, at least, the many
instances occurring in Roman poetry may point to a
practice of the ordinary individual and family.[14]   So too,
if we may judge by many passages in the plays of Plautus
and Terence,[15]—if here we have genuine Roman usage,
as is probable,—the feeling of dependence on a Power
manifesting itself in the affairs of daily life is shown also
in the expression of *thankfulness* which followed success
or escape from peril.   Gratitude was not a prominent
characteristic of the Roman, but I have already remarked
on the presence of it in the practice of the *votum*, and
there is at least some evidence that it was recognised as
due to benignant deities as well as human beings.[16]

In public life, throughout Roman history, the forms of
religious rites were maintained on all important occasions.
When Varro wrote a little manual of Senatorial procedure
for the benefit of the inexperienced Pompeius when
consul in 70 B.C., he was careful to mention the preliminary sacrifice and *auspicatio*, performed by the presiding magistrate, who also had to see that the business
de rebus divinis came first on the paper of agenda.[17]   At
one time every speaker invoked the gods at the beginning
of his oration, as well indeed he might in a situation so
unusual and trying for a Roman before the days of Greek
education ; and the earliest speeches preserved in the
literary age, *e.g.* those of Cato and the Gracchi, retained
the religious exordium.[18]   We have a trace of the Gracchan
practice in a famous passage at the end of the work called
Rhetorica ad Herennium of *circ.* 82 B.C., where the death
of Ti. Gracchus is graphically described.[19]   But there is
no need to multiply examples of public religious formalism
on occasions of all kinds, on entering on an office, founding

a colony, leaving Rome for a provincia, and so on ; some
of them I have already mentioned, others are familiar to
all classical students.

So let us not hesitate for a moment to give this people
credit for their religiousness.   True, their neighbours,
Greeks like Polybius, approved of it only with an ironical
smile on their lips, as we may smile at the devoted
formalism of extreme Catholic or Protestant, while we
secretly— if we have some sympathy with strangely
varying human nature—admire the confidence and regularity that we cannot ourselves claim.   At the moment
where I have thus paused before beginning my second
story, at the end, that is, of the regal period, I believe that
this religious system, though perhaps beginning to harden,
still meant a profound belief in the Power thus manifested
in many forms, and an ardent and effective desire to be
in right relation to it.   I believe that it contained the
germ of a living and fruitful growth ; but that growth
was at this very moment arrested by the beginning of a
process of which I shall have much to say in the next
two or three lectures.

But it is hard to realise this better side of the religion
of a hard and practical people, and all the more so since
it is the worse side that is almost always presented to us
in modern books.   It is hard to realise that it was not
merely a system of insurance, so to speak, against all
kinds of material evils,—and here again all the more so
because there is a tendency just now to reduce both
religion and law to an origin in magic, leaving the
religious instinct, the *feeling of dependence*, the progenitor of conscience, quite out of account.   One must
indeed be thoroughly familiar with Roman literature and
antiquities to overcome these difficulties, to discover the
spiritual residuum in the Roman character beneath all
its hardness and utilitarianism.   Before we pass on to
the task before us, let me make two suggestions for
the help of those who would endeavour to find this
spiritual residuum.   The first is that they should consider

the history and true meaning of three great words which the Latin language has bequeathed to modern speech,— *religio*, the feeling of awe, taking practical shape in the performance of authorised ceremonies ; *sacrum*, that which by authoritative usage is made over without reserve to the divine inhabitants of the city ; and last but not least, *pietas*, the sense of duty to god and man alike, to all divine and human beings having an authorised claim upon you. And this word *pietas* shall introduce my second suggestion — that there is no better way of getting to understand the spirit of the Roman religion than by continual study of the *Aeneid*, where the hero is the ideal Roman, *pius* in the best and widest sense. What makes the *Aeneid* so helpful in this way is the poet's intimate and sympathetic knowledge of the religious ideas of the Italians, in which we may see reflected those of the Roman of the age we are now dealing with : his love too of antiquity and of all ancient rites and legends ; and his conviction that the great work of Rome in the world had been achieved not only by *virtus* but by *pietas*. What has been won by *virtus* must be preserved by *pietas*, by the sense of duty in family and State,—that is the moral of the *Aeneid*. In no other work of Roman genius is this idea found in anything like the same degree of prominence and consistency ; and when a student has steeped his mind well in the details of the Roman worship, and begins to weary of what must seem its soulless Pharisaism, let him take up the *Aeneid* and read it right through for the story and the characters. I will venture to say that he will think better both of the Romans and their poet than he ever did before. But of the *Aeneid* I shall have more to say later on ; at present let us turn to the less inspiring topics which must occupy us for the next few lectures.

The last fact of Roman religious history which I mentioned last year was the building of the great Capitoline temple of Jupiter, Juno, and Minerva, and I then explained why this constituted a religious revolution.

The next temple of which tradition tells us was destined for another trias, Ceres, Liber, and Libera ; the traditional date was 493 B.C., the cause a famine, and the site was at the foot of the Aventine, the plebeian quarter outside the pomoerium, close to the river where corn-ships might be moored.[20]   Ceres, Liber, and Libera are plainly neither more nor less than the three Greek corn deities, Demeter, Dionysus, and Persephone, in a Latin form,[21] whose worship was prominent in South Italy and Sicily ; and unless we throw tradition overboard entirely, as indeed has often been done, the inference is obvious that this trias came from the Greeks of the south with an importation of corn to relieve a famine which pressed especially on the plebs.   It is a fact that the temple and its cult remained always closely connected with the plebs ; they were under the charge of the plebeian aediles, who also in historical times had the care of the corn-supply necessary for the city population.[22]   Thus, though we need not accept in full Livy's statement that the very next year corn was imported from Etruria, Cumae, and Sicily, it cannot be denied that there is a strong consensus in the various traditions about the temple, which taken together suggest a Greek, non-patrician, and early origin.   That the cult had at all times a Greek character is undisputed fact.

But I am not so much concerned with the temple itself as with the date and the manner of its foundation.   It was said to have been founded in the year 496, and dedicated in 493, in obedience to directions found in " the Sibylline books," which books, according to the well-known tradition, had been acquired by the last Tarquin, after some haggling, from an old woman, and placed in the charge of *duoviri sacris faciundis*.   The story itself is worthless in detail ; but the question for us is whether it can be taken as showing that the Sibylline influence then pervading the Greek world gained a footing at Rome in any form so early as this.   Was the temple really founded in 496, or at some time thereabout ?   And was it founded in obedience to some Sibylline direction ?   These questions are of real importance, for upon our answer to them depends the date of the beginning of a gradual metamorphosis of the Roman religious practice.   The so-called Sibylline books and their keepers were responsible, as we shall see directly, for the introduction at Rome of what was known as the *Graecus ritus*,—for the foundation of temples to deities of Greek origin, and for other rites which initiated an entirely new type of religious feeling. We need to be sure when all this began.

In the first place, so far as I can judge, it is almost impossible to dissociate the origin of the temple from Sibylline influence.   As we have seen, the cult was Greek, and all such Greek cults of later times were introduced by the keepers of the Sibylline books ; and further, the records of temple foundations were among the most carefully preserved facts in Roman annals.[23]   I think it is hardly possible to suppose that a cult which came, not from Latium or southern Etruria, like those of Diana, Minerva, and the Capitoline deities, but from some Greek region to the south, and probably from Sicily, could have been introduced by Roman authorities unaided by Greek influence.   If that be so, and if we can show that the temple really belongs to this early age, then we have a strong probability that the Sibylline influence gained a footing at Rome at the very beginning of the republican period.[24]

There is one curious fact in connection with the temple that in my opinion goes far to prove that the traditional date is not far out.   Pliny tells us explicitly that the two Greek artists who decorated the temple, Damophilus and Gorgasus, inscribed their names on the walls, and he added that the work of the former would be found on the right and that of the latter on the left.[25]   Nothing more is known about them ; but I am assured that the fact that they signed their names and added these statements suits the character of Greek art in the archaic age 580 to 450 B.C. No signatures of artists are known earlier than about 580 ; then comes a period when signatures are found, sometimes with statements such as these. And lastly, about 450, we begin to find simple signatures without any other words.[26] Thus the presumption is a strong one that the temple belongs to a time earlier than 450 ; and if that be so, then I think the inference holds good that the Sibyl first gained a footing at Rome about the same time. There are indeed some reasons why we should not put this event in the period of the kings ;[27] but if we accept the traditional date of the temple we may put it any time between 509 and 496.

I have purposely used vague terms, such as Sibylline *influence*, instead of speaking in the old manner of Sibylline *books* or oracles, because it is almost incredible that at so early a date it could have been possible to divulge any contents of a store of writings such as must have been most carefully treasured and concealed. This has been shown conclusively to be out of the question in Diels' now famous little book "*Sibylline Leaves.*" But we may also follow Diels in assuming that about the end of the sixth century some kind of Greek oracle or oracular saying did actually arrive at Rome, purporting to be an utterance of the famous Sibyl of Cumae.[28]

But what *was* this Sibylline influence which thus penetrated to Rome, if I am right, at the beginning of the fifth century? It is no part of my design to discuss the history of Greek mysticism, though we shall hear something more of it in a later lecture. It will be enough to remind you that in the sixth century Greece was not only full of Orphism and Pythagoreanism, but of floating oracular *dicta* believed to emanate from a mystic female figure, a weird figure of whom it is hard to say how far she was human or divine ; and of whose origin we know nothing, except that her original home was, as we might expect, Asia Minor. She was inspired by Apollo,[29] it was said, like the Pythia, and like her too became ἔνθεος (*possessed*) when uttering her prophecies ; this is the earliest fact we know about her, for a famous fragment of Heracleitus represents her as uttering sayings

S

"with frenzied lips," [30]—a tradition of which Virgil has made good use in the sixth *Aeneid*:

> non vultus, non color unus,
> non comptae mansere comae ; sed pectus anhelum,
> et rabie fera corda tument.

But more to our purpose is the sober judgment of Plato a century after the first Roman experience of her, who in the *Phaedrus* classes her among those who have wrought *much good* by their inspired utterances.[31] This passage may help us to understand how ready men were at that time to turn for aid in tribulation to what they believed to be divine help, to an inspired wisdom beyond the range of the local deities of their own city-states.

This Sibyl became gradually localised in certain Greek cities, and thereby broke up, as it were, into several Sibyls. One of these Sibylline homes was at Cumae in Campania, the oldest Greek city in Italy, and this enables us to explain easily how the name and fame of the Sibyl reached Rome. Dim as is all early Roman history, the one clear fact of the sixth century is, as we have seen, the rapid advance of the Etruscans, their occupation of Rome, Praeneste, and other Latin cities, and their conquest of Campania, which is now ascribed to that same age.[32] Legend told in later days how the last Etruscan king had taken refuge at Cumae after his expulsion from Rome, and it is just possible that it may here be founding upon some dim recollection of a fact. However this may be, it is plain that it was through the great Etruscan disturbance of that period that Rome came to make trial of Sibylline utterances. In a moment of distress—the famine of which I spoke just now, and which I take to be historical because the remedy, the temple under the Aventine, was so closely connected with the corn-supply— she sent for or admitted an utterance of the Sibyl of Cumae, with whom she had come into some kind of contact through her Etruscan kings.

Let us consider that this foreign dynasty must have

brought a new population to the city on the Tiber, the chief strategic point of middle Italy,—a new element of plebs, whatever the old one may have been.[33]   We have seen signs, even in the religious history of this age, that commerce and industry were increasing, and that their increase was due to a movement from without, rather than to the old patrician *gentes*.   When the Etruscan dynasty fell and the old patrician influence was restored, the government must have been face to face with new difficulties, and among them the supply of corn for an increasing population in years of bad harvest.   With a fresh source of supply from the south came the cult of the Greek corn-deities at the bidding of a Sibylline utterance; and henceforward that remedy was available for other troubles.   But the patrician rulers of Rome were true, it would seem, as far as was possible, to the old ways, and for a long time they used this foreign remedy very sparingly.   At what date the utterances were collected in "books" and deposited in the Capitoline temple we do not know, nor have we any certain knowledge of their original nature or form.   Tradition said that the collection dated from the last king's reign, and that it was placed in the care of *duoviri sacris faciundis*, as we have seen, who in 367 B.C. gave way to *decemviri*, five of whom might be members of the plebs.   I am myself inclined to conjecture that this comparatively late date may be the real date of the origin of a *permanent collection* and a *permanent college of keepers*, and that the earlier *duoviri* were only temporary religious officers, *sacris faciundis*, *i.e.* for the carrying out of the directions of Sibylline utterances specially sought for at Cumae.   They would thus be of the same class as other special commissions appointed by the Senate for administrative purposes;[34] while the decemviri, though retaining the old title, were permanent religious officers appointed to collect and take charge of a new and important set of regulations for the benefit of the community, and one which concerned the plebs at least as much as the patricians.

But I must turn to the more important question how far, down to the war with Hannibal, when I shall take up the subject afresh, the Roman religion was affected for good or harm by these utterances and their keepers. They took effect in two ways : either by introducing new deities and settling them in new temples, or by ordering and organising new ceremonies such as Rome had never seen before.

The introduction of a new deity now and again was not of great account from the point of view of religion, except in so far as it encouraged the new ceremonies ; the Romans had never taken much personal interest in their deities, and the arrival (outside the pomoerium in each case) of Hermes under the name of Mercurius, or Poseidon bearing the name of the old Roman water *numen* Neptunus, or even of Asclepios with a Romanised name Aesculapius, would not be likely to affect greatly their ideas of the divine.   These facts have rather a historical than a religious significance ; Hermes Empolaios, for example, suggests trade with Greek cities, perhaps in grain,[35] and belongs therefore to the same class as Ceres, Liber, Libera, of whom I have already spoken.   The arrival of Poseidon-Neptune may mean, as Dr. Carter has suggested, a kind of " marine insurance " for the vessels carrying the grain from Greek ports.[36]   The settling of Aesculapius in the Tiber island in 293, as the result of a terrible pestilence, is interesting as being the first fact known to us in the history of medicine at Rome ; the temple became a kind of hospital on the model of Epidaurus, where the god had been brought in the form of a snake by an embassy sent for the purpose, and the priests who served it were probably Greeks skilled in the healing art.[37] This last case is a curious example of new Roman religious experience, but it can hardly be said to have any deep significance in the religious history of Rome.   Of the obliteration of the old *numen* Neptunus by the Greek god who took his name we know nothing for good or ill ; we are ignorant of the real meaning of the old *numen,* an'd cannot tell whether the loss of him was compensated by the usefulness of his name in Roman literature to represent the Greek god of the sea.

Let us turn to the much more important subject of the new ceremonies ordered by the Sibylline " books." The first authentic case of such innovation occurred in 399 B.C., during the long and troublesome siege of the dangerous neighbour city Veii ; I call it authentic because all the best modern authorities so reckon it, though it occurred before the destruction of old records during the capture of the city by the Gauls. The circumstances were such as to fix them-selves in the memory of the people, and in one way or another they found their way into the earliest annals, probably those of Fabius Pictor, composed during the Second Punic War.[38]

The previous winter, Livy tells us,[39] was one of extra-ordinary severity ; the roads were blocked with snow, and navigation on the Tiber stopped by the ice. This miser-able winter was followed too suddenly by a hot season, in which a plague broke out which consumed both man and beast, and continued so persistently that the Senate ordered the Sibylline books to be consulted. This per-sistence is the first point we should notice ; " Cuius insana-bili pernicie quando nec causa nec finis inveniebatur,"—so wrote Livy, evidently meaning to express an extremity of trouble which would not give way to ordinary religious remedies. We may compare his account of the next recorded consultation of the books (Livy vii. 2), when neither the old rites nor even the new ones were sufficient to secure the *pax deorum* and abate another pestilence, and recourse was had to yet another remedy in the form of *ludi scenici.* The times were out of joint,—the peace of the gods was broken, and thus the community was no longer in right relation to the Power manifesting itself in the universe. The result was a revival of *religio*, of the feeling of alarm and anxiety out of which the whole religious system had grown. The old deities might seem to be forsaking their functions, since the old rites had ceased to appeal to them.   Mysterious and persistent pestilence is a great tamer of human courage ; it is a new experience that man knows not how to meet, and in ancient life it was also a new *religious* experience.

The remedy was as new as the pestilence, and almost as pernicious.   During eight days Rome saw three pairs of deities reclining in the form of images on couches, before which were spread tables covered with food and drink.   Whether in this first case they were taken out of the temples and exposed to view in certain places, *e.g.* the forum, is not clear ; later on, in the days of *supplicationes*, of which more will be said presently, they were visited in procession.   The three pairs were Apollo and Latona, Diana and Hercules, Mercurius and Neptunus ; all of them Greek, or, as in the case of Diana, Mercurius, and Neptunus, Roman deities in their new Greek form. We cannot trace the special applicability of all of them to the trouble they were thus invoked to appease,—another point that suggests a complete revolution in the Roman ways of contemplating divine beings.   These are not functional *numina*, but foreigners whose ways were only known to the manipulators of the Sibylline utterances. They seem like quack remedies, of which the action is unknown to the consumer.

New also, but better in its effect, was the publicity of these proceedings, and the part taken in them by the whole population, patrician and plebeian, men, women, and children.   If we can trust Livy's further statements, every one left his door open and kept open house, inviting all to come in, whether known or unknown ; all old quarrels were made up, and no new ones suffered to begin ; prisoners were freed from their chains, and universal good-will prevailed.   These eight days were in fact kept as holidays, and doubtless by the novelty of the whole scene the astute authorities hoped to inspire fresh hope and confidence, and to divert attention from the prevailing misery, just as our soldiers in India are induced to forget the presence of cholera in a station by

constant games and amusements. That this was really
one leading object of the whole show is not generally
recognised by historians; but it seems fully explained by
the fact I mentioned just now, that in the similar trouble
of 349 B.C. recourse was had for the first time to *ludi
scenici* in order to amuse the people. In the history of
the Hannibalic war we shall have plenty of opportunity
of noting this kind of expedient. The Roman people,
we must remember, were getting more and more to be
inhabitants of a large city, and, as such, to seek for enter-
tainment, like all citizens in all ages. The religious rites
of the old calendar were perhaps by this time getting too
familiar, losing their original meaning; whether they had
ever been very entertaining to a city population may be
doubted. Something more showy was needed; processions had always been to the taste of the Roman,
and banquets, such as the epulum Iovis, which I have
already noticed, often accompanied the processions.

Now, this love of show and novelty, of which we
have abundant evidence later on as a Roman characteristic, taken together with the anxiety and alarm—the
new *religio*—arising from the pestilence, will sufficiently
explain the *lectisternia*, as these shows were called. We
have here in fact the first appearance, constantly recurring
in later Roman history, of a tendency to seek not only
for novelty, but for a more emotional expression of
religious feeling than was afforded by the old forms of
sacrifice and prayer, conducted as they were by the priest
on behalf of the community without its active participation. Those old forms might do for the old patrician
community of farmers and warriors, but not so well for
the new and ever-increasing population of artisans and
other workmen, whether of Roman or foreign descent.
It would seem, indeed, as if the sensitiveness of the
human fibre of a primitive community increases with its
increasing complexity, and with the greater variety of
experience to which it is exposed; and in the case of
Rome, as if the simple ancient methods of dealing with

the divine inhabitants of the city were no longer adequate
to the needs of a State which was steering its way to
empire among so many difficulties and perils.   It is not
indeed certain that the new rites, or some points in them,
may not have had their prototypes in old Italian usage,
though the *lectisternia*, the actual display of gods in
human form and in need of food like human beings, are
almost certainly Greek in origin.[40]   But so far as we can
guess, the emotional element was wholly new.   True,
Livy tells us in two passages of his third book of
occasions when men, women, and children flocked to all
the shrines (*omnia delubra*) seeking for the *pax deorum*
at the invitation of the senate ; but the early date, the
great improbability of the senate taking any such step,
and the absence of any mention of the priesthoods, makes
it difficult to believe that these assertions are based
on any genuine record.   We must be content to mark
the first *lectisternia* in 399 as the earliest authentic
example of the emotional tendency of the Roman plebs.[41]

If we can judge of this period of Roman religious
history by the general tendency of the policy of the
Roman government, we may see here a deliberate attempt
to include the new population in worship of a kind that
would calm its fears, engage its attention, and satisfy its
emotion, while leaving uncontaminated the old ritual that
had served the State so long.   If this conclusion be a
right one, then we must allow that the new ceremonial
had its use.   Dr. Frazer has lately told us in his eloquent
and persuasive way, of how much value superstition has
been in building up moral habits and the instinct of submission to civil order.   His thesis might be illustrated
adequately from the history of Rome alone.   But from a
purely religious point of view the story of the *lectisternia*
is a sad one.   The old Roman invisible *numen*, working
with force in a particular department of human life and
its environment, was a far nobler mental conception, and
far more likely to grow into a power for good, than the
miserable images of Graeco-Roman full-blown gods and

goddesses reclining on their couches and appearing to partake of dinner like a human citizen. Such ideas of the divine must have forced men's religious ideas clean away from the Power manifesting itself in the universe, and must have dragged down the Roman *numina* with them in their corrupting degradation. According to our definition of it, religion was now in a fair way to disappear altogether ; what was destined to take its place was not really religion at all. Nor did it in any way assist the growth of an individual conscience, as perhaps did some of the later religious forms introduced from without. It was of value for the moment to the State, in satisfying a population greatly disturbed by untoward events ; and that was all.

Closely connected with the *lectisternia*, and following close upon them in chronological order, were the processional ceremonies called *supplicationes*. The historical relation between the two is by no means clear ; but if we conclude, as I am fairly sure we may, that the *lectisternia* were shows of a joyful character, accompanied, as Livy describes the first one, with private entertainments, and meant to keep up the spirits of the plebeian population, and if we then turn to the early *supplicationes*, in which men, women, and children, *coronati*, and carrying laurel branches, went in procession to the temples, and there prostrated themselves after the Greek fashion, the women "crinibus passis aras verrentes," we shall be disposed to look on them as, in origin at least, distinct from each other.[42] We may conjecture that the appearance of the gods in human form at the doors of their temples suggested to the plebeian women a kind of emotional worship which was alien to the old Roman feeling, but familiar enough to those (and they must have been many) who knew the life of the Greek cities of Italy. It may be that they had tried it even in earlier times ; but anyhow, in the fourth and third centuries B.C. advantage was taken of the *pulvinaria* to use them as stopping-places in the procession of a *supplicatio*, and the phrase becomes a common one in the annals, " supplicatio ad omnia pulvinaria indicta." The *lectisternia* were ordered five times in the fourth century; [43] by that time, it would seem likely, the *supplicationes* had become an authorised institution, and had perhaps embodied the practice of *lectisternia* in the way suggested above. We shall meet with them again when we come to the religious history of the war with Hannibal.

One word more before I leave this subject for the present. In all this innovation we must not forget to note the growth of individual feeling as distinguished from the old worship of civic grouping, in which the individual, as such, was of little or no account. I pointed out the first signs of this individualism when speaking of the temple of the Capitoline Jupiter, and we shall have reason to mark its rapid growth further. We are now, in fact, and must realise that we are, in a period in which, throughout the Graeco-Roman world, the need was beginning to be felt of some new rule of individualistic morality. The Roman population, now recruited from many sources, was but reflecting this need unconsciously when it insisted on new emotional rites and expiations. The Roman authorities were forced to satisfy the demand ; but in doing so they made no real contribution to the history of Roman religious experience. It was impossible that they should do so ; they represented the old civic form of religion, "bound up with the life of a society, and unable to contemplate the individual except as a member of it." [44] The new forms of worship, the *supplicatio* and *lectisternium*, could not be, as the old forms had in some sense been, the consecration of civic and national life. They were to the Romans as the worship of Baal to the Jews of the time of the Kings ; and, unlike that poisonous cult, they could never be rooted out.

NOTES TO LECTURE XI

1. This is the expression of Sallust, *Catil.* 12. 3.

2. See my paper on the Latin history of the word *religio*, in *Transactions of the Congress for the History of Religions*, 1909, vol. ii. p. 172. W. Otto in *Archiv*, 1909, p. 533 foll.

3. Cic. *de Nat. Deorum*, ii. 8.

4. Cic. *Harusp. resp.* 19.

5. Livy xliv. 1. 11 ; Sallust, *l.c.* ; Gellius, *Noct. Att.* ii. 28. 2.

6. Polyb. vi. 56.

7. Posidonius ap. Athenaeum vi. 274 A ; Dion. Hal. ii. 27. 3.

8. Gell. ii. 28.

9. Marquardt, iii. 126.

10. Cato, *R.R.* 142.

11. Calpurnius, *Eclogue*, v. 24. I have described a similar scene in the Alps in *A Year with the Birds*, ed. 2, p. 126.

12. Petronius, *Sat.* 117 : " His ita ordinatis, quod bene feliciterque eveniret precati deos, viam ingredimur." I owe this reference, as others in this context, to Appel's treatise *de Romanorum precationibus*, p. 56 foll.

13. Varro, *R.R.* i. 1.

14. *e.g.* Virg. *Aen.* v. 685 (Aeneas during the burning of the fleet) ; *Aen.* xii. 776 (Turnus in extremity). Cp. Tibull. iii. 5. 6 (in sickness).

15. A good example is *Captivi*, 922 : " Iovi disque ago gratias merito magnas quom te reducem tuo patri reddiderunt," etc.

16. For gratitude to human beings see Valerius Maximus v. 2. A good example of gratitude to a deity is in Gell. *N.A.* iv. 18 ; but it is told of Scipio the elder, who was eccentric for a Roman. When accused by a tribune of peculation in Asia he said, " Non igitur simus adversum deos ingrati et, censeo, relinquamus nebulonem hunc, eamus hinc protinus Iovi Optimo Maximo gratulatum." Public gratitude to the gods is frequent in later *supplicationes*, *e.g.* Livy xxx. 17. 6.

17. Gellius, *N.A.* xiv. 7. 9.

18. Servius ad *Aen.* xi. 301 (" praefatus divos solio rex infit ab alto ").

19. This was in a *contio* : " Cum Gracchus deos inciperet precari." See above, Lecture VII. note 13.

20. See *R.F.* p. 74 foll. ; Wissowa, *R.K.* p. 243. For the relation of the pomoerium to the wall, see above, p. 94.

21. The process is amusingly explained by Carter in *The Religion of Numa*, p. 72 foll.

22. *R.F.* p. 75.

23. See Aust, *De aedibus sacris P.R.*, passim.

24. Lately this has been denied by Pais, *Storia di Roma*, i. 339

25. Pliny, *N.H.* 35, 154.

26. I owe the information to my friend Prof. Percy Gardner.

27. See Carter, *op. cit.* p. 66 ; but I am not sure that his reasons are conclusive.

28. Diels, *Sibyllinische Blätter*, p. 6 foll., and cp. 79.

29. It should be noted that the cult of Apollo in Rome was older than the introduction of Sibylline influence ; so at least it is generally assumed. Wissowa, however (*R.K.* p. 239), puts it as "gleichzeitig." The date of the Apollinar in pratis Flaminiis, the oldest Apolline fanum in Rome (outside pomoerium), is unknown ; that of the temple on the same site was 431 (Livy iv. 25 and 29). There is little doubt that the Apollo-cult spread from Cumae north-wards, and was by this time well established in Italy. (The founda-tion of the temple of 431, consisting of opus quadratum, still in part survives : Hülsen-Jordan, *Rom. Topographie*, iii. 535).

30. Heracleitus, *fragm.* xii., ed. Bywater.

31. *Phaedrus*, p. 244.

32. So Korte in Pauly-Wissowa, *Real-Encycl., s.v.* "Etrusker."

33. The present tendency is to take the plebs as representing an older population of Latium before the arrival of the patricians ; see, *e.g.*, Binder, *Die Plebs*, p. 358 foll. But the plebs of later days is not to be explained on one hypothesis only.

34. *e.g.* in religious matters the *duoviri aedi dedicandae*; Mommsen, *Staatsrecht*, ii. 601 foll.

35. Carter, *Religion of Numa*, p. 77 foll. It is uncertain whether there was a Roman Mercurius of earlier origin, or whether the name Mercurius (*i.e.* concerned in trade) was a new invention to avoid using the Greek name, as in the case of the trias Ceres, Liber, Libera.

36. Carter, *op. cit.* 81. The connection of this Poseidon-Neptunus and Hermes-Mercurius is confirmed by the fact that the two were paired in the first *lectisternium*, 399 B.C. Livy v. 13.

37. Wissowa, *R.K.* p. 254.

38. See Diels, *Sib. Blätter*, p. 12, note 1.

39. Livy v. 13.

40. I have discussed the possibility of the epulum Iovis being an old Italian rite in *R.F.* p. 215 foll. For the Greek origin of these shows see *Dict. of Antiquities*, ed. 2, *s.v.* "lectisternia."

41. Livy iii. 5. 14, and 7. 7.

42. The plebeian tendencies of the time are suggested, *e.g.*, by the fact that immediately before the first *lectisternium* a plebeian was elected military tribune (Livy v. 13). The fourth century is of course the period of plebeian advance in all departments, and ends with the opening of the priesthoods to the plebs by the lex Ogulnia, and the publication of the Fasti. Plebeian too, I suspect, was the keeping open house and promiscuous hospitality which is

recorded by Livy of the first *lectisternia* ; this was the practice of the plebs on the Cerealia (April 19), and was perhaps an old custom connected with the supply of corn and the temple of Ceres (see above, p. 255).   It was not imitated by the patrician society, with its reserve and exclusiveness, till the institution of the Megalesia in 204 B.C.   See Gellius xviii. 2. 11.

43. The expression *crinibus demissis* is found in a lex regia (Festus, *s.v.* "pellices"); the harlot who touches Juno's altar has to offer a lamb to Juno "crinibus demissis."   This is therefore Roman practice.

44. For the *supplicationes* see Wissowa, *R.K.* 357 foll.; Marq. 48 and 188; and the author's article in *Dict. of Antiquities.*   The passages already referred to as doubtful evidence (Livy iii. 5. 14, 7. 7) describe all the features of the *supplicatio* as early as the first half of the fifth century.   A list of later passages in Livy will be found in Marq. 49, note 4.   On the whole I doubt if much was made of these rites before the third century and the Punic wars.

45. Wissowa, *R.K.* 356, note 7.

46. Caird, *Gifford Lectures*, vol. ii. p. 46.

LECTURE XII

THE PONTIFICES AND THE SECULARISATION OF RELIGION

IN the last lecture we saw how the new experiences of the Roman people, during the period from the abolition of the kingship to the war with Hannibal, led to the introduction of foreign deities and showy ceremonies of a character quite strange to the old religion. But there was another process going on at the same time. The authorities of that old religion were full of vigour in this same period; it may even be said, that as far as we can trace their activity in the dim light of those early days, they made themselves almost supreme in the State. And the result was, in brief, that religion became more and more a matter of State administration, and thereby lost its chance of developing the conscience of the individual. It is indeed quite possible, as has recently been maintained,[1] that it stood actively in the way of such development. I have no doubt that there was a germ of conscience, of moral feeling, in the *religio* of old days—the feeling of anxiety and doubt which originally suggested the *cura* and *caerimonia* of the State; but the efforts of the authorities in this period were spent in gradually destroying that germ. True, they did not interfere with the simple religion of the family, which had its value all through Roman history; but the attitude of the individual towards public worship will react on his attitude towards private worship, which may also have lost some part of its vitality in this period.

The religious authorities of which I speak are of course the two great colleges of pontifices and augurs. Of the latter, and of the system of divination of which they held the secrets, I will speak in the next lecture. Here we have to do with the pontifices and their work in this period, a thorny and somewhat technical subject, but a most important one for the history of Roman religious experience.

I have so far assumed that this college existed in the age of the kings, and assisted the Rex in the administration of the *ius divinum*. It is legitimate to do this, but as a matter of fact we do not know for certain what was the origin of the college itself, or of its mysterious name. In the period we have now reached we come, however, upon a striking fact, which is luckily easy to interpret ; the king's house, the *Regia*, has become the office of the head of the college, the pontifex maximus, and also the meeting-place of the college for business.[2] Obviously this head, whether or no he existed during the kingly period, has stepped into the place of the Rex in the control of the *ius divinum*. Again, we know that in the third century B.C., when written history begins, the pontifices and their head had reached a very high level of power, as we shall presently see more in detail ; the process of the growth of this power must therefore lie in the two preceding centuries, during which Rome was slowly attaining that paramount position in Italy in which we find her at the time of the Punic wars. Thirdly, we know that in that third century B.C. the college was laid open to plebeians as well as to members of the old patrician gentes, and that one of the most famous of all its many distinguished heads was not only not a patrician, but a Latin from Cameria, Ti. Coruncanius. Putting these three facts together we can divine in outline the history of the pontifices during these two centuries. With the instinct for order and organisation that never failed them, the Romans have constructed a *permanent* power to take charge of their *ius divinum, i.e.* all their relations to the deities with whom they must maintain a *pax*; the circumstances of their career during two centuries have exalted this power to an extraordinary degree of influence, direct and indirect, internal and external; and, lastly, in a period which saw the gradual amalgamation into a unified whole of privileged and unprivileged, *patres* and *plebs*, they have with wonderful wisdom thrown open to all citizens the administration of that *ius* which was essential to the welfare of the united community. These are indisputable facts; and they are thoroughly characteristic of the practical wisdom of the Roman people in that early age.

In order to understand how the pontifices attained their great position, the one thing needful is to examine the nature of their work. This I propose to do next, and then to attempt to sum up the result of their activity on the Roman religious system.

It is impossible to exaggerate the importance of the college in the early history of Roman law; and for us in particular that importance lies in the fact that they were the sole depositaries of the religious law in the period during which the civil law was being slowly disentangled from it. If we look at the so-called *leges regiae*, which are probably the oldest rules of law that have come down to us (though they may have been made into a collection as late as the very end of the Republic),[3] we see at once that they belong to the *ius divinum*; and there is little doubt that they were extracted from those books of the pontifices which I shall have to explain later on.[4]   In other words, it is the maintenance of the *pax deorum* that they are chiefly concerned with; the crime of the citizen is a violation of that *pax*, and the deity most concerned will punish the community unless some expiatory step is taken to re-establish the right relation between the human and divine inhabitants of the city. "Pellex aram Iunonis ne tangito; si tanget, Iunoni crinibus demissis agnum feminam caedito." "Si parentem puer verberit, ast olle plorassit, puer divis parentum sacer esto."[5]   The harlot who touches the altar of Juno, the deity of married women,

breaks the *pax* with that deity, and she must offer a
piacular sacrifice to renew it ; the son who strikes a
parent is made over as the property of the *divi parentum*,
i.e. those of the whole community,[6] the peaceful relation with whom his act has imperilled. With such rules
as these the civil magistrate of the republic can have had
nothing to do ; they belong to an older period of thought
and of government, and survived in the books of the
college which under the republic continued to administer
the *ius divinum* ; for these rules doubtless continued to
exist side by side with the civil law as it gradually
developed itself, and the necessary modes of expiation
were known to the pontifices only. Roman society was
indeed so deeply penetrated for many ages with the idea
of *religio*—the dread of violating the *pax deorum*,—that the
idea of law as a matter of the relation of man to man, as
" the interference of the State in the passions and interests
of humanity only," must have gained ground by very
slow degrees. This primitive religious law then, *i.e.* the
regulation of the proper steps to be taken to avoid a
breach of the *pax deorum*, was entirely in the hands of the
religious authorities, the Rex at first and then the
pontifices, as the only experts who could know the secrets
of the *ius divinum* ; and from their decisions and prescriptions there could be no appeal, simply because there
was no individual or body in the State to whom an
appeal was conceivable. But after the rule of the
Etruscan kings, with all its disturbing influences, and
after the revolution which got rid of them, there must
have been an age of new ideas and increased mental
activity, and also of increasing social complexity, the
signs of which in the way of trade and industry we have
already found in certain facts of religious history. In
the domain of law this meant new problems, new difficulties ; and these were met in the middle of the fifth
century B.C., if the received chronology is to be accepted,[7]
by the publication of the XII. Tables.

In order to get some idea of the work of the pontifices

T

at this time, let us consider one or two of these difficulties and problems.

Within the family every act, every relation, was matter of religion; the *numina* had to be considered in regard to it. The end and aim, then as throughout Roman history, was the maintenance of the *sacra* of the family, without which it could not be conceived as existing—the due worship of its deities, and the religious care of its dead. Take marriage as an example: "the entry of a bride into the household—of one who as yet had no lot in the family life—meant some straining of the relation between the divine and human members,"[8] and the human part of the family must be assured that the divine part is willing to accept her before the step can be regarded as complete. She has to enter the family in such a way as to share in its *sacra*; and if *confarreatio* was (as we may believe) the oldest form of patrician marriage,[9] the bride was subjected to a ceremony which was plainly of a sacramental character—the sacred cake of *far* being partaken of by both bride and bridegroom in the presence of the highest religious authority of the State. In the simplest form of society there would be no call for further priestly interference in marriage; but in a society growing more numerous and complex, exceptions, abnormal conditions begin to show themselves, and new problems arise, which must be solved by new expedients, prescriptions, permissions, devices, or fictions. For these the religious authorities are solely responsible; for what is a matter of religious interest to the family is also matter of religious interest to the State, simply because the State is composed of families in the same sense as the human body is composed of cellular tissue. All this, we believe, was once the work of the Rex, perhaps with the college of pontifices to help him; when the kingship disappeared it became the work of that college solely, with the pontifex maximus as the chief authority.

So, too, in all other questions which concerned the maintenance of the family, and especially in regard to the devolution of property. I am here only illustrating the way in which the pontifical college acquired their paramount influence by having a quantity of new and difficult work forced upon them, and it is not part of my plan to explain the early history of adoptions and wills ; but I may give a single concrete illustration for the benefit of those who are not versed in Roman law. It must constantly have happened, in that disturbed period which brought the kingship to an end, that by death or capture in war a family was left without male heirs. Daughters could not take their place, because the *sacra* of a family could not be maintained by daughters, who would, in the natural order of things, be sooner or later married and so become members of other families. Hence the expedient was adopted of making a *filius familias* of another family a member of your own ; and this, like marriage, involved a straining of the relations between the human and divine members of your family, and was thus a matter for the religious authorities to contrive in such a manner as to preserve the *pax* between them. The difficulty was overcome by the practical wisdom of the pontifical college, which held a solemn inquiry into the case before submitting it to the people in specially summoned assembly (*comitia calata*) ;[10] and thus the new *filius familias* was enabled not only to renounce his own *sacra* (*detestatio sacrorum*), but to pass into the guardianship of another set of *sacra*, without incurring the anger of the *numina* concerned with the welfare of either.

Such difficult matters as these, and many more connected directly or indirectly with the devolution of property, such as the guardianship of women and of the incapable, the power to dispose of property otherwise than by the original rules of succession, the law of burial and the care of the dead,—all these, at the time of which I am speaking, must have been among the secrets of the pontifices ; and we can also suspect, though without being sure of our facts, that the great increase of the importance of the *plebs* under the Etruscan dynasty offered further opportunities for the growth alike of the work and influence of the college.[11]   Above all, we must remember that this work was done in secret, that the mysteries of adjustment were unknown to the people when once they had passed out of the ken of family and gens, and that there could have been no appeal from the pontifices to any other body.   Nay, more, we must also bear in mind that this body of religious experts was *self-electing*.   Until the lex Domitia of 104 B.C. both pontifices and augurs filled up their own colleges with persons whom they believed qualified both by knowledge and disposition.   Thus it would seem that there was every chance that in that early Rome, where neither in family nor State could anything be undertaken without some reference to the religious authority, where the *pax deorum* was the one essential object of public and private life, a power might be developed apt one day not only to petrify religion and stultify its worshippers, but thereby also to cramp the energies of the community, acting as an obstacle to its development within its walls and without.   Had Roman law remained entirely in the hands of this self-electing college, one of two things must have happened: either that college would have become purely secular in character, or the wonderful legal system that we still enjoy would never have had space to grow up.   But this was not to be; with the publication of the XII. Tables a new era opens.

If we reject, as we conscientiously may, the latest attempts of criticism to post-date the drawing up of the Tables,[12] and in fact to destroy their historical value for us, what is their significance for our present purpose? It is simply that in the middle of the fifth century B.C. the pontifices lost a monopoly—ceased to be the sole depositaries of the rules of law affecting the *pax deorum*, and that new rules are being set down in writing, on the basis of old custom, which more especially affect the relations between the human citizens.   For both the *ius divinum* and the *ius civile* are to be found in this collection, but the latter is beginning to assert its independence.   I think we may say, without much hesitation, that this event, however doubtful its traditional details, did actually save Rome from either of the two consequences to which I alluded just now. The constitution developed itself on lay and not on ecclesiastical lines, leaving the pontifices other work to do, and Roman civil law was eventually able to free itself from the trammels of the *ius divinum*.

But for another century the college still found abundant legal work to do, for it was not likely that at Rome, the most conservative of all city-states, it could be quickly set aside, or that the old ideas of law could so speedily disappear. What then was this work?

When rules of civil law were written down, it was still necessary to deal with them in two ways which were open to the pontifices, and indeed at this early time to no one else. First, it was necessary to make their provisions effectual by prescribing in each case the proper method of procedure (*actio*). Now it is most important to grasp the fact that procedure in the *ius civile* was originally of precisely the same nature as procedure in the *ius divinum*, and that precisely the same rigid exactness is indispensable in both. Action and formula in civil law belong to the same class of practices as sacrifice and prayer in religious law, and spring from the same mental soil. Thus, for example, the most familiar case of action and formula in civil law, the *sacramentum*, was, as the name proves, a piece of religious procedure, *i.e.* the deposition in a sacred spot of a sum of money which the suitor in the case would forfeit if he lost it, together with the utterance of a certain formula of words which must be correctly spoken. If we choose to go back so far, we may even see in this combination of formularised act and speech a survival of magical or quasi-magical belief;[13] but this is matter rather for the anthropologist than the historian of religion. The point for us at this moment is that these acts and formulae (*legis actiones*, as they are known in Roman law) could not suddenly or rapidly pass out of the hands of that body of skilled experts which had so long been in sole possession of them ; the publication of old and new rules of law in the XII. Tables made no immediate difference in this respect. The consuls, the new civil executive, were still in no sense necessarily skilled in such matters, and were without the prestige of the former executive, the Rex ; they were also doubtless busy with other work, especially in the field. Nothing could be more natural than that the pontifices should continue to provide the procedure for the now written law, just as they had formerly supplied it for the unwritten.[14]

So, too, with the *interpretation* of the Tables ; this was the second part of the work that still remained to them. Writing was in that age a mystery to the mass of the population, and doubtless the idea was still in their minds that there was something supernatural about it. Writing, in fact, as well as formularised action and speech, may have had the flavour of magic about it. However that may be, there can be no doubt that the interpretation of a legal document was in those days a much more serious, if a less arduous business, than it is now. Here again, then, it seems perfectly natural that there should be no rapid or violent change in the *personnel* of those deemed capable of such interpretation ; there was no other body of ex- perts capable of the work ; the pontifices remained *iuris- consulti*, *i.e.* interpreters and advisers, and in the course of two and a half centuries accumulated an amount of material that formed a basis for the first published system of Roman law, the *ius Aelianum* or *tripartita* of 200 B.C. It is most useful to remember, as proof of this, that one member of the college was selected every year for the special purpose of helping the people with advice in matters of civil law, both in regard to interpretation and the choice of *legis actiones* ; so we are expressly told by Pomponius, who adds that this practice continued for about a hundred years after the publication of the Tables, *i.e.* till the election of the first praetor in 366.[15] After that date the *ius civile* emerges more distinctly from the old body of law, which included also the *ius divinum*, and its interpretation was no longer a matter purely for religious experts.   In 337 we hear of the first *plebeian* praetor—truly a momentous event, showing that the old profound belief is dying out, which demanded a religious and patrician qualification for all legal work.   And at the end of the fourth century comes the publication, not only of the *legis actiones*, but of the Fasti, *i.e.* even of that most vital part of the *ius divinum*, which distinguished the times and seasons belonging to the numina from those belonging to the human citizens.[16]   One might well suppose that the power of the pontifices was on the wane, for they had lost another monopoly.

And indeed in one sense this was so.   It must have been so, for as the range of the State's activity increased, the sphere of religious influence became relatively less. Marriage, for example, though it still needed a religious ceremony in common opinion, ceased to need it in the eye of the law—a change which is familiar to us in our own age.   The pontifex was no longer indispensable to the suitor at law, nor to the citizen who wished to know on what day he might proceed with his suit.   The college undoubtedly ceased to be the powerful secretly-acting body in whose hands was the entire *religio* of the citizen, *i.e.* the decision of all points on which he might feel the old anxious nervousness about the good-will of the gods. But now we mark a change which gave the old institution new life and new work.   At the end of this fourth century (300 B.C.) it was thrown open to plebeians by the lex Ogulnia; and, as I have already mentioned, within a few years we come upon a plebeian pontifex maximus, who was not even a Roman by birth, yet one of the most famous in the whole series of the holders of that great office.   Most probably, too, the numbers of the members have already been increased from five to nine, of whom five must be plebeian.   These members begin to be found holding also civil magistracies, and the pontifex maximus was often a consul of the year.   It is quite plain then that this priestly office is becoming more and more secularised ; it expands with the new order of things instead of shrinking into itself. It leaves religion, in the proper sense of the word, far behind. The sacrificing priests, the flamines, etc., who were the humbler members in a technical sense of the same college, go on with their proper and strictly religious work under the supervision of the pontifex maximus,[17] but they steadily become of less importance as the greater members become secularised in their functions and their ambitions. And these greater members, instead of becoming stranded on a barren shore of antique religion, boldly venture into a new sphere of human life, and add definite secular work to their old religious functions.

The events of the latter part of the fourth century B.C., culminating in the publication of the Fasti and the *legis actiones*, probably meant much more for the Romans than we can divine by the uncertain light of historical imagination. It is the age of expansion, internal and external ; the old patrician exclusive rule was gone beyond recall ; the plebeians had forced their way into every department of government, including at last even the great religious *collegia* ; the old Latin league had been broken up, and the Latin cities organised in various new relations to Rome, each one being connected with the suzerain city by a separate treaty, sealed with religious sanctions. After the Samnite wars and the struggle with Pyrrhus, further organisation was necessary, and there arose by degrees a loose system of union which we are accustomed to call the Italian confederation. The adaptation of all these new conditions to the existing order of things at Rome was the work of the senate and magistrates so far as it concerned human beings only ; but so far as it affected the relations of the divine inhabitants of the various communities it must have been the work of the pontifices. That work is indeed almost entirely hidden from us, for Livy's books of this period are lost, and Livy is the only historian who has preserved for us in any substance the religious side of Rome's public life. But what we have

learnt in the course of these lectures will have made it plain
that no political changes could take place without involving
religious adaptation, and also that the only body qualified
to undertake such adaptation was the pontifical college.

We may thus be quite certain, that though they had
lost their old monopoly of religious knowledge, the pontifices found plenty of fresh work to do in this period.
It is my belief that they now became more active than
they ever had been.   From this time, for example, we
may almost certainly date their literary or quasi-literary
activity; I mean the practice of recording the leading
events of each year, which may have had its origin a
century earlier, with the eclipse of the sun in or about
404 B.C.[18]   I should guess that after the admission of the
plebeians to the college in 300 B.C., the new members put
fresh life and vigour into the old work, and developed it
in various directions.   It is in this period that I am
inclined to attribute to the college that zeal for compiling
and perhaps inventing religious formulae of all kinds,
which took shape in the *libri* or *commentarii pontificum*,
and embodied that strange manual of the methods of
addressing deities, which we know as *Indigitamenta*.   And
again, in the skilled work of the admission of new deities
and the dedication of their temples, occasioned by the
new organisation and condition of Italy, and lastly, in the
supervision of the proper methods of expiating *prodigia*,
which (though the habit is doubtless an old one) began
henceforward to be reported to the Senate from all parts
of the ager Romanus and even beyond, their meetings in
the Regia must have been fully occupied.   Our loss is
great indeed in the total want of detail about the life
and character of the great plebeian pontifex maximus
of the first half of the third century B.C., that Titus
Coruncanius whom I have already mentioned as being a
Latin by birth; for Cicero declares that the *commentarii*
of the college showed him as a man of the greatest
ability,[19] whose reputation remained for ages as one who
was ready with wise counsel in matters both public and

private. Coupling him with two other memorable holders of the office, he says that " et in senatu et apud populum et in causis amicorum et domi et militiae consilium suum fidemque praestabant." [20]   This passage should be remembered as a valuable illustration of the way in which the college and its head were becoming more and more occupied with secular business ; it is worth noting, too, that this great man was himself consul in the year 280, and took a useful part in the first campaign against Pyrrhus.[21]   Yet Cicero makes it plain that he looked on him also as a great figure in religious matters—nay, even as a man whom the gods loved.[22]

I will finish this lecture by illustrating briefly this renewed and extended activity of the pontifices, so far as we can dimly trace it in this third century B.C.   Most of it is connected more or less directly with the State religion, yet with a tendency to become more and more secular and perfunctory ; the word *cura* would express it better than *caerimonia*, and *caerimonia* better than *religio*.   The care of the calendar, for example (a technical matter which lies outside my province in these lectures), was originally of religious importance, because the oldest religious festivals marked operations of husbandry, and these, when fixed in the calendar, must occur at the right seasons.[23]   It was the duty of the pontifices so to adjust the necessary intercalations as to effect this object—a duty to which they were, as it turned out, quite unequal. But continued city life broke the connection between the festivals and the agricultural work to which they originally corresponded, and what was once a *cura* of religious import became a secular matter of which the value was not appreciated.   So too with another duty, for which both the Romans and ourselves have more reason to be grateful to them—the recording of the leading events of national history.

It is uncertain what prompted the college, or rather its head, to begin making these records, though there is

no doubt about the fact. But it would be natural enough
that those who had charge of the calendar, which would
necessitate some record of years for purposes of inter-
calation, should go on to mark the names of the consuls
and such striking events as would make a year memorable. In any case this was what actually happened. The
pontifex maximus, we are told with precision, kept a
tabula, or whited board, on which these events were noted
down, with the consuls' names attached to them, or possibly a kind of almanac, made out for the whole year, on
which they could append their notes to particular days.[24]
This yearly *tabula* was no doubt at first kept secret, like
all the pontifical documents, but sooner or later, perhaps
at the same time as the publication of the *fasti* and *legis
actiones*, it was exposed to public view in or at the Regia.[25]
This went on for at least two centuries, and the records,
which in the nature of things must have grown in length
and detail as events became more startling and numerous,
were edited in eighty books by the pontifex maximus P.
Mucius Scaevola in 123 B.C. — the year of the first
tribunate of C. Gracchus. The large number of these
books has long been a stumbling-block to the learned,
for we are expressly told that the *annales maximi*, as the
records were called, were (in spite of their name) of a
very meagre character ; and many conjectures have quite
recently been made to explain it.[26] But guessing is almost
useless, seeing that there are no data for it. The editor
may have added matter of his own, amplifying and
adorning after the manner of writers of his day ; or he
may have worked in the contents of other pontifical books,
libri or *commentarii pontificales*. The point for us is simply
the continued activity of the pontifex maximus in this
work, which must have become almost entirely secular in
character. The notes may have been jejune, but they
were probably accurate, and free from the perversions of
family vanity or such lengthy rhetorical ornamentation as
became the universal fashion among private writers of
annalistic history. They were, we may suppose, exactly

what our modern historical conscience demands. But all that is left of them, or almost all, is the list of consuls (*fasti consulares*) and of triumphs (*fasti triumphales*) which in their present form must, or at least may, have been extracted from them.[27]   On the whole, we may reckon them as the most valuable work of the college ; and they may be taken as marking a growing sense of the importance of Rome and her history, the commemoration of which is thus committed to an official who, as an individual, had invariably served the State well, and in whom all classes had perfect confidence.[28]

One important part of the work of the college in this century must have been the adjustment of the civic religion of the Italian communities to that of Rome. What deities were to be made citizens of Rome ? Which were to be left in their old homes undisturbed ? No doubt many other questions must have called for attention in religious matters after the conquest of Italy, but this is the one of which we know most. The temple foundations of this period have all been carefully put together (chiefly from Livy's invaluable records) by Aust,[29] and show that there was a certain tendency to bring in deities from outside, not so much because they represented some special need of the Romans, corn or art or industry, as two centuries earlier, but simply because they were deities of the conquered whom it might be prudent to adopt. The great Juno Regina of Veii was long ago induced by *evocatio* to migrate to Rome ; Fors Fortuna from Etruria, Juturna from Lavinium, Minerva Capta from Falerii, Feronia, a famous Latin goddess from Capena, Vortumnus from Volsinii,[30] all attest the same liberal tone in religious matters which on the whole marks the secular Italian policy of the Senate in this period. If we had but more information about the former, we should be able to understand the latter far better. We should like to know why in some cases the chief deity of a community came to Rome, while in others there is not trace of migration. The famous Vacuna of Reate, for example, never left her

home in the Apennines, possibly because she was a kind
of Vesta, who could not be spared from Reate, and was
not wanted at Rome.[31]

The list of foundations also points to other tendencies
and experiences of the time.   We might guess that there
was some attempt, with the aid of pontifical skill, to
encourage agriculture or give it a fresh start after the
invasion of Pyrrhus; for between 272 and 264, the years
of the pacification of Italy, we find temples built to four
agricultural deities, three indigenous Roman ones, Consus
Tellus Pales, and one Etruscan garden god, Vertumnus.[32]
Then we have a group of foundations in honour of deities
connected with water——Juturna, Fons, Tempestates, which
seem to have some reference to the naval activity of the
first Punic war; they all fall between 259 and 241 B.C.[33]
Lastly, we notice a fresh accession of deified abstractions,
——Salus (an old deity in a new form), Spes, Honos et
Virtus, Concordia, and Mens [34]   I am glad to find that
the latest investigator of these religious abstractions is
at one with me in believing that they simply mark a
developed stage in the religious bent of the earliest
Roman.   If the old Romans had the habit of spiritual-
ising a great variety of material objects, in other words,
if they were in an advanced animistic stage, there seems
to be no reason why they should not have begun to
spiritualise mental concepts also (for which they had
words, as for the material objects), even at a very early
period.   The whole psychological aspect of such abstractions is most interesting, but I must pass it over
here, merely suggesting that each of these abstractions
was doubtless deified for some particular reason, under
the direction, or with the sanction, of the pontifices.[35]

But we have not as yet reached what is, after all, for
our purposes the most instructive part of the work of the
pontifices——I mean the archives or memoranda (*libri* or
commentarii) which they kept, and from which, indirectly, much of what I have had to say about the *ius
divinum* has been drawn.   It is here that we see the

policy of maintaining the *pax deorum* carried to its highest point.   These books contained a vast collection of formulae for every kind of process in which the deities were in any way concerned ; here was the complete *pharmacopoeia* of the *ius divinum*.[36]   We must remember that the pontifex maximus and his assessors had to be ready at any moment with the correct formula for all religious acts, whether extraordinary, like the *devotio* of Decius or the expiation of some startling " prodigium," or belonging to the ordinary course of city life, such as prayers in sacrificial ritual, *vota* both public and private, charters (*leges*) of newly founded temples, and so on. The idea that the spoken formula (ultimately, as we saw, derived from an age of magic) was efficient only if no slip were made, seems to have gained in strength instead of diminishing, as we might have expected it to do with advancing civilisation ; and the pontifices not only responded to its importunity, but actually stimulated it. *Vires acquirit eundo* are words which apply well in all ages to the passion for organisation and precision.   Though we cannot prove it, I myself have little doubt that the members of the college, or some of them, collected and invented formulae simply for the pleasure of doing it, and that the work became as congenial to them as the systematisation of the law to Jewish scribes after the captivity, or as casuistry to the confessors of the middle ages.   When the art of writing became familiar to experts, the natural and primitive desire of the Roman to have exactness in the spoken word affected him also in his relations with the word as written.   The scribe and the Pharisee found their opportunity.   The whole public religion of the State, and to some extent also the private religion of the family, became a mass of forms and formulae, and never succeeded in freeing itself from these fetters.

We can best illustrate this superfluity of priestly zeal in that strange list of forms of invocation called *Indigitamenta*, which I have already explained with the help of

Wissowa.[37]   Working upon the old Roman animism,
and the popular fondness for formulae, the pontifices
drew up those lists in the fourth and third centuries
B.C., which have so seriously misled scholars as to the
genuine primitive religious ideas of the Romans.   They
are in the main priestly inventions, the work of ingenious
formulators.   We may even be tempted to look on them
as an attempt to rivet the yoke of priestly formalism on
the life of the individual as well as on the life of the
State as a whole.   But if ever this was the intention,
it was too late.   A people that was beginning to get
into touch with the civilisation of Hellas could not possibly
bear such a yoke.   In the last lecture we have already
seen a tendency towards emotional religion independent
of the old State worship ; the philosophy of individualism was to complete the work of emancipation in
the last two centuries B.C.   The old State religion remained, but in stunted form and with paralysed vitality ;
Rome was the scene of an *arrested religious development.*
The feeling, the religious instinct (*religio*) was indeed
there, though latent ; the Romans were human beings,
like the rest of us.   But as we go on with the story we
shall find that, when trouble or disaster brought it out of
its hiding-place, it was no longer possible to soothe it on
Roman principles or by Roman methods.   These methods
—in other words, the *ius divinum* as formulated by the
authorities—had been meant to soothe it, and had indeed
so effectually lulled it to sleep, that when at last it awoke
again they had lost the power of dealing with it.   When
the craving did come upon the Roman, which in time of
peril or doubt has come upon individuals and communities
in all ages, for support and comfort from the Unseen, it
had to be satisfied by giving him new gods to worship in
new ways, gods from Greece and the East, some of them
concealed under Latin names, but still aliens, not citizens
of his own State, aliens with whom he had little or
nothing in common, who had no home in his patriotic
feeling, no place in his religious experience.[38]   As I said

at the beginning of the last lecture, we must not under-rate the religiousness of the Roman character, which was never entirely lost ; but the secret of its comparative use-lessness lies in this—that the natural desire to be right with the Power manifesting itself in the universe, and to know more of that Power, became weakened and destroyed by an over-scrupulous attention to the means taken to realise it, and by the introduction of foreign methods which had no root in the mental fibre of the people, and reflected no part of its experience. Religion was effectually divorced from life and morality.

NOTES TO LECTURE XII

1. See Mulder, *De notione conscientiae, quae et qualis fuerit Romanis*, Leyden, 1908, cap. 2.   On p. 56 he quotes Luthard (*Die antike Ethik*, p. 131), who says of the Roman religion that it was even more an affair of the State than with any other people ; hence its peculiar legal character.   Though Mulder overworks his point, his chapter (especially p. 61 foll.) is full of interest.

2. Wissowa, *R.K.* p. 431.   The first chapter of Ambrosch's *Studien und Andeutungen*, in which the nature and history of the Regia was first really investigated, is still valuable.   An excellent short account is given by Mr. Marindin in his article in the *Dict. of Antiquities*, ed. 2.   It is now generally maintained that the Regia in historical times was rather a building for sacred purposes than a residence for a man and his family, and this I hold to be correct ; but it may for all that have originally been the residence of the Rex and of the Pont. Max. when the Rex had disappeared.

3. See Schanz, *Gesch. der röm. Literatur*, i. 43, where a succinct account is given of modern opinion as to the so-called *ius Papirianum*. The main argument for the late date of the collection is that Cicero does not seem to have known of it when he wrote the letter *ad Fam.* ix. 21 in 46 B.C.   This of course in no way affects the primitive character of the rules themselves.

4. The inference that the rules were found in the *Libri pontificum* is inevitable in any case, but seems proved by the fact that one of them, that relating to the *spolia opima*, is stated by Festus, p. 189 (*s.v.* "opima"), to have been extracted from those books.

5. Festus, *s.v.* "pellices" and *s.v.* "plorare," which latter word is interpreted as = *inclamare*.

6. The *divi parentum* are here generally taken as those of the particular family, and this may have been so; but cf. Wissowa, *R.K.* 192.

7. For the attempts of Pais in Italy and Lambert in France to date the Tables at the end of the fourth century or later, see Schanz, *op. cit.* i. 41. In Germany opinion is universally in favour of the traditional date.

8. See *Social Life at Rome in the Age of Cicero*, p. 135.

9. On the religious character of *confarreatio* see De Marchi, *La Religione nella vita privata*, i. p. 145 foll.

10. Cic. *de Domo*, 12. 14 ; Gellius, v. 19.

11. See, *e.g.* Launspach, *State and Family in Early Rome*, p. 256 foll. The last three chapters of this little book, on Patria potestas, Marriage, and Succession, will be found useful by those who cannot enter into the many disputes and difficulties which have arisen out of the attempts of writers on Roman law to adjust legal ideas to the dim early history of Rome. Binder, in his work *Die Plebs*, starts from the improbable hypothesis that the plebs was the population of the Latin part of the city as distinct from that Sabine part on the Quirinal, which he believes to have been the only patrician body ; and he further believes that the plebs lived originally under " Mutter-recht," the patres under "Vaterrecht." Such a condition of society would, of course, have greatly added to the pontifical work of religious adjustment ; it would have been more than even the pontifices could have successfully achieved.

12. See above, note 7. Binder, *Die Plebs*, p. 488 foll., discusses, and in the main rejects, the arguments of Pais and Lambert.

13. So Huvelin, in a paper in *L'Année sociologique*, 1905-6, p 1 foll., criticised by Hubert et Mauss, *Mélanges d'histoire des religions*, p. xxiii. foll.

14. From the religious point of view the *legis actiones* are best explained in Marquardt, 318 foll. Cp. Muirhead, *Roman Law*, ed. 1899, pp. 246-7 ; Greenidge, *Roman Public Life*, index *s.v.* "legis actio," and especially p. 87.

15. The famous passage of Pomponius is in the *Digest*, i. 2. 2, sec. 6 (for the work of Aelius, see *Dig.* i. 2, 2, 38) "ex his legibus . . . actiones compositae sunt, quibus inter se homines disceptarent : quas actiones ne populus prout vellet institueret, certas sollemnesque esse voluerunt. . . . Omnium tamen harum et interpretandi scientia et actiones apud collegium pontificum erant, ex quibus constituebatur, quis quoquo anno praeesset privatis."

16. Livy ix. 46 "civile ius, repositum in penetralibus pontificum, evulgavit (Cn. Flavius), fastosque circa forum in albo proponit, ut quando lege agi posset sciretur." Cp. Val. Max. ii. 5. 2. *Civile ius* is here usually taken as meaning the procedure ; but this is a passage which may give some countenance to those who would put the publication of the XII. Tables later than the traditional date.

17. For the relation of the Flamines, Vestals, and Rex sacrorum to the pontifex maximus, see Wissowa, *R.K.* 432 foll.

18. See above, p. 283. For the eclipse. Cic. *Rep.* i. 16. 25 ; and

for the various scientific determinations of its exact date, Schanz, *Gesch. der röm. Lit.* vol. i. (ed. 2) p. 37. " Ex hoc die," writes Cicero, " quem apud Ennium et in maximis annalibus consignatum videmus, superiores solis defectiones reputatae sunt."

19. Cic. *Brutus*, 55 " longe plurimum ingenio ualuisse."

20. *De Orat.* iii. 33. 134.

21. See *Dict. of Classical Biography*, *s.v.* " Coruncanius."

22. *Nat. deor.* ii. 165. Coruncanius is mentioned as one of those whom the gods love, if indeed they take an interest in human affairs.

23. See above, p. 100 foll. ; and *Roman Festivals*, p. 3.

24. Our knowledge of this *tabula* chiefly depends on a passage in the Danielian scholiast on Virg. *Aen.* i. 373 : " ita enim annales conficiebantur. Tabulam dealbatam quotannis pontifex maximus habuit, in qua praescriptis consulum nominibus et aliorum magistratum, digna memoratu notare consueverat domi militiaeque terra marique gesta per singulos dies. Cuius diligentiae annuos commentarios in octoginta libros veteres retulerunt, eosque a pontificibus maximis, a quibus fiebant, annales maximos appellarunt." The explanation of the name is no doubt wrong ; but all the rest of this passage can be relied on; cp. Cic. *de Orat.* ii. 12. 52 ; Dion. Hal. i. 73, 74 ; Gell. ii. 28. 6 ; Cic. *Legg.* i. 2. 6. For the idea of the almanac, see Cichorius in Pauly-Wissowa, *Real-Encycl.*, *s.v.* " annales maximi."

25. *Proponebat tabulam domi*, Cic. *de Orat.* ii. 12. 52. This must refer to the official residence of the Pont. Max. ; see above, p. 271.

26. These attempted solutions of an insoluble problem may be found in brief in Schanz, *Gesch. der röm. Lit.* i. 37. Perhaps the boldest is that of Cantorelli, that the annales were constructed not out of the tabula but out of the commentarii ; but this is in conflict with the passage in the scholiast on Virgil. To me the difficulty does not seem overwhelming ; events occurring " domi militiaeque, terra marique," may have filled considerable space, and yet have been meagre in the eyes of the rhetoricians of the last century B.C.

27. Schanz, *op. cit.* p. 35.

28. The great authority of the Pont. Max. is well shown in the story of Tremellius the praetor, who in the middle of the second century B.C. was fined (by a tribune ?) " quod cum M. Aemilio pontifice maximo iniuriose contenderat, sacrorumque quam magistratuum ius potentius fuit." Livy, *Epit.* 47.

29. *De aedibus sacris populi Romani*, p. 10 foll.

30. Aust, *op. cit.* p. 14 foll. See also *R.F.* p. 340 foll.

31. For Vacuna, Wissowa, *R.K.* pp. 44 and 128. She was later, but probably without good reason, identified with Victoria. The conjecture that she was a hearth deity rests on the lines of Ovid, *Fasti*, vi. 305, which I have before referred to in another context :

ante focos olim scamnis considere longis
  mos erat et mensae credere adesse deos.
nunc quoque cum fiunt antiquae sacra Vacunae,
  ante Vacunales stantque sedentque focos.

32. Aust, p. 14.   For Vertumnus the *locus classicus* is Propert.
v. 2.   It is not certain that the connection with gardens was
primitive.

33. *R.F.* p. 341.

34. *R.F.* p. 341.

35. See Axtell, *The Deification of Abstract Ideas in Roman
Literature and Inscriptions* (Chicago, 1907), p. 59 foll., where the
views of Mommsen, Boissier, Marquardt, and Wissowa are discussed.
Axtell's own conclusion is given on p. 62 foll.   In the main it seems
to agree with that hazarded in my *Roman Festivals*, p. 190.

36. For the evidence as to the contents of the *commentarii*, which
are now generally identified with the *libri*, see Wissowa, *R.K.*
32 and 441 ; Schanz, *op. cit.* i. 32 ; and the article " Commentarii "
in Pauly-Wissowa, *Real-Encycl.*   As Wissowa remarks (p. 441,
note 6), we are greatly in need of a complete collection of all
fragments of these archives.

37. See above, p. 159 foll.   The conviction that these lists are of
comparatively late and priestly origin, which has long been growing
on me, was originally suggested by the learned article " Indigitamenta " by R. Peter in Roscher's *Lexicon*, vol. ii. p. 175 foll.

38. I have here adopted some sentences from my article in the
Hibbert Journal for 1907, p. 854.

LECTURE XIII

THE AUGURS AND THE ART OF DIVINATION

" THE one great corruption to which all religion is exposed
is its separation from morality. The very strength of the
religious motive has a tendency to exclude, or disparage,
all other tendencies of the human mind, even the noblest
and best. It is against this corruption that the prophetic
order from first to last constantly protested. . . . Mercy
and justice, judgment and truth, repentance and goodness—not sacrifice, not fasting, not ablutions,—is the
burden of the whole prophetic teaching of the Old
Testament." [1]

The over-formalising, or ritualising, of any religion is
sure to bring about that result against which the Jewish
prophets protested. We saw at the end of the last lecture
how the pontifices contributed to such a result. We are
now to study the contribution of the other great college,
the augurs. For instead of developing, as did the wise
man or seer of Israel, into the mouthpiece of God in His
demand for the righteousness of man, the Roman diviner
merely assisted the pontifex in his work of robbing religion
of the idea of righteousness. Divination seems to be a
universal instinct of human nature, a perfectly natural
instinct, arising out of man's daily needs, hopes, fears ;
but though it may have had the chance, even at Rome,
it never has been able, except among the Jews, to emerge
from its cramping chrysalis of magic and become a really
valuable stimulant of morality.

By divination I mean the various ways and methods

by which, in all stages of his development, man has persuaded himself that what he is going to do or suffer will
turn out well or ill for him.   It is probably judicious, with
Dr. Tylor and with the majority of recent anthropologists,
to consider it as belonging to the region of magic ; [2] and
it is obvious that it affords excellent examples of that
inadequacy which characterises magical attempts to overcome the difficulties man meets with in his struggle for
existence.[3]   It belongs, like other forms of magic, to a
stage in which man's idea of his relation to the Power
manifesting itself in the universe is both rude and rudimentary.   But it shares with magic the power or property
of surviving, in form at least, through the animistic stage
into that of religion, and it is largely practised at the
present day even among highly civilised peoples.

But I must observe, before I go on, that divination as
an object of anthropological inquiry still stands in need of
a thorough scientific examination.   At present it seems
to puzzle anthropologists ; [4] and the reason probably is
that the material for studying it inductively has not as yet
been collected and sifted.   Strange to say, it does not
appear in the index to Dr. Westermarck's great work,
which I have so often quoted : it is hardly to be found
even in the *Golden Bough* : nor can I find a thoroughgoing treatment of it in any other books about the early
history of mankind.   And any sort of guesswork under
these circumstances only increases our difficulties.   Some
years ago the great German philosophical lawyer, von
Jhering, in an interesting work called the *Evolution of the
Aryan*, made some most ingenious attempts to explain
the origin of Roman divination.   He fancied that the
practice of examining the entrails of a victim, for example,
began in the course of Aryan migration, because when
you encamped in a new region you would catch and kill
some of the native cattle in order to see whether they
were wholesome enough to tempt you to stay.[5]   Again,
the study of the flight of birds was prompted by the desire
to get information about the mountain passes and the

course of great rivers ; and this study grew into an elaborate art as the leader of the host, the prototype of the Roman augur, gained experience by constant observation from elevated ground.[6]   Such a theory as this last might be worth something if it were based upon known facts ; as it is, it is only most ingenious guesswork.   This great legal writer did not know, as we do now, that divination by both these methods is found all over the world, and cannot be explained by any supposed needs of migrating Aryans.

Whatever be the origin of the several forms of divination, the object of the practice in ancient Italy and Greece is beyond doubt—to find out whether the Power with whom you wish to be in right relation is favourable to certain human operations, or willing to aid in removing certain forms of human suffering.   According to our definition, it was a part of religion, whether or no it belonged originally to magic.   It was a practical expression of that doubt or anxiety to which I believe the Romans attached the word *religio*.   In the agricultural period it must have been specially useful and even inevitable,[7] because the tiller of the soil is always in need of knowledge as to the best times and seasons for his operations, and his out-of-door life gives him constant opportunity of observing natural phenomena, *diosemeia*, signs from heaven, and the utterances and movements of birds and other animals.   It is interesting to reflect that these last may often be of real service in foretelling the weather, which is so important to the farmer.   As I write this on a December day I recall the fact that I have myself within the last week successfully foretold a spell of cold after observing a great arrival of winter thrushes from the north.   This particular branch of augury is, in fact, neither so inadequate nor so absurd as most others.   Von Jhering may turn out to be right in his notion that at least some forms of divination have their origin in practical needs and in the skill of uncivilised man in discerning the signs of the weather—a skill which it is well to remember

far exceeds that of the house-dweller of modern civilisation.   But with the growth of the City-state and the
habits of life in a town, these early instincts and methods
of the agriculturist came to be caught up into a system
of religious practice, adapted to the conditions of civil and
political existence ; thus they gradually lost their original
meaning and such real value as they ever possessed.   I
have pointed out that the Roman festivals and the ritual of
the oldest calendar gradually got out of relation with the
agricultural life in which they for the most part originated :[8] so it was with divination, which in the hands of
the State authorities became formalised into a set of rules
for ascertaining the good-will of the gods, and obtaining
their sanction for the operations of the community, which
had no scientific basis whatever, no relation to truth and
fact.   Of all the methods for putting yourself in right
relation with the Power, this was the least valuable, and
indeed the most harmful ; it came in course of time to be
a positive obstacle to efficiency and freedom of action, it
wasted valuable time, and it often served as the means of
promoting private ends to the detriment of the public
interest.

Before I go on to consider the development of the
highly formalised system of public divination, let me clear
the ground by a few remarks about such forms of the
practice as were not sanctioned by the State.   That these
existed throughout Roman history there is no doubt, as
they existed in Greece, among the Jews, and elsewhere in
the East, alongside of the advanced and organised methods
of official and authorised experts.

Our information about private divination is scattered
about in Roman literature, and even when brought together there is not a great deal of it.   What is prominent
both in Roman literature and Roman history is the
divination authorised by the State and systematised by
its authorities ; even in Cicero's treatise *de Divinatione*,
though the subject-matter is of a general kind, drawn
from Greece as well as Rome, it is, I think, apart from

philosophical questions, chiefly the art of augurs and haruspices that interests the writer, who was himself an augur when he wrote it. In Greek literature exactly the opposite is the case ; there we hear little of State-author-ised divination, and a great deal of wandering sooth-sayers, soothsaying families, and oracles which (except at Delphi) were not under the direct control of a City-state.[9] The methods of divination are much the same in both peninsulas, and indeed vary little all the world over ; the difference lies simply in this,—that at Rome the adoption and systematisation by the State of certain methods, especially those which dealt with birds and lightning, had the effect of discrediting, if not excluding, an immense amount of private practice of this kind. I mean that if the State strongly sanctions some forms of divination, working them by its own officials, it casts a shadow of discredit over the rest. As the *ius divinum* tended to exclude magic and the barbarous in ritual, so did the *ius augurale*, which was a part of it, exclude the quack in divination. And in this particular department of human delusion the result may be said to have been happy ; for though divination belongs to religion as having survived from an earlier stage into a religious one, yet it is the least valuable, the least fruitful, part of it.[10] True, the augural systematisation, as we shall see, had a sinister effect on political progress ; but even there the very emptiness and absurdity of the whole business helped to bring contempt on it, and, as Cicero tells us in a well-known passage, even old Cato declared that he could not imagine why a *haruspex* did not laugh when he met a brother of the craft.[11] In Greece, on the contrary, it might, I believe, be shown that the absence of system-atisation by the State only served to prolong the credit and influence of the professional quack.

Greece was at all periods full of these quacks ; did the sham prophet exist at Rome in the period we have now under review ? Later on the Oriental soothsayer found his way there ; of these *Chaldaei* and *mathematici* I shall have a word to say in another lecture, and we shall see how the State authorities made occasional attempts to exclude them. Of the *frantic* type of diviner, the ἔνθεος, so common in Greece, we hear nothing in the sober Roman annals ; the idea of a human being " possessed by a spirit of divination " seems foreign to the Roman character.[12] The only soothsayer, so far as I know, who appears in Roman legend in a private capacity is that Attus Navius who gave Tarquinius Priscus the benefit of his knowledge; and he is represented as a respectable Sabine, and his art as an augural one learnt from the Etruscans.[13] There are, indeed, ancient traces of a prophetic art at Rome, but, as the historian of divination has well observed, they are all connected not with human beings, but with divinities, a fact which explains the Latin word *divinatio*.[14] To take what is perhaps the best example, the ancient deity Carmenta, who had a flamen and a double festival in the month of January, may very probably represent some dim tradition of a *numen* at whose shrine women might gain some knowledge as to their fortunes in childbirth, just as outside Rome, at Praeneste and Antium, Fortuna seems to have had this gift in historical times.[15] So St. Augustine interpreted Carmenta,[16] probably following Varro ; and to Virgil she was the " *vates fatidica*, cecinit quae prima futuros Aeneadas magnos et nobile Pallanteum."

But Carmenta, Picus, Faunus, are dim mythical figures which for us can have no bearing on Roman religious experience ; it would be more to the point to ask what was the original meaning and history of the word *vates*, if the question were answerable in the absence of an early Roman literature. All we can say about this is that this word had, as a rule, a certain dignity about it, which enabled it eventually to stand for a poet, and that it rarely has a sinister sense, unless accompanied by some adjective specially used in order to give it.[17] The real word for a quack is *hariolus*, and the fact that it is comparatively rare suggests that the character it expresses was not a common one. It occurs here and there in fragments of old plays, where, unluckily, we cannot be quite sure whether it represents a Greek or a Latin idea. The following lines from the Telamo of Ennius shows us the *hariolus*, as well as the word *vates* with a discreditable adjective attached :

> sed superstitiosi vates impudentesque harioli
> aut inertes, aut insani, aut quibus egestas imperat,
> qui sibi semitam non sapiunt, alteri mostrant viam,
> quibu' divitias pollicentur, ab iis drachmam ipsi petunt.[18]

A more satisfactory bit of evidence as to the existence of the quack in the second century B.C., when Greece and the East were beginning to pour their unauthorised religionists into Italy, is the interesting passage in old Cato's book on agriculture, in which he urges that the bailiff of an estate should not be permitted to consult either a *haruspex, augur, hariolus*, or *Chaldaeus*.[19] But on the whole, such little evidence as we possess seems to confirm the view I hazarded just now, that the overwhelming prestige of State authority at Rome discouraged and discredited the quack diviner both in public and private life. His work in private life was largely that of fortune-telling, of foretelling the future in one sense or another ; and this was exactly what the State authorities never did and never countenanced, at any rate until the stress of the Hannibalic war, and then only in a very limited sense. Their object was a strictly religious one, to get the sanction of the divine members of the community for the undertakings of the human ones. Even the so-called Sibylline oracles, as we saw, were not prophecies ; and the augural art never provided an answer to the question, " What is going to happen ? " but only to that much more religious one, " Are the deities willing that we should do this or that ? "[20]

But before I leave the subject of private divination, I must note that there was a department of it which may be called legitimate, as distinguished from that of the quack. I mean the *auspicia* of the family religion, and also the comparatively harmless folklore about omens of all sorts and kinds.

Naturally we have little information about legitimate *auspicia* in the life of the family ; but we have seen that the religious instinct of the Roman forbade him to face any important undertaking or crisis without making sure of the sanction of the *numina* concerned, and among the methods of insurance (if I may use a convenient word) the *auspicia* must have had a place from the earliest times. No important thing was done, says Cicero in the *de Divinatione*, "nisi auspicato, ne privatim quidem." [21] Valerius Maximus says the same in so many words, and some other evidence has been collected by De Marchi in his work on the private religion of the Romans.[22] But only in the case of marriage do we hear of *auspicia* in historical times, and even there they seem to have degenerated into a mere form. "Auspices nuptiarum, re omissa, nomen tantum tenent"—so Cicero wrote of his own time ; [23] he seems to be thinking of augury by means of birds, for he adds, "nam ut nunc extis sic tunc avibus magnae res impetrari solebant." As we have already seen, the object of the examination of a victim's entrails was simply to ascertain its fitness to be offered ; but by Cicero's time the Etruscan art of divination by this method must have penetrated into private life. I think we may conjecture that in the life of the family on the land the *auspicia*, as the word itself implies, were worked chiefly by observation of birds. Nigidius Figulus, the learned mystic of Cicero's time, wrote a book, *de Augurio Privato*, of which one fragment survives which has to do with this kind of divination, and with the distinction between omens from birds seen on the right or left, and from high or low flyers.[24] In the familiar ode of Horace beginning, "Impios parrae recinentis omen," [25] the *corvus* and *cornix* are mentioned besides the *parra*, and in that wholesome old out-of-door life of the farm, as I said just now, there was a certain basis of truth and fact in the observation of such presages. But Horace mentions other animals, wolf, fox, and snake, and some at least of the folklore about omens which is to be found in Pliny's descriptions of animals may help us to appreciate the nature of the old Roman ideas on this subject. The tiller of the land and the shepherd on the uplands used their eyes and ears, not wholly without advantage to themselves; but in the life of the city such observation became gradually formal and meaningless, and degenerated into the superstition reflected in Horace's ode. I must parenthetically confess to a personal feeling of regret that this people, who in their early days had good opportunities, made little or no contribution to the knowledge of animals and their habits.[26] But I must pass on to the more important subject of divination as developed and formalised by the authorities of the State.

In explaining the ritual of the *ius divinum* I laid stress on the fact that its main object was to maintain the *pax deorum*, the right relation between the divine and human citizens.[27] To make this *pax* secure, it was necessary that in every public act the good-will of the gods should be ascertained by obtaining favourable auspices—it must be done *auspicato*. To take the first illustration that occurs, Livy describes a dictator about to fight a battle as leaving his camp *auspicato*, after sacrificing to obtain the *pax deorum*.[28] It is for this reason that the *auspicia* have a leading place in the foundation legends of the city. We are all familiar with the story of the *auspicia* of Romulus and Remus, which goes back at least as far as Ennius; [29] and we find them also in the foundation of *coloniae* in historical times.[30] I do not know that I can better express the place which the *auspicia* occupied in the mind of the Roman than by quoting the words which Livy puts into the mouth of Appius Claudius in 367 B.C., when supposed to be inveighing against the opening of the consulship to plebeians: "Auspiciis hanc urbem conditam esse, auspiciis bello ac pace, domi militiaeque, omnia geri, quis est qui ignoret?" He goes on to argue that these *auspicia* belong to patricians only, that no plebeian magistrate is created *auspicato*, that the man who wants to allow plebeians to become curule magistrates, *tollit ex civitate auspicia*. "Nunc nos, tanquam iam nihil pace deorum opus sit, omnes caerimonias polluimus." [31]   This is, of course, only Livy's rhetoric, but it represents the fundamental Roman idea of the public *auspicia.*

The passage is also useful because it alludes to the fact that the right of taking the *auspicia* belonged ultimately to the whole patrician body of fully qualified citizens.[32] But so far as we can discern in the dim light of the earliest period, this body entrusted the right and duty to its chief magistrate, the Rex, exactly as it entrusted him with the *imperium*, the supreme power of command in civil matters.   Thus the *auspicia* and the *imperium* were indissolubly connected ; as Dr. Greenidge says,[33] " they are the divine and human side of the same power," and may be found together in a thousand passages in Roman literature and inscriptions.   But at the side of the Rex we find, according to tradition, two helpers or advisers called *augures*, the three together perhaps forming a *collegium.*[34]   Now there was certainly an important difference between the Rex and the augurs ; the latter were aiders and interpreters, but the Rex only was said *habere auspicia*, just as the whole patrician body had this right, though they delegated it to the Rex during his lifetime, and on his death received it again.   The man who " habet auspicia " has the right of *spectio, i.e.* of taking the auspices in a particular case,[35] of watching the sky or the conduct of the sacred fowls in eating ; this right the augurs never had.   Their power was limited to guidance and interpretation.   This follows necessarily from the fundamental principle that the *auspicia* and the *imperium* were indissolubly connected ; for the augur, of course, never possessed the *imperium* by virtue of his office.   It is true that of the augur in the regal period we know almost nothing ; his art, as we shall see directly, was kept strictly secret, and he was bound by oath not to reveal it.[36] But we may safely argue back in general terms from the relation of magistrate and augur under the later Republic to the relation of augur and Rex, from whom descended the magistrate's *imperium*.   The one essential thing to remember is that *it was in all periods the magistrate who was responsible*, under the sanction and advice of his assistants the pontifices and augurs, for the maintenance of the *pax deorum*.   The lay element in the actual working of the constitution never lost this prerogative.   Rome was never hierarchically governed.

It would be going beyond the scope of these lectures if I were to plunge at this point into the thorny question of the exact relation between magistrate and augur in respect of details.   Nor do I propose to go into the minutiae of augural lore, which are not instructive, like those of sacrifice, for our survey of Roman religious experience.   It will be sufficient to state in outline what I believe to be necessary for our purpose.[87]   The person who had the *auspicia, i.e.* originally the Rex, like the later magistrate, had to watch for signs from heaven ; in order to do so he marked out a *templum*, a rectangular space, by noting certain objects, trees or what not, beyond which, whether he looked at earth or sky, he need take no notice of what he saw.   The spot where he took up his position for this purpose was itself a rectangular space,[88] marked out on a similar principle ; in each case the space was *liberatus effatus, i.e.* freed from previous associations by a form of words, and ready, if need were (as in the case of *loca sacra*) to be further handed over to the deities as their property ; this consecration, however, did not, of course, follow in the ordinary procedure of the *auspicia*. In the *urbana auspicia* all *loca effata* must be within the sacred boundary of the *pomoerium*.   Within this the magistrate watched in silence at the dead of night for such signs as he especially asked for (*auspicia impetrativa*) ; those which offered themselves without such specification (*oblativa*) he was not bound to take cognisance of unless some one claimed his attention for them.   The signs were originally in the regal period, if we may guess from the word *auspicium*, only such as birds supplied, and the space in which they were watched for was not complicated by the divisions of the later augural art.[39]   The business of the augur was, we may suppose, to see that the details were carried out correctly, and to interpret the signs ; but those signs were not sent to *him*, for he was not the actual representative of the State in this ritual.

If the constitutional position and duty of the augurs have now been made sufficiently clear, I may go on to explain briefly, as in the case of the pontifices, how the office became gradually secularised, and the duty formalised, so that if there ever had been anything of a really religious character in this art, any genuine belief in the manifestation by the Power of his will in matters of State life, such character, such belief, had become by the second century B.C. entirely paralysed and destroyed. But the history of the augurate is much more difficult to follow than that of the pontificate.   The work of the pontifices touched the life of every day, public and private, at many points, with the result that their secrets ceased to be secrets by the end of the fourth century B.C. The work of the augurs was occasional, and more technical than that of the other college ; it can hardly be said to have affected the religion of family life, nor did it continually bear upon public life, as did the pontifical knowledge of the *ius divinum* and the calendar.   Hence the augural lore was never published, under pressure of public opinion, and neither ancient nor modern scholars have had to waste their time in investigating it.   Books were indeed written about it in later times by one or two curious students, but in the time of Cicero, who was himself an augur, the neglect of it was general, even by members of the college.[40]

This mysterious augural lore was preserved in books, like that of the pontifices ; and in all probability these books were put together in the same period as the latter, viz., the two centuries immediately following the abolition of the kingship.[41]   I think there is a strong probability that the augurate emerged from the age of Etruscan rule which marks the latter part of the kingly period, with increased importance and fresh activity, the result of immediate contact with Etruscan methods of divination.[42] It is likely that they began in this way to cultivate the art of divination by lightning, which was peculiarly Etruscan, and to divide their *templum* into *regiones*, which, as I said just now, were not apparently needed for the observation of omens from birds.   How far they carried this art we cannot tell, owing to the loss of their books and the commentaries upon them ; but about the Etruscan discipline we do know something.   Those who wish to have a glimpse of it may consult the first chapter of the fourth volume of Bouché-Leclercq's *History of Divination*, as a more intelligible account than any known to me.[43]   But all I need to insist on now is the likelihood that the augurs began the Republican period with a power of interpretation which was the more important because the art was changed ; it is now the depository not only of the old bird lore, but of the new lightning lore.   And as this last became the peculiar characteristic of the art of public divination, and as the augurs were, like the pontifices, a close self-electing corporation until 104 B.C. and a close self-electing *patrician* body until the lex Ogulnia of 300 B.C., holding secret meetings every month on the *arx*,[44] and recording their lore in books which were never made public, they might well have grown into a powerful hierarchy, *if they had only been possessed of the right of spectio*.   What saved Rome from this fate was simply the fact that the college was a body of interpreters only, or, in other words, the principle that the *auspicia* belonged exclusively to the magistrate.   The *auspicia* were in fact a matter of public law, not of religion, properly speaking ; the idea on which they were based, that the sanction of the deities was needed for every public action, very early lost its true significance, and the process of taking them became a mere form, the religious character of which was almost entirely forgotten. They ceased to be matter of religion just as the amulet

or any other form of preventive magic fails to be
reckoned as within the sphere of religion; the feeling
was there that they must be attended to (though even
that feeling lost its strength in course of time), but only
as a matter of custom, not because the Power was really
believed to sanction an act in this way.

Thus it seems that the importance of the augurs
belongs to Roman public law, and not to the history of
Roman religious experience.   It will be found fully
explained, in that connection, in Mommsen's *Staatsrecht*,
or in Dr. Greenidge's volume on *Roman Public Life*.[45]
All we have to note here is the complete secularisation
of what was once really a part of the Roman religion;
the augurs themselves were public men and could hold
magistracies, and their art of interpretation came to be
used for secular and political purposes only.   They
could declare a magistrate *vitio creatus*, whether they
had been present at the taking of the auspices or not;
they could also on appeal stop the proceedings at a
public assembly, whether for election or legislation; it
may be said of them that in one way or another they
had a veto on every public transaction.[46]   As Cicero
expresses it in his *ius divinum*, in the second book of his
work on the constitution: " Quae augur iniusta nefasta
vitiosa dira defixerit inrita infectaque sunto, quique non
paruerit, capital esto." [47]   But in spite of the fine words
iniusta nefasta vitiosa, there was no religious principle
involved in this solemn injunction.   When Bibulus in 59
B.C. sought as consul to stop Caesar's proceedings by
using his right of *spectio*, all he had to do was to announce
that he was going to look for lightning (*obnuntiare*);
and if there had been the smallest remnant of religious
belief left in the Roman mind about such transactions,
it would quietly have acquiesced, in the conviction that
Jupiter would send lightning to the Roman magistrate
who asked for it; as it was, Caesar took no notice, and
the Roman people only laughed.   Caesar was at the
time, let us note, the head of the Roman religion, ponti-

fex maximus. So with the augurs as the interpreters of the magisterial *spectio* ; proud as Cicero was of becoming an augur, with all the old surviving elective ritual,[48] he never, we may be sure, believed for a moment that he had the power of interpreting the will of the gods. A century before his augurship the whole business of public divination had been regulated by statute, like any other secular matter ; and in his own day it was an open question with men of education whether there were such a thing as divination at all.[49] True, as we shall see, the *illegitimate* forms of divination were at this very time gaining ground, as the current of superstition increased in strength which marks this last period of the republic ; but the augur's art and the *spectio* of the magistrate were still surviving as mere constitutional fossils, and were not destined to share largely in Augustus' heroic attempt to put fresh life into the *ius divinum*. *Vile damnum*, as Tacitus said of the foreign quacks banished to Sardinia by Tiberius ; for neither in the sphere of religion nor later in that of politics can the art of divination be said to have had any lasting value.

I have not dealt at any length with the augurs and the State system of divination, but I hope I have said enough to show that, as I hinted at the beginning of this lecture, it affords an excellent illustration of the way in which the religious instinct, the desire to be in right relation with the Power manifesting itself in the universe, was first soothed and satisfied, then hypnotised and paralysed, by the formalisation and gradual secularisation of religious processes. The desire to obtain the sanction of the Power by seeking for favourable signs or omens seems to be a universal instinct of human nature, though a perverse one ; if left to itself it will apparently pass into the region of harmless folklore, where it does not seriously interfere with human progress, either secular or religious ; but where, as at Rome, it is taken up into the ritual of a religious system, and is further allowed to express itself mechanically in the region of public law, it exhausts itself rapidly, loses all its original significance, and becomes a clog on human progress.

In ancient Italy this instinct for divination was nowhere so strongly and so perversely developed into a mechanical system as in Etruria, and it is highly probable that this development contributed largely to the rapid political and moral decay of the Etruscan people. The narrow aristocratic constitution of the Etruscan cities, worked by a kind of priestly nobility, seems to have afforded great opportunities for the cultivation of the perverse art which (as we are now beginning to recognise) this people had brought with them from the East.[50] I have already suggested that an Etruscan dominion at Rome had very probably unfortunate results in developing and formalising the art of the augurs. But the age of the Tarquinii was not the only one in which the sinister influence of this strange people was brought to bear on Roman religious institutions ; and before I close this lecture I must say a very few words about a second invasion of Etruscan perversity, which began some two centuries and a half later. This was the result of that renewed *religio*, that feeling of anxiety and sometimes of despair characteristic of the last half of the third century B.C., the perilous era of the Punic wars, with which I shall deal more particularly in the next lecture. The state religion could not soothe it ; neither pontifices nor augurs had any sufficient native remedy for it, and as the ritual of worship was reinforced from Greece and the East, so the ritual of divination was reinforced from Etruria.

The Etruscans seem to have educated their diviners with care and system. We do not know the details of such education, but it seems likely that there were schools of these prophets, by means of which the art was handed down and developed.[51] The word for the person thus trained was *haruspex* in its Italian form as known to us, though it had an Etruscan original.[52] The art acquired was of three kinds—the interpretation of lightning ; the explanation and interpretation of the entrails of victims, and especially of the liver ; and, thirdly, the explanation and expiation of portents and prodigia.[53]   All three departments seem to have been carried to an extreme degree of perverse development.   To give an idea of it I need but refer to recent discussions of the relation between the divisions marked on a bronze model of a victim's liver (found in 1877 at Piacenza), in which are written the Etruscan names of a great number of deities, and the somewhat similar divisions of the templum of the heavens as given by Martianus Capella in explanation of the celestial dwellings of the Italian deities.   A study of this unprofitable subject, of which the only interest lies in the illustration it offers of the prostitution of human ingenuity, will be found in a little work by Carl Thulin, published in the series called *Religionsgeschichtliche Versuche und Vorarbeiten.*[54]

Just as the Roman authorities had recourse from time to time to the Sibylline books, so also they occasionally, though not apparently before the Punic wars, sought the help of the trained Etruscan diviners.   We shall come across instances of this in the next two lectures, and I need not specify them now.   They seem to have used their art in all its departments ; and in the most degraded of these, the examination of entrails, it was found so convenient to have their services in a campaign that in course of time one at least seems to have accompanied every Roman army.[55]   The complicated art of augury might in fact be dispensed with if you had a *haruspex* ready and willing at a moment's notice to give you a good report of the victim's liver.   To keep up the supply of experts, the senate, probably in the second century B.C., determined to select and train ten boys of noble family in each Etruscan city.   This was the last service that the degenerate Etruscan people rendered to its conquerors, and a more degrading one it is impossible to imagine. These foreign diviners were never admitted to the dignity of a *collegium* ;[56] they rather played the part of the domestic chaplain kept to say grace before meat.   For a moment they attract our attention in connection with the persecution of Cicero by his political enemies, and the *consecratio* after his exile of the site of his house on the Palatine hill.[57]   For a moment again we meet with them in the reign of Claudius, who was interested in the Etruscans and wrote a work about them, and once raised the question in the senate of the revival of the haruspices and their art—such part of it, at least, as might seem worth preserving—" ne vetustissima Italiae disciplina per desidium exolesceret." [58]   And strange to say, though in fact no part of this ancient Italian discipline was in the least worth preserving, it survived in outward form into the fourth century of the empire.[59]   We read with astonishment in the code of the Christian emperor Theodosius, that if the imperial palace or other public buildings are struck by lightning the haruspices are to be consulted, according to ancient custom, as to the meaning of the portent.[60]   Thirteen years after the death of Theodosius, in 408, Etruscan experts offered their services to Pompeianus, prefect of Rome, to save the city from the Goths.   Pompeianus was tempted, but consulted Innocent, the Bishop of Rome, who " did not see fit to oppose his own opinion to the wishes of the people at such a crisis, but stipulated that the magic rites should be performed secretly."   What followed is uncertain.   " The Christian historian says that the rites were performed, but were unavailing ; the pagan Zosimus affirms that the aid of the Tuscans was declined." [61]   So hard died the futile arts of the most unfruitful of all Italian races.

NOTES TO LECTURE XIII

1. Stanley's *Jewish Church* (ed. 1906), vol. i. p. 398 foll.

2. *Hist. de divination dans l'antiquité*, vol. i. p. 7 foll. ; divination is " contemplative," magic " active."   But this learned author did not deal with divination except as it existed in Greece and Italy ; and in view of our present extended knowledge this differentia is not instructive.

3. See Tylor's article in the last edition of the *Encyclopaedia Britannica*, and his *Gifford Lectures*, Pt. ii. ch. iv. ; Haddon, *Magic and Fetishism*, p. 40. Bouché-Leclercq, *Hist. de divination dans l'antiquité*, vol. i. p. 7, distinguishes divination from magic ; but his knowledge of the subject was limited to civilised races.

4. Mr. Marett seems doubtful about it : see his *Threshold of Religion*, pp. 42 and 83. In the latter passage he says that it may or may not be treated as a branch of magic, and may be " originally due to some dim sort of theorising about causes, the theory engendering the practice rather than the practice the theory." I should doubt whether, when the facts have been fully collected, this will be the conclusion to which they point.

5. *Evolution of the Aryan*, Drucker's translation, p. 369.

6. *Ib.* pp. 364, 374.

7. A curious survival of divination from the agricultural period, which was taken over by the State, but not fixed to a day in the calendar, is the *augurium canarium*. The exta of red puppies which had been sacrificed were consulted, apparently with a view to ascertain the probability of the corn ripening well (Festus, p. 285, quoting Ateius Capito). See *R.F.* p. 90, and the references there given ; also Cic. *de Legibus*, ii. 20 ; Fest. 379 ; and Wissowa in Pauly-Wissowa, p. 2328.

8. See above, p. 102.

9. See Dr. Jevons' account in Gardner and Jevons, *Manual of Greek Antiquities*, ch. vii.

10. Bouché-Leclercq in the introduction to his first volume (p. 3) expresses a different opinion. He thinks that the benefit conferred by divination in the conduct of life was the most valuable part of religion. With this I entirely disagree.

11. Cic. *de Divinatione*, ii. 51.

12. See Bouché-Leclercq, iv. 119 foll. In a recently published essay, *De antiquorum daemonismo*, by J. Tamburnino (Giessen, 1909), the only genuine Roman evidence adduced of possession is Minucius Felix, *Octavius*, ch. 27, *i.e.* it belongs to the late second century A.D. In the so-called Italian oracles there is no question of it : *e.g.* the lots at Praeneste were worked by a boy (Cic. *de Div.* ii. 86).

13. Livy i. 36 ; Cic. *de Div.* i. 17. It is Dion. Hal. iii. 70 who says that his art was Etruscan.

14. Bouché-Leclercq, iv. 120.

15. For Carmenta see *R.F.* 167 and 291 foll. For Fortuna, *ib.* 223 foll. ; cp. 170 foll.

16. Aug. *de Civ. Dei*, iv. 11 ; he uses the plural *Carmentes* ; see *R.F.* as above. Virgil, *Aen.* viii. 336.

17. As " superstitiosi vates " in the passage of Ennius quoted below. In his imaginary *ius divinum* Cicero uses the word for " fatidici " authorised by the State (*de Legg.* ii. 20). He is perhaps thinking of the haruspices.

18. Ribbeck, *Fragm. tragicorum Romanorum*, p. 55. For
hariolus outside the play-writers, Cic. *de Nat. Deor.* i. 20. 55, where
it is combined with haruspices, augures, vates, and coniectores (interpreters of dreams).   *Ad Att.* viii. 11. 3.

19. Cato, *R.R.* ch. 54 ; cp. Columella, i. 8 and xi. 1.

20. See P. Regell, *De augurum publicorum libris*, p. 6 "Omnia
illa auguria quae futurarum rerum aliquid predicunt . . . augurum
publicorum disciplinae abroganda sunt : aut privati sunt augurii, aut
Tuscorum disciplinae." Cp. Cic. *de Har. Resp.* 9. 18.

21. Cic. *de Div.* i. 16. 28 ; Val. Max. ii. 1. 1.

22. *La Religione nella vita domestica*, i. 153 foll. ; 232 foll.

23. Cic. *de Div.* i. 16, 28.

24. This fragment is preserved in Gellius vii. 6. 10. Nigidius
may be responsible for many of Pliny's omens. Regell, *op. cit.* p. 8.

25. Hor. *Odes*, iii. 27. 1 foll.

26. Exactly the same misfortune occurred in the middle ages.
The monks had abundant opportunity of observation, but were
occupied with other matters, and have left behind them no works on
natural history.

27. See above, p. 169 foll.

28. Livy vi. 12.

29. See the fragment of Ennius' *Annales* in Cic. *de Div.* i. 107.

30. Wissowa, *R.K.* p. 450 ; *Lex coloniae Genetivae*, 66 and 67.

31. Livy vi. 41.

32. See a good account in the *Dict. of Antiquities*, vol. i. 252 and
255 ; and Wissowa in Pauly-Wissowa, *s.v.* "auspicia."

33. *Roman Public Life*, p. 162.

34. Wissowa, *R.K.* 451, note 2 ; Marq. 241.

35. Mommsen, *Staatsrecht*, i. 86.

36. Wissowa, *R.K.* 451, note 7 ; Plut. *Quaest. Rom.* 99 ; Pliny,
Ep. 4. 8. Plutarch asks why an augur can never be deprived of his
office, and answers that the secrecy of his art made it impossible.
Cp. Paulus, 16.

37. The latest authoritative account of the auspicia is in Pauly-
Wissowa, *s.v.*, where the necessary literature and material will be
found for a study of an extremely complicated subject.

38. The technical term was *templum minus*, in contradistinction
to the *templum maius*, *i.e.* the space in which he was to look for
signs. See Bouché-Leclercq, iv. 197 ; Fest. 157. The usual place
was the *arx*, where was the *auguraculum*, on which the magistrate
taking the auspices "pitched his tent" (*tabernaculum*), looking to
the east, with the north as his left or lucky side. Von Jhering, *op.
cit.* p. 364, makes some ingenious use of this procedure to support
his theory that the origin of such institutions is to be found in the
period of migration.

39. That the division of the *templum* into *regiones* was necessary
only for the *auguria caelestia*, and not for the observation of birds,

is the conclusion drawn by Wissowa (*R.K.* 457, note 2) from the words of Cicero (*de Legibus*, ii. 21) in his *ius divinum* : " caelique fulgura regionibus ratis temperanto " (*i.e.* the magistrates).

40. Cicero expressly says that even old Cato complained of the neglect of the auspicia by the college : *de Div.* i. 15. 28 ; above, in sec. 25, he had said the same thing of the augurs of his own day, *i.e.* including himself. We know of a work on the *auspicia* by M. Messalla, an augur, from which Gellius, xiii. 15, quotes a lengthy extract (cp. ch. 14). This man was consul in 53 B.C. ; Schanz, *Gesch. der röm. Lit.*, ii. 492. Just at the same time Appius Claudius, Cicero's predecessor as governor of Cilicia, wrote *libri augurales*, to which Cicero more than once alludes in his correspondence with Appius : *ad Fam.* iii. 9. 3 and 11. 4. It is plain that the old augural lore is now treated only as a curiosity, of which the secrecy need no longer be respected.

41. P. Regell, *De augurum publicorum libris*, whose excellent little work has never been superseded, thinks (p. 19) that the *libri* were the result of the neglect of the art, *i.e.* that it was necessary to put it in writing, because otherwise it would be forgotten. " Tota eius vita," he says, "lenta est mors." The lore was complete about the time of the decemvirate, but *decreta* must have been continually added (p. 23). The nucleus may be represented in Cicero, *de Legibus*, ii. 20. 21, and perhaps existed in Saturnian verse (Festus, 290). The additions in the way of decree or comment would probably range over the fourth and third centuries B.C. like those of the pontifices. No doubt the Hannibalic war had the effect of diminishing the importance of the lore, as the next lecture should show. On the whole we may put the great period of the college between the decemvirate and the war with Hannibal.

42. This is the opinion of Bouché-Leclercq, *op. cit.* vol. iv. p. 205 foll. ; cp. Wissowa, *R.K.* p. 457. Cicero calls the augurs "interpretes Iovis Optimi maximi" (*de Legibus*, ii. 20), and herein could hardly have made a mistake, as he was himself an augur. As the great deity was of Etruscan origin in this form, I should conjecture that the college took new ground and gained new influence under the Etruscan dynasty.

43. Cp. also Müller-Deecke, *Die Etrusker*, ii. 165 foll. Our knowledge comes chiefly from the learned but obscure writer Martianus Capella (ed. Eyssenhardt), who wrote under the later Empire.

44. For these meetings see Cic. *de Div.* i. 41. 90 ; Regell, p. 23. They were obsolete in Cicero's time, but seem to have still existed in the time of Scipio Aemilianus : Cic. *Lael.* 2. 7.

45. *Staatsrecht*, i. 73 foll. ; Greenidge, *Roman Public Life*, p. 172 foll.

46. The best account of the constitutional power of the augurs is in Pauly-Wissowa, *Real-Encyclopädie*, *s.v.* "augur," vol. i. p. 2334 foll.; cp. Wissowa, *R.K.* 457-8.

47. *De Legibus*, ii. 21.

48. The outward form of *co-optatio* was still preserved, like our "election" of a bishop by a chapter. Cicero was co-opted by Hortensius after nomination by two other augurs. See his interesting account of this in his *Brutus*, ch. i. The survival may be taken as throwing light on the original secrecy and closeness of the *collegium*.

49. For the *leges Aelia et Fufia*, cf. Greenidge, *op. cit.* p. 173. The Stoics of the last century B.C. were divided on this point. See below, p. 399. In the second book of his *de Divinatione*, following the Academic or agnostic school, he himself confutes his brother Quintus' argument for divination contained in Bk. I.

50. This is the view of Thulin, *Die Götter des Martianus Capella und der Bronzeleber von Piacenza* (Giessen, 1906), p. 7 foll., and it seems at present to hold the field : see Gruppe, *Die mythologische Literatur aus den Jahren 1898-1905*, p. 336.

51. Müller-Deecke, vol. ii. p. 7 foll.

52. See Deecke's note on p. 12 of Müller-Deecke, vol. ii. It is possibly connected with *hariolus*.

53. Wissowa, *R.K.* p. 470, and Müller-Deecke, vol. ii. 165 foll.

54. See above, note 50.

55. References to Livy will be found in Wissowa, *R.K.* p. 473, note 11. One of these, to Livy xxvii. 16. 14, is worth quoting as suggesting that a *haruspex* might give useful advice in spite of his art : "Hostia quoque caesa consulenti (Fabio) deos haruspex, cavendum a fraude hostili et ab insidiis, praedixit."

56. They were not *sacerdotes publici Romani*, nor is a *collegium* mentioned till the reign of Claudius : Tac. *Ann.* xi. 15. The proper term seems to have been *ordo*, which occurs in inscriptions of the Empire : Marq. p. 415.

54. See the oration *De haruspicum responsis* (especially 5. 9), the genuineness of which is now generally acknowledged. Asconius quotes it as Cicero's (ed. Clark, p. 70) : so also Quintilian, v. 11. 42.

58. Tac. *Ann.* 11. 15.

59. The *haruspices* mentioned in inscriptions (above, note 56) were not the genuine article ; they were Romans and *equites*. Probably this was only one of the many ways of finding dignity or employment for persons of good birth under the Empire.

60. *Cod. Theod.* xvi. 10. 1 (of the year 321 A.D.), quoted by Wissowa, *R.K.* p. 475, note 1. In ix. 16. 3. 5, however, the practice of consulting such experts is strictly prohibited.

61. The story is told in Prof. Dill's *Roman Society in the Last Century of the Western Empire*, ed. 1, p. 41.

LECTURE XIV

THE HANNIBALIC WAR

WE have noticed two different, if not opposing, tendencies in Roman religious experience since the disappearance of the kingship. First, there was a tendency towards the reception of new and more emotional forms of worship, under the direction of the Sibylline books and their keepers; secondly, we have seen how, in the hands of pontifices and augurs, religious practice became gradually so highly formularised and secularised that the real religious instinct is hardly discernible in it, except indeed in the degraded form of scruple as to the exact performance of the ritual laid down. There was also, towards the end of that period, a third tendency beginning to show itself, which was eventually to complete the paralysis of the old religion—a tendency to neglect and despise the old religious forms. This need not surprise us, if we keep in mind two facts : (1) that Rome is now continually in close contact with Greece and her life and thought; (2) that it seems to be inevitable in western civilisation that a hard and fast system of religious rule should eventually arouse rebellion in certain minds. Already there are a few signs that the regulations of the *ius divinum* are not invariably treated with respect.

As long ago as 293 B.C. and the last struggle with the Samnites, we find a trace of this neglect or carelessness. One of the chicken-keepers (*pullarii*) reported falsely to the consul Papirius that the sacred chickens had given good omen in their eating : this was discovered by a

314

young nephew of Papirius, " iuvenis ante doctrinam deos spernentem natus," as Livy calls him, and came to the consul's ears.   Papirius' reception of the news was characteristic of the way in which a Roman could combine practical common-sense with the formal respect claimed by his *ius divinum* ; he declared that the omen had been reported to him as good, and therefore " populo Romano exercituique egregium auspicium est."   The umpire had decided favourably for him, and there was an end of the matter, except indeed that that umpire was placed in the forefront of the battle that the gods might punish him themselves, and there of course he died.[1]   A generation later we have a case of far more pronounced contempt in the familiar story of P. Claudius Pulcher and his colleague Junius, each of whom lost a Roman fleet after neglecting the warning of the *pullarius* : of Claudius it is told that he had the sacred chickens thrown into the sea.[2]   Another well-known story is that of Flaminius, the democrat consul who, as we shall learn directly, was defeated and killed at Trasimene after leaving Rome with none of his religious duties performed.[3]   The famous Marcellus of this second Punic war, though himself an " augur optimus," according to Cicero, declined to act upon an *auspicium ex acuminibus*—electric sparks seen at the end of the soldiers' spears—and was accustomed to ride in his litter with blinds drawn, so that he should not see any evil omen.[4] Assuredly the transition from superstition to reason had its ludicrous side even in public life.

But it is not the gradual approach of rationalism that is the subject of this lecture.   For years after the death of Flaminius we have no trace of it : that was no time for speculating, and it would have been dangerous.   The religious history of the time, as recorded by Livy, shows on the contrary that *religio* in the old sense of the word is once more occupying the Roman mind—the sense of awe in the presence of the Unknown, the sense of sin or of duties omitted, or merely a vague sense of terror that suggested recourse to the supernatural.   No wonder : for

though Italy had been invaded within the memory of
living man, it was not then invaded by one who had
sworn to his father in infancy to destroy the enemy root
and branch.   Instinctively both Romans and loyal Italians
knew that they were face to face with a struggle for life
and death.   It is hard for us to realise the terror of the
situation as it must have been in those days of slow communication and doubtful news.   It is to Livy's credit that
he recognised it fully, and all who look on history as
something more than wars and battles must be eternally
grateful to him for searching the records of the pontifices
for evidence of a people's emotion and the means taken
to soothe it.   Polybius has nothing to tell us of this but
a few generalisations, drawn from his own experience a
century later.[5]   In all essential attributes of a Roman
historian Livy is far the better of the two.   I propose to
follow his guidance in trying to gain some knowledge of
the revived *religio* of the age and the way in which it was
dealt with by the authorities.

It is in the winter of 218-17, when Hannibal was
wintering in north Italy after his victory at the Trebbia,
that Livy first brings the matter before us.[6]   He uses the
word I have just now and so often used : men's minds
were *moti in religionem*, and they reported many *prodigia*
which were uncritically accepted by the vulgar.   He
begins with Rome, and here it is worth noting that these
portents issue from the crowded haunts of the markets,
the *forum olitorium*, and the *forum boarium*, both close to
the river and the quays.   In the latter place, for example,
an ox was said to have climbed to the third story of a
house, whence it threw itself down, terrified by the panic
of the inhabitants — a story which incidentally throws
light on the housing of the lower population at the time.[7]
Other wonders were announced from various parts of
Italy,[8] and the decemviri were directed to have recourse
to the Sibylline books, except for the *procuratio* of one
miracle, common in a volcanic country, the fall of pebble-
rain.[9]   This had a *procuratio* to itself by settled custom,

the *novendiale sacrum*,[10] an expiation parallel with that
which, in the religion of the family, followed a birth or a
death.   For the rest, the whole city was subjected to
lustratio,[11] and, in fact, the whole population was busy with
the work.   A *lectisternium* was ordered for Iuventas,[12] the
deity of the young recruits, a *supplicatio* for Hercules at one
of his temples, and five special victims were ordered for
Genius—directions which have been variously interpreted.
I am disposed to think of them as referring to the capacity
of the State to increase its male population in the face of
military peril.   That the authorities were looking ahead
is clear from the fact next stated, that one of the praetors
had to undertake a special vow if the State should survive
for ten years.   These measures, ordered by the books,
"magna ex parte levaverant religione animos."   Unfortunately, the wayward consul Flaminius spoilt their
endeavours by wilfully neglecting his religious duties at
the Capitol, and also at the Alban mount, where he should
have presided at the Latin festival, and hurrying secretly
to the seat of war, lest his command should be interfered
with by the aristocrats.

Spring came on, and with the immediate prospect
of a crisis the *religio* broke out afresh.[13]   Marvels were
reported from Sicily and Sardinia, as well as Italy and
Rome.   We need not trouble ourselves with them, except
so far as to note that one, at least, was pure invention ; at
Falerii, where there was an oracle by lots,[14] one tablet fell
out of the bundle with the words written on it, *Mavors
telum suum concutit*.   The mental explanation of all
this is lost to us ;[15] it would be interesting to know how
the reports really originated and were conveyed to Rome.
That a widely spread *religio* is really indicated we can
hardly doubt.   The steps taken to soothe it, the religious
prescriptions, are of more value to us.   The Senate received
the reports, and the consul then introduced the question
of procuration.   Besides decreeing, no doubt with the
sanction of the pontifices, certain ordinary measures, the
Senate referred the matter to the decemviri and the Sibyl-

line books. A *fulmen*, weighing fifty pounds, was awarded to Jupiter, and gifts of silver to his consorts in the Capitoline temple. Then follow directions which show that the *religio* of women was to be particularly cared for. Juno Regina of the Aventine was to have a tribute collected by matrons, and she and the famous Juno Sospita of Lanuvium were to have special sacrifices ; and it is probable that another Juno Regina, she of Ardea, was the object of a sacrifice, which the decemviri themselves undertook in the forum of that city.[16] This prominence of Juno may be a counterpart, I think, to the special attention shown to Hercules and Genius in the previous winter.[17] And it is interesting to notice that the libertinae were directed to collect money for their own goddess Feronia.[18]

It is evident that Livy, in detailing these directions from the books of the pontifices,[19] took them in the chronological order in which they were to be carried out ; for the day sacred to Juno Regina of the Aventine is September 1, that of Feronia November 13, and the last instruction he mentions is in December, when Saturnus was to have a sacrifice and *lectisternium* at his own temple in the forum (prepared by senators), and a *convivium publicum*. This meant, we note with interest, the Graecising of this old Roman cult, which now took the form which is so familiar to us of public rejoicing by all classes, including slaves.[20] But long before these dates the terrible disaster of Trasimene had forced the Senate, at the urgent persuasion of the dictator Fabius, to have recourse to the sacred books again.[21] Never before had they been so frequently consulted ; the ordinary *piacula* of the pontifices were not thought of ; a consul had grievously broken the *pax deorum*, and what remedy was possible no Roman authority could tell. The prescriptions of the books were many and various ; the most interesting of them is the famous *ver sacrum*, an old Italian custom, already referred to, but here prescribed by a Greek authority. This was submitted to the people in Comitia, and carried with quaint provisions suited to protect them against any unconscious mistake in carrying out the vow, such as might produce further *religio*. We will only notice that though, according to the old tradition, it was to Mars that the Italian stocks were wont in time of famine and distress to dedicate the whole agricultural produce of the year, together with the male children born that spring,[22] in this crisis it is to Jupiter that the vow is made. It is the Roman people only who here make the vow, and they make it, I doubt not, to that great Jupiter of the Capitol who for 300 years has been their guardian, and in whose temple are kept the sacred books that ordered it.[23]

But the authorities were determined to make now a supreme effort to still the alarm, and to restore the people to cheerfulness. They went on to vow *ludi magni, i.e.* extra games beside the usual yearly *ludi Romani,* at a cost of 333,333 and one-third asses, three being the sacred number. Then a *supplicatio* was decreed, which was attended not only by the urban population, but by crowds from the country, and for three days the decemviri superintended a *lectisternium* on a grand scale, such as had never been seen in Rome before, in which twelve deities in pairs, Roman and Greek indistinguishable from each other, were seen reclining on cushions. If Wissowa interprets this rightly,[24] as I think he does, it marks a turning-point in the religious history of Rome. The old distinction between *di indigetes* and *di novensiles* now vanishes for good ; the showy Greek ritual is applied alike to Roman and to Greek deities ; the Sibylline books have conquered the *ius divinum,* and the decemviri in religious matters are more trusted physicians than the pontifices. The old Roman State religion, which we have been so long examining, may be said henceforward to exist only in the form of dead bones, which even Augustus will hardly be able to make live.

So far, however, all had been orderly and dignified. But after Cannae we begin to divine that the stress of disaster is telling more severely on the nervous fibre of the people. Two Vestals were found guilty of adultery—

always a suspicious event ; in such times a wicked rumour once spread would have its own way.   One killed herself ; the other was buried alive at the Colline gate.   A *scriba pontificis*, who had seduced one of them, was beaten to death by the pontifex maximus.   Such a violation of the *pax deorum* was itself a prodigium, and again the books were consulted, and an embassy was sent to Delphi with Fabius Pictor as leader.[25]   Greece is looming ever larger in the eyes of the frightened Roman.

Under such circumstances it is hardly astonishing to read of a new (or almost new) and horrible rite, in which a Greek man and woman and a Gallic man and woman (slaves, no doubt) were buried alive in the *forum boarium* in a hole closed by a big stone, which had already, says Livy, been used for human victims—"minime Romano sacro."   As in the case of the Vestals, blood-shedding is avoided, but the death is all the more horrible.   What are we to make of such barbarism?   Technically, it must have been a sacrifice to Tellus and the Manes, like the *devotio* of Decius, and like that also, it probably had in it a substratum of magic.[26]   As regards the choice of victims it baffles us, for if we can understand the selection of a Gallic pair at a time when the Gauls of North Italy were taking Hannibal's side, it is not so easy to see why the Greeks were just now the objects of public animosity. Diels has suggested that Gelo, son of Hiero of Syracuse, deserted Rome for Carthage after Cannae,[27] and wanting a better explanation we may accept this, and imagine, if we can, that the cruel death of a pair of Greek slaves need not be taken as expressing any general feeling of antagonism or hatred for things Greek.   But, after all, the most astonishing fact in the whole story is this—that the abominable practice lasted into the Empire ; Pliny, at least, emphatically states that his own age had seen it, and heard the solemn form of prayer which the magister of the quindecemviri used to dictate over the victims.[28]   Pliny, we may note, also speaks of the *forum boarium* as the scene of the sacrifice, where also the first gladiatorial games were exhibited.[29]   Rome was already accustomed to see horrors there.

As we have now reached the climax of the religious panic of these years, I may pause here for a moment to refer to an interesting matter which I mentioned in my third lecture.   At this very time, if we accept Wissowa's conjecture, the twenty-seven puppets of straw known as Argei, which were thrown over the *pons sublicius* by the Vestals on the ides of May, were being substituted as surrogates for the sacrifice by drowning of the same number of Greeks (Argei) ; an atrocity which he fancies actually took place somewhere in the interval between the first and second Punic wars, under orders found in the Sibylline books.[30]   All scholars know that there were in the four regions of the old city twenty-seven (or twenty-four) chapels, *sacella*, which were also called Argei, and have caused great trouble to topographers and archaeologists.[31]   To complete his hypothesis, Wissowa conjectures that these too date from this same age, and were distributed over the city in order to take away the miasma caused by some great pestilence or other trouble, of which, owing to the loss of Livy's second decade, we have no information.   But neither have we a scrap of information about the building of the chapels, or the drowning of the twenty-seven Greeks, an atrocity so abominable that the only way in which we might conceivably account for its disappearance in the records would be the hypothesis of a conspiracy of silence, an impossible thing at Rome. The loss of Livy's second decade cannot of itself be an explanation ; such an event is just what an epitomator would have seized on, yet there is no trace of it in the surviving epitomes, nor in any other author who may have had Livy before him.   Varro knew nothing of it, so far as we can tell ; where he refers to the Argei he makes no mention of such an astonishing origin either of puppets or chapels.   If there had been a record in the books of the pontifices, it is impossible to imagine that he was not aware of it.

Y

On the contrary, he quotes no official record, but a line of Ennius which attributes the origin of the Argei to Numa : [32]

libaque fictores Argeos et tutulatos.

Now Ennius was born in 239 [33] B.C., and was, therefore, living when the whole astonishing business began. How does he come to ascribe to Numa institutions which were to himself exactly as the building of the Forth Bridge might be to an Edinburgh man of middle age ?   Why, too, if these institutions were of such recent date, did the Romans of the last two centuries B.C. invent all sorts of wild explanations of them, at which Wissowa very properly scoffs ?   It is for him to explain why these explanations were needed.   It is inconceivable that in a large city, with colleges of priests preserving religious traditions and formulae, all memory of the remarkable origin of *sacella* and puppets should have so completely vanished as to leave room for the growth of such a crop of explanations.   These will be found in my *Roman Festivals*, p. 112, and whoever reads them will conclude at once, I am sure, that the Romans knew nothing at all about the true history of the Argei.   We may still class this curious ceremony with some of the primitive magical or quasi-magical rites of the ancient settlement.   We are not entitled to cite it as an example of the growing savagery of this trying period ; and if it be argued that it is an example rather of humanity, because for the original victims straw puppets were substituted, the answer is that even if we were to grant the human sacrifice, the surrogation of puppets is a most unlikely thing to have happened. [34]   It is a rare practice ; Wissowa himself judiciously rejects it as an explanation of such objects as *oscilla* and *maniae*.   You cannot adopt it when you choose, to explain a difficulty, and then reject it when you choose.   Why, one may ask, was this humane method not applied also to the two pairs of Gauls and Greeks just mentioned ?   But I need not pursue the subject further ; we may be satisfied to reflect that from an

anthropological point of view the Argei need never have
been anything more than puppets.[35]

But to return to the religious history of the war. It
would seem that the extraordinary series of performances
ordered during the depression and despair that followed
Cannae had succeeded for the time in quieting the *religio*.
Fabius Pictor too had returned from Delphi,[36] and brought
home in what seems to be hexameter verse instructions as
to the worship of certain deities, with injunctions to the
Romans to send gifts to the Pythian Apollo if prosperity
should return to them, and ending with the significant
words, "lasciviam (disorderly excitement) a vobis prohibete,"
which may be interpreted as " keep quiet, and do not get
into a religious panic." The hexameters were Greek, but
were translated for the benefit of the people ; and Fabius
publicly told how he had himself obeyed the voice of the
oracle by sacrificing to the deities it named, and had
worn the wreath, the sign that he was accomplishing
religious work, during the whole of his journey home.
This wreath he now deposited on the altar of Apollo.
This was in 216, and it is remarkable that we hear of no
new outbreak of *prodigia*, the normal symptom of *religio*,
till the next year. Then we have a list ; as Livy says,[37]
" simplices et religiosi homines " were ready with them
at any time. A panic arose in Rome, not strictly of
a religious kind, which shows the nervousness of the
population ; a rumour went about that an army had
been seen on the Janiculum, but men who were on the
spot refuted it. In this case the Sibylline books were
not consulted, but Etruscan haruspices were called in,
who simply ordered a *supplicatio* of the new kind, at
the *pulvinaria*. This is the first, or almost the first
instance of these experts being consulted ; earlier statements of the kind are probably apocryphal, as I pointed
out in the last lecture. It is not clear why the authorities
had recourse to them at this moment ; but I am inclined
to think that the old remedies even of the Sibylline books
and their keepers were getting stale, and that while it was

thought undesirable to excite the people by new rites, it was felt that the familiar ones might gain some new prestige by being recommended by new experts. The old prescription, given by a new physician, may gain in authority. The next year again, 213, brought another crop of *prodigia*, but Livy dismisses them with the simple words, " His procuratis ex decreto pontificum." [38] It is reasonable to suppose that a reaction was taking place in the minds of the senators and pontifices, and that they were determined to take as little notice as possible of disturbing symptoms, relying on the prestige of the Delphic oracle, and acting on its advice to suppress *lascivia*.

But in this same year the *lascivia* broke out again with unprecedented force. The cause was not only, as Livy explains it, the dreary continuance of the war with varying success; if we read between the lines we may guess that the break-up of family life occasioned by the deaths of so many heads of houses and their sons, had opened the way for *feminine* excitement and for the introduction of external rites such as an old Roman *paterfamilias* would no more have tolerated than the pontifices themselves. " Tanta religio," says Livy,[39] " et ea magna ex parte externa, civitatem incessit, *ut aut homines, aut dii repente alii viderentur facti*" ; it seemed as if the old religious system, in spite of all its highly formalised apparatus of expiation, was being deliberately set aside. " Nec iam in secreto modo atque intra parietes abolebantur Romani ritus : sed in publico etiam ac foro Capitolioque (this is the hardest cut of all) *mulierum* turba erat, nec sacrificantium nec precantium deos patrio more." To understand such an amazing religious rebellion against the *ius divinum* we must remember that 80,000 men had fallen at Cannae, besides great numbers in the two previous years, and that therefore the real effective human support of that *ius* had in great part given way. Private priests and prophets, vermin to be found all over the Graeco-Roman

world, had captured for gain the minds of helpless
women, and of the ruined and despairing population of
the country now flocking into Rome. The aediles and
triumviri capitales, responsible for the order of the city,
could do nothing ; the Senate had to commission the
praetor urbanus to rid the people of these *religiones*.
When in those days the Senate and magistrates took
such a matter in hand, further rebellion was impossible.
All we are told is that the praetor issued an edict
ordering that all who possessed private forms of prophecy
or prayer, or rules of sacrifice, should bring them to
him before the kalends of April next ; and that no one
should sacrifice in public with any strange or foreign
rite. I do not know that the wonderful good sense
of this decree has ever been commented on. To take
violent or cruel measures would have been dangerous
in the extreme at such a psychological moment. Livy
tells this story at the very end of the year 213, and
the kalends of April referred to must be those of the
next year ; there was, therefore, plenty of time to obey
the order, and in the meantime the excitement might
subside of itself. The mischief was not absolutely and
suddenly stopped ; in private houses the new rites
were allowed to go on,—a policy adhered to in time
to come,—but the *ius divinum* of the Roman State,
the public worship of the Roman deities, must not be
tampered with. This wise policy seems to have succeeded for the time ; for even after the capture of
Tarentum by Hannibal, and the prospect of an attack in
that direction from Macedonia, we do not hear of any
renewed outbreak. *Prodigia* are reported as usual, but
the remedy thought sufficient is only a single day's
supplicatio and a *sacrum novendiale.* The consuls, however, in the true Roman spirit, devoted themselves for
several days to religious duties before leaving Rome
for their commands.

This was at the beginning of the year 212. But after
the Latin festival at the end of April we hear of a new

religio, and a very curious one.[40]   It looks as though certain Latin oracles, written in Saturnian verse, and attributed to an apocryphal *vates* of the suspicious name of Marcius, had got abroad in the panic of the previous year, and had been confiscated by the praetor urbanus charged, as we saw, with the suppression of religious mischief.   He had handed them on to the new praetor urbanus of 212. One of them prophesied the disaster of Cannae which had already happened ; the other gave directions for instituting games in honour of Apollo, including one which placed the religious part of these *ludi* in the hands of the decemviri.   I strongly suspect that the whole transaction was a plan on the part of the Senate and the religious colleges, in order to quiet the minds of the people by a new religious festival in honour of a great deity of whose prestige every one had heard, for he had been long established in Rome ; he is now to take a more worthy place there, to be incorporated in the *ius divinum* in a new sense, in gratitude perhaps for his recent advice given to Fabius Pictor at Delphi. Possibly also he is to be regarded here as the Greek deity of healing, though we do not hear of any pestilence at the time ; but four years later it was in consequence of an epidemic that these *ludi* were renewed and made permanent.   The main object of the moment was no doubt to amuse the people and occupy their minds.   The whole population took part in the games, wearing wreaths as partakers in a sacred rite ; the matrons were not left out ; and every one kept his house door open and feasted before the eyes of his fellow-citizens.[41]

If it be asked why these games in honour of a Greek god should have been suggested by a Latin oracle, the answer is, I think, that the latter was used rather as a pretext for a pre-conceived plan ; if it be true that the Marcian verses had won some prestige among the vulgar, it was an adroit stroke to invent one that might be used in this way.   This is the only way in which we can

satisfactorily account for the direction to the decemviri
to undertake the necessary sacrifices. The government
seizes a chance of taking the material of *religio* out of
the hands of the vulgar and utilising it for its own
purposes. It was clever too to give the alleged Latin
oracles the sanction of the *Graecus ritus*; "decemviri
Graeco ritu hostiis sacra faciant," says the oracle. The
keepers consulted the sacred books as to the projected
ludi, and henceforward, as it would seem, these Latin
oracles were placed in their keeping to be added to
the Sibylline books in the collection on the Capitol.
The amalgamation of Roman and Greek religion is
complete. If there were any doubt of it after the
lectisternia to the twelve gods which we noticed just now,
all such doubt is removed by the religious events of
this year 212—that famous year in which Hannibal
came within sight of Rome, and fell away again, never
to return.

The student of Roman religious history, and of all
religious psychology, as he follows carefully the extracts
from the priestly records which Livy has embodied in
his story of the last years of the great struggle, will
find much to interest him. Even little things have
here their significance. He will still find relics of the
scruple about the minutiae of the *ius divinum* to which
the Romans had become habituated under priestly rule
—*religio* in that sense in which it is least really religious.
He will find a Flamen Dialis resigning his priesthood
because he had made a blunder in putting the *exta* of
a victim on the altar;[42] only too ready, it may have
been, to take an opportunity of getting free of those
numerous taboos which deprived the priest of Jupiter
of all possibility of active life. Such a conjecture finds
support in the curious fact that his successor was a youth
of such bad character that his relations induced the
pontifex maximus to select him for the sacred post, in
hopes that the restrictive discipline he would have to
undergo might improve his morals and make him a

better citizen.[43]   About the later history of this youth
I may have something to say in the next lecture.
Again, we find *religio* of the scrupulous kind sadly
worrying the stout old warrior Marcellus shortly before
his death [44] : " Aliae atque aliae obiectae animo religiones
tenebant."   One of these *religiones* was a curious one ;
he had vowed a temple of Honos and Virtus — two
deities together ; and the pontifices made difficulties,
insisting that two deities could not inhabit the same
cella, for if it should be struck by lightning, how were
you to tell, in conducting the *procuratio*, to which of
them to sacrifice ?   The difficulty was solved by building
two temples.   Such quaintnesses of the old type of
religious idea are thus still found, but they are becoming
mere survivals.

The *prodigia* continue, and occasionally, as a new crisis
in the war was known to be approaching, became exacer-
bated.   In 208, just before the old consul Marcellus left
the city to meet his death, he and his colleague were
terribly pestered with them, and could not succeed in their
sacrificing (*litare*).   For many days they failed to secure
the *pax deorum*.[45]   When it was known that Hasdrubal was
on his way from Spain, and that the greatest peril of the
war was approaching, special steps were taken to make
sure of that *pax*.[46]   The pontifices ordered that twenty-
seven maidens—a number of magical significance both in
Greece and Italy [47]—should chant a *carmen* composed by
the poet Livius Andronicus ; and in the elaborate ritual
that followed, as the result of the striking of the temple of
Juno on the Aventine by lightning, the decemviri and
haruspices from Etruria also had a share.   The procession
of the maidens, singing and dancing through the city till
they reached the temple of Juno by the Clivus Publicius,
was a new feature in ritual, and must have been a striking
one.   Doubtless it was all a part of a deliberate policy to
keep the women of the city in good humour, and in touch
with the religion of the State, instead of going after other
gods, as they had already gone and were again to go with

amazing and perilous fervour. For Juno Regina of the Aventine was their special deity; and in this case they were authorised—all *matronae* living within ten miles of the city—to contribute in money to a noble gift to the temple.

Hasdrubal was defeated and killed (207), and the danger passed away. Then, when the news reached Rome (if Livy's account may be relied on), there followed such an outburst of gratitude to the deities as we have never yet met with, and shall not meet with again in Roman history.[48] It was not only that the State ordered a *supplicatio* of three days thanksgiving; men and women alike took advantage of it to press in crowds to the temples, the materfamilias with her children, and in her finest robes: "cum omni solutae metu, perinde ac si debellatum foret, deis immortalibus grates agerent." I would draw attention to the fact that here is no mere fulfilment of a vow, of a bargain, as some will have it; in this moment of real religious emotion the first thought is one of thankfulness that the *pax deorum* is restored, and that the Power manifesting itself in the universe, though in the humble form of these dwellers in Roman temples, would permit the long-suffering people once more to feel themselves in right relation to him. As we go on with our studies in the two centuries that follow, let us bear this moment in mind; it will remind us that the religious instinct never entirely dies out in the heart of any people.

I would fain stop at this point, and have done with the war and its religious troubles; but there is one more event which cannot be omitted,—the solemn advent of a new deity, this time neither Greek nor Italian. After the Metaurus battle, the dreaded Hannibal yet remained in Italy, and so long as he was there the Romans could know no security. So far as religion could help them every possible means had been used; there seemed no expedient left. In 205 a pretext for inspecting the Sibylline books was found in an unusual burst of pebble-rain; and there, as it was given out, an oracle was deciphered, which foretold that Hannibal would have to leave Italy if the Magna Mater of Pessinus were brought to Rome.[49]   In whose brain this idea originated we do not know, but it was a brilliant one.   The eastern cult was wholly unknown at Rome, was something entirely new and strange, a fresh and hopeful prescription for an exhausted patient.   The project was seized on with avidity, and supported by the influence of Delphi and of that strange soldier mystic the great Scipio.[50]   The best man in the State was to receive the goddess, and when, after many months, she came to Italy in the form of a black stone, it was Scipio who was chosen for the duty. For Attalus, king of Pergamus, had consented to let her go from her Phrygian home ; and when she arrived at Ostia, Scipio with all the Roman matrons went thither by land ; alone he boarded the ship, received the goddess from her priests, and carried her to land, where the noblest women of the State received her,—received the black stone, that is,—and carried it in their arms in turns, while all Rome poured out to meet her, and burned incense at their doors as she passed by.   And praying that she might enter willingly and propitiously into the city, they carried her into the temple of Victory on the Palatine on the 4th of April, henceforward to be a festal day, the popular Megalesia.

This Magna Mater was the first Oriental deity introduced into Rome, and the last deity introduced by the Sibylline books.   It is probable that no Roman then knew much about the real nature of her cult and its noisy orgiastic character and other degrading features ; it was sufficient to have found a new prescription, and once more to have given the people, and especially the women, a happy moment of hope and confidence.   But the truth came out soon enough ; and though the goddess must have her own priests, it was ordered by a *Senatusconsultum* that no Roman should take part in her service.[51]   Though established in the heart of the city, and ere long to have her own temple, she was to continue a foreign deity outside the *ius divinum*. As such she belongs to those worships with which I am not called upon by the plan of these lectures to deal.

Hannibal withdrew at last from Italy, and in 202 the war came to an end. Looking at the divine inhabitants of the city in that year, we may see in them almost as much a *colluvies nationum* as in the human population itself. Under such circumstances neither the old City-state nor its religion could any longer continue to exist. The decay of the one reflects that of the other ; the failure to trust the *di indigetes*, the constant desire to try new and foreign manifestations of divine power, were sure signs that the State was passing into a new phase. In the next two centuries Rome gained the world and lost her own soul.

NOTES TO LECTURE XIV

1. The story is told in Livy x. 40 and 41, and must have been taken by him from the records of the pontifices, which had almost certainly begun by this date (see above, p. 283). While on these chapters the reader may also note the curious vow of this Papirius to Jupiter Victor at the end of ch. xlii. ; and the description of the religious horrors of the Samnites witnessed by the army, and especially the words "respersae fando infandoque sanguine arae" (see above, p. 196), which clearly indicate a practice abhorrent to Romans.

2. Val. Max. i. 5. 3 and 4 ; Cic. *de Div.* i. 16. 29 ; Livy, *Epit.* xix.

3. The *locus classicus* is Livy xxi. 63.

4. Cic. *de Div.* ii. 36. 77. I find an illustration of this effect of lightning in Major Bruce's *Twenty Years in the Himalaya*, p. 130 : "Directly the ice-axes begin to hum (in a storm) they should be put away."

5. He notices it in connection with the war only in iii. 112. 6, after the battle of Cannae : a striking passage, but cast in general language.

6. Livy xxi. 62 foll. Wissowa comments on this passage in *R.K.* p. 223.

7. See the author's *Social Life at Rome in the Age of Cicero*, p. 28 foll.

8. The rule seems to have been that no *prodigia* were accepted, and *procurata* by the authorities, which were announced from beyond

the ager Romanus. See Mommsen in O. Jahn's edition of the *Periochae* of Livy's books, and of Iulius Obsequens, preface, p. xviii. But this does not appear from the records of this war; and, at any rate, the religious panic was Italian as well as Roman.

9. Red sand still occasionally falls in Italy, brought by a sirocco from the Sahara, and this accounts for the *prodigium*, "*pluit sanguine*," which is often met with. I have a record of it in the *Daily Mail* of March 11, 1901. But the *lapides* were probably of volcanic origin.

10. Wissowa, *R.K.* p. 328.

11. This must have been a special performance of the yearly Amburbium, of which unluckily we known hardly anything (Wissowa, *R.K.* 130).

12. *R.F.* p. 56, where unfortunately the word is misprinted Pubertas. Wissowa, *R.K.* 126, thinks of Hebe in a Latin form; in his view it must be a Greek deity, being brought in by the decemviri and the books. But we shall find that these begin now to interfere with Roman cults, and in such a crisis we need not wonder at it. Wissowa allows that we do not know where this Hebe can have come from, nor, I may add, why she should have come. That there was some special meaning in the combination Juventas, Hercules, Genius I feel sure, and I conjecture that it may be found in the urgent need of a supply of *iuvenes*. Hercules and Genius seem both to represent the male principle of life (*R.F.* 142 foll.). Juventas speaks for herself, but we may remember that the *tirones* sacrificed to her on the day of the Liberalia (17th March), and that Liber is almost certainly another form of Genius (*R.F.* 55).

13. Livy xxii. 1.

14. It is only from this passage that we know of the oracle. See Bouché-Leclercq, *Hist. de divination*, iv. 146. That of Caere is mentioned in Livy xxi. 62. Both cities were mainly Etruscan.

15. Livy xxvii. 37 betrays some knowledge of the infectious nature of prodigy-reporting: "Sub unius prodigii, ut fit, mentionem, alia quoque nuntiata."

16. Pliny, *N.H.* xxxv. 115, where the verses are quoted as inscribed on the paintings in her temple at Ardea. Note that Juno is here called the wife of Jupiter by a Greek artist from Asia.

17. For Juno as the woman's deity and guardian spirit, see above, p. 135. To refer this prominence of the goddess to her connection with Carthage and mythical enmity to the Romans, as we see it in the *Aeneid*, is premature; we must suppose that each Juno was still a local deity, and no general conception in the later Greek sense is as yet possible.

18. For Feronia, see *R.F.* 252 foll.

19. The *procurationes* ordered were doubtless recorded in the *annales maximi*. The books of the decemviri, we must suppose, were burnt with the oracles in 38 B.C. (Diels, *Sib. Blätter*, p. 6 note).

20. Wissowa, *R.K.* 170; Marq. 586 foll.

21. Livy xxii. 9-10.

22. See above, p. 204 foll. ; Strabo, p. 250 ; Festus, p. 106.

23. If it be asked why Jupiter is here without his titles Optimus Maximus, the answer is that just below, where *ludi magni* are vowed to him, as all such *ludi* were, he is also simply Jupiter.

24. *R.K.* 356. In his view the new amalgam of twelve gods was known as *di Consentes*, an expression of Varro's which has been much discussed. See Müller-Deecke, *Etrusker*, ii. 83 ; *C.I.L.* vi. 102 ; Wissowa, *Gesammelte Abhandlungen*, 190 foll. In *de Re Rust.* i. 1, Varro speaks of twelve *dei consentes, urbani*, whose gilded statues stood in the forum.

25. Livy xxii. 57.

26. See above, p. 207. Orosius' account of this is worth reading ; he calls it "obligamentum hoc magicum" (iv. 13). He mentions a Gallic pair and a Greek woman, and dates it in 226 (227 according to Wissowa, *Gesammelte Abhandlungen*, p. 227). Cp. Plut. *Marcell.* 3. Livy's words, "iam ante hostiis humanis, minime Romano sacro, imbutum," agree with this. There must have been an outbreak of feeling and recourse to the Sibylline books in the stress of the Gallic war.

27. *Sib. Blätter*, p. 86.

28. Pliny, *N.H.* xxviii. 12 and 13. Plutarch, *l.c.*, confirms him. Pliny, it may be noticed, is here writing of spells, etc., among which he classes the *precatio* of this rite.

29. The first gladiatorial show was in 264 B.C. (Val. Max. ii. 4. 7).

30. The arguments are stated fully in his *Gesammelte Abhandlungen*, 211 foll.

31. The best account of these, or rather of the Argean itinerary, of which fragments are preserved in Varro, *L.L.* v. 45 foll., is still that of Jordan in his *Römische Topographie*, ii. 603 foll. The extracts seem to be from a record of directions for the passage of a procession round the *sacella* (or *sacraria*, Varro v. 48). Though quoting these, Varro has nothing to say of their origin, which would be strange indeed if they were of such comparatively late date.

32. In Varro, *L.L.* vii. 44. There is no doubt that the line is from Ennius ; it is also quoted as his in Festus, p. 355.

33. Schanz, *Gesch. der röm. Literatur*, vol. i. ed. 3, p. 110.

34. Some examples of substitution will be found in Westermarck, *Origin and Development of the Moral Ideas*, i. 469. It is of course a well-known phenomenon, but is now generally rejected as an explanation of *oscilla, maniae*, etc. (see Wissowa, *R.K.* p. 355, and Frazer, *G.B.* ii. 344). I know of no case of it on good evidence at Rome, unless it be one in the *devotio*, of an effigy for the soldier, ("ni moritur," Livy viii. 10).

35. See *Roman Festivals*, p. 117, with references to Mannhardt ; Frazer, *G.B.* ii. 256 ; Farnell, *Cults of the Greek States*, v. 181.

36. Livy xxiii. 11. See also Diels, *Sib. Blätter*, pp. 11 and 92.

37. Livy xxiv. 10.

38. *Ib.* xxiv. 44.

39. *Ib.* xxv. 1.

40. *Ib.* xxv. 12. On the Marcian oracles and their metre, see Bouché-Leclercq, *Hist. de divination*, iv. 128 foll. ; Wissowa, *R.K.* 463 note 2 ; Diels, *op. cit.* p. 7 foll.

41. See above, Lect. xi. p. 262. For the Apolline games, *R.F.* p. 179 foll.

42. Livy xxvi. 23.

43. *Ib.* xxvii. 8.

44. *Ib.* xxvii. 25 ; Plut. *Marcellus*, p. 28.

45. *Ib.* xxvii. 23.

46. *Ib.* xxvii. 37.

47. The idea that this number was "chthonic" and a monopoly of the Sibylline utterances was started by Diels, *Sib. Blätter*, p. 42 foll., with imperfect anthropological knowledge, and has led Wissowa and others into wrong conclusions, *e.g.* as to the Argei. See an article criticising Wissowa in *Classical Rev.* 1902, p. 211. On the whole subject of the number three and its multiples, see Usener, "Dreizahl," in *Rheinisches Museum* for 1903, and Goudy, *Trichotomy in Roman Law* (Oxford, 1910), p. 5 foll.

48. Livy xxvii. 51. For gratitude among Romans, see above, p. 202. A gift of thanksgiving was sent to Delphi (Livy xxviii. 45).

49. *Ib.* xxix. 10 foll. For other references see *R.F.* p. 69 foll.

50. *Ib.* xxix. 10.

51. Dion. Hal. ii. 19 ; *R.F.* p. 70.

LECTURE XV

AFTER THE HANNIBALIC WAR

THE long and deadly struggle with Hannibal ended in 201 B.C., and no sooner was peace concluded than the Senate determined on war with Macedon. This decision is a critical moment in Roman history, for it initiated not only a long period of advance and the eventual supremacy of Rome in the Eastern Mediterranean, but also an age of narrow aristocratic rule which remained unquestioned till revolution broke out with Tiberius Gracchus. But we cannot safely deny that it was a just decision. Hannibal was alive, and his late ally, Philip of Macedon, now in sinister coalition with Antiochus of Syria, might be capable of invading exhausted Italy. To have an enemy once more in the peninsula would probably be fatal to Rome and Italy, and one more effort was necessary in order to avert such a calamity ; an effort that must be made at once, while Carthage lay prostrate.

It is necessary to grasp fully the danger of the moment if we are to understand the part played by religion (if I may use the word) in bringing about the desired result. It was most difficult to persuade a people worn out by one war that it was essential for their safety that they should at once face another. Historians naturally look on the success of the Senate in this task as due to its own prestige, and to the skilful oratory of the Consul in the speech to the people which Livy has reproduced in his own admirable rhetoric. But a closer examination of the chapters at the beginning of the historian's thirty-first book will show that religion too was used, in accordance with the experience of the late war, to put pressure on the voters and to inspire their confidence.   As we saw in the last lecture, they had been constantly cheered and braced by religious expedients,—their often-recurring *religio* had been soothed and satisfied ; now the same means were to be used positively rather than negatively, to help in urging them to a definite course of action.   Some sixty years later Polybius, writing of the extreme religiousness of the Romans, expressed his conviction that religion was invented for political objects, and only serves as the means of bridling the fickle and unreasoning Demos ; for if it were possible to have a State consisting of wise men only, no such institution would be necessary.[1]   The philosophic historian is here thinking mainly of the way in which religion was turned to account by the Roman authorities in his own lifetime.   We cannot have a better illustration of this than the events of the year 200 B.C.

Already, in the autumn of the previous year, the ground had been prepared.   To the plebeian games in November there had been added a feast of Jupiter (*Iovis epulum*), as had been done more than once during the late war.[2]   Jupiter, in the form of his image in the Capitoline temple, lay on his couch at the feast of the outgoing plebeian magistrates, with his face reddened with minium as at a triumph, and Juno and Minerva sat each on her *sella* on either side of him ; and to give practical point to this show, corn from Africa was distributed at four asses the modius, or at most one quarter of the normal price.   When the new consuls entered on office on the ides of the following March, further religious steps were at once taken ; the political atmosphere was charged with religiosity.   On the first day of their office the consuls were directed by the Senate, doubtless with the sanction of the pontifices, to *sacrifice to such deities as they might select*, with a special prayer for the success of the new war which Senate and people (the latter by a clever anticipation) are contemplating. Haruspices from Etruria had been adroitly procured, and no doubt primed, who reported that the gods had accepted this prayer, and that the examination of the victims portended extension of the Roman frontier, victory, and triumph.[3] Yet, in spite of all this, the people were not yet willing ; in almost all the centuries, when the voting for the war took place, they rejected the proposal of the Senate. Then the consul Sulpicius was put up to address them, and at the end of Livy's version of his speech we find him clinching his political arguments with religious ones. " Ite in suffragium, bene iuvantibus dis, et quae Patres censuerunt, vos iubete. Huius vobis sententiae non consul modo auctor est, sed etiam di immortales ; qui mihi sacrificanti . . . laeta omnia prosperaque portendere." Thus adjured, the people yielded ; and as a reward, and to stifle any *religio* that might be troubling them, they are treated to a *supplicatio* of three days, including an "*obsecratio circa omnia pulvinaria*" for the happy result of the war ; and once more, after the levy was over,— a heavy tax on the patience of the people,—the consul made vows of *ludi* and a special gift to Jupiter, in case the State should be intact and prospering five years from that day.[4]

Exactly the same religious machinery was used a few years later to gain the consent of the people for a war of far less obvious necessity,—that with Antiochus of Syria. It was at once successful. The haruspices were again on the spot and gave the same report ; and then, *solutis religione animis*, the centuries sanctioned the war. The vow that followed, of which Livy gives a modernised wording, was for *ludi* to last ten continuous days, and for gifts of money at all the *pulvinaria*, where now, as we gather from these same chapters, the images of the gods were displayed on their couches during the greater part of the year.[5]

We may realise in accounts like these how far we

have left behind us the old Roman religion we discussed in earlier lectures. That religion did not any longer supply the material needed ; it was not suited to be the handmaid of a political or military policy ; it was a real religion, not invented for political purposes, to use Polybius' language, but itself a part of the life of the State, whether active in war, or law, or politics. In the ceremonies I have just been describing almost all the features are foreign,—the *pulvinaria*, the haruspices, perhaps even the *Iovis epulum* ; and we feel that though the *religio* in the minds of the people is doubtless a genuine thing, yet the means taken to soothe it are far from genuine,— they are *mala medicamenta*, quack remedies. Such is the method by which a shrewd, masterly government compels the obedience of a *populus religiosus*. After long experience of such methods, can we wonder that Polybius could formulate his famous view of religion, or that a great and good Roman lawyer, himself pontifex maximus, could declare that political religion stands quite apart from the religion of the poets, or that of the philosophers, and must be acted on, whether true or false ? [6]

The reporting of *prodigia* goes on with astonishing vigour in this period, and seems to have become endemic. I only mention it here (for we have had quite enough of it already) because the question arises whether it is now used mainly for political purposes, or to annoy a personal rival or enemy. This does not appear clearly from Livy's accounts, but in an age of personal and political rivalries, as this undoubtedly was, it can hardly have been otherwise. Certain it is that the interests of the State were grievously interfered with in this way. The consuls at this time, and until 153 B.C., did not enter on office until March 15, and they should have been ready to start for their military duties as soon as the levies had been completed ; instead of which, they were constantly delayed by the duty of expiating these marvels. In 199 Flamininus, whose appointment to the command in Macedonia had of course annoyed the friends of the man he was super-

seding, was delayed in this way for the greater part of the
year, and yet he is said to have left Italy at an earlier
date than most consuls.[7] Thus the change to January 1
for the beginning of the consular year, which took place
in 153 B.C., was an unavoidable political necessity. Even
the Sibylline books came to be used for personal and
political purposes. In the year 144 the praetor Marcius
Rex was commissioned to repair the Appian and Aniensian
aqueducts and to construct a new one. The *decemviri
sacris faciundis*, consulting the books, as it was said, for
other reasons, found an oracle forbidding the water to be
conveyed to the Capitoline hill, and seem on this absurd
ground to have been able to delay the necessary work.
Our information is much mutilated, but the real explanation seems to be that there was some personal spite
against Marcius, who, however, eventually completed the
work.[8] Nearly a century later a Sibylline oracle, beyond
doubt invented for the purpose, was used to prevent
Pompeius from taking an army to Egypt to restore
Ptolemy Auletes to his throne. But all students of Roman
history in the last two centuries B.C. are familiar with
such cases of the prostitution of religion or religious
processes, and I have already said enough about it in the
lecture on divination.[9]

I do not, of course, mean to assert that personal and
political motives account for all or the greater number
of *prodigia* reported. There is plenty of evidence that
the genuine old *religio* could be stirred up by real marvels,
which the government were bound to expiate in order to
satisfy public feeling. Thus in 193 B.C. earthquakes were
so frequent that the Senate could not meet, nor could any
public business be done, so busy were the consuls with
the work of expiation. At last the Sibylline books were
consulted and the usual religious remedies applied ; but
the spirit of the age is apparent in the edict of the consuls, prompted by the Senate, that if *feriae* had been
decreed to take place on a certain day for the expiation
of an earthquake, no fresh earthquake was to be reported

on that same day.[10]   This delicious edict, unparalleled in
Roman history, caused the grave Livy to declare that the
people must have grown tired, not only of the earthquakes,
but of the *feriae* appointed to expiate them.

Let us turn to another and more interesting feature of
this age, which is plainly visible in the sphere of religion,
as in other aspects both of private and public life : I mean
the growth of *individualism*.   Men, and indeed women
also, as we shall see, are beginning to feel and to assert
their individual importance, as against the strict rules and
traditions, civil or religious, of the life of the family and
the State.   This is a tendency that had long been at
work in Greece, and is especially marked in the teaching
of the two great ethical schools of the post-Alexandrian
period, the Epicureans and Stoics.   The influence of
Greece on the Romans was already strong enough to have
sown the seeds of individualism in Italy ; but the tendency
was at the same time a natural result of enlarged experience and expanding intelligence among the upper classes.
The second century B.C. shows us many prominent men
of strong individual character, who assert themselves in
ways to which we have not been accustomed in Roman
history, *e.g.* Scipio the elder, Flamininus, Cato, Aemilius
Paulus and his son, Scipio Aemilianus ; and among lesser
and less honourable men we see the tendency in the
passionate desire for personal distinction in the way of
military commands, triumphs, and the giving of expensive
games.   This is the age in which we first hear of statues
and portrait busts of eminent men ; and magistrates
begin to put their names or types connected with their
families on the coins which they issue.[11]

In religion this tendency is seen mainly in the attempts
of the individual, often successful, to shake himself free
of the restrictions of the old *ius divinum*.   I pointed out
long ago that it was a weak point in the old Roman
religion that it did little or nothing to encourage and
develop the individual religious instinct ; it was formalised
as a religion of family and State, and made no appeal, as

did that of the Jews, to the individual's sense of right
and wrong.[12]   The sense of sin was only present to the
Roman individual mind in the form of scruple about
omissions or mistakes in the performance of religious
duties.   Thus religion lost her chance at Rome as an
agent in the development of the better side of human
nature.   As an illustration of what I mean I may recall
what I said in an early lecture, that the spirit of a dead
Roman was not thought of as definitely individualised ;
it joined the whole mass of the Manes in some dimly
conceived abode beneath the earth ; there is no singular
of the word Manes.   It is only in the third century B.C.
that we first meet with memorial tombstones to individuals, like those of the Scipios, and not till the end
of the Republican period that we find the words Di Manes
representing in any sense the spirit of the individual
departed.[13]

In practical life the quarrel of the individual with the
ius divinum takes the form of protest against the restrictions placed on the old sacrificing priesthoods, these of
the Flamines and the Rex sacrorum, who, unlike the
pontifices and augurs, were disqualified from holding a
secular magistracy.[14]   These priesthoods must be filled
up, and when a vacancy occurred, the pontifex maximus,
who retained the power of the Rex in this sphere, as a
kind of *paterfamilias* of the whole State, selected the
persons, and could compel them to serve even if they were
unwilling.   But the interests of public life are now far
more attractive than the duties of the cults,—the individual wishes to assert himself where his self-assertion
will be noted and appreciated.

These attempts at emancipation from the *ius divinum*
were not at first successful.   In 242 a flamen of Mars
was elected consul ; he hoped to be in joint command
with his colleague Lutatius of the naval campaign against
Carthage.   But the *ius divinum* forbade him to leave Italy,
and the pontifex maximus inexorably enforced it.[15]   Of
this quarrel we have no details ; but in 190 a similar case

is recorded in full.   A flamen Quirinalis, elected praetor, who had Sardinia assigned him as his province, was stopped by the *ius divinum* administered by another inexorable pontifex maximus ; and it was only after a long struggle, in which Senate, tribunes, and people all took part, that he was forced to submit.   So great was his wrath that he was with difficulty persuaded not to resign his praetorship.[16] Naturally it became difficult to fill these priesthoods, for it was invidious to compel young men of any promise to commit what was practically political suicide.   The office of *rex sacrorum* was vacant for two years between 210 and 208 ;[17] and in 180 Cornelius Dolabella, a *duumvir navalis*, on being selected for this priesthood, absolutely refused to obey the pontifex maximus when ordered to resign his secular command.   He was fined for disobedience, and appealed to the people ; at the moment when it became obvious that the appeal would fail, he contrived to escape by getting up an unlucky omen.   *Religio inde fuit pontificibus inaugurandi Dolabellae* ; and here we have the strange spectacle of the *ius divinum* being used to defeat its own ends.   Such a state of things needs no comment.[18]

But the most extraordinary story of this kind is that of a flamen of Jupiter,—a story which many years ago I told in detail in the *Classical Review.*   Here I may just be allowed to reproduce it in outline.   In the year 209 a young C. Valerius Flaccus, the black sheep of a great family, was inaugurated against his will as Flamen Dialis by the pontifex maximus P. Licinius.[19]   It was within the power of the head of the Roman religion to use such compulsion, but it must have been difficult and unusual to do so without the consent of the victim's relations.   In this case, as Livy expressly tells us, it was used because the lad was of bad character,—*ob adolescentiam negligentem luxuriosamque* ; and it is pretty plain that the step was suggested by his elder brother and other relations, in order to keep him out of mischief.   For, as we have seen, the taboos on this ancient priesthood were numerous and strict, and among the restrictions laid on its holder was one which forbade him to leave his house for a single night. Thus we learn not only that this priesthood was not much accounted of in those days, but also that for the *cura* and *caerimonia* of religion a pure mind was no longer needed. But it might be utilised as a kind of penal settlement for a libertine noble ; and it is not impossible that a century and a quarter later the attempt to put the boy Julius Caesar into the same priesthood, though otherwise represented by the historians, may have had the same object.[20] But the strange thing in the case of Flaccus is that this very *cura* and *caerimonia*, if Livy's account is to be trusted, had such a wholesome disciplinary effect, that the libertine became a model youth, the admiration of his own and other families.   Relying on his excellent character he even asserted the ancient right of this flamen to take his seat in the Senate, a right which had long been in abeyance *ob indignitatem flaminum priorum* ; and he eventually gained his point, in spite of obstinate opposition on the part of a praetor.   Some years later, in 200, this same man was elected curule aedile.[21]   This was clearly the first example of an attempt to combine the priesthood with a magistracy, for a difficulty at once arose and was solved in a way for which no precedent is quoted.   Among the taboos on this priest there was one forbidding him to take an oath ; yet the law demanded that a magistrate must take the usual oath within five days of entering on office.[22]   Flaccus insisted on asserting his individuality in spite of the *ius divinum*, and the Senate and people both backed him up.   The Senate decreed that if he could find some one to take the oath for him, the consuls might, if they chose, approach the tribune with a view to getting a relieving *plebiscitum* ; this was duly obtained, and he took the oath by proxy.   In his year of office as aedile we find him giving expensive *ludi Romani* ; and in 184 he only missed the praetorship by an unlucky accident.[23] In this story we find the self-assertion of an individual supported by Senate, consuls, and people in breaking loose from the antiquated restrictions of a bygone age, and we cannot but sympathise with it.   But Roman history is full of surprises, and among these I know none more amazing than the successful attempt of Augustus two centuries later to revive this priesthood with all its absurdities.[24]

The self-assertion of members of the great families against the *ius divinum* was inevitable, and in the instances just noticed the attitude of compromise taken up by the government was only what was to be expected in an age of stress and change and new ideas.   But in less than twenty years after the peace with Carthage this government found itself suddenly face to face with what may be called a religious rebellion chiefly among the lower orders, including women ; and the authorities unhesitatingly reverted to the position of conscientious guardians of the religious system of the City-state.   They began to realise that they had been holding a wolf by the ears ever since the beginning of the Hannibalic war ; that they had a population to deal with which was no longer pure Roman or even pure Italian, and that even the genuine Romans themselves were liable to be moved by new currents of religious feeling.   During the war they had done all that was possible to meet the mental as well as the material troubles of this population, even to the length of introducing the worship, under certain restrictions, of the great Phrygian Mother of the gods.   But now, in 186, the sudden outbreak of Dionysiac orgies in Italy showed them that all their remedies were stale and insufficient, and that the wolf was getting loose in their hands.

Dionysus had long been housed at Rome, under the name of Liber, in that temple of Ceres, Liber, and Libera which was discussed in detail in my eleventh lecture.[25] But it is not likely that many Romans recognised the identity of Liber and Dionysus, and it is quite certain that the characteristic features of the Dionysiac ritual were entirely unknown at Rome for three centuries after the foundation of the temple.   That ritual, as it existed in Greece from the earliest times, retaining the essential features which it bore in its original Thracian home,[26] has lately been thoroughly examined and clearly expounded by Dr. Farnell in the fifth volume of his *Cults of the Greek States*, and the student of the Roman religious history of this period would do well to study carefully his fifth chapter. In most Greek states, as at Athens, in spite of occasional outbreaks, the wilder aspects of the cult had not been encouraged, but at Delphi and at Thebes, *i.e.* on Parnassus and Cithaeron, the more striking phenomena of the genuine ritual are found down to a late period. Dr. Farnell has summed these up under three heads at the beginning of his account : " The wild and ecstatic enthusiasm that it inspired, the self-abandonment and communion with the deity achieved through orgiastic rites and a savage sacramental act, and the prominence of women in the ritual, which in accordance with a certain psychic law made a special appeal to their temperament."[27] It meant in fact exactly that form of religious ecstasy which was peculiarly abhorrent to the minds of the old Romans, who had built up the *ius divinum* with its sober ritual and its practical ideas of the supernatural powers around them. We found nothing in our studies of this religion to lead us to suppose for an instant that it had any mental effect such as " the transcending of the limits of the ordinary consciousness and the feeling of communion with the divine nature." [28] The Latin language indeed had no native words for the expression of such emotions.[29]

But it would be a great mistake to suppose that there was no soil in Italy, or even at Rome, where such emotional rites might take root. We may believe that the dignity and sobriety of the Roman character was in part at least the result of the discipline of ordered religion in family and state ; but this is not to say that the Romans were never capable of religious indiscipline,—far from it. The Italian rural festival, then as now, was lively and indecorous, so far as we can guess from the few glimpses we get of it; and at Rome the ancient festival of Anna Perenna, in which women took part, was a scene of revelry as Ovid describes it,[30]—of dancing, singing, and intoxication, and we need not wonder that it found no place in the ancient calendar of the *ius divinum*.   And we have lately had occasion to notice, in the new ritual instituted under the direction of the Sibylline books, and more especially during the great war, clear indications that the natural emotions of women, even of Roman women, had to be satisfied by shows and processions in which they could share, and that the ideal dignity of the Roman matron had often given way under the terrible stress of public and domestic anxiety and peril.   No wonder then that when Roman armies had been for years in Greece, and Greeks were flocking into Rome in larger numbers every year, the Dionysiac rites should find their way into Italy, and no wonder too that they should instantly find a congenial soil, exotics though they were.

The story of the Bacchanalia is told by Livy in his best manner, and whether or no it be literally true in every particular, is full of life and interest.   It is the fashion now to reject as false whatever is surprising; and the latest historian of Rome dismisses Livy's account of the discovery of the mischief as "an interesting romance."[31] Fortunately we are not now concerned with this romance, if such it be; I only propose to dwell on one or two points more nearly concerned with our subject.

First, let us note that the seeds of this evil crop were sown in Etruria, the most dangerous neighbour of the Romans from a religious point of view; for it is hardly too much to say that all Greek influences that filtered through Etruria on their way to Rome were contaminated in the process.   According to the story,[32] a common Greek religious quack (*sacrificulus et vates*, as Livy calls him), of the type held up to scorn by Plato in the *Republic*,[33] came to Etruria and began to initiate in the rites; drunkenness was the result, and with drinking came crime and immorality of all kinds.   From Etruria the mischief spread to Rome, and was there discovered accidentally. According to the evidence given, it began with a small association of women, who met openly in the daytime only three times a year. Then it fell under the direction of a priestess from Campania,—Rome's other most dangerous neighbour in regard to religion and morals,—who gave it a sinister turn. The meetings were held at night, and were accompanied not only by the characteristic features of the old Thracian ritual, but, as in Etruria, by the most abominable wickedness. It was said to have infected a large part of the population, including young members of noble families ; for with the true missionary instinct, young people only were admitted by the hierophants. We need not necessarily believe all this ; but it is certain, from the steps taken by the government, about which there is no doubt, that it is in the main a true account. The storm and stress of the long war with Hannibal would be enough to account for the phenomena, even if they were not in keeping with well-known psychical facts.

Let us now turn for a moment to the attitude of the government in this extraordinary episode of Roman religious experience. The danger is dealt with entirely by the Senate and the magistrates ; the authorities of the *ius divinum* as such have nothing to do with it. It is characteristic of the age that it is not dealt with as a matter of religion merely, but as a conspiracy—*coniuratio*.[34] This is the word used by Livy, and we find it also in the document called *Senatusconsultum de Bacchanalibus*, part of which has most fortunately come down to us. This is the word also used, we may note, of the conspiracy of Catiline in the century following, and it always conveys the idea of *rebellion* against the order and welfare of the State. In this case it was rebellion against the whole body of the *mos maiorum*, the ἦθος of the City-state of Rome. For it was an attempt to supersede the ancient religious life of that State by *externa superstitio, prava religio—prava*, because *deorum numen praetenditur scele-*

ribus; and hence, as Livy expresses it in the admirable speech put into the mouth of the consul, the Roman gods themselves felt their *numen* to be contaminated.[85] All the speeches in Livy, except perhaps the military ones, are worth careful study by those who would enter into the Roman spirit as conceived by an Augustan writer; and this is one of the most valuable of them.

Lastly, let us note the steps taken by the government in this emergency. It is treated as a matter of police, both in Rome and Italy; the guilty are sought out and punished as conspirators against the State, and a precedent of tremendous force is hereby established for all future dealings with *externa superstitio*, which held good even to the last struggle with Christianity. Where foreign rites are believed to be dangerous to the State or to morality, they must be rigidly suppressed in the Roman world; when they are harmless they may be tolerated, or even, like the cult of the Magna Mater, received into the sacred circle of Roman worships.[86] But there is yet another lesson to be learnt from the conduct of the government at this crisis. Who would have suspected, while reading the horrible story, and noting the almost arbitrary energy with which the *coniuratio* was stamped out, that the Dionysiac rites would even now be tolerated under certain conditions? That this was so is a fact attested not only by Livy, but by the *Senatusconsultum* itself.[87] The government was now forced to recognise the fact that there were Romans for whom the *ius divinum* no longer sufficed, and who needed a more emotional form of religion. If any one (so ran in effect the *Senatusconsultum*) felt conscientiously that he could not wholly renounce the new religion, he might apply in person to the praetor urbanus; and the praetor would lay the matter before a meeting of the Senate, at which not less than a hundred must be present. The Senate may give leave for the worship, provided that no more than five persons be present at it; and that there be no common fund for its support, nor any permanent priest to preside at it.

These clauses, says Aust,[38] are a concession to the strong spiritual current of feeling which sought for something fresher and better to take the place of the old religion of forms ; and on the whole we may agree with him.   All religious revivals are liable to be accompanied by moral evil, but they all express unmistakably a natural and honourable yearning of the human spirit.

Not long after this, in 181, the government put its foot down firmly on what seems to have been another attempt, though in this case a ludicrous one, to introduce strange religious ideas at Rome.   We have the story of this on the authority not only of Livy, but of the oldest Roman annalist, Cassius Hemina, from whose work Pliny has preserved a fragment relating to this matter.[39]   Cassius must almost certainly have been alive in 181, and would remember the event ;[40] and though his account and Livy's differ in details, we may take the story as in the main true.   A secretary (*scriba*), who had land on the Janiculan hill, dug up there a stone coffin with an inscription stating that the king Numa was buried in it.   No remains of a body were found, but in a square stone casket inside the coffin were found books written on paper (*charta*) and supposed to be writings of Numa about the Pythagorean philosophy.   These writings were read by many people, and eventually by a praetor, who at once pronounced them to be subversive of religion.   That anything supposed to emanate from Numa should have this character was of course impossible ; and it is plain that the writings were believed even at the time to be absurd forgeries, drawn up with the idea of investing strange doctrines with the authority of Numa's name ; for the legend of a religious connection between Numa and Pythagoras must have been known at the time.   The discoverer appealed to the tribunes, who referred the matter to the senate ; and the senate authorised the praetor to burn the books in the Comitium, which was done in the presence of a large assembly.

In a later lecture I shall have something to say of the

revival of Pythagoreanism in the time of Cicero, and I
need not now attempt to explain what such a revival
might mean.   All we need to note is that something
subversive of the Roman religion was believed to be
circulating in 181 in Roman society under the assumed
authority of Numa's name, and that the senate, warned
by recent experience, determined to stamp it out at once.
They seem to have suddenly become alive to the fact
that Greece, and in this instance mainly Magna Graecia,
was sending clever agents to Rome for the propagation
of ideas which might make the people less tractable to
authority.   In the stress of the great war, indeed for years
afterwards, they had probably never had leisure to reflect
on the inevitable result of the writings of a man like
Ennius, who was not improbably responsible for the
propagation of these very Pythagorean notions.[41]   Now
a reaction seems to set in against the flowing tide of
admiration for everything Greek ;[42] but it was too late
to arrest the flood.   All that could be hoped for was that
in the lives and minds of the wiser Romans the new
Greek civilisation might so leaven the old Roman ignorance that no permanent harm should be done to the
instincts of *virtus* and *pietas* : and to some extent this
hope was realised.   But for the masses there was no such
hope.   What Greek teaching reached their minds was
almost wholly that of the *ludi scenici* ; and I must now
say a word in conclusion about this unwholesome influence—unwholesome, that is, so far as it affected the
old religious ideas.

I had occasion, when dealing with Dr. Frazer's notion
that the Roman religion admitted such ideas as the
marriage of the gods with all its natural consequences,[43]
to point out that his evidence was almost wholly derived
from the play-writers of the very period on which we are
now engaged.   I said that he seems to be justified in
concluding that there was a popular idea of such a kind,
which the State religion did not recognise ; but that it
can very easily be explained as the natural effect of a

degenerate Greek mythology, popularised by Greek dramas adapted to the Roman stage, upon certain peculiarities of the Roman theology, and especially the functional combination of male and female divine names in Italian invocations of the deities.   Nothing could be more natural than that playwrights should take advantage of such combinations to invent or translate comic passages to please a Roman audience, " now largely consisting of semi-educated men who had lost faith in their own religion, and a host of smaller people of mixed descent and nationality." We do not know enough of the older comedies to be at all sure how far they had gone in this direction, though we are certain, to use the words of Zeller,[44] that it was impossible to transplant Greek poetry to Roman soil without bringing Greek mythology with it ; or, as I should put it, without subordinating the old reasonable idea of the Power manifesting itself in the universe to the Greek fancy for clothing that Power in the human form and endowing it with human faults and frailties.

But of the two great literary figures of the age we have now reached, Ennius and Plautus, we know beyond all doubt that they taught the ignorant Roman of their day not only to be indifferent to his deities, but to laugh at them.   Just at the very time when the forged books of Numa were being burnt in the Comitium, Ennius' famous translation of the *Sacred History of Euhemerus* was becoming known at Rome, in which was taught the doctrine of the human origin of all deities ; and though we have hardly a fragment left of the comedies of Ennius, we may presume that he would not have hesitated for a moment to make the gods ridiculous on the stage.   It was he who wrote the celebrated lines in his tragedy of Telamo :[45]

ego deum genus esse semper dixi et dicam caelitum,
sed eos non curare opinor quid agat humanum genus,

which (as I have said elsewhere)[46] strike a direct blow at

the efficacy of sacrifice and prayer by openly declaring that
the gods did not interest themselves in mankind.   This
is the same Epicurean doctrine afterwards preached by
Lucretius, and I must return to it in the next lecture.
At present let us select a couple of specimens of the
more explicit evidence of the extant plays of Plautus,
which began to be exhibited at Rome just about the end
of the war with Hannibal.

Here is an example of the way in which the family
relationships of Greek gods could be made amusing
under Roman names.   Alcesimarchus in the *Cistellaria*
wishes to make a strong asseveration, and begins : [47]

> at ita me di deaeque, superi et inferi et medioxumi,

but immediately goes on to specify these deities more
particularly by their names and relationships—*and gets
the latter wrong*.   Melaenis corrects him in a way which
(as Aust notes) [48] could only have seemed comical to a
Roman audience if they had already some acquaintance
with the divine family gossip.

> itaque me Iuno regina et Iovi' supremi filia
> itaque me Saturnus eiius patruos—ME. ecastor, pater.
> AL. itaque me Ops opulenta, illius avia—ME. immo mater quidem.

Perhaps it was the fancy of the age for divine
genealogy that is here being made fun of rather than
the gods themselves ; but in any case the passage shows
how irrecoverably lost was the real impersonal character
of the old Roman *numen*, and how impossible it must
have been in such an age to believe that anything was
really to be gained by the once solemn rites of the *ius
divinum*.

But the most remarkable evidence is in the Amphitruo,[49] where Jupiter and Mercurius are among the
dramatis personae.   This comedy is extremely amusing,
and was quite capable of entertaining the Parisians in
the form given it by Molière ; but for them it could
hardly have been so funny as for the Greeks in the age
of the New Comedy and their disciples the Romans of

Plautus' day, who saw Zeus and Hermes, Jupiter and Mercurius, brought by their own misdoings into absurd and degrading situations. Jupiter personates Amphitruo, and so gains admission to his wife, Alkmene! Comment is needless, unless we take the last line of the play as a comment :—

> Nunc, spectatores, Iovi' summi causa clare plaudite!

I do not propose to follow further the downfall of the old Roman ideas about the objects of worship, or the neglect and decay of the *ius divinum*. They do not fall within the scope of my subject—the religious experience of the Roman people. So long as there was any life in these ideas and in the cult which was the practical expression of them, they formed part of that experience. But I think I have sufficiently proved that the life has gone out of the ideas, and that the worship has consequently become meaningless. Ideas about the divine may be discussed by philosophers as the Romans begin to read and in some degree to think ; and the outward forms of the cult may be maintained in such particulars as most closely concern the public life of the community ; but as a religious system expressing human experience we have done with these things.

NOTES TO LECTURE XV

1. Polybius vi. 56.

2. Livy xxxi. 4 *ad fin.*, cp. xxv. 2, xxvii. 36, etc. For the *Iovis epulum* see *R.F.* 216 foll. and the references there given. Wissowa, *R.K.* foll. 111. 385 foll. I am not sure that I am right in limiting the human partakers of the epulum of Nov. 13 to the plebeian magistrates.

3. Livy xxxi. 5. The importance of the words "prolationem finium" does not seem to have been noticed by historians. If they are genuine they indicate an undoubtedly aggressive attitude.

4. Livy xxxi. 7 and 8.

5. Livy xxxvi. 1.

6. Augustine, *Civ. Dei*, iv. 27 : "Relatum est in litteras doctissimum pontificem Scaevolam disputasse tria genera tradita deorum : unum a poetis, alterum a philosophis, tertium a principibus civitatis.

Primum genus nugatorium dicit esse, quod multa de diis fingantur indigna, etc.   Expedire igitur falli in religione civitates."

7. Livy xxxii. 9, cp. 28.   In connection with these *prodigia* it may be worth noting that in xxxii. 30 we are told that a consul vowed a temple to Juno Sospita, who had in her famous seat at Lanuvium been a constant centre of marvel-mongering.   Livy xxxiv. 53 places the building of this temple *in foro olitorio* three years later, if we may read there Sospitae instead of the Matutae of the MSS. with Sigonius : (cp. Aust, *de Aedibus*, p. 21, and Wissowa, *R.K.* 117).   This interesting deity had been taken into the Roman worship in 338 B.C., but not moved from Lanuvium, which had peculiar religious relations with Rome.   See *Myth. Lex.* vol. ii. p. 608, where the attributes of this Juno in art are described by Vogel.   The date of the temple at Rome was 194.   Whether the object of it was to diminish the portents at Lanuvium it is impossible to say, but judging from the records of *prodigia* in Julius Obsequens it had that effect.   I find only four *prodigia* reported from Lanuvium after this date.

8. See the passage in Frontinus, *de Aqueductibus*, i. 7 (C. Herschel's edition gives the reading of the best MS.), and the mutilated passage in the new epitomes of Livy found by Grenfell and Hunt in Egypt (*Oxyrrhyncus Papyri*, vol. iv. pp. 101 and 113). The general bearing of the two passages taken together seems to me to be that given in the text.

9. Cic. *ad Fam.* i. 1 and 2.   A somewhat similar case in 190 B.C. will be found in Livy xxxviii. 45, where the oracle forbade a Roman army to cross the Taurus range.

10. Livy xxxiv. 55.

11. Livy xxxviii. 56, mentions statues which were believed to be those of Scipio the elder, his brother Lucius, and Ennius, "in Scipionum monumento" outside the Porta Capena, and another of Scipio at Liternum, where he had a villa ; this one Livy says that he saw himself blown down by a storm.   On statues and busts at Rome, see Pliny xxxiv. 28 foll. ; Mrs. Strong, *Roman Sculpture*, p. 28 foll. ; *Cambridge Companion to Latin Studies*, p. 550 foll. ; and for coins, p. 456.

12. See above, p. 240, for the remarkable exception in the case of the elder Scipio, whose practice when in Rome was to go up to the Capitoline temple before daybreak and contemplate the statue of Jupiter ; the dogs never barked at him, and the aedituus opened the *cella Iovis* at his summons.   I see no good ground for rejecting this story, which is not likely to have been invented.   It can be traced back to two writers, Oppius, the friend of Caesar, and Julius Hyginus, the librarian of Augustus (Gell. vi. 1. 1), and was probably based on tradition.   Livy mentions it in xxvi. 19, and suggests that this and other ways of Scipio were assumed to impress the multitude. The Roman mind was naturally averse from such individualism in

religion ; but Scipio was beyond doubt more familiar than his contemporaries with Greek ideas.   In a chapter on Idealism in his little book on *Religion and Art in Ancient Greece*, Professor Ernest Gardner writes : " The statue (of Athene) by Phidias within the Parthenon offered not merely that form in which she would choose to appear if she showed herself to mortal eyes, but actually showed her form as if she had revealed it to the sculptor. To look upon such an image helped the worshipper as much as— perhaps more than—any service or ritual, to bring himself into communion with the goddess, and to fit himself, as a citizen of her chosen city, to carry out her will in contributing his best efforts to its supremacy in politics, in literature, and in art."   That Scipio had some feeling of this kind need not be doubted, though the statue was not a great work of art like that of Phidias.   Cp. Lucretius, vi. 75 foll.

13. See below, p. 386.

14. Marquardt, 332, and Mommsen, *Staatsrecht*, i. ed. 2, p. 463 foll.

15. Livy, *Epit.* xix.

16. Livy xxxvii. 51 : " Religio ad postremum vicit, ut dicto audiens esset flamen pontifici."   Here *religio* is used in the sense of obligation to the *ius divinum*.

17. Livy xxvii. 6 ; cp. 36.

18. This story is told in Livy xl. 42.

19. Livy xxvii. 8.   For the compelling power (*capere*) of the Pont. Max., see Marq. 314.   The story may have come from the annals of the Valerii Flacci, and also from those of the pontifices ; it was apparently well known, as Valerius Maximus knew it (vi. 9. 2).

20. Velleius ii. 43.

21. Livy xxxi. 50.

22. For the oath see " Lex incerta reperta Bantiae," lines 16 and 17, in Bruns, *Fontes Iuris Romani.*   The oath taboo is mentioned by Gellius 10. 15. 3. ; Festus 104, and Plutarch, *Quaest. Rom.* 113.

23. Livy xxxii. 7 ; xxxix. 39.

24. Tac. *Ann.* iv. 16.

25. See above, p. 255.

26. Farnell, *Cults of the Greek States*, vol. v. p. 85 foll.   Very interesting is the modern survival of Dionysiac rites recently discovered in Thrace by Mr. Dawkins (*Hellenic Journal*, 1906, p. 191).

27. Farnell, *op. cit.* vol. v. p. 150.

28. Quoted by Farnell, p. 151, from Rohde's *Psyche.*

29. It is possible that *superstitio* may originally have had some such meaning ; see W. Otto in *Archiv für Religionswissenschaft*, 1909, p. 548 foll. ; Mayor's edition of Cic. *de Nat. Deorum*, note on ii. 72 foll.

30. Ovid, *Fasti*, iii. 523 foll. See also *Roman Society in the Age of Cicero*, p. 289.

31. See Mr. Heitland's *History of the Roman Republic*, vol. ii. p. 229 note, and cp. Wissowa in Pauly-Wissowa, *Real-Encycl. s.v.* " Bacchanalia."

32. Livy xxxix. 8 foll.

33. Plato, *de Rep.* 364 B ; cp. *Laws*, 933 D.

34. " Quaestio de clandestinis coniurationibus decreta est," Livy xxxix. 8 ; so also in chs. 14 and 17. Cp. *Sctm. de Bacchanalibus*, line 13, " conioura (se)." This document is, strictly speaking, a letter to the magistrates " in agro Teurano" in Bruttium embodying the orders of the Senatus consultum.   It will be found in Bruns, *Fontes Iuris Romani*, or in Wordsworth, *Fragments and Specimens of Early Latin.*

35. Livy xxxix. 16 : " Omnia, dis propitiis volentibusque, faciemus, qui quia suum numen sceleribus libidinibusque contaminari indigne ferebant," etc.

36. Mommsen, *Strafrecht*, p. 567 foll.

37. Livy xxxix. 18 *ad fin. Sctm. de Bacch.* lines 3 foll.

38. *Religion der Römer*, p. 78.

39. Livy xl. 29 seems to have put his account together from Cassius Hemina and other annalists, so far as we can judge from the reference to them in Pliny, *N.H.* xiii. 84 ; Valerius Antias, who simply stated that the writings were Pythagorean as well as Numan, Livy rejects as ignorant of the chronological impossibility of making the king contemporary with the philosopher.   The fragment of Cassius Hemina is quoted in Pliny, sec. 86 ; Val. Max. i. 1, and Plutarch, *Numa* 22, add nothing to our knowledge of the incident.

40. See Schanz, *Gesch. der röm. Literatur*, i. 268 ; Pliny, *loc. cit.*, calls him " vetustissimus auctor annalium," but his work was later than the *Annals* or *Origines* of Cato.

41. Ennius came from South Italy (Rudiae in Messapia), the home of Pythagoreanism.   For traces of it in his works, see Reid on Cicero, *Academica priora*, ii. 51.

42. This is the view taken by Colin, *Rome et la Grèce, 200-146 B.C.*, p. 269 foll.   This reaction was probably only a part of the general reversion to conservatism which we have been noticing in the action of the government in religious matters.

43. See above, p. 149 foll.

44. Quoted by Aust, *Religion der Römer*, p. 64.   The passage is in Zeller's *Religion und Philosophie bei den Römern*, a short treatise reprinted in his *Vorträge und Abhandlungen*, ii. 93 foll.

45. Ribbeck, *Fragmenta Tragicorum Latinorum*, p. 54.

46. *Social Life at Rome in the Age of Cicero*, p. 334.

47. *Cistellaria*, ii. 1. 45 foll.

48. Aust, *op. cit.* p. 66.

49. See Schanz, *Gesch. der röm. Literatur*, vol. i. p. 75.

LECTURE XVI

I SAID at the end of the last lecture that ideas about the Divine might be discussed at Rome by philosophers, as the Romans began to read and in some degree to think. At the era we have now reached, the latter half of the second century B.C., this process actually began, and I propose in this lecture to deal with it briefly. But my subject is the Roman religious experience, and I can only find room for philosophy so far as the philosophy introduced at Rome had a really religious side. Another reason forbidding me to give much space to it is that it was at Rome entirely exotic, did not spring from an indigenous root in Roman life and thought, and never seriously affected the minds of the lower and less educated population. And I must add that the types of Greek philosophy which concern us at all have been fully and ably dealt with, the one in vol. ii. of Dr. Caird's lectures on this foundation on *The Evolution of Theology in the Greek Philosophers*, a work from which I have learnt much, and the other by Dr. Masson in his most instructive work on the great Epicurean poet Lucretius.

We have seen in the two last lectures that in that second century B.C. the Roman was fast becoming religiously destitute—a castaway without consolation, and without the sense that he needed it. He was destitute, first, in regard to his idea of God and of his relation to God ; for if we take our old definition of religion, which seems to me to be continually useful, we can hardly say of that age that it showed any effective desire to be in right relation with the Power manifesting itself in the universe. The old idea of the manifestation of the Power in the various *numina* had no longer any relation to Roman life ; the kind of life in which it germinated and grew, the life of agriculture and warlike self-defence, had passed away with the growth of the great city, the decay of the small farmer, and the extension of the empire ; and no new informing and inspiring principle had taken its place. Secondly, he was destitute in regard to his sense of duty, which had been largely dependent on religion, both in the family and in the State.   No new force had come in to create and maintain conscience.   In public life, indeed, the religious oath was still powerful, and continued to be so, though there are some signs that its binding force was less strong than of yore, especially in the army.[1]   But in a society so complex as that of Rome in the last two centuries B.C. much more was wanted than a bond sanctioned by civil and religious law ; there was needed a sense of duty to the family, the slave, the provincials, the poor and unfortunate.   There was no spring of moral action, no religious consecration of morality, no stimulus to moral endeavour.   The individual was rapidly developing, emancipating himself from the State and the group-system of society ; but he was developing in a wrong direction.   The importance of self, when realised in high and low alike, was becoming self-seeking, indifference to all but self.   We have now to see whether philosophy could do anything to relieve this destitution of the Romans in regard both to God and duty.

The first system of philosophy actually to make its appearance at Rome was that of Epicurus[2] ; but it speedily disappeared for the time, and only became popular in the last century B.C., and then in its most repulsive form.   It was indeed destined to inspire the noblest mind among all Roman thinkers with some of the greatest poetry ever written ; but I need say little of it, for it was never really a part of Roman religious experience. Though capable of doing men much good in a turbulent and individualistic age, it did not and could not do this by establishing a religious sanction for conduct. The Epicurean gods were altogether out of reach of the conscience of the individual. They were superfluous even for the atomic theory on which the whole system was pivoted;[3] and what Epicurus himself understood by them, or any of his followers down to Lucretius, is matter of subtle and perplexing disputation.[4] One point is clear, that they had no interest in human beings;[5] and the natural inference would be that human beings had no call to worship them ; yet, strange to say, Epicurus himself took part in worship, and in the worship of the national religion of his native city. Philodemus, the contemporary of Lucretius, expressly asserts this,[6] and even insists that Epicurism gave a religious sanction to morality which was absent in Stoicism.[7] Lucretius himself clearly thought that worship was natural and possible. ' If you do not clear your mind of false notions," he says, " nec delubra deum placido cum pectore adibis."[8] Man might go on with his ancestral worship, but entirely without fear, and as with " placid mind " he took part in the rites of his fathers, a mysterious divine influence might enter his mind ; " the images of a Zeus, a Heracles, an Athene, might pass in and impress on him the aspect and character of each deity, and carry with them suggestions of virtue, of courage, of wise counsel in difficulty."[9] Evidently both Epicurus and his followers had felt the difficulty and the peril of breaking entirely with the religious habits of the mass of the people, and had conscientiously done their best to reconcile their own belief with popular practice—an attempt which has its parallel in the religious speculation of the present day.

But for the Roman follower of Epicurus, wholly unused to such subtle ideas as the passage of divine influence into the mind by means of religious contemplation, this lame attempt to bring apathetic gods into relation with human life must have been quite meaningless. Cicero well expresses the common sense of a Roman at the very beginning of his treatise on the *Nature of the Gods*.[10] " If they are right who deny that the gods have any interest in human affairs, where is there room for *pietas*, for *sanctitas*, for *religio* ? " What, he adds, is the use of worship, of honour, of prayer ? If these are simply make-believes, *pietas* cannot exist, and with it we may almost assume that *fides* and *iustitia*, and the social virtues generally, which hold society together, must vanish too. Such criticism is characteristically Roman, and we may take it as representing accurately the feeling of the old-fashioned Roman of Cicero's day, as well as of the Stoic or Academic critic of Epicurism. On the other hand, the believing Epicurean at Rome was not more likely to accept the compromise ; he had done with his own gods and their worship, and such a " ficta simulatio " was not likely to attract him. Even Lucretius, whose mind was in a sense really religious, does no more in the passage I quoted just now than *allude* to actual worship of the gods, and he makes it quite clear that the tranquillity and happiness coming from contemplation, and the punishment that follows misdoing, are both purely subjective ; the gods are not active in influencing man's life, but man influences that life himself by opening his mind to the contemplation of the gods. This passage of Lucretius (vi. 68 foll.) is, if I am not mistaken, the nearest approach to real religion that we find in the history of Roman Epicurism ; yet so far as we know it bore no fruit. It seems to me to express a genuine feeling, a *religio*, but the expression is blurred by a consciousness of inconsistency.

The fact is that in the system of Epicurus the Power manifesting itself in the universe is not a divine Power, but a mechanical one ; the gods have nothing to do with it, they cannot be active, their perfection is found in repose ; they are an adjunct, an after-thought in the system. Thus all attempts to reconcile the Power with the popular religion must inevitably be failures, and more especially

so in the Roman world. At best the Epicurean gods
could but set an example of quietism which could not
possibly be a force for good in that active world of
business and government.[11] The real force of Epicurism,
for the Roman at least, if I am not mistaken, was
analogous to a religious force, though far indeed from
being one in reality—I mean the profound and touching
belief in the Founder himself as a saviour, which is so
familiar to all readers of Lucretius.[12] And the real
legacy of Lucretius himself to Roman religion is only
indirectly a religious one—I mean the wholesome contempt for "*superstitio*" and all the baser side of religious
belief and practice, old and new.[13] If his devotion to the
Master had been rooted more in the love of goodness
and less in the admiration for his speculations, and if his
contempt for *superstitio* had been less harshly dogmatic,
had he been more sympathetic and generous in his
attitude to the Italian ideas of the divine—the power of
Lucretius might possibly have been strong and permanent.

Thus for the Roman's destitution in regard to God
Epicurism could find no remedy, and as a consequence
it could provide no religious sanction for his conduct in
life. What power it had upon conduct as a system of
ethics is a question outside the range of my subject. No
doubt a certain type of mind, naturally pure and good,
and apt to retire upon itself, might find in Epicurism
not only no harm but even positive help ; perhaps the
best way to appreciate this fact, too often overlooked, is
to read the defence of the Epicurean ethics put into the
mouth of Torquatus, in the first book of the *de Finibus*,[14]
by one who was far from being in sympathy with the
creed. But for the Roman of that age, when ideas of
duty and discipline were losing strength, this enticing
faith, with pleasure as its *summum bonum*, and with
quietism as its ideal of human life,[15] could hardly be
a real stimulus to active virtue ; the Roman needed
bracing, and this was not a tonic, but a sedative. Far
more valuable in every way, and far better suited to the

best instincts of the Roman character, was the rival creed
of Stoicism, and I must devote the rest of this lecture to
the consideration of its religious aspect.

It was most fortunate for Rome that her best and
ablest men in the second century B.C. fell into the hands,
not of Epicureans, but of Stoics—into the hands, too, of a
single Stoic of high standing, fine character, and good
sense. For destitute as the Roman was both in regard
to God and to Duty, he found in Stoicism an explanation
of man's place in the universe,—an explanation relating
him directly to the Power manifesting itself therein, and
deriving from that relation a *binding* principle of conduct
and duty. This should make the religious character of
Stoicism at once apparent. It is perfectly true, as the
late Mr. Lecky said long ago,[10] that "Stoicism, taught
by Panaetius of Rhodes, and soon after by the Syrian
Posidonius, became the true religion of the educated
classes. It furnished the principles of virtue, coloured
the noblest literature of the time, and guided all the
developments of moral enthusiasm." To this I only
need to add that it woke in the mind an entirely new
idea of Deity, far transcending that of Roman *numina*
and of Greek polytheism, and yet not incapable of being
reconciled with these ; so that it might be taken as an
inpouring of sudden light upon old conceptions of the
Power, glorifying and transfiguring them, rather than,
like the Epicurean faith, a bitter and contemptuous negation of man's inherited religious instincts. But before
we go on to consider this illumination more closely, let
me say a few words about Panaetius the Stoic missionary,
and Scipio Aemilianus, his most famous disciple.

Scipio, born 184, was a happy combination of the
best Roman aristocratic character and the receptive intelligence which for a Roman was the chief result of a
Greek liberal education. He had been educated by his
famous father, Aemilius Paulus, in a thoroughly healthy
way ; he was no mere book-student, but a practical
courageous Roman, with a solid mental foundation of

moral rectitude (*pietas*) fixed firmly in the traditions and
instincts of his own family. On this foundation, as has
been well said,[17] a superstructure of intellectual culture
might be built securely without destroying it, and this
was exactly what did take place, both for Scipio and for
that circle of friends of his which has become so famous
in Roman history. In very early life he became the
intimate friend of Polybius, whose account of their first
unreserved intercourse is one of the most delightful passages in all ancient literature;[18] and from Polybius he
doubtless learnt to think. He must have learnt to understand the real nature of the Roman empire, to appreciate
the forces which had called it into being,[19] the qualities
which had preserved it through the fearful struggle with
Hannibal, and the duty of a noble Roman in regard to
it. From Polybius, indeed, it is not likely that he gained
much light on matters either of religion or morality; but
that statesman and historian must inevitably have accustomed him, in the course of their long intercourse, to think
more deeply than Roman had ever yet thought, about
the world in which he lived and was to act for many
years the leading part. Thus he was well prepared for
the friendship of a more spiritual guide.

Panaetius, who was probably about the same age as
Scipio, had the advantage, as a visitor at Rome, of being
a Rhodian, *i.e.* a citizen of the one Greek State which had
been almost continuously on good terms with Rome, and
of great value to her. He was also a scion of an old and
honoured family in that city, and was thus in every way
a fit friend and companion for a great Roman noble.
When their friendship began we do not know for certain;
but it is a fact that he lived for some two years, together
with Polybius, in the house of Scipio, and these years
were probably between 144 and 141 B.C., after Scipio's
return from the conquest of Carthage.[20] When Scipio in
141 was commissioned by the Senate to go and set
things in order in the eastern Mediterranean, he took
Panaetius with him,[21] and brought him home to live with

him again as a guest, perhaps until he left for the Numan-
tine war in 134, after which it is not likely that they met
again before Scipio's sudden death in 129. I am particular about the extent of their intimacy, because I wish
to make it clear that this was no ordinary or fleeting
friendship between a commonplace Greek philosopher
and an average Roman statesman. Both statesman and
philosopher were far above the usual level of their kind,
and in the course of this long intimacy must have had
full opportunity of learning from each other. From
Scipio Panaetius would learn the secrets of the Roman
temperament, and divine the right methods of dealing
with it, and the result of this was a happy modification
of the old rigidity of the Stoic principles—an adaptation
of them to the Roman character which had far-reaching
consequences. From Panaetius Scipio and his friends
would learn a new and illuminating conception of man's
place in the universe, and of his relation to the Power
manifested in it. To understand the power of Stoicism
on the mind of these Romans and their intellectual
successors, it is necessary to have a clear idea of this
illumination.

Hitherto there had been nothing in the religion of
Rome, or of any other city-state, to make it inevitable,
reasonable, that man should worship the Power, except
tradition and self-interest, involved in the tradition and
self-interest of the family and the city. The gods belonged, as we saw, to family or city as divine inhabitants,
and if you neglected them they would show their anger
against you. Originally it was *religio*, the feeling of awe
for something distinct from man and unknown to him,
which forced him to propitiate that which he might fear,
but had no reason, except the instinct of self-preservation,
to reverence; and later on, as he came to know his
numina better, to make them, so to speak, his own, and
to formulate the methods of propitiating them, he gradually came also to take them for granted, and to worship
them as a matter of traditional duty. The idea of con-

forming his life to the will of any of these *numina* would,
of course, be absolutely strange to him—the expression
would have no meaning whatever for him. The help
which he sought from them was not moral help, but
material.[22]   But now, when the *religio* has been hypnotised
and soothed away, and when the tradition of ceremonial
observance was growing dim and weak, when he is left
alone with his fellow-men, and without any binding
reason for right conduct towards them, he may learn
from Stoicism that there is a Power above and beyond
all his *numina*, yet involving and embracing them all, to
which, and by the help of which, as a man endowed with
reason, he *must* conform his life.

The theology held and taught by Panaetius, in common
with all Stoics at all periods, was based upon two leading
thoughts, in the correlation of which lay the kernel of the
Stoic ethical system.   The first of these thoughts is this :
the whole universe, in all its forms and manifestations,
shows unmistakably the work of Reason, of Mind ; without mind, reason, *spiritus*, as Cicero calls it,[23] the universe
could not exist. I need not go here into the origin and
history of this thought ; what is important for us is to
make clear the theological consequences of it. Obviously
it was natural that the Stoic should be led on to the
conviction that this universe endowed with Reason—
with a Reason far transcending all human capacity—
must itself be God. The Stoic arguments in support of
this further step are indeed lame, as they inevitably must
be ; they are well set forth at the beginning of Book ii.
of Cicero's work *de Natura Deorum* (based upon one by
Posidonius, the successor and disciple of Panaetius), where
they seem to us rather cold and formal. That step is
indeed incapable of being made convincing by any
syllogism ; it is only when we try to think with the
minds of those old thinkers, living in a world of unmeaning worship, that we begin to realise the nobility of a
conviction which they tried in vain to reduce to a
syllogism. *Sapiens a principio mundus, et deus habendus*

est;[24] these words, which sound like an article of a creed, suffice for us without the laborious arguments of Cleanthes and Chrysippus which we may read in the fifth and sixth chapters of Cicero's book. Cicero has added to these a characteristic illustration from city life, which I may quote as more useful for us. "If a man enters a house or a gymnasium or a forum, and sees reason, method, and discipline reigning there, he cannot suppose that these came about without a cause, but perceives that there is someone there who rules and is obeyed: how much more, when he contemplates the motions and revolutions to be seen in the universe (*e.g.*, in the heavenly bodies), must he conclude that they are all governed by a conscious Mind!" And this Mind can be nothing else but God.

This sounds like the Deism of the eighteenth century, and might be described as "natural religion"; but the Stoics took yet another step, and developed their thought into Pantheism. The idea of a personal Deity, distinct from the universe and its Creator, was obnoxious to them; it would have committed them to a dualism of Mind and Matter which, from the very outset of their history, they emphatically repudiated; their conviction was of a Unity in all things, and to this they consistently held in spite of constant and damaging criticism. The theological result of this conviction has lately been well expressed by Dr. Bussell.[25] He is speaking of Seneca in particular, but what he says applies to all Stoics equally well: "Though he yearns to see God in 'the moral order of the Universe,' he is forced in the interests of Unity to identify Him with every other known force. As He is everything, so any name will suit Him. He is the sum of existence: or the secret and abstract law which guides it: He is Nature or Fate. The partial names of special deities are all His, and together they make up the fulness of the divine title; but *they disappear in the immense nothingness*, rather than colour or qualify it." This is a point of immense importance for the study of Stoicism at

Rome ; it was fully developed by Posidonius, and copied from him both by Cicero and Varro. " God," says Cicero in the book I have been quoting, " pervading all nature (*pertinens per naturam cuiusque rei*), can be understood as Ceres on the land, as Neptune on the sea, and so on, and may be and should be worshipped in all these different forms ; " not in superstitious fear and grovelling spirit— the mental attitude which Lucretius had condemned years before this treatise was written—but with pure heart and mind, following the one and true God in all his various manifestations.[26]   Thus the Stoic Pantheism, in spite of its weak points, could find room for the deities of the city-state, and put new illuminating life into them. To us it may seem, as it seems to Dr. Bussell, that they would disappear in an immense nothingness ; but to the Roman mind of Scipio's age, if I am not mistaken, they might, on the contrary, save the great Pantheistic idea from so itself disappearing.   I cannot but think that the Roman's idea of divinity, the force or will-power which he called *numen*,[27] would find here a means of reviving its former hold on the Roman mind, and enabling it to grasp as a concrete fact, and not merely as an abstract idea, the " deus pertinens per naturam cuiusque rei."   In particular the Roman conception of the great Jupiter, the father of heaven, might gain new life for the people who had so long been used to call him " the Best and Greatest."   Almost from the very beginning of Stoicism the school had seized upon Zeus to convey, under the guise of a personality and a name, some idea of the Reason in the universe ;[28] and the same use might just as well, perhaps even better, be made of the great deity of the Capitoline temple, whom his people recognised as the open heaven with all its manifestations, the celestial representative of good faith and righteous dealing, and the special protector of the destinies of Rome and her empire.

The second thought which lies at the base of the religion or theology of Stoicism, is this : that Man himself, alone in all the Universe, shares with God the full possession of Reason.   In other words, Man alone, besides God, is strictly individual, self-conscious, capable of realising an end and of working towards it ; he is so utterly different from the animals, so far above them (or if we call him an animal, he is, in Cicero's language,[29] *animal providum, sagax, multiplex, acutum, memor, plenum rationis et consilii*), that he must surely be of the same nature as God.   And this is what, in strict conformity with all Stoic teaching, Cicero in this same passage expressly says—man is *generatus a deo*.   So too in the famous hymn of Cleanthes,[30] quoted by St. Paul at Athens ("For we are also his offspring,") :—

Chiefest glory of deathless Gods, Almighty for ever,
Sovereign of Nature that rulest by law, what name shall we give thee ?
Blessed be Thou, for on Thee should call all things that are mortal.
For that we are Thy offspring : nay, all that in myriad motion
Lives for its day on the earth bears one impress, Thy likeness, upon it ;
Wherefore my song is of Thee, and I hymn Thy power for ever.

In these splendid lines it is plain that not Man only is thought of, but all living things, animals included with Man ; and this is in accordance with the true Stoic Pantheism.   But none the less on this account did the Stoics believe Man to be the one living thing in the universe comparable with God, and capable of communion with him by virtue of the possession of Reason.   As Cicero says, a few lines farther on in the work I am quoting, "virtus eadem in homine ac deo est, neque ullo alio ingenio praeterea."   And since every creature seeks to maintain and augment its own being, to bring it to perfection, to express it fully, by an innate law of its nature, Man being endowed with Reason above all other creatures, strives, or should strive, to bring himself to a perfect expression, by identifying himself with the divine principle which he shares with God.   As Dr. Caird puts it,[31] "the ruling power of Reason so dominates his nature that he cannot be described as anything but a self-conscious *ego* (*i.e.* in contrast with other animals) ; and just because of this, all his impulses become concentrated in one great effort after self-realisation." But the self that he tries to realise must be his true self, not his irrational impulses : the self which is a part of the divine principle. He must desire to realise himself as having Reason, and so to come into close communion with God, the Reason of the universe. Those who are at all familiar with the later Roman Stoics, Seneca and Marcus Aurelius, and Epictetus, if we may include him among them, will recognise in this inspiring thought, vague and impalpable as it may seem, the germ of many beautiful expressions of the relation of Man to God, which seem to bring Stoicism into closer spiritual connection with Christianity than any other doctrine of the ancient world.

The work of Cicero from which I have been quoting, the first book of his treatise on the Laws, *i.e.* the Roman constitution, is very probably based on one by Panaetius himself,[82] of whom we are expressly told that he used to discuss that constitution together with Polybius and Scipio in the days of their happy intimacy at Rome.[83] In any case we may find it helpful, taken together with the earlier fragmentary work *de Republica,* in trying to form some idea of the effect of this second leading Stoic thought on the best Roman minds of the last ages of the Republic. We find, as we might expect, that it is not on Man simply as individual that stress is here laid. Man is not thought of as hoping to realise his own Reason in isolation ; the Stoics, though, like their rivals, they represent a reaction of the individual against the State, were all along perfectly clear that man in isolation would be helpless, and that his own reason bade him realise himself in association with his fellow-men.[84] It is the position of Man, as associated, 1, with God, 2, with other men, that is here made prominent ; and the bond of connection is in each case Law, which is indeed only one name for the Supreme Reason and the highest Good. I must say a word about these two aspects of Man's

2 B

position in the world, in order to explain what I believe to have been the effect of this teaching on the Roman mind.

1. In explaining the relation of Man to God Cicero uses an expression which some years before he had developed in a fine passage in the Republic : *true law*, he says, *is right reason*.[35]   In the Laws he takes it up again, and argues that as both God and Man have reason, there must be a direct relation between them.[36]   And as Law and right reason are identical, we may say that Law is the binding force of that relation.   And again, this means that the universe may be looked on as one great State (*civitas*), of which both God and Man (or gods and men) are citizens, or in another way as a State of which the constitution is itself the Reason, or God's law, which all reasonable beings must obey.   Such obedience is itself the effort by which Man realises his own reason : he is a part of a reasonable universe, and he cannot rebel against its law without violating his own highest instinct.   It is not hard to see how this way of expressing the Stoic theological principle would appeal to the Roman mind. That mind was wholly incapable of metaphysical thinking ; but it could without effort understand, with the help of its social and political principles and experience, the idea of supreme intelligent rule—a supreme *imperium*, as it were, to rebel against which would be a moral *perduellio*, high treason against a supreme Law, unwritten like his own, and resting, as he thought of his own as resting, on the best instincts, tradition, reason, of his community ; from his own constitution and laws he could lift his mind without much difficulty to the constitution and law of the *communis deorum et hominum civitas.*   The idea of God in any such sense as this was indeed new to him ; but he could grasp it under the expression " universal law of right reason " when he would have utterly failed, for example, to conceive of it as " the Absolute."   He can feel himself the citizen of a State whose maker and ruler is God, and whose law is the inevitable force of Reason ;

he can realise his relationship to God as a part of the same State, gifted with the same power of discerning its legal basis, nay, even helping to administer its law by rational obedience.

2. Reason as thus ruling the universe can also provide a basis for Man's reasonable association with his fellow-men, and a religious basis if conceived as God ; for Man's recognition of the divine law, the *recta ratio*, as binding on him, is followed quite naturally by his recognition of the application of that law to the world he lives in.   " Human law comes into existence," says Zeller explaining this point,[37] " when man becomes aware of the divine law, and recognises its claim on him."   Here, again, it is easy to see how illuminating would be this conception of law for the Roman of Scipio's time.   So far the Roman idea and study of law (as I have elsewhere expressed it) [38] had been of a crabbed, practical character, wanting in breadth of treatment, destitute of any philosophical conception of the moral principles which lie behind all law and government.   The new doctrine called up life in these dry bones, and started Roman lawyers, many of whom were Stoics more or less pronounced, on a career of enlightened legal study which has left one of the most valuable legacies inherited by the modern world from ancient civilisation.   In another way too it had, I think, an immediate effect on Scipio himself and his circle, and on their mental descendants, of whom Cicero was the most brilliant : it made them look on the law and constitution of their State as eminently reasonable, and on rebellion against it as unreason, or as the Romans call it, *lascivia*, wanton disregard of principle.   So far as I know, no great Roman lawyer was ever a revolutionary like Catiline or Clodius, nor yet an obstinate conservative like Cato, whose Stoicism was of the older and less Romanised type ; the two of whom we know most in the century following the arrival of Panaetius were both wise, just, and moderate men, Mucius Scaevola and Servius Sulpicius, of whom it may be truly said they

contributed as much to civilisation as the great military and political leaders of the same period.

There now remains the question whether this noble Stoic religion, as we may fairly call it, with its ideas of the relation of Man to God and to his fellow-men, had, after all, sufficient definiteness for a Roman to act as a grip on his conscience and his conduct in his daily dealings with others. It could deduce the existence and beauty of the social virtues from its own principles; if Man partakes of the eternal Reason, or, as they otherwise put it, if he is through his Reason a part of God himself in the highest sense, and if God and Reason are in the highest sense good, then in realising his own Reason, in obeying the voice of the God within him,[40] he must be himself good by the natural instinct of his own being. Accordingly, these social virtues, duties, *officia*, as the Romans called them, were set forth by Panaetius in two books, which in a Latinised form we still fortunately possess,— the first two of Cicero's work *de Officiis*,—and without the uncompromising rigidity which characterised the original Stoic ethical doctrine inherited from the Cynics.[42] In the first book he treated of the good simply (*honestum*), in the second of the useful (*utile*), and in a third, which it was left for Cicero to execute, of the cases of conflict between these two. In this charming work there is much to admire, and even much to learn : the social virtues— benevolence, justice, liberality, self-restraint, and so on, are enlarged upon and illustrated by historical examples [42] in perfect Latin by Cicero ; and as we read it we cannot but feel that the influence of Panaetius upon his educated Roman pupils must have been eminently wholesome.

But at the same time we inevitably feel that there is something wanting. What power could such a discussion really have to constrain an ordinary man to right action ? The constraint, such as it is, seems purely an intellectual process, and this is indeed noticeable in the Stoic ethics of all periods. No Stoic brought his doctrine nearer to a religious system than Epictetus ; yet this is how Epictetus

puts the matter : [43] " If a man could be thoroughly penetrated, as he ought to be, with this *thought*, that we are
all in an especial manner sprung from God, and that God
is the Father of men as well as gods, full sure he would
never conceive aught ignoble or base of himself. . . .
Those few who *hold* that they are born for fidelity,
modesty, and unerring rightness in dealing with the things
of sense, never conceive aught base or ignoble of themselves." He means that, for the real Stoic, *self-respect is
the necessary consequence of his intellectual conception of his
place in the universe,* and that self-respect must as inevitably result in virtue. Can this intellectual attitude really
act as a constraining force on the will of the average
man ? This is far too complicated a question for me
to enter upon here, and I can but suggest the study of
it for anyone who would wish to test the actual life-
giving moral power of this philosophy. Suffice it to
say that their idea of the universe as Reason and God
naturally led the Stoics into a kind of Fatalism, a destined
order in the world which nothing could effectually oppose ; [44]
and they were naturally in some difficulty in reconciling
this with the freedom of Man's will. That freedom they
constantly and consistently asserted ; but it comes after
all to this, that Man is free to bring his will into conformity, *through knowledge,* with the Power and the universal Reason ; or, as Dr. Caird puts it, [45] Man has the
choice whether he will be a willing or an unwilling servant
(of the universal Reason) : unwilling, if he makes it his
aim to satisfy his particular self, an aim which he can
only attain so far as the general system of things allows
him ; willing, if he identifies himself with the divine
reason which is manifested in that system." But that
identification of himself with the divine Reason is again
an intellectual process ; it can only be realised by minds
highly trained in thinking ; it could not have the smallest
grip on the conduct of the ordinary ignorant man, or on
the minds of women and children.

And here we come upon another weak point in Stoicism

as presented to the Roman world in this last century B.C.
It was an age in which gentleness, tenderness, pity, and
the philanthropic spirit were most sadly needed, and it
cannot be said of Stoicism that it had any mission to
encourage their growth.   The Stoics looked on the mass
of men as ignorant and wicked,[46] and it never occurred to
them that it was a duty of the Good Man to teach and
redeem them,—to sacrifice his life, if need be, in the work
of enlightenment.   They seem to have thought even of
women and children as hardly partaking of Reason ; their
ideally good man was virtuous in a strictly virile way,[47]
and it never occurred to them that training in goodness
must begin from the earliest years, and be gradually
developed with infinite sympathy and tenderness.   If a
man is to learn that there is something within him which
partakes of God, and which should naturally lead him to
right conduct, he must begin to learn this truth in his
infancy.[48]   But the absence of a place for emotion and
sympathy in the Stoic system, resulting from the purely
intellectual nature of their central doctrine of Reason,
meant also the absence of any spirit of enthusiastic propa-
ganda.   Their notion that emotion or passion is "a movement of mind contrary to reason and nature,"[49] lamed
their whole system as a progressive force in the world of
that day.   Such religious power as it could exercise
worked simply through the radiating influence of a few
wise and good men, by nature pure and unselfish, who
gradually familiarised the educated part of society with a
nobler idea of God than the old religion had ever been
able to supply, and with that other inspiring idea of the
near relation of Man to God as partaking of His nature.
But the active enthusiasm of a real religion—the *effective*
desire to be in right relation with the Power—was strange
to Stoicism.   In one way or another it had many excellent results ; it cleared the ground, for example, for a
new and universal religion by putting into the shade, if
not altogether out of the way, the old local cults with
their narrow and limited civic force : it glorified the idea

of law and order in an age when the Roman world seemed to be forgetting what these sacred words meant ; *but a real active enthusiasm of humanity was wanting in it.* Hence there is a certain hopelessness about Stoicism, which increased rather than diminished as the world went on, and such as is seen in a kind of sad grandeur in Marcus Aurelius, the Stoic emperor. Of him it may be said, both as emperor and philosopher, as has been said of the Stoic in general, that "he was essentially a soldier left to hold a fort surrounded by overpowering hosts of the enemy. He could not conquer or drive them away, but he could hold out to the last and die at his post."

NOTES TO LECTURE XVI.

1. See, *e.g.* Livy iii. 20 : "Sed nondum haec, quae nunc tenet saeculum, neglegentia deum venerat ; nec interpretando sibi quisque iusiurandum et leges aptas faciebat, sed suos potius mores ad ea accommodabat." Cp. Cic. *de Off.* iii. 111.

2. Two Epicureans were expelled from Rome in 173 (probably), Athenaeus, p. 547. Cicero, *Tusc.* iv. 3, 7, gives some idea of the later popularity of the school in the first half of the last century B.C.

3. So Masson, *Lucretius,* i. 263, 271.

4. See Masson i. ch. xii. and ii. p. 141 foll. ; Mayor's *Cicero de Nat. Deor.* vol. i. xlviii. and 138 foll.; Guyau, *La Morale d'Épicure* (ed. 4), p. 171 foll.

5. Cic. *N.D.* i. 19, 49 foll., and many other passages ; Diog. Laert. x. 55 ; Zeller, *Stoics, Epicureans, and Sceptics,* p. 441 foll. ; Masson i. 292, who aptly quotes Cotta the academic critic in Cicero's dialogue : "When Epicurus takes away from the gods the power of helping and doing good, he extirpates the very roots of religion from the minds of men" (Cic. *N.D.* i. 45. 121). One may add with Dr. Masson (i. 416 foll.) that a machine cannot command worship ; the *Natura* of Lucretius, *i.e.,* was really a machine.

6. Masson i. p. 284, and citations of Philodemus there given.

7. Mayor's Cic. *N.D.* vol. i. p. xlix.

8. Lucr. vi. 68 foll.

9. Masson i. p. 285.

10. Cic. *N.D.* i. 2. 3.

11. Cic. *N.D.* i. 37. 102 ; to believe the gods idle "etiam homines inertes efficit."

12. For this profound reverence for Epicurus see also Cic. *N.D.*

i. 8. 18. It amounted to a faith. In this passage the Epicurean is described as "nihil tam verens quam ne dubitare aliqua de re videretur, tanquam modo ex deorum concilio et ex Epicuri intermundiis descendisset." See also sec. 43 and Mayor's note; Cic. *de Finibus*, i. 5. 14 : Masson i. 354-5, who quotes the most striking passages from Lucretius, *e.g.* v. 8-10 :

> deus ille fuit, deus, inclyte Memmi,
> qui princeps vitae rationem invenit eam quae
> nunc appellatur sapientia, etc.

In a paper entitled "Die Bekehrung (conversion) im klassischen Altertum," by W. A. Heidel (*Zeitschrift für Religionspsychologie*, vol. iii. Heft 2), the author, an American disciple of W. James, argues that the exordium of Bk. iii. indicates a psychological conversion of Lucretius.

13. See Masson's chapter (p. 399 foll.) on the teaching and personality of Lucretius. *Social Life at Rome in the Age of Cicero*, p. 327 foll., and references there given. I may note here that the power of Epicurism as a faith depended also largely on the directness, downrightness, and audacity of its system, working on minds weary of philosophers' disputations and political quarrels.

14. Cic. *de Finibus*, i. viii. to end (translation by J. S. Reid, Camb. Univ. Press). The following sentence in ch. 18, sec. 57, puts the Epicurean ethics in a nutshell : " Clamat Epicurus, is quem vos nimis voluptatibus esse deditum dicitis, non posse iucunde vivi nisi sapienter, honeste, iusteque vivatur, nec sapienter, honeste, iuste, nisi iucunde."

15. What this quietism might mean for a Roman may be gathered from the following passage in Cic. *de Finibus*, i. 13. 43, in which *sapientia* is practical wisdom, the Aristotelian φρόνησις, or the *ars vivendi*, as Cicero has explained it just before : " Sapientia est adhibenda, quae, et terroribus cupiditatibusque detractis et omnium falsarum opinionum temeritate derepta, certissimam se ducem praebeat ad voluptatem. Sapientia enim est una, quae maestitiam pellat ex animis, quae nos exhorrescere metu non sinat ; qua praeceptrice in tranquillitate vivi potest, omnium cupiditatum ardore restincto. Cupiditates enim sunt insatiabiles, quae non modo singulos homines, sed universas familias evertunt, totam etiam labefactant saepe rempublicam. Ex cupiditatibus odia discidia discordiae seditiones bella nascuntur." And so on to the end of the chapter. The message of Lucretius to the Roman was practically the same. The remedy was the wrong one in that age ; though it does not necessarily entail withdrawal from public life with all its enticements and risks, it must inevitably have a strong tendency to suggest it ; and such withdrawal had, as a matter of fact, been one of the characteristics of the Epicurean life. See Zeller, *Stoics*, etc., ch. xx. ; Guyau, *La Morale d'Épicure*, p. 141 foll.

16. *History of European Morals* (1899), vol. i. p. 225. The treatment of Stoicism in this work, though not, strictly speaking, philosophical, is in many ways most instructive.

17. F. Leo, *Die griechische und lateinische Literatur*, p. 337. See the author's *Social Life at Rome in the Age of Cicero*, p. 105.

18. Polybius xxxii. 9-16

19. See a discussion by the author of the meaning of τύχη in Polybius, *Classical Review*, vol. xvii. p. 445, and the passages there quoted relating to the growth of the Roman dominion.

20. See Schmekel, *Die mittlere Stoa*, p. 3 foll.

21. *Ib.* p. 6, note 3.

22. See above, p. 251.

23. Cic. *N.D.* ii., end of sec. 19. He is translating the Greek πνεῦμα, which in Stoicism is not a spiritual conception, but a material one, in harmony with their theory of the universe as being itself material, including reason and the soul. This is one of the weak points of the Stoic idea of Unity. For the meaning of *spiritus* see Mayor's note on the passage; it is "the ether or warm air which penetrates and gives life to all things, and connects them together in one organic whole."

24. Cic. *N.D.* ii. xiii. 36 *ad fin.* On all this department of the Stoic teaching see Zeller, *Stoics*, etc., p. 135 foll.; Caird, *Gifford Lectures*, vol. ii., Lectures 16 and 17.

25. *Marcus Aurelius and the Later Stoics*, by F. W. Bussell p. 42.

26. Cic. *N.D.* ii. ch. 28 (secs. 70-72), with Mayor's commentary; Zeller, *op. cit.* p. 327 foll.; Mayor, introduction to vol. ii. of his edition of Cic. *N.D.* xi. foll.; *Social Life at Rome in the Age of Cicero*, p. 334 foll. It is important to note the distinction drawn by Cicero between religion and superstition; what Lucretius called *religio* as a whole Cicero (and Varro too, cf. Aug. *Civ. Dei*, vi. 9) thus divided. See Mayor's valuable note, vol. ii. p. 183. Some interesting remarks on the Stoic way of dealing with popular mythology will be found in Oakesmith's *Religion of Plutarch*, p. 68 foll.

27. See above, p. 118 foll.

28. See Mayor's note on Cic. *N.D.* ii. 15. 39 (vol. i. p. 130), with quotation from Philodemus. Zeller, *Stoics*, etc., p. 337 foll.

29. Cic. *de Legibus*, i. 7. 22.

30. *Fragmenta Philosophorum Graecorum*, Paris, 1883. I have borrowed the beautiful translation of my friend Hastings Crossley, printed p. 183 foll. of his *Golden Sayings of Epictetus*, in Macmillan's Golden Treasury Series.

31. *Gifford Lectures*, ii. p. 94.

32. So Schmekel, *Die mittlere Stoa*, p. 61 foll. The evidence is

not conclusive, and the process of argument is one of elimination, but it raises a fairly strong probability.

33. Cic. *de Rep.* i. 21. 34.

34. See Zeller, *Stoics*, etc., p. 294 foll.

35. Cic. *de Rep.* iii. 22. 33.

36. Cic. *de Legibus*, i. 7. 22 foll. : "Est igitur, quoniam nihil est ratione melius, eaque in homine et in deo, prima homini cum deo rationis societas.   Inter quos autem ratio, inter eosdem etiam recta ratio communis est," etc.

37. Zeller, *Stoics*, etc., p. 226 foll.

38. *Social Life at Rome*, p. 117.

39. *Ib.* p. 118 foll.

40. I may take this opportunity of noting that a Roman might better understand this notion of his Reason as the voice of God within him, or conscience, from his own idea of his " other soul," or genius ; see above, p. 75.   But we do not know for certain that it was presented to him in this way by Panaetius, though Posidonius (*ap. Galenum*, 469) used the word δαίμων in this sense, as did the later Stoics ; see Mulder, *de Conscientiae notione*, p. 71.   Seneca, *Ep.* 41. 2, uses the word *spiritus* : " Sacer intra nos spiritus sedet . . . in unoquoque virorum bonorum, quis deus incertum est, habitat deus " (from Virg. *Aen.* viii. 352).   Cp. Marcus Aurelius iii. 3.   Seneca uses the word genius clearly in this sense in *Ep.* 110 foll.   On the Stoic daemon consult Zeller, *Stoics*, etc., p. 332 foll. ; Oakesmith, *Religion of Plutarch*, ch. vi.

41. See, *e.g.*, Zeller, p. 268.

42. This habit of illustrating by historical examples had an educational value of its own, but serves well to show how comparatively feeble was the appeal of Stoicism to the conscience.   It may be seen well in Valerius Maximus, whose work, compiled of fact and fiction for educational purposes, is far indeed from being an inspiring one.   See *Social Life at Rome*, p. 189.

43. Arrian, *Discourses*, i. 3. 1-6 (*Golden Sayings of Epictetus*, No. 9).

44. Schmekel, *Die mittlere Stoa*, p. 190 foll. (Panaetius), and 244 foll. (Posidonius), Zeller 160 foll.   This is the Fate or Providence on which the moral lesson of the *Aeneid* is based ; see below, p. 409 foll. Aeneas is the servant of Destiny.   If he had persisted in rebelling against it by remaining at Carthage with Dido, that would not have changed the inevitable course of things, but it would have ruined him.

45. *Gifford Lectures*, ii. 96.

46. Zeller, *Stoics*, etc., p. 255.   This, of course, did not diminish the duty of general benevolence, *ib.* p. 310 and references, where fine passages of Cicero and Seneca are quoted about duties to one's inferiors.   But an enthusiasm of humanity was none the less wanting in Stoicism, and this was largely owing no doubt to their hard and fast

distinction between virtue and vice, and their want of perception of a growth or evolution in society.   See Caird, *op. cit.* ii. 99 ; Lecky, *Hist. of European Morals*, i. 192 foll. ; Zeller 251 foll.

47. See some excellent remarks in Lecky, *op. cit.* i. p. 242 foll.

48. See above, note 40.

49. Zeller, *Stoics*, etc., p. 229.   Cic. *de Finibus*, iii. 10, 35 ; *Tusc. Disp.* iv. 28, 60.

LECTURE XVII

MYSTICISM—IDEAS OF A FUTURE LIFE

WE have now reached the end of the period of the Republic ; but before I go on to the age of Augustus, with which I must bring these lectures to an end, I must ask attention to a movement which can best be described by the somewhat vague term Mysticism, but is generally known to historians of philosophy as Neo-pythagoreanism. The fact is that such tendency as there ever was at Rome towards Mysticism—which was never indeed a strong one till Rome had almost ceased to be Roman[1] —seems to have taken the form of thinking known as Pythagorean. The ideas at the root of the Pythagorean doctrine, the belief in a future life, the conception of this life as only preparatory to another, the conviction of the need of purgation in another life and of the preparatory discipline and asceticism to be practised while we are here,—these are truly religious ideas ; and even among Romans the religious instinct, though it might be hypnotised, could never be entirely destroyed. When it awoke from time to time in the minds of thinking men it was apt to express itself in Pythagorean tones. With the ignorant and vulgar it might find a baser expression in superstition pure and simple,—in the finding of portents, in astrology, in Dionysiac orgies ; but with these Pythagoreanism must not be reckoned. These, as they appeared on the soil of Italy, were the bastard children of quasi-religious thought. But the movement of which I speak marks a reaction, among men who could both feel and think, against the

whole tendency of Roman religious experience as we have
been tracing it; against the extreme formalism, now
meaningless, of the Roman State religion; against the
extreme scepticism and indifference so obvious in the last
century and a half of the republican era; against the
purely intellectual appeal of the ethical systems of which
I have been recently speaking. Stoicism indeed, as we
shall see, held out a hand to the new movement, simply
because Stoicism had a religious side which was wanting
in Epicurism. But the thought that our senses and our
reason are not after all the sole fountains of our knowledge, a thought which is the essence of mysticism, was
really foreign to Stoicism; and when this thought did
find a soil in the mind of a thinking Roman of this age,
it was likely to spring up in a transcendental form which
we may call Pythagoreanism.

South Italy was indeed the true home of the
Pythagorean teaching. There its founder had established
it, and there, mixed up with more popular Orphic doctrine
and practice, it must have remained latent for centuries.[2]
"Tenuit magnam illam Graeciam," says Cicero of Pythagoras, "cum honore disciplinae, tum etiam auctoritate;
multaque saecula post sic viguit Pythagoreorum nomen,
ut nulli alii docti viderentur."[3] To South Italy Plato is
said to have travelled to study this philosophy, and to
learn the doctrine of the immortality of the soul; and the
story is generally accepted as true.[4] But of any missionary
attempt of Pythagoreanism on Rome we know nothing—
and probably there was nothing to tell—till that mysterious
plot to introduce it after the Hannibalic war which I
mentioned in a recent lecture.[5] That war brought Rome
into close contact with Tarentum and southern Italy, and
it is likely enough that the attempt to connect King Numa
with the philosopher, both in the familiar legend and in
the alleged discovery of the stone coffin with its forged
manuscripts, had its origin in this contact. The Senate
could not object to the legend, but it promptly stamped
out this grotesque attempt at propagandism. Then we

hear no more of the doctrine for a century at least ; but in the last century B.C. we know that there appeared a number of Pythagorean writings, falsely attributed to the founder himself or his disciples,[6]—a method of propagandism which, like that of the previous century, may perhaps be taken as marking the religious nature of the doctrine, which needed the *ipse dixit* of the founder or something as near it as possible.[7]   But of the immediate influence of these writings we know nothing.   The person really responsible for the tendency to this kind of mysticism was undoubtedly the great Posidonius, philosopher, historian, traveller, who more than any other man dominated the Roman world of thought in the first half of the last century B.C., and whose writings, now surviving in a few fragments only, lie at the back of nearly all the serious Roman literature of his own and indeed of the following age.[8]   Panaetius, there can be little doubt, had done something to leaven Stoicism with Platonic-Aristotelian psychology,[9] the general tendency of which was towards a dualism of Soul and Body.   The Stoics, in the strict sense of the name, " could not be content with any philosophy which divided heaven from earth, the spiritual from the material."   " They rebelled against the idea of a transcendent God and a transcendent ideal world, as modern thought has rebelled against the supernaturalism of mediaeval religion and philosophy." [10]   In their passion for unity they would not separate soul and body.   But when once Panaetius had hinted at a reversion to the older mode of thought, it was natural and easy to follow his lead in a society which had long ago abandoned burial for cremation, and bidden farewell to the primitive notion that the body lived on under the earth : in a society, too, which had always believed in that " other soul," the *Genius* of a man, as distinct from his bodily self of this earthly life.[11]

Now as soon as this dualism of body and soul was suggested, it was taken up by Posidonius into what we may call his neo-Stoic system, and at once gave mysticism,

—or transcendentalism, if we choose so to call it—its chance. For in such a dualistic psychology it is the soul that gains in value, the body that loses. Life becomes an imprisonment of the soul in the body; the soul seeks to escape, death is but the beginning of a new life, and the imagination is set to work to fathom the mysteries of Man's future existence, nay, in some more fanciful minds, those of his pre-existence as well. This kind of speculation, half philosophic, half poetical, is the transcendental side of the Platonic psychology, and in the last age of the Republic was able to connect Platonism and Pythagoreanism without deserting Stoicism.[12] We can see it reflected from Posidonius in the Dream of Scipio, the beautiful myth, imitated from those of Plato, with which Cicero concluded his treatise on the State, written in the year 54 B.C., after his retirement from political life. In this, and again in the first book of his *Tusculan Disputations*, composed nearly ten years later, Cicero is beyond doubt on the tracks of Posidonius, and therefore also of Pythagoreanism.[13] Listen to the words put into the mouth of the elder Scipio and addressed to his younger namesake: "Tu vero enitere et sic habeto, non esse te mortalem, sed corpus hoc; non enim tu es, quem forma ista declarat; sed *mens cuiusque is est quisque,* non ea figura quae digito demonstrari potest."[14] Here is the body plainly losing, the soul gaining importance. But he goes still further: "*deum igitur te scito esse*: si quidem deus est qui viget qui sentit qui meminit: qui providet, qui tam regit et moderatur et movet id corpus cui propositus est, quam hunc mundum ille princeps deus, et ut mundum ex quadam parte mortalem ipse deus aeternus, sic fragile corpus animus sempiternus movet."[15]

With such a view of the soul in relation to the body, we can understand how in this myth it is described as flying upwards, released from corporeal bondage, and ascending through heavenly stations to pure aether, if at least (and here we may note the characteristic Roman touch) its abode on earth has been the body of a good citizen.[16] All that

is of earth earthy, all old ideas of burial, all notions of a
gloomy abode below the earth, are here fairly left behind.
So too in the first book of the *Tusculans*, written after the
death of his beloved daughter, Cicero would persuade himself and others that death cannot be an evil if we once allow
the soul to be immortal: for from its very nature it must
rise into aethereal realms, cannot sink like the body into
the earth.[17]   Into its experiences in the aether I do not
need to go here.   Enough has been said to show that, as
it were, the heavens were opened, and with the psychological separation of soul from body the imaginative
faculty was released also; not indeed that any Roman,
or even Posidonius himself, could revel in cosmological
dreams as did Plato, but they found in him all they
needed, and it would seem that they made much use of
it.   Plato's *Timaeus* was made by Posidonius the subject
of a commentary,[18] and by Cicero himself it was in part
at least translated, about the time when he was writing
the *Tusculans*, and still deeply moved by his recent loss.
Of this translation a fragment survives; and in the introductory sentences he indicates a second stimulus to his
Pythagorean tendencies, besides Posidonius.   He tells how
he had met at Ephesus, when on his way to his province
of Cilicia, the famous Pythagorean Nigidius Figulus, and
had enjoyed conversation with him.[19]   Nigidius was an
old friend, who had helped Cicero in his consulship; he
was one of those " polyhistores " who are characteristic of
the age, like Posidonius and Varro, and wrote works on
all kinds of subjects of which but few fragments remain.
But his reputation as a Pythagorean survived for centuries;[20] and this mention of him by Cicero is only
another proof of the direction the thoughts of the latter
were taking in these last two years of his life.

Clearly, then, Cicero in his philosophical writings of
these years was affected by the current of mysticism that
was then running.   But to me it is still more interesting
to find it moving him in a practical matter of which he
has himself left the truth on record; for Cicero is a real

human being for whom all who are familiar with his
letters must have something in the nature of affection,
and with whom, too, we feel genuine sympathy in the
calamity which now fell upon him. It was early in
45 B.C. that he lost his only and dearly loved daughter
and the blow to his sensitive temperament, already hardly
tried by political anxiety, was severe. We still have the
private letters which he wrote to Atticus after her death
from his solitude at Astura on the edge of the melancholy
Pomptine marshes;[21] and here, if our minds are sufficiently divested of modern ideas and trained to look on
death with Roman eyes, we may be startled to find him
thinking of her as still in some sense surviving, and as
divine rather than human : as a deity or spirit to whom a
fanum could be erected. He makes it clear to Atticus,
who is acting as his business agent at Rome, that he does
not want a mere tomb (*sepulcrum*), but a *fanum*, which as
we have seen was the general word for a spot of ground
sacred to a deity. " I wish to have a *fanum* built, and
that wish cannot be rooted out of my heart. I am
anxious to avoid any likeness to a tomb, not so much on
account of the penalty of the law, as in order to attain as
nearly as possible to an *apotheosis*. This I could do if I
built it in the villa itself, but . . . I dread the changes of
owners. Wherever I construct it on the land, I think
that I could secure that posterity should respect its
sanctity."[22] The word here translated sanctity is *religio* ;
we may remember that all burial places were *loca religiosa*,
not consecrated by the State, yet hallowed by the feeling
of awe or scruple in approaching them ; but Cicero is
probably here using the word rather in that wider sense
in which it so often expresses the presence of a deity in
some particular spot.[23]

Atticus was a man of the world and probably an
Epicurean, and his friend in two successive letters half
apologises for this strong desire. " I should not like it to
be known by any other name but *fanum*,—unreasonably,
you will perhaps say." And again, " you must bear with

these silly wishes (*ineptiae*) of mine." [24]   But this only makes
the intensity of his feeling about it the more plain and
significant ; he really seems to want Tullia to be thought
of as having passed into the sphere of divinity, however
vaguely he may have conceived of it.   Perhaps he remembered his own words in Scipio's dream, " Deum te esse
scito."   The ashes of Tullia rested in the family tomb,
but the godlike thing imprisoned in her mortal body was
to be honoured at this *fanum*, which, strange as it may
seem to us, her father wished to erect in a public and
frequented place.   She does not fade away into the common herd of Manes, but remains, though as a spirit, the
same individual Tullia whom her father had loved so dearly.

I long ago explained the old Roman idea of Manes,[25]
a vague conception of shades of the dead dwelling below
the earth, and hardly, if at all, individualised.   But in
Tullia's case we meet with a clear conception of an
individual spirit ; and this alone would lead us to suspect
a Pythagorean influence at work, such as that under
which Virgil wrote the famous words " Quisque suos
patimur Manes," which simply mean " Each individual of
us must endure his own individual ghosthood." [26]   This
process of individualisation must have been gradually
coming on, but the steps are lost to us ; we only know
that the earliest sepulchral inscription which speaks to it,
in the vague plural Di Manes so familiar in later times, is
dateable somewhere about this very time.[27]   My friend
Dr. J. B. Carter would explain it, in part at least, by the
Roman conception of Genius to which I alluded just now,
and doubtless this must be taken into account.   For
myself I would rather think of it as the natural result of
the growth of individualism in the living human being
during the last two centuries B.C.   Surely it was impossible for personality to grow as it did in that period without a corresponding growth of the idea of individual
immortality in the minds of all who believed in a future
life of any kind at all.   The Epicureans did not so
believe ; but Roman Stoics instructed by Panaetius and

Posidonius might not only believe in immortality but in an immortality of the individual.

Let me take this opportunity of noting that there was, of course, no sort of restriction on a man's belief about this or any other religious question. It was perfectly open to every one to hold what view best pleased him about the state of the dead: all that the State required of him was that he should fulfil his obligations at the tombs of his own kin. No dogma reigned in the necropolis, only duty, *pietas*,— and that *pietas* implied no conviction. The Parentalia in February were originally, so far as we can discern, only a yearly renewal of the rite of burial on its anniversary ; [28] this implies civilisation and some kind of calendar, but not a creed. Later on, in the Fasti of the City-state, the day was fixed for all citizens without regard of anniversaries ; and here the rites become a matter of *ius*, the *ius Manium*, to the observance of which the Manes are entitled. Still there is no creed, though Cicero speaks of this *ius* as based on the idea of a future life. [29] As a fact these rites are a survival from an age in which the dead man was believed to go on living in the grave, but that primitive idea was no longer held by the educated. Each man was free in all periods to believe what he pleased about the dead, and as the Romans began to think, this freedom becomes easy to illustrate. Cicero himself is usually agnostic, as is in keeping with his Academic tendency in philosophy ; even in one of these very letters he seems to speak of his own non-existence after death. [30] So, too, the excellent Servius Sulpicius, in the famous letter of condolence written to Cicero at this time from Athens, seems to be uncertain. [31] We all know the words of Caesar (reported by Sallust), which are often quoted with a kind of holy horror, as though a pontifex maximus might not hold any opinion he pleased about death, and as though his doubt were not the common doubt of innumerable thinking men of the age. [32] Catullus wrote of death as "nox perpetua dormienda" ; Lucretius, of course, gloried in the thought that there is no life beyond.

In the following century the learned Pliny could write of death as the relapsing into the same nothingness as before we were born, and could scoff at the absurdities of the cult of the dead.[33]

But when a man like Cicero was deeply touched by grief, his emotional nature abandoned its neutral attitude, and turned for consolation to mysticism. As I have said, he was persuading himself that Tullia was still living,—a glorified spirit. We can gain just a momentary glimpse of what was in his mind by turning to the fragments of the *Consolatio* which he was now writing at Astura.

This was a *Consolatio* of the kind which was a recognised literary form of this and later times,[34] though in this case it was addressed by the writer to himself; to write was for Cicero second nature, and he was sure to take up his pen when he had feelings that needed expression. It is unfortunately lost, all but one fragment, which he quotes himself in the first book of his *Tusculans*, and one or two more preserved by the Christian writer Lactantius, a great admirer of Cicero, who came near to catching the beauty of his style. The passage quoted by himself is precious.[35] It insists on the spiritual nature of the soul, which can have nothing in common with earth or matter of any kind, seeing that it thinks, remembers, foresees : " ita quicquid est illud, quod sentit, quod sapit, quod vivit, quod viget, caeleste et divinum, ob eamque rem aeternum sit necesse est." And in the concluding words he hints strongly at the *divinity* of the soul, which is of the same make as God himself,—of the same immaterial nature as the only Deity of whom we mortals can conceive. His daughter, therefore, is not only still living in a spiritual life, but she is in some vague sense divine ; that word *apotheosis*, which he twice uses in the letters, has a real meaning for him at this moment ; and in a fragment of the *Consolatio* quoted by Lactantius he makes this quite plain ; " Te omnium optimam doctissimamque, approbantibus dis immortalibus ipsis, in eorum coëtu locatam, ad opinionem omnium mortalium consecrabo." [36]

Undoubtedly Cicero is here under the influence of the Pythagoreans as well as of his own emotion. In another chapter Lactantius seems to make this certain ;[37] he begins by combining Stoics and Pythagoreans as both believing the immortality of the soul, goes on to deal with the Pythagorean doctrine (or one form of it) that in this life we are expiating the sins of another, and ends by quoting Cicero's *Consolatio* to that effect : " Quid Ciceroni faciemus ? qui cum in principio Consolationis suae dixit, luendorum scelerum causa nasci homines, iteravit id ipsum postea, quasi obiurgans eum qui vitam poenam non esse putet." Another lost book, the *Hortensius*, which was written immediately after the *Consolatio*, March to May 45,[38] shows in one or two surviving fragments exactly the same tendency of thought and reading.[39] Our conclusion then must be that Cicero, always impressionable, and in his way also religious, had in this year 45 a real religious experience. He was brought face to face with one of the mysterious facts of life, and with one of the great mysteries of the universe, and the religious instinct awoke within him. How many others, even in that sordid and materialistic age, may have had the like experience, with or without a mystical philosophy to guide their thoughts ? In the last words of the famous Laudatio Turiae, of which I have written at length in my *Social Life in the Age of Cicero*,[40] we may perhaps catch an echo of a similar religious feeling : " Te di Manes tui ut quietam patiantur atque ita tueantur opto " (I pray that thy divine Manes may keep thee in peace and watch over thee). These words, expressing the hope of a practical man, not of a philosopher, are very difficult to explain, except as the unauthorised utterances of an individual. They hardly find a parallel either in literature or inscriptions. We must not press them, yet they help us to divine that there was in this last half-century B.C. some mystical yearning to realise the condition of the loved ones gone before, and the relation of their life to that of the living. This religious instinct, let us note once for all, is not identical with the old one which we expressed by the formula about the Power manifesting itself in the universe. The religious instinct of the primitive Roman was concerned only with this life and its perils and mysteries; the religious instinct of Cicero's time was not that of simple men struggling with agricultural perils, but that of educated men whose minds could pass in emotional moments far beyond the troubles of this present world, to speculate on the great questions, why we are here, what we are, and what becomes of us after death.

But what of the ordinary Roman of this age—what of the man who was not trained to think, and had no leisure or desire to read? What did he believe about a future life, or did he believe anything? This brings us to a curious question about which I must say a very few words—did this ordinary Roman, as Lucretius seems to insist, believe in Hades and its torments? Not in one passage only does Lucretius insist on this. "That fear of Hell" (so Dr. Masson translates him) "must be driven out headlong, which troubles the life of man from its inmost depth, and overspreads everything with the blackness of death, and permits no pleasure to be pure and unalloyed." [41]   I need not multiply quotations; evidently the poet believed what he said, though he may be using the exaggeration of poetical diction. And to a certain extent he is borne out by the literature of his time. In fact Polybius, writing nearly a century earlier of the Romans and their religion, implies that such notions were common, and that they were invented by "the ancients" to frighten the people into submission. [42] Cicero, though he of course thinks of them as merely the fables of poets, seems to suggest that the ordinary man did believe in them; thinking of his own recent loss, he says that our misery would be unbearable when we lose those we love, if we really thought of them as "*in iis malis quibus vulgo opinantur.*" [43]   Of course all these fables were Greek, not Roman. There is no reason to believe that the old Romans imagined their own dead experiencing any miseries in Orcus—the old name, as it would seem, for the dimly imagined abode of the Manes, afterwards personified after the manner of Plutus.[44] No doubt they believed that the dead were ghosts, desiring to get back to their old homes, who, in the well-ordered religion of the City-state, were limited in this strong desire to certain days in the civic year.[45] But their first acquaintance with Hades and its tortures may probably be dated early, i.e. when they first became acquainted with Etruscan works of art, themselves the result of a knowledge of Greek art and myth.[46] Early in the second century B.C. Plautus in the *Captivi* alluded to these paintings as familiar; [47] and we must not forget that the Etruscans habitually chose the most gruesome and cruel of the Greek fables for illustration, and especially delighted in that of Charon, one likely enough to strike the popular imagination. The play-writers themselves were responsible for inculcating the belief, as Boissier remarked in his work on the Roman religion of the early empire.[48] In the theatre, with women and children present, Cicero says in the first book of his *Tusculans*, the crowded auditorium is moved as it listens to such a "grande carmen" as that sung by a ghost describing his terrible journey from the realms of Acheron; and in another passage of the same book he mentions both painters and poets as responsible for a delusion which philosophers have to refute.[49] I need not say that the Roman poets too continually use the imagery of Tartarus; but they use it as literary tradition, and in the sixth *Aeneid* it is used also to enforce the idea of duty to the State which is the real theme of the poem.

As Dr. Masson truly observes, we have the literature but we have not the folklore of the age of Cicero and Virgil; and it must be confessed that without the folklore such scanty literary evidence as I have just mentioned does not come to much. Dr. Masson indeed concludes on this evidence that the fear of future torments played a considerable part in the religious notions both of the common people and possibly of some of the educated.   I think it may have been so, but on other grounds, which I must briefly explain.

From all that I have said in these lectures about the religious ideas represented in the earliest calendar, *i.e.* those of the governing Romans of the earliest City-state, it will be plain that a gruesome eschatology was an impossibility for them.   Just the same may be said of the Greek ideas represented in the Homeric poems ; for with the exception of the Nekuia of the *Odyssey*, which almost all scholars agree in attributing to a later age than the bulk of the two Homeric epics, in this poetry *il se fait grand jour*.[50]   This is not the first time that I have compared the religion of the Roman patricians to that of Homer ;[51] and there is a growing conviction among experts that we have in each case the ideas of a comparatively civilised immigrant population, whose religion, though it has developed in very different ways, has the common characteristic of cleanness and brightness.   In Italy it is practical, in Homer imaginative ; but in both it is free from the brutal and the grotesque.   Even the eschatology of the eleventh *Odyssey* is not cruel, it is comparatively colourless ; and, as I said just now, this also may be said of the Roman ideas of Orcus and the Manes.

In each case it is life, not death, that is of interest to the living ; death is rather a negation than anything distinctly realised.   The state of the dead in Homer is shadowy and *triste*, a state not to be desired, as Achilles so painfully expresses it in a famous passage ; but the *life* of the Achaean in the poems is vivid—nay, such a vivid realisation of life can alone account for the production of such poems.   So, too, the immigrant population at Rome, to whom is due the regulation of the religion as we know it, and the inspiring force that made for ordered government and warlike enterprise, was too full of practical if not of imaginative vitality to be apt to dwell upon the possibilities of existence after death, to conceive of such existence as either happy or miserable, the reward or the punishment for things done in this world.

But in each peninsula this immigrant race was living in the midst of a far more primitive population ; and it is perhaps to this population that we must look for the origin of the more detailed and imaginative notions of the life of the dead. Of the Greeks in this matter I have not space here to speak, nor am I competent to do so. But the conviction is steadily gaining ground that in early Rome we have to recognise the existence of two races ; whether the older of these was Ligurian, as Prof. Ridgeway thinks, or primitive Latin, *i.e.* old Italic, as Binder believes, does not matter for our present purpose ;[52] nor are the arguments drawn from religion which these writers have used at all convincing to my intelligence. But they have not noticed what is to me a really valid argument, viz. the double festival of the dead in the calendar of Numa. In February we find the cheerful and orderly festival of the Parentalia, the yearly renewal of the seemly rite of burial; in May, on the other hand, the student of the calendar is astonished to find three several days called Lemuria, the rites belonging to which are never mentioned, except where Ovid treats us to a grotesque account of the driving out of ancestral spirits from the house.[53] No one doubts, I think, that the Lemuria represents an older stratum of thought about the dead than the other festival,[54] but no one, so far as I know, has ventured to claim the Lemures and their three days as belonging to the religion of the more primitive race. If I make this suggestion now, it must be taken as a hypothesis only, but as a hypothesis it can at least do no harm. If I am asked why Lemuria should have been admitted into the patrician calendar, I answer that I have long held that a few of the non-patrician religious customs were absorbed into the religion of the city of the four regions, the Lupercalia, for example ;[55] and nothing could be more likely than that the old barbarous ideas about the dead should win this amount of respect, seeing that by the limitation to three days in the year order and decency might be brought into their service. I may repeat, with a slight addition, what I wrote ten years ago about these two Roman festivals of the dead : " If we compare Ovid's account of the grotesque domestic rites of the Lemuria with those of February, which were of a systematic, cheerful, and even beautiful character, we may feel fairly sure that the latter represent the organised life of a City-state, the former the ideas of an age when life was wilder and less secure, and the fear of the dead, of ghosts and demons, was a powerful factor in the minds of the people.   If we may argue from Ovid's account, it is not impossible that the Lemuria may have been one of those periodical expulsions of demons of which we hear so much in the *Golden Bough*, and which are performed on behalf of the community as well as in the domestic circle among savage peoples.   It is noticeable that the offering of food to the demons is a feature common to these practices, and that it also appears in those described by Ovid." [56]   To this I should now add the suggestion above made, that the Lemuria represents the ideas of the older race that occupied the site of Rome, while the Parentalia is orginally the festival of the patrician immigrants.

But what has all this to do with the eschatology which Lucretius attributes to the common people at Rome in his own day ?   Simply this, that the ideas at the root of the Lemuria may well have provided the raw material for such an eschatology, while those at the root of the Parentalia could not have done this.   Dr. Westermarck has recently shown that primitive religions do spontaneously generate the idea of moral retribution after death, *e.g.* the notion that the souls of bad people may reappear as evil spirits or obnoxious animals. [57]   We have no proof whatever of the existence of such notions at Rome ; but I contend that the permanence of this type

of belief about the dead which is represented by the
Lemuria — a permanence which is attested by Ovid's
description—raises a presumption that the lower stratum
of the Roman population, if the chance were given it,
would the more readily understand the pictures of
Etruscan artists and the allusions of Greek playwrights,
and the more easily become the prey of the eschatological
horrors which Lucretius describes as terrifying them.   The
material was there from the earliest times, and all that
was needed was for Greeks and Etruscans to work
upon it.

Before leaving this point it may be worth while to
remember that though the well-to-do and educated classes
cremated their dead, the poor of the crowded city population of the period I am now dealing with enjoyed no such
orderly and cleanly funeral rites.   The literary evidence
is explicit on this point, and has been confirmed by
modern excavation on the Esquiline, where we know from
Varro and Horace that the poor and the slaves were
thrown *en masse* into *puticuli, i.e.* holes where it was
impossible that any memorial ceremonies could be kept
up.[58]   Horace's lines are familiar (*Sat.* 8. 8):

> huc prius angustis eiecta cadavera cellis
> conservus vili portanda locabat in arca.
> hoc miserae plebi stabat commune sepulcrum, etc.

It is dangerous to be too confident about the effect on
the religious imagination of different ways of dealing
with the dead ; but it is at least not improbable that
any inherited tendency to believe in a miserable future
for the soul would be confirmed and maintained by so
miserable a fate for the body.   The mass of the population had little chance of ridding itself of eschatological
superstition.

Thus I am inclined to come to Dr. Masson's conclusion, though on somewhat different grounds.   I think
it quite possible that the uneducated in the age of the
poet may have really been inoculated with these ideas of
cruel retribution, and that in many cases this may have

resulted in despair or at least discomfort.   Only we must remember that in a great city like Rome, as in Paris or London to-day, both the miseries and the enjoyments of life would tend to accustom the minds of the lower strata to consider the present rather than the future ; the necessities and pleasures of the moment are with them the only material of thought.   Neither comfort nor remonstrance could reach them from pulpit or from missioner ; neither fear nor hope could largely enter into their lives. In fact I half suspect that most of them were, after all, so long as they were healthy and active, much what Lucretius would have them be—free from all religious scruple ; but, alas, utterly destitute of the intellectual support which he claimed from the study of philosophy. We can well understand how it was among the lower population of the great cities that early Christianity found its chance.   They had no education or philosophy to stand between them and the gospel of redemption.

I must say one word about another kind of transcendentalism which was pushing its way into favour in Roman society at this time—I mean astrology.   One may call it transcendental because it was based, in its original home in the East, on a mystical notion of sympathy between the phenomena of the starry heavens and the phenomena of human life ; [59] and that this notion was carefully inculcated by those who taught the " science " at Rome is shown by the long and wearisome poem on astrology written by Manilius in the succeeding age.   But it is not likely that this form of mysticism had become really popular before the period of the Empire, and in any case it can hardly be called a part of Roman religious experience.   I only mention it here as helping to illustrate the way in which men's minds were now beginning to turn with interest to speculations altogether beyond the range of that practical ethical philosophy which was natural and congenial to the Roman, altogether beyond the horizon of man's daily prospect in this world.   The growing interest in Fortuna, both as natural force and deity, which became intense under the Empire, is another indication of the same tendency.[60]

As soon as Rome had come into close contact with Greece, which had long before been overrun by the eastern astrology—by the Chaldaeans or *mathematici*, as they are so often called—these experts began to appear also in Italy. We first hear of them from old Cato, who advises that the steward of an estate should be strictly forbidden to consult *Chaldaei, harioli, haruspices*, and such gentry.[61] In 139 B.C.—a year in which there happened to be in Rome an embassy from Simon Maccabaeus—Chaldaeans were ordered to leave Rome and Italy within ten days; but I think there is some evidence that these were really Jews who were trying to propagate their own religion.[62] For some time we hear nothing more of these intruders; but they probably gained ground again in the course of the Mithridatic wars, which were responsible for the introduction of much Oriental religion into Italy. They are mentioned in 87, together with θῦται and Sibyllistae, as persuading the ill-fated Octavius to remain in Rome to meet his death, as it turned out, at the hands of the Marians.[63] But no Roman seems to have taken up astrology as a quasi-scientific study till that Nigidius, of whom I have already said a word, was persuaded thus to waste his time and brains. He is said to have foretold the greatness of Augustus at his birth in 63 B.C.;[64] and from this time forward the taking of horoscopes or *gene-thliaca* became a favourite pursuit at Rome—unfortunately for the people of Europe, who caught the infection and kept it endemic for at least fifteen centuries.

Astrology is in no sense religion, and I must leave it with these few remarks. It represents the individual and his personal interests, not even the advantage of the community, and it was for this reason that the Chaldaei were disliked by the Roman government. The individual is not satisfied with legitimate Roman means of divination; he is employing illegitimate ways when he entrusts himself to these Orientals, who, most of them doubtless, well deserved the scathing contempt which Tacitus has contrived to put into six words : " Genus hominum potentibus infidum, sperantibus fallax," adding, with no less contempt for the Roman authorities who had to deal with them, that they will always be forbidden, and always will be found at Rome.[65]

NOTES TO LECTURE XVII

1. For the Pythagoreanism of the Neo-platonic movement in the third century A.D. consult Bussell, *Marcus Aurelius and the Later Stoics* (Edin. 1910), p. 30 foll., who explains the reaction from Stoicism to Neo-Platonism.   See also Caird, *Gifford Lectures*, ii. 162 foll.

2. Schmekel, *Die mittlere Stoa*, p. 403, says that it had ceased to exist for centuries as a philosophy, but cautiously adds in a note that the knowledge of it was not extinct.   The famous Orphic tablets from South Italy are taken as dating from the third and fourth centuries B.C., and if not actually Pythagorean, they are next door to being so.   See Miss Harrison, *Prolegomena to the Study of Greek Religion*, p. 660.

3. *Tusc. Disp.* i. 38.

4. See, *e.g.*, Prof. Taylor's little book on Plato (Constable), p. 11.

5. See above, p. 349.

6. Sextus Empiricus, *adv. Physicos*, ii. 281 foll.

7. For the devotion of the believers to the founder and his *ipse dixit*, see Cicero, *Nat. Deor.* i. 5. 10.

8. The relation of Posidonius to Roman literature has been much discussed of late.   See, *e.g.*, Norden, Virgil, *Aen.* vi., index, *s.v.* " Stoa " ; Schmekel, *Die mittlere Stoa*, 85 foll., 238 foll.

9. For Panaetius' enthusiasm for Plato and his teaching, see Cic. *Tusc. Disp.* i. 32. 79 ; the whole passage indicates, though it does not exactly prove, an approach to the Platonic pyschology.

10. Caird, *Gifford Lectures*, vol. ii. p. 85.

11. See above, p. 75.   The idea that the practice of cremation influenced the ideas of the Roman about the soul was first, I think, suggested by Boissier, *Religion romaine*, i. 310.   Cicero himself hints at this conclusion in *Tusc. Disp.* i. 16. 36 : " In terram enim cadentibus corporibus, hisque humo tectis, e quo dictum est humari, sub terra censebant reliquam vitam agi mortuorum.   Quam eorum opinionem magni errores consecuti sunt; quos auxerunt poetae."

12. This point is well put by Dill, p. 493 of *Roman Society from Nero to Marcus Aurelius*.   See also Dieterich, *Eine Mithras-Liturgie*, p. 200 fol. ; Stewart, *Myths of Plato*, 352-53.

13. Schmekel, *Die mittlere Stoa*, p. 400 foll.

14. *De Rep.* vi. 26.

15. *Ib.* The word *providet* reminds us that this transcendental philosophy supplied the later Stoics with an explanation of divination. See Bouché-Leclercq, *Hist. de divination*, i. 68 ; Dill, *op. cit.* p. 439 ; Seneca, *Nat. Quaest.* ii. 52, fully accepted divination. Cp. Cic. *Tusc. Disp.* i. 37. 66, where he quotes his own *Consolatio* ; see above, p. 388. Panaetius, however, had courageously denied divination : Cic. *Div.* i. 3. 6 ; Zeller, *Stoics*, etc., p. 352.

16. *De Rep.* vi. 15, 26, and 29.

17. *Tusc. Disp.* i. 16. 36 foll. On the whole subject of the rise of the soul after death see Dieterich, *Eine Mithras-Liturgie*, p. 179 foll.

18. Schmekel, *op. cit.* p. 438 ; Stewart, *Myths of Plato*, p. 300.

19. For Nigidius, see Schanz, *Gesch. der röm. Literatur* (ed. 2), vol. ii. p. 419 foll.

20. "Nigidius Figulus Pythagoreus et magus in exilio moritur" is the notice of him in St. Jerome's Chronicle for the year 45 B.C.

21. These letters are in the 12th book of those to Atticus, Nos. 12-40.

22. *Ad Att.* xii. 36. The translation is Shuckburgh's.

23. A good example is Virg. *Aen.* viii. 349, but it is needless to multiply instances of the *religio loci*. Serv. *ad Aen.* i. 314 defines *lucus* as "arborum multitudo cum religione."

24. *Ad Att.* xii. 36 ; cp. 35. He uses the Greek word ἀποθέωσις in 35. 1, which seems to have come into use in his own time ; see Liddell & Scott, *s.v.*

25. See above, p. 58.

26. *Aen.* vi. 743. The meaning of these words seems to be quite plain, though commentators have worried themselves over them from Servius downwards. The mistake has been in not sufficiently considering the force of *quisque*, and puzzling too much over the vague word *Manes*. Henry discerned the true meaning in our own time. See his *Aeneidea*, vol. iii. p. 397. Cp. the words quoted above from *Somn. Scip.* : "mens cuiusque is est quisque." M. S. Reinach (*Cultes*, etc. ii. 135 foll.) is not far out : "Nous souffrons chacun suivant le degré de souillure de nos âmes."

27. *C.I.L.* i. 639, with Mommsen's note.

28. See *R.F.* p. 308.

29. *Tusc. Disp.* i. 12. 27. For the "ius Manium," *de Legibus*, ii. 22 and 54 foll.

30. *Ad Att.* xii. 18 : "Longum illud tempus *cum non ero* magis me movet quam hoc exiguum," etc. Cp. *Tusc.* i. *ad fin.*

31. *Ad Fam.* iv. 5. 6 : "Quod si quis apud inferos sensus est, qui illius in te amor fuit pietasque in omnes suos, hoc certe illa te facere nonvult."

32. Sall. *Cat.* ch. 51 : "Mortem cuncta mortalium dissolvere,

ultra neque curae neque gaudio locum esse." This is the Epicurean doctrine, which Caesar was said to hold.

33. Catull. 5. 6 ; Pliny, *N.H.* vii. 188. The whole passage is worth quoting : " Post sepulturam vanae Manium ambages. Omnibus a supremo die eadem quae ante primum, nec magis a morte sensus ullus aut corpori aut animae quam ante natalem. Eadem enim vanitas in futurum etiam se propagat et in mortis quoque tempora sibi vitam mentitur, alias immortalitatem animae, alias transfigurationem, *alias sensum inferis dando et Manes colendo deumque faciendo qui iam etiam homo esse desierit,* ceu vero ullo modo spirandi ratio ceteris animalibus praestet, aut non diuturniora in vita multa reperiantur quibus nemo similem divinat immortalitatem," etc.

34. There is an essay on this form of literature in the *Études morales sur l'antiquité* of Constant Martha, p. 135 foll.

35. *Tusc. Disp.* i. 27. 66.

36. Lact. *Inst.* i. 15. 20.

37. Lact. iii. 18.

38. See Schanz, *Gesch. der röm. Literatur,* vol. ii. p. 376.

39. Fragments 54 and 55.

40. P. 158 foll.

41. Lucr. vi. 764 foll. Cp. iii. 966 foll. ; Masson, *Lucretius,* i. p. 402. Mr. Cyril Bailey also reminds me of Lucr. iii. 31-93, and 1053 to end ; and adds a decided opinion that the poet is not here thinking of the common Roman, but of the educated Roman brought up on Greek and Graeco-Roman poetry and philosophy.

42. Polyb. vi. 56.

43. *Tusc.* i. 46. 111.

44. See Roscher's *Myth. Lex. s.v.* "Orcus" ; Wissowa, *R.K.* p. 192.

45. See above, p. 107.

46. Müller-Deecke, *Etrusker,* ii. 108 foll. Illustrations can be seen in Dennis, *Cities and Cemeteries of Etruria,* ed. 2.

47. *Captivi,* v. 4. 1.

48. *La Religion romaine d'Auguste aux Antonins,* vol. i. p. 310.

49. Cic. *Tusc.* i. 16. 37. For the eschatology of the sixth *Aeneid,* a curious mélange of religion, philosophy, and folklore, see Norden's work on Virgil, *Aeneid,* vi. (index, p. 468). Norden believes, I may note, that the philosophical and religious elements in it are mainly derived from Posidonius. Cp. also Glover, *Studies in Virgil,* ch. x. (Hades). For popular beliefs in Hades, etc., under the Empire, see Friedländer's *Sittengeschichte,* vol. iii. last chapter.

50. Weil, *Études sur l'antiquité grecque,* p. 12, quoted by Glover, p. 218.

51. See above, p. 105.

52. Since this lecture was written a most interesting discussion of Greek ideas, Achaean and Pelasgic, about the relation of soul and body after death, has appeared in Mr. Lawson's *Modern Greek Folk-*

lore and Ancient Greek Religion, especially in chapters v. and vi., confirming me, to some extent at least, in the conjecture I had here hazarded.   The working of the imagination in regard to a future state is in Greece, in his view, peculiar to the older or Pelasgic population ; and if the Etruscans were of Pelasgic stock, as is now believed by many, their imaginative grotesqueness, a degraded form perhaps of the original characteristic, acting on the ideas of a still more primitive population of which the Lemuria is a survival, might explain the later prevalence of a gruesome eschatology at Rome. But whoever studies Mr. Lawson's chapters closely will find serious difficulties in the way even of such a hypothesis as this.

53. Ovid, *Fasti,* v. 430 foll. ; *R.F.* p. 109.   Wissowa, *R.K.* p. 192, attributes the ideas of larvae (ghosts) and of Orcus, not to religion, but to popular superstition.   If he here means by religion the State religion and the *Parentalia* in particular, I can agree with him.

54. Dr. Carter allows this in Hastings' *Dict. of Religion and Ethics,* vol. i.   (Roman section of article " Ancestor Worship.")

55. See *R.F.* p. 334.

56. *R.F.* p. 107.

57. *Origin and Development of Moral Ideas,* ii. 693 foll.

58. Varro, *L.L.* v. 25 ; Paulus p. 216; Hülsen-Jordan, *Röm. Topogr.* iii. p. 268 foll.   The remains of these puticuli were unluckily very imperfectly reported, and have been lost in the building of the Rome of to-day.   On the question of the religious aspect of the two ways of disposing of the dead, burial and cremation, it is as well to remember Dieterich's warning in *Mutter Erde,* p. 66, note : " den Versuch, aus der Verbreitung und dem Wechsel der Sitte des Verbrennens und Begrabens für meine Untersuchung Schlüsse zu gewinnen, habe ich völlig aufgegeben, als ich angesichts der ungeheueren Materialen meines Kollegen von Duhn die Unmöglichkeit solcher Schlüsse einsehen musste."   In Mr. Lawson's book quoted above it seems to me to be proved that the object of both methods is the same, viz. to destroy the body as quickly as possible in order to prevent the soul from re-entering it and annoying the survivors.

59. This is well explained by Cumont in his *Religions orientales dans le paganisme romain,* p. 196 foll., following Bouché-Leclercq's work on astrology in Greece.   Cumont thinks that astrology took over the business of the augurs and haruspices, which was now dropped, and this is true in the main as regards the individual, but not as regards the State ; see above, p. 308 foll.

60. For Fortuna in the writings of Caesar, etc., see *Classical Review,* vol. xvii. p. 153.   The *locus classicus* for Fortuna as a deity under the early empire is Pliny, *N.H.* ii. 22.

61. Cato, *R.R.* ch. v. 4.

62. Val. Max. i. 3. 2, who no doubt was following Livy ; for in the Epitomes of some lost books of Livy discovered at Oxyrrhyncus

402 ROMAN RELIGIOUS EXPERIENCE

by Grenfell and Hunt (*Oxyrrh. Papyri*, vol. iv. p. 101), the same fact is alluded to.   For the embassy, Maccab. i. 14. 24 ; xv. 15-24. Two extracts from the text of Valerius, which is here lost, both state that proselytising Jews were at this time driven from Rome ; the Jupiter Sabazius, whose cult they were propagating, can hardly be other than that of Jehovah ; see Schürer, *Jewish People in the Time of Christ*, pt. ii. vol. ii. p. 233 of the English translation.   The expulsion of Chaldaei may, however, have been a separate measure of the praetor Hispalus.

63. Plutarch, *Marius*, 42.

64. Suet. *Aug.* 1.   I have seen a learned work about a century old, now entirely forgotten, in which it is maintained that Virgil's fourth Eclogue is simply a genethliacon of Augustus ; the arguments, which are ingenious but futile, are drawn from the poem of Manilius.

65. Tacitus, *Hist.* i. 22.

LECTURE XVIII

RELIGIOUS FEELING IN THE POEMS OF VIRGIL

MY justification for devoting a whole lecture to Virgil
must be that this great poet, more warmly and sym-
pathetically than any other Latin author, gives expression
to the best religious feeling of the Roman mind.   And
this is so not only in regard to the tendencies of religion
in his own day ; he stands apart from all his literary
contemporaries in that he sums up the past of Roman
religious experience, reflects that of his own time, and
also looks forward into the future.   No other poet, no
historian, not even Livy, who sprang from the same
region and in his tone and spirit in some ways resembles
Virgil, has the same broad outlook, the same tender interest
in religious antiquity, the same all-embracing sympathy
for the Roman world he knew, and the same confident
and cheerful hope for its future.   Each of the Augustan
poets—Horace, Ovid, Propertius, Tibullus—has his own
peculiar gift and charm ; but those who know Virgil
through and through will at once acknowledge the difference between these and the man possessed of spiritual
insight.   They are helpful in various ways to the student
of Roman religion, and Tibullus especially has a simple
reverence for the old religion which has inspired a few
exquisite descriptions of this aspect of Italian life.   But,
if I may use the word, they had no mission ; they were
true poets, yet not poets of the prophetic order ; they had
not thought deeply and reached conviction, like Lucretius
and Virgil.   A few words from the conclusion of an

Edinburgh professor's admirable work on Virgil will sufficiently express what I mean. " His religious belief," says Sellar, " like his other speculative convictions, was composite and undefined ; yet it embraced what was purest and most vital in the religions of antiquity, and in its deepest intuitions it seems to look forward to the belief which became dominant in Rome four centuries later." [1] In fact, Virgil gathers up what was valuable in the past of Rome and adds to it a new element, a new source of life and hope. It was this that made it possible for a great French critic to assert that for those who have read Virgil there is nothing astonishing in Christianity.[2] Let us try and realise what these writers mean. The Scotsman is sober and earnest, the Frenchman epigrammatically exaggerating ; but the feeling that underlies both utterances is a true one.

We have traced the gradual paralysis of the secularised State religion. We have glanced at the two types of philosophical thought which took the place of that religion in the minds of the cultivated section of Roman society, neither of which could adequately supply the Roman and Italian mind with an expression of its own natural feeling, never wholly extinct, of its relation to the Power manifesting itself in the universe. Stoicism came near to doing what was needed, by rehabilitating itself on Italian soil and indulging Roman preconceptions of the divine ; but it could not greatly affect the mass of men, and its appeal was not to feeling, but to reason. Epicurism, though perhaps more popular, was in reality more in conflict with what was best in the Italian nature, and the passionate appeal of Lucretius to look for comfort to a scientific knowledge of the *rerum natura* had no enduring power to cheer. Lastly, we have examined the tendency of the same age towards mysticism and Cicero's doubting and embarrassed expression of it, and we found that this tendency rather illustrates a sense of something wanting than hopefully satisfies it. We may well feel ourselves, now we have arrived at the close of the Republican era, just as the best men of that

day felt, that there *is* something wanting.   In their minds
this feeling almost amounted to despair ; in ours, as we
read the story of the troublous time after the death of
Caesar, it is pity and wonder.   There was, in fact, more
than a sense of weariness and discomfort, moral and
material, in the Roman mind of that generation—there
was also what we may almost call a sense of sin, such a
feeling, though doubtless less real and intense, as that
which their prophets, from time to time, awoke in the
Jewish people, and one not unknown in the history of
Hellas.   It was essentially a feeling of neglected duty—
of neglected duty to the Power and of goodwill wanting towards men.   Lucretius had been unconsciously a
powerful witness to this feeling, but had not found the
remedy.   In the early Augustan age it is again expressed
by Horace, by Sallust, and more deeply and truly in the
beautiful preface to Livy's History.[8]   Livy there says that
he devoted himself to the early annals of Rome that he
might shut his eyes to the evils of his own time—" tempora quibus nec vitia nostra nec remedia pati possumus.'

This something wanting was then a feeling, a *religio*, if
we can venture to use the old word once more in the
sense which I have so often attributed to it.   Not an
unreasonable or ungovernable feeling, not a *superstitio*,
but a feeling of happy dependence on a higher Power,
and a desire to conform to His will in all the relations of
human life.   This is the kind of feeling that had always
lain at the root of the Roman *pietas*, the sense of duty to
family and State, and to the deities who protected them.
In the jarring of factions, the cruelty and bloodshed of
tyrants, and the luxurious self-indulgence of the last two
generations, the voice of *pietas* had been silenced, the
better instincts of humanity had gone down.   We have
to see what was done by our poet to awake that voice
again and to put fresh life into those instincts.   Only let
us remember that more permanent good is done in this
world by a beautiful nature giving itself its natural expression, than by precept or denunciation ; and beware of

attributing to Virgil more direct consciousness of his
mission than he really felt.   It is the nature of the man
that is of value to us in our studies, as it was to the
Romans in their despair, a nature ruled by sweet, calm
feeling, full of sympathy and full of hope.

The something wanting in others which we find in
Virgil only, or in him more convincingly felt and more
resonantly expressed, is a kindly and hopeful outlook on
the world, with a deep and real sympathy for all sorrow
and pain.   It is not the result of any definite religious
conviction ; it is in the nature of the man, and is of the
very fibre of his being ; but it made him a better religious
teacher than the rest, just because real religion is not a
matter of reason only, or of convention, or of art, but of
feeling.   This was the true antidote to despair or depression—a sympathy with man in all he does or suffers, not
an indignant cry of remonstrance like that of Lucretius.
Virgil's sympathetic outlook includes not only Man, but
the animal world, and there can be no better proof that
his feeling was genuine.   The nightingale robbed of her
young,[4]

> quem durus arator
> observans nido implumes detraxit : at illa
> flet noctem, ramoque sedens miserabile carmen
> integrat et maestis late loca questibus implet ;

the cattle smitten by the plague,[5] the migrating birds
coming in from the sea,[6] and many another tender
touch, all show us the feeling of which I am speaking ; for
he who could so feel towards animals must needs have a
soul of pity for man.   So, too, with the inanimate nature
of Italy ; the land in which Virgil's shepherds and husband-
men live and work is one full of such detailed loveliness
as might suggest a beneficent Power presiding over it all,
inviting man to lift up his heart in gratitude or prayer.
As Sellar has well remarked,[7] the sense of natural beauty
is in the *Georgics* intertwined with the toil of man, raising,
as it were, the toiler to a higher level of humanity as he
lifts his eyes from his work.   And this natural beauty is

made real for the reader by the life and force that everywhere pervades it; all nature is alive and full of feeling;
the fruit trees, for example, in the second *Georgic* seem
instinct with an almost human life.[8]   The moment this
comes home to us we see how it harmonises with all we
have learnt of the old Italian conception of the divine, of
the forceful *numina* working for man's benefit if properly
propitiated.   And even when Virgil is using the language
of the Stoics to explain the life of nature, we feel that
behind the philosophical theory there lies this feeling of
the Italian :

> deum namque ire per omnes
> terrasque tractusque maris caelumque profundum :
> hinc pecudes, armenta, viros, genus omne ferarum.[9]

This is the religious spirit of the *Georgics* ; the divine
forces are everywhere, and a man must submit himself to
them and seek their aid.   He finds his true resource
rather in prayer than in philosophy, his part in the world
is "laborare et orare."   The hard lot of the Hesiodic
labourer is not that of the *agricola* of the *Georgics*, who
carries on his campaign of toil with a cheerful heart and
a clear conscience, for he is in right relation with the
Power manifesting itself in the life around him.

This, then, so far as I can describe it without going too
far into detail, is the feeling, the *religio*, which was needed
in the Italy of that day.   We may, perhaps, venture to
compare its revival in the work of Virgil with the return
to nature in the English poetry of a century ago, which
also brought with it a revival of religious fervency.
Though Virgil and Wordsworth are in many ways as
unlike as two poets can be, they are alike in the possession of that gentle and trustful outlook on the world of
nature which stimulates the mind to think of itself in its
relation to the Power.   We do not need to analyse the
process or to put it into any logical shape ; we may rest
content with it as a fact in the history of Roman religious
experience.

In Virgil's case, as in Wordsworth's, this feeling had

the effect of reconciling the poet's mind to the old forms
of religious worship.   Reconcile is, perhaps, hardly the
right word ; we may doubt whether he had ever quar-
relled with them.   As he believed in the Power and its
manifestations, so too he believed in the traditional modes
of propitiating it, not asking himself the *raison d'être* of
this or that ceremony, still less looking on them with pity
and contempt, like Lucretius, but accepting them in his
broad humanity as part of the life and thought of man
in Italy.

fortunatus et ille Deos qui novit agrestes.[10]

Let us mark the word *novit*.   The husbandman has come
to recognise these emanations of the Power and to know
them as friends ; the word could not have been used of
malignant spirits.   As I said in an early lecture, man
advances in his knowledge of the Power as he advances
in civilisation.   So the rural rites have a claim on his
sympathy no less than the men who performed them ; he
knew them in their detail, and he knew them in the spirit
which animated them.   He must have studied them in
detail, and not only the rural cults, but those of the city
too ; every gesture in worship has an interest for him,
and so great is our respect for his accuracy that we accept
what he tells us even if we cannot explain it.[11]   His
careful learning in all these details has been the means of
preserving for us large sources of knowledge ; for Servius,
Macrobius, and other commentators accumulated stores of
it in endeavouring to interpret him.

Now, this is not mere antiquarianism in Virgil, any
more than is the detail of old life which abounds in Scott's
poems and novels.   These two men had the same wide,
sympathetic outlook on the world.   Scott was interested
in everything and everybody, whether living or dead long
ago, and in all they did ; and I think we may say the
same of Virgil, though he is said to have been rather
reserved and shy than genial and talkative like Scott.
Virgil's mind was not so much " curious," I think, as

sympathetic, and his delight in these religious details arises from his love of Italy and all that man did in it. He caught the spirit of the old Italian worship, which, as we saw, demanded that each act should be performed accurately according to rules laid down. He recognises the necessity, and with true Italian instinct he acts upon it as he writes. He knows that these acts of cult are one outward expression of that quality which had made Rome great—*pietas*, the sense of duty to family, State, and Deity.

So far I have been considering what I may call the psychological basis of Virgil's religion—the man's sympathetic nature and wide outlook, which included in its love of Italy even the old practical worship of Italians. I have now to go on to the poet's greatest work, in which the idea of duty was not merely recognised in religious acts but exemplified in an ideal Roman. It is mainly in the *Aeneid* that we see him looking forward as well as backward, for it is there that we have the chart of the Roman's duty drawn to the scale of his past history, and meant to guide him in the future in still more glorious travel.

There are two ways in which we may contemplate the *Aeneid* as a whole and the teaching it offered the Roman of that day. We may think of it (if I may for a moment use musical language) as a great fugue, of which the leading subject is the mission of Rome in the world. Providence, Divine will, the Reason of the Stoics, or, in the poetical setting of the poem, Jupiter, the great protecting Roman deity, with the Fates behind him somewhat vaguely conceived,[12] had guided the State to greatness and empire from its infancy onwards, and the citizens of that State must be worthy of that destiny if they were to carry out the great work. This mighty theme pervades the whole poem and, like the subject of a fugue, enters and re-enters from time to time in thrilling tones. It is given out in the prophecy put into the mouth of Jupiter himself at the beginning of the first book; it is heard

in still more magnificent music from the shade of old
Anchises in the last moments of the hero's visit to Hades
in the sixth book, and again in the description of the
shield which Venus gives her son.[18]   Though the poem
is unequal and some parts of it are left without the final
touches, yet whenever the poet comes upon this great
theme the tone is that of a full organ.   This is, I think,
apart from those exquisite beauties of detail which are
for those only who have been initiated in the Virgilian
mysteries, what chiefly moves the modern reader of Virgil.
There are drawbacks which, for us moderns at least,
detract from the general effect : the intervention of gods
and goddesses after the Homeric manner, but without the
charm of Homer ; the seeming want of warm human
blood in the hero ; the stern decrees of Fate overruling
human passions and interests ; but he who keeps the
great theme ever in mind, watching for it as he reads, as
one watches for the new entry of a great fugue-subject,
will never fail to see in the *Aeneid* one of the noblest
efforts of human art—to understand what makes it the
world's second great epic.

But this great destiny of Rome has been accomplished
by the service of man ; by his loyalty, self-sacrifice, and
sense of duty ; by that quality known to the Romans as
pietas ; and the second lesson or reminder of the *Aeneid*
lies in the exemplification of this truth in the person and
character of the hero.   We moderns find it hard to
interest ourselves in the character of Aeneas.   But as Prof.
Nettleship remarked long ago,[14] a Roman reader would
not have thought him dull or uninteresting ; if that had
been so, the poem could hardly have become popular
from the moment of its publication.   I am inclined to
think that the *development* of the character of Aeneas
under stress of perils, moral and material, was much more
obvious to the Roman than it is to us, and much more
keenly appreciated.   For him it was the chief lesson of
the poem, which makes it as it were a " whole duty of the
Roman " ; and as this lesson is really a part of Roman

religious experience I am going to occupy the rest of this
lecture with it.

The development of the character of Aeneas, under
the influence of perils and temptations through which he
is guided by Jupiter and the Fates, is not a subject which
has received much attention from modern criticism.[15]
Yet to me, at least, it would be surprising if the leading
character of the poem were, so to speak, a statue once
and for all conceived and executed by the artist, instead
of a human being subjected to various experiences which
work upon his character as well as his career. There
were circumstances in Virgil's time which made it natural
that a poet of a serious and philosophical turn of mind
should be interested in the development of character and
make it part of his great subject. We have more than
once had occasion to notice the growth of individualism
in the last two centuries B.C. Beyond doubt personal
character had a great interest at this time for thinking
men, apart from its development; the world was ruled
by individuals, and at no time has so much depended on
the disposition of individuals. Men had long begun to
take themselves very seriously, and to write their own
biographies. So entirely had the individual emancipated
himself from the State, that he had almost forgotten that
the State existed and claimed his *pietas* ; he worked
and played for his own ends.[16] Even the armies of that
melancholy age were known and thought of, not as the
servants of the State, but as Sullani, Pompeiani, and so
on. This almost arrogant self-assertion of the individual
was a fact of the time, and could not be suppressed
entirely ; it was henceforward impossible to return to the
old times when the State was all in all and the individual
counted for little.

But in the *Aeneid*, if I am not mistaken, there is
an almost perfect balance between the two conflicting
interests. The State is the pivot on which turns all that
is best in individual human character ; in other words,
Aeneas is not playing his own game, but fulfilling the

order of destiny which was to bring the world under Roman dominion.   Individualism of the wrong type, that of Dido, Turnus, Mezentius, has to be escaped or over-come by the hero, for whom the call of duty is that of the State to be ; but, all the same, the hero is an *individual*, and one conceived not merely as a type or a force. True, he is typical of Roman *pietas*, and bears his constant epithet accordingly ; but if we look at him carefully we shall see that his *pietas* is at first imperfect, and that his individualism has to be tamed and brought into the service of the State *with the help of the State's deities*.   This is what makes the *Aeneid* a religious poem ; the character of Aeneas is pivoted on religion ; religion is the one sanction of his conduct.   There is no appeal in the *Aeneid* to knowledge, or reason, or pleasure,—always to the will of God.   *Pietas* is Virgil's word for religion, as it had been Cicero's in his more exalted moments. In the Dream of Scipio we read that "*piis* omnibus retinendus est animus in custodia corporis : nec iniussu eius a quo ille est vobis datus, ex hominum vita migrandum est, *ne munus humanum adsignatum a deo defugisse videa-mini.*" [17]   In these words, as is shown by those that follow, the *munus hominum* is exactly what it is in the *Aeneid*, duty to Man and the State, and as it is laid down for man by God, it is also duty to Him.   The State finds its perfection in the individual so long as he thus fulfills the will of God.[18]

Let us now go on to watch Aeneas as he gradually develops this perfect balance of motive.

Aeneas is marked at the very outset of the poem as "insignem pietate virum" ; the key-note of his character is sounded here at once with skill, and the key thus suggested (to use musical metaphor once more) is main-tained steadily throughout it.   The quality demanded by the gods from every true Roman who would take his part in carrying out the divine mission of Rome must be emphasised in the ideal Roman.   Yet, as we read on, we soon discover that Aeneas was by no means as yet a perfect character. It can hardly be by accident that the poet has described him as yielding to despair and bewailing his fate on the first approach of danger—forgetting the mission before him and the destiny driving him on, and wishing that he were lying dead with Hector under the walls of Troy (i. 92 foll.). It would have been easy enough for Virgil to have taken up at once the heroic vein in the man, as it was left him by Homer,[19] and to have made him urge his men to bestir themselves or to yield bravely to fate. And this is precisely what Aeneas does *when the storm is over and the danger past* (198 foll.) ; yet even then he is not whole-hearted about it :

> talia voce refert, curisque ingentibus aeger
> *spem voltu simulat*, premit alto corde dolorem.

At the very moment, that is, when he expresses his belief in his destiny and the duty of making for Italy, he still has misgivings, though he dare not express them.

Heinze has remarked[20] that before this, at the sack of Troy, he had shown a want of self-control, and yielded to a mad passion of desperate fighting that is not to be found in the Aeneas of the last six books (ii. 314 foll.) :

> arma amens capio nec sat rationis in armis.

Furor and *ira* drive him headlong ; we are reminded of the mad fury of Mezentius or Turnus.

Again, after the death of Priam Venus has to remind him of his duty to his father, wife, and son (ii. 594 foll.), reproaching him for his loss of sanity and self-control :

> nate, quis indomitas tantus dolor excitat iras ?
> quid furis, aut quonam nostri tibi cura recessit ?
> non prius aspicies ubi fessum aetate parentem
> liqueris Anchisen, superet coniunxne Creusa
> Ascaniusque puer ?[21]

During the wanderings narrated in the third book it is Anchises who leads, and who receives and interprets the divine warnings ; he seems to be the guardian and guide of his son : to that son he is " omnis curae casusque levamen " (iii. 709), and he is " felix nati pietate " (iii. 480).

He is, in fact, the typical Roman father, who, unlike Homer's Laertes, maintains his activity and authority to the end of his life, and to whom even the grown-up son, himself a father, owes reverence and obedience. As Boissier has pointed out,[22] the death of Anchises is postponed in the story as long as possible, and it is only after his death that Aeneas is exposed to a really dangerous temptation ; it is immediately after this event that, as we saw, he loses heart at the first storm, and then, on landing in Africa, falls a victim for the moment to the queenly charms of Dido. We may notice that up to this point his *pietas* has been a limited one, hardly called upon for exercise beyond the bounds of family life and duty ; when he is himself at the head, not only of the family, but, so to speak, of the State, it has to take a wider range, and to be put to a severe test.

To all that has at different times been written about Virgil's treatment of the Dido legend I must venture here to add another word. Heinze has shown [23] that no certain origin can be discovered for the form of the story as Virgil tells it ; it may have been Naevius who first took Aeneas to Sicily, but we do not know whether he or any successor of his invented the essential point of Virgil's story,—the suicide of Dido as a consequence of her desertion by Aeneas.[24] In any case the question arises, why our poet should have deliberately abandoned the current and popular version, and exposed his hero to such imminent danger of deserting the path which Jupiter and the Fates had marked out for him,—of sacrificing his great mission to the passion of a magnificent woman, and to the prospect of illicit ease and unsanctioned dominion. Heinze is of opinion that Virgil's motive was here a purely artistic one ; he wanted an opportunity to introduce the pathetic element into his epic. " There was no lack of models ; the latest bloom of Greek poetry had been in nothing more inventive than in dealing with all the phenomena of the passion of love,—its agony, shame, and despair, and the self-immolation of its victims." [25]   He

enforces this view with great learning, and all he writes
about it is of value ; but I must confess that he has not
convinced me that this was Virgil's chief motive.   He
seems to me to leave out of account two important con-
siderations : first, that though the poet drew freely on
every available source, Greek and Roman, for the enrich-
ment of his subject and its treatment, yet the whole
design and purpose of the *Aeneid* is Roman and not
Greek, and the introduction of a love-story *as such* would
have been foreign to that design, and also to the aims
and hopes of Augustus and the best men of the age.
Secondly, Heinze seems to forget, like so many others
who have written about the Dido episode, that Virgil had
before his very eyes facts sufficiently striking, a romance
quite sufficiently appalling, to suggest the adoption of
the form of the story as we have it in the fourth book.
Twice in his own lifetime did a single formidable woman
work a baleful spell upon the destinies of the Roman
empire.   In neither case did the spell take fatal effect ;
Julius escaped in time from the wiles and the splendour
of Cleopatra ; Antony failed indeed to escape, but brought
himself and her to fortunate ruin.   It is to me inexplicable, considering how all Virgil's poems abound with
allusions to the events of his time, and with side-glances
at the chief agents in them, that neither Heinze nor
Norden should have even touched on the possibility that
Cleopatra was in the poet's mind when he wrote the
fourth book.   It is perhaps difficult for one who puts the
poem on the dissecting-board, and whose attention is
continually absorbed in the investigation of minute points
in the fibre of it, to bear in mind the extraordinary events
of the poet's lifetime,—the civil war, the murder of Julius,
the division of the Roman world, the distraction of Italy,
the attempt of Antony, or rather, indeed, of his enslaver,
to set up a rival Oriental dominion, and the rescue of
Romanism and civilisation by Augustus.   Had Lucretius
himself lived in that generation, he could hardly have
escaped the influence of these appalling facts.   Whoever

will turn to the late Prof. Nettleship's essay on the poetry of Virgil, appended to his *Ancient Roman Lives of Virgil*, [26] can hardly fail to be convinced that on the later poet's mind they had produced a profound impression, the effects of which are traceable throughout the whole mass of his work. His Roman readers, whose state and empire had been brought to the verge of ruin by the exaltation of individual passions and ambitions, would look for these constant allusions and understand them far better than we can.

I maintain, then, that the poet adopted his version of the story of Dido not simply as an affecting and pathetic episode, but (in keeping with his whole design) to emphasise the great lesson of the poem by showing that the growth and glory of the Roman dominion are due, under providence, to Roman *virtus* and *pietas*— that sense of duty to family, State, and gods, which rises, in spite of trial and danger, superior to the entice- ments of individual passion and selfish ease. Aeneas is sorely tried, but he escapes from Dido to perform the will of the gods ; it is Jupiter, ruler of the Fates and the Roman destinies, who rescues him, and thus the divine care for Rome, an idea of which Augustus wished to make the most, is carefully preserved in the tale. If for us the character of Aeneas suffers by his desertion of Dido, that is simply because the poet, seized with intense pity for the injured queen, seems for once, like his own hero, to have forgotten his mission in the poem, and at the very moment when he means to show Aeneas performing the noblest act of self- sacrifice, renouncing his individual passion and listening to the stern call of duty, human nature gets the better of him, and what he meant to paint as a noble act has come out on his canvas as a mean one.

In Virgil's story, then, we have in contrast and conflict the opposing principles of duty and pleasure, of patriotism and selfishness, and the victory of the latter in the person of Aeneas by the help of the great god who was the guardian of the destinies of Rome, and of the goddess who was the mother of the hero and the reputed progenitor of the Julian family. When once this great trial is over, the way is clear for the accomplishment of Aeneas' mission, though he still has trials to face, and as yet is not fully equipped for meeting them.

Whoever, after reading the stormy scenes of the fourth book, will go straight on to the fifth, cannot but be struck with a change of tone which would have been doubly welcome to a man of that true Roman feeling which Virgil was counting on as well as inculcating through-out his work — doubly welcome, because he would find it not only in the incidents, but in the character of Aeneas. We here leave self and passion behind, and are introduced to scenes where the careful performance of religious and family duties seems to produce ease of mind and the tranquillity that comes of a soothed conscience. For the first time in the poem we meet with a characteristic of that best Roman life which was dear to the heart of Augustus, and with which we may be quite certain that the poet himself was entirely in sympathy. Strange, indeed, it is that this should be the case in a book so wholly based for its externals on Greek poetical traditions ; but it is none the less true, and it is a striking example of Virgil's wonderful genius for transforming old things with new light and meaning.[27]

It is not only then, or even mainly, the traditional necessity of describing games in an epic poem, that is the *raison d'être* of the fifth book ; the object was rather, as I understand it, to gain the needful contrast to the stormy passion of the fourth, and a relief for the mind of the Roman reader before he approached the awful scenery and experiences of the sixth, while at the same time there could be indicated—and for a Roman reader more than indicated—the *first beginning of a change* in the character of the hero. All this is effected with wonderful skill by making Aeneas perform with detailed carefulness the Roman ritual of the *Parentalia* as it was known to the

Romans of the Augustan age. The *Parentalia*, as I have said elsewhere,[28] were not days of terror or ill-omen, but rather days on which the performance of duty was the leading idea in men's minds ; that duty was a pleasant and cheerful one, for the dead were still members of the family, and there was nothing to fear from them so long as the living performed their duties towards them under the due regulations of the *ius divinum*. The ritual indicates the idea of the yearly renewal of the rite of burial, with the propitiation of the departed which was necessary for the welfare of the family ; and when the liturgical nine days were over, the living members met together in the *Caristia*, a kind of love feast of the family, at which all quarrels were to be forgotten, and from which all guilty members were excluded. In families of wealth and distinction in Virgil's time the days of mourning might be followed by *games in honour of the departed*. Thus a Roman would at once recognise the fact that Aeneas is here presented to us for the first time as a Roman father of a family, discharging the duties essential to the continuance and prosperity of that family with cheerfulness as well as with *gravitas* ; and that his *pietas* here takes a definite, practical, and truly Roman form, though it is not as yet extended to its full connotation as the performance of duty towards the State and its gods.

All this is quite in keeping with the little touches of characterisation which we can also notice in this book. In the second line Aeneas pursues his way *certus*, even while he gazes at the flames of Dido's funeral pyre, not knowing what they meant. He presides at the games with the dignity of a Roman magistrate, and reproachingly consoles the beaten Dares with words which seem to reflect his late experience at Carthage (v. 465) :

> infelix, quae tanta animum dementia cepit ?
> non vires alias conversaque numina sentis ?
> *cede deo.*

When the ships are burnt, he does not give way to despair, as in the storm of the first book, but prays for help to the omnipotent Jupiter, in whose hand were the destinies of his descendants (v. 687 foll.).   But he is not yet perfect in his sense of duty ; he feels the blow severely, and for a moment wavers (v. 700 foll.) :

> . . . casu concussus acerbo
> nunc huc ingentis, nunc illuc pectore curas
> mutabat versans, Siculisne resideret arvis
> oblitus fatorum, Italasne capesseret oras.

It needs the cheering advice of old Nautes (*quicquid erit, superanda omnis fortuna ferendo est*), and the appearance of the shade of Anchises, to confirm his wavering will with renewed sense of his mission.   This appearance of his father, " omnis curae casusque levamen," with the summons to meet him in Hades, is, as Heinze has seen,[29] a turning-point in the fortunes and the character of Aeneas, and prepares us for the final ordeal and initiation which he undergoes in the following book.

I here use the word initiation because I have no doubt that Virgil had in his mind when writing it the Greek idea of initiation into mysteries preparatory to a new life.   An actual initiation was, of course, out of the question ; on the other hand a *catabasis*, a descent into Hades, was part of the epic inheritance he derived from Homer, and this, like the funeral games in the fifth book, he might use with an earnestness of purpose wanting in Homer, to work in with the great theme of his poem, not merely as an artistic effort.   The purpose here was to make of Aeneas a new man, to regenerate him ; to prepare him by mystic enlightenment for the toil, peril, and triumph that await him in the accomplishment of his divine mission.   We must not look too closely into the process ; it is a strange mélange of popular and philosophic ideas and scenery, made at once intelligible and magnificent by the wonderful resources of the poet ; but we may be sure that it has the same general meaning as the visions of Dante long afterwards.   As Mr. Tozer has said, Dante's conversion and ultimate salvation were the primary object of his journey through the three realms of the spiritual world.[80]   In this sense it can be called an initiation, an ordeal, a sacrament.

So much has been written about this wonderful book that I do not need to dwell upon it here.   I will content myself with pointing out very briefly a fact which struck me when I last read it.   The ordeal of preparation is not complete till the very end of the book, when the shade of Anchises has shown his son all the great things to come, the due accomplishment of which depends on his sense of duty, his *pietas*.   Up to that moment Aeneas is always thinking and speaking of the past, while in the last six books he is always looking ahead, absorbed in the work each hour placed before him, and in the prospect of the glory of Rome and Italy.   The poet had contrived that his hero should himself narrate the story of the sack of Troy and his subsequent wanderings, and narrate them to the very person who would have made it impossible for him ever again to look forward on the path of duty. Surely this is significant of a moral as well as an artistic purpose ; the passionate love of the queen urges her to keep his mind fixed on the past, to engage him in the story of events that concerned himself and not his mission (i. 748):

> necnon et vario noctem sermone trahebat
> infelix Dido, longumque bibebat amorem
> multa super Priamo rogitans, super Hectore multa, etc.

After the shade of Creüsa had told him of his destiny, which she was not to share, the past was still in his mind, and he seems to have forgotten the warning ; he calls himself an exile (iii. 10):

> litora cum patriae lacrimans portusque relinquo
> et campos ubi Troia fuit.   Feror exsul in altum—

I find an exception after the meeting with Andromache, when he thinks of the future for a moment, but even then half-heartedly as it seems to me, with a very distinct reluctance to face the dangers to come, and with a touching envy of those who could " stay at home at ease " (iii. 493

foll.).   His want of faith in the future is again shown in
Book v., in the passage quoted just now ; and even in
Book vi. he is at first purposely depicted as "slack," as
having his attention caught by what is for the moment
before him, or with the figures of old friends and enemies
whom he meets, until the last awakening revelation of
Anchises.   Thus no sooner has he landed in Italy than
he is attracted by the pictures in the temple of Apollo and
incurs a rebuke from the priestess (vi. 37 foll.) :

> non hoc ista sibi tempus spectacula poscit ;'
> nunc grege de intacto septem mactare iuvencos
> praestiterit, etc. ;

so also a little farther on she has to warn him again
(50 foll.) at the entrance to the cave :

> " cessas in vota precesque,
> Tros " ait " Aenea, cessas ? "

It may be fancy in me to see even in his prayer which
follows a leaning to think of Troy and his past troubles
(56 foll.).   But I cannot but believe that in this book he
is meant to take a last farewell of all who have shared
his past fortunes, have helped him or injured him ; he
meets Palinurus, Dido, Tydeus, Deiphobus, and the rest,
and while meditating over these he has once more to be
hurried by his guide (538) :

> sed comes admonuit breviterque adfata Sibylla est :
> nox ruit, Aenea, nos flendo ducimus horas.

When Anchises appears the whole tone changes, and
his famous words seem to me to show conclusively that
hesitation and want of fixed, undeviating purpose had
been so far his son's chief failing (806) :

> et dubitamus adhuc virtutem extendere factis,
> aut metus Ausonia prohibet consistere terra ?

The father's vision and prophecy are of the *future* and
the great deeds of men to come, and henceforward Aeneas
makes no allusion to the past and the figures that peopled
it, abandons talk and lamentations, " virtutem extendit

factis." At the outset of Book vii. we feel the ship moving
at once ; three lines suffice for the fresh start ; Circe is
passed unheeded. " Maior rerum mihi nascitur ordo,"
says the poet in line 43 ; " maius opus moveo ; " for the
real subject of the poem is at last reached, and a heroic
character by heroic deeds is to lay the foundation of the
eternal dominion of Rome.

A very few words shall suffice about the Aeneas of the
later books. Let us freely allow that he is not strongly
characterised ; that for us moderns the interest centres
rather in Turnus, who is heroic as an individual, but not
as a pioneer of civilisation divinely led ; that there is no
real heroine, for feminine passion would be here out of
place and un-Roman, and the courtship of Lavinia is
undertaken, so to speak, for political reasons. The rôle
of Aeneas, as the agent of Jupiter in conquest and civilisation, would appeal to a Roman rather than to a modern,
and it was reserved for the modern critic to complain of a
lack of individual interest in him. So, too, it is in Jewish
history; we feel with Esau more than with Jacob, and with
David more than with Moses, who is none the less the
grandest typical Israelite in the Old Testament. And,
indeed, Virgil's theme here is less the development of a
character or the portraiture of a hero than the idealisation
of the people of the Italy which he loved so well, who
needed only a divinely guided leader and civiliser to enter
upon the glorious career that was in store for them.

I cannot escape the belief, as I read again through
these books, that Virgil did intend to depict in Aeneas
his ideal of that Roman character to which the leading
writers of his day ascribed the greatness of their race.
His *pietas* is now confirmed and enlarged, it has become a
sense of duty to the will of the gods as well as to his
father, his son, and his people, and this sense of duty never
leaves him, either in his general course of action or in the
detail of sacrifice and propitiation. His courage and
steadfastness never fail him ; he looks ever forward, confident in divine protection ; the shield he carries is adorned

—a wonderful stroke of poetic genius—with scenes of the future, and not of the past (viii. 729 foll.) :

> talia per clipeum Volcani, dona parentis,
> miratur rerumque ignarus imagine gaudet
> attollens umero famamque et fata nepotum.

He is never in these books to be found wanting in swiftness and vigilance ; when he cheers his comrades it is no longer in a half-hearted way, but as at the beginning of the eleventh book, with the utmost vigour and confidence, " Arma parate, animis et spe praesumite bellum" (xi. 18).

His *humanitas* again is here more obvious than in his earlier career, and it is plainly meant to be contrasted with the heroic savagery of Mezentius and Turnus. So keenly did the poet feel this development in his hero's character, that in his descriptions of the death of Lausus and the burial of Pallas—noble and beautiful youths whom he loved in imagination as he loved in reality all young things—his tenderness is so touching that even now we can hardly read them without tears. And not only is the hero heroic and humane, but he is a just man and keeps faith ; when, in the twelfth book, the Rutulians break the treaty, and his own men have joined in the unjust combat (xii. 311) :

> at pius Aeneas dextram tendebat inermem
> nudato capite atque suos clamore vocabat :
> " quo ruitis ? quove ista repens discordia surgit ?
> o cohibete iras ; ictum iam foedus et omnes
> compositae leges : mihi ius concurrere soli."

He claims for himself alone, under the guiding hand of providence, the right to deal with Turnus, the enemy of humanity and righteousness. And we may note that when it came to that last struggle, though conquering by divine aid, he was ready to spare the life of the conquered till he saw the spoils of the young Pallas upon him.

The character of Aeneas, then, though not painted in such strong light as we moderns might expect or desire, is

intentionally developed into a heroic type in the course of
the story—a type which every Roman would recognise as
his own natural ideal.   And this growth is the direct
result of religious influence.   It is partly the result of the
hero's own natural *pietas*, innate within him from the first,
as it was in the breast of every noble Roman ;   partly the
result of a gradually enlarged recognition of the will of
God, and partly of the strengthening and almost sacramental process of the journey to Hades, of the revelation
there made of the mysteries of life and death, and of the
great future which Jupiter and the Fates have reserved
for the Roman people.   In these three influences Virgil
has summed up all the best religious factors of his day :
the instinct of the Roman for religious observance, with
all its natural effect on conduct ;   the elevating Stoic
doctrine which brought man into immediate relation with
the universal ;   and, lastly, the tendency to mysticism,
Orphic or Pythagorean, which tells of a yearning in the
soul of man to hope for a life beyond this, and to make
of this life a meet preparation for that other.

Only one word more.   We can hardly doubt the truth
of the story that the poet died earnestly entreating that
this greatest work of his life should perish with him, and
this may aptly remind us that though I have been treating
the Aeneid as a poem of religion and morals, yet, after
all, Virgil was a poet rather than a preacher, and thought
of his Aeneid, not as a sermon, but as a work of art.   Had
he thought of it as a sermon he could hardly have wished
to deprive the Roman world of it.   The true poet is never
a preacher except in so far as he is a poet.   If the Greeks
thought of their poets as teachers, says the late Prof.
Jebb, "this was simply a recognition of poetry as the
highest influence, intellectual and spiritual, that they
knew."   " It was not merely a recreation of their leisure,
but a power pervading and moulding their whole existence."   Surely this is also true of Virgil, and of the best
at least of his Roman readers.   No one can read the sixth
Aeneid, the greatest effort of his genius, without feeling

that poetry was all in all to him; that learning, legend, philosophy, religion, whatever in the whole range of human thought and fancy entered his mind, emerged from it as poetry and poetry only.

NOTES TO LECTURE XVIII

1. Sellar, *Virgil*, p. 371.

2. Sainte-Beuve, *Étude sur Virgile*, p. 68.

3. Horace, *Epode* 16, where, however, he is not quite so much in earnest as in *Odes* iii. 6. Sallust, prefaces to Jugurtha and Catiline: these do not ring quite true.

4. *Georg.* iv. 511 foll.

5. *Georg.* iii. 440 foll. The famous lines (498 foll.) about the horse smitten with pestilence will occur to every one.

6. *Aen.* vi. 309.

7. *Op. cit.* p. 231. He cites *Georg.* i. 107 and 187 foll.

8. Sellar, *Virgil*, p. 232.

9. *Georg.* iv. 221 foll.

10. *Georg.* ii. 493.

11. Prof. Hardie recently asked me an explanation of the double altar that we meet with more than once in Virgil in connection with funeral rites: *e.g.*, *Ecl.* 5. 66; *Aen.* iii. 305; v. 77 foll. Servius tries to explain this, but clearly did not understand it. Of course I could offer no satisfactory solution. Yet we are both certain that there is a satisfactory one if we could only get at it.

12. Much has been written about the part of the Fates in the *Aeneid* and their relation to Jupiter. See Heinze, *Vergils epische Technik*, p. 286 foll.; Glover, *Studies in Virgil*, 202 and 277 foll. I may be allowed to refer also to my *Social Life at Rome in the Age of Cicero*, p. 342 foll.

13. *Aen.* i. 257 foll., vi. 756 foll., viii. 615 foll.

14. *Suggestions preliminary to a Study of the Aeneid*, p. 36.

15. It is not likely to strike us unless we read the whole *Aeneid* through, without distracting our minds with other reading, and this few of us do. I did it some ten years ago; before that the development of character had not dawned on me fully. I later on found it shortly but clearly set forth in Heinze's *Vergils epische Technik*, p. 266 foll.; and this caused me to read the poem through once more, with the result that I became confirmed in my view, and read a paper on the subject to the Oxford Philological Society, which I have in part embodied in this lecture.

16. This is dwelt on in *Social Life at Rome in the Age of Cicero*, p. 124 foll.

17. *De Republica*, vi. 15.

18. It may be as well to note here that the actual representation of God in the *Aeneid* is its weakest point.   It was an epic poem, and could not dispense with the Homeric machinery : hence Jupiter is practically the representative of the Stoic all-pervading deity, with the Fates behind him.   But it is not unlikely that Virgil may thus have actually helped to make the way clear for a nobler monotheistic idea by damaging Jupiter in the course of this treatment ; see *Social Life at Rome in the Age of Cicero*, p. 341 foll.

19. On the Homeric Aeneas there are some good remarks in Boissier's *Nouvelles Promenades archaeologiques* (*Horace et Virgile*), p. 130 foll.   Of all the Homeric heroes he seems to come nearest, though but slightly sketched, to the Roman ideal of heroism.

20. Heinze, *Vergils epische Technik*, p. 17.

21. I should be disposed to consider this passage as decisive of the point, but that it immediately follows upon the doubtful lines 567-588, in which Aeneas is tempted in his mad fury to slay Helen ; and if these lines are not Virgil's, we have not sufficient explanation of the rebuke which Venus here administers to her son.   On the other hand, if they were really Virgil's, and omitted (as Servius declares) by the original editors Tucca and Varius, we should have a convincing proof that the poet meant his hero, in these terrible scenes, to come so short of the true Roman heroic type as to be capable of slaying a woman in cold blood, and while a suppliant at an altar of the gods.   Into this much-disputed question I must not go farther, except to note that while Heinze is absolutely confident that Virgil never wrote these lines, the editor of the new Oxford text of Virgil is equally certain that he did.   My opinion is of no value on such a point ; but I am disposed to agree with Mr. Hirtzel that " versus valde Vergilianos, ab optimis codicibus omissos, iniuria obleverunt Tucca et Varius."   They are certainly in keeping with the picture of Aeneas' *impotentia* which is generally suggested in Book ii.   If it should be argued that this *impotentia*, *i.e.* want of self-control, is only put into the mouth of Aeneas in order to heighten the effect of his stirring narrative, it will be well to remember the remonstrances of Venus, which make such a hypothesis impossible.

22. *Op. cit.* p. 231.

23. *Vergils epische Technik*, p. 113 foll.

24. The original story was, that unable to escape from an enforced marriage with Iarbas, she killed herself to mark her unflinching faithfulness to her first husband Sicharbas.   Servius quotes Varro as stating that it was not Dido, but Anna who committed suicide for love of Aeneas (on *Aen.* iv. 682) ; and as Varro died before the Aeneid was begun, this may be taken as proving that Virgil's version of the love-story was not his own invention. But it is quite possible that Servius here only means that Varro's version differed in this point from that which the poet soon after-

wards adopted ; it may be that the story in the poem is thus practically his own.

25. *Op. cit.* p. 116.

26. *Ancient Lives of Vergil*, Clarendon Press, 1879.

27. The critics have, I think, been weaker in dealing with the fifth book than with any of the others.   Prof. Tyrrell is too violent in his contempt for it to admit of quotation here.   Heinze has some good and acute remarks on Virgil's motive in placing the book where it is, but seems to me to miss the real importance of it (*op. cit.* 140 foll.).   Even Boissier, whose delightful account of the scenery of Eryx should be read by every one who would appreciate this book (*op. cit.* p. 232), goes so far as to say that it is the one book with which we feel we might easily dispense so far as the story is concerned.

28. *Roman Festivals*, p. 307.

29. *Op. cit.* p. 270.

30. *Commentary on Dante's Divina Commedia*, pp. 615 foll.   I am indebted for this reference to Stewart's *Myths of Plato*, p. 367.

31. Nettleship remarked most truly that there is no better way of appreciating the heroic Aeneas of these last books than by studying carefully the early part of the eleventh.

LECTURE XIX

THE AUGUSTAN REVIVAL

IT is a long descent from the inspiring idealism of Virgil to the cool, tactical attempt of Augustus to revive the outward forms of the old religion. It seems strange that two men so different in character and upbringing should have been working in the same years in the same direction, yet on planes so far apart. How far the two were directly connected in their work we cannot know for certain. It is said that the subject of the Aeneid was suggested to Virgil by Augustus, and it is quite possible that this may be true ; but it by no means follows from this that the inspiration of the poem came from any other source but Virgil's own thought and feeling. We also know that Augustus from the first appreciated the Aeneid, and that he saved it for all time ; but it is by no means clear that it inspired him in his efforts towards moral and religious regeneration. Perhaps the truth is that both were moved by the wave of mingled depression and hope that swept over Italy for some years after the death of Julius, and that each used his experience in his own way and according to his opportunities. They had at least this in common, that they utilised the past to encourage the present age, and that by filling old forms and names with new meaning they set men's minds upon thinking of the future.[1]

Yet the revival of the State religion by Augustus is at once the most remarkable event in the history of the Roman religion, and one almost unique in religious history. I have repeatedly spoken of that State religion as hypnotised or paralysed, meaning that the belief in the efficacy of the old cults had passed away among the educated classes, that the mongrel city populace had long been accustomed to scoff at the old deities, and that the outward practice of religion had been allowed to decay. To us, then, it may seem almost impossible that the practice, and to some extent also the belief, should be capable of resuscitation at the will of a single individual, even if that individual represented the best interests and the collective wisdom of the State. For it is impossible to deny that this resuscitation was real ; that both *pax deorum* and *ius divinum* became once more terms of force and meaning. Beset as it was by at least three formidable enemies, which tended to destroy it even while they fed on it, like parasites in the animal or vegetable world feeding on their hosts,—the rationalising philosophy of syncretism, the worship of the Caesars, and the new Oriental cults,—the old religion continued to exist for at least three centuries in outward form, and to some extent in popular belief.

We must remember the tenacious conservatism of the Roman mind : the emotional stimulus of the age of depression and despair which preceded this revival : and the conscientious care with which the successors of Augustus, Tiberius in particular, carried out his religious policy.[2] Then as we become more familiar with the Corpus of inscriptions and the writings of the early Christian fathers, we begin to appreciate the fact that the natural and inherited religion of a people cannot altogether die, and that to describe this old Roman religion as *dead* is to use too strong a word. The votive inscriptions of the Empire show us overwhelming proof of surviving belief in the great deities of the olden time, and of the care taken of their temples. Antoninus Pius is honoured " ob insignem erga caerimonias publicas curam et religionem." [3] Marcus Aurelius himself did not hesitate in times of public distress to put in action the whole

apparatus of the old religion.[4]   Constantius in A.D. 329
was shown round the temples when he visited Rome for
the first time, and in spite of his Christianity took a
curious interest in them.[5]   That the private worship, too,
went on into the fourth century we know from the
Theodosian code, where in the interest of Christianity
the worship of Lares Penates and Genius is strictly
forbidden.[6]   Again, the constant ridicule with which the
Christian writers speak of the *minutiae* of the heathen
worship makes it quite plain that they knew it as actually
existing, and not merely from books like those of Varro.
They do not so much attack the Oriental religions of
their time as the genuine old Roman cults ; more especially is this the case with St. Augustine, from whose *de
Civitate Dei* we have learnt so much about the latter.   The
very necessity under which the leaders of Christianity
found themselves of suiting their own religious character,
and in some ways even their own ceremonies, to the
habits and prejudices of the pagans, tells the same story.
But the question how far Latin Christianity was indebted
to the religion of the Romans must be postponed to my
last lecture ; I have said enough to indicate in which
direction we must go for evidence that the work of
Augustus was not in vain, that it gave fresh stimulus to
a plant that still had some life in it.

If, then, the Augustan revival was not a mere sham,
but had its measure of real success, how are we to
account for this ?   I think the explanation is not really
difficult, if we bring to bear upon the problem what we
have learnt from the beginning about the religious experience of the Romans.   Let us note that Augustus troubled
himself little about the later political developments of
religion, which we have lately been examining,—about
pontifices, augurs, and Sibylline books ; these institutions,
which had been so much used in the republican period for
political and party purposes, it was rather his interest to
keep in the background.   But in one way or another he
must have grasped the fundamental idea of the old

Roman worship, that the prosperity and the fertility of man, and of his flocks and herds and crops on the farm, and the prosperity and fertility of the citizen within the city itself, equally depended on the dutiful attention (*pietas*) paid to the divine beings who had taken up their abode in farm or city.[7]   The best expression of this idea in words is *pax deorum*,—the right relation between man and the various manifestations of the Power,—and the machinery by which it was secured was the *ius divinum.*[8] We shall not be far wrong if we say that it was Augustus' aim to re-establish the *pax* by means of the *ius* ; but if we wished to explain the matter to some one who has not been trained in these technical terms, it would be better to say that he appealed to a deeply-rooted idea in the popular mind,—the idea that unless the divine inhabitants were properly and continually propitiated, they would not do their part in supporting the human inhabitants in all their doings and interests.   This popular conviction he deliberately determined to use as his chief political lever.

This has, I think, been insufficiently emphasised by historians, who contemplate the work of this shrewd statesman too entirely from the political point of view.   I am sure that he had learnt from his predecessors in power that reform on political lines only was without any element of stability, and that he knew that it was far more important to touch a spring in the feeling of the people, than to occupy himself, like Sulla, in mending old machinery or inventing new.   If he could but induce them to believe in him as the restorer of the *pax deorum*, he knew that his work was accomplished.   And I believe that we have what is practically his own word for this conviction ; not in his Res Gestae, the *Monumentum Ancyranum*, which is a record of facts and of deeds only, but in the famous hymn which Horace wrote at his instance and to give expression to his ideas, for use in the Secular Games of 17 B.C., to which I am coming presently. Ferrero has lately described that hymn as a magnificent poem,[9] an opinion which to me is incomprehensible.   It is neat, and embodies the necessary ideas adequately, but it is far too flat to be the genuine offspring of such a poet as Horace.   To me it reads as though Augustus had written it in prose and then ordered his poet to put it into metre ; and assuredly it expresses exactly what we should have expected Augustus to wish to be sung by his youthful choirs.   I shall refer to it again shortly to illustrate another point ; all I need say now is that he who reads it carefully and thinks about it will find there the conviction of which I have been speaking, that prosperity and fertility, whether of man, beast, or crop, depend on the Roman's attitude toward his deities ; religion, morality, fertility, and public concord are the points which the astute ruler wished to be emphasised.[10]   That this hymn was a really important part of the ceremony is certain from the fact that it was given to the best living poet to write, and that his name is mentioned as its author in the inscription, discovered not many years ago, which commemorated the whole performance : " CARMEN COMPOSUIT Q. HORATIUS FLACCUS." [11]

If, then, I am right, this strange movement was not merely a revival of religious ceremonies, but an appeal through them to the conscience of the people.   A revival of religious *life* it, of course, was not, for what we understand by that term had never existed at Rome ; but it was an attempt to give expression, in a religious form and under State authorisation, to certain feelings and ideas not far removed in kind from those which in our own day we describe as our religious experience.   Whether Augustus himself shared in these feelings and ideas it is, of course, impossible to conjecture.   But as a man's religious convictions are largely the result of his own experience and of that of the society in which he lives, and as Augustus' own experience for the twenty years before he took this work in hand had been full of trial and temptation, I am disposed to guess that he was rather expressing a popular conviction which he shared himself than merely standing apart and administering a remedy.   And this view seems to me to be on the whole confirmed by the tone and spirit of the great literary works of the age.

Augustus did not become pontifex maximus till the year 12 B.C., nineteen years after he had crushed Antony at Actium ; he waited with scrupulous patience until the headship of the Roman religion became vacant by the death of Lepidus.[12] But this did not prevent him from pursuing his religious policy with great earnestness before that date, for he had long been a member of the pontifical college, as well as augur and quindecemvir. No sooner had he returned to Rome from Egypt than the work of temple restoration began, the outward and visible sign to all that the *pax deorum* was to be firmly re-established. The fact of the restoration he has told us in half a dozen words in his own Res Gestae :[13] "Duo et octaginta templa deum in urbe ex decreto senatus refeci," adding that not one was neglected that needed repair. Among them was that oldest and smallest temple of Jupiter Feretrius on the Capitol to which I referred in a former lecture ;[14] and his personal interest in the work is attested by Livy, who says that he himself heard Augustus tell how he had found an inscription, relating to the second *spolia opima* dedicated there, when he went into the temple bent on the work of restoration.[15] It needs but a little historical imagination to appreciate the psychological importance of all this work. We have to think not only of the by-standers who watched, but of the very workmen themselves, rejoicing at once in new employment and in the revival of an old sense of religious duty. Little more than twenty years earlier, no workman could be found to lay a hand upon the newly-built temple of Isis, when the consul Aemilius Paulus gave orders for its destruction as a centre of *superstitio* ;[16] now abundant work was provided which every man's conscience would approve. When I think of the Rome of that year 28, with all its fresh hope and confidence taking visible shape in this way, even Horace's famous lines seem cold to me (*Od.* ii. 6. 1):

delicta maiorum immeritus lues
Romane, donec templa refeceris
aedesque labentis deorum et
foeda nigro simulacra fumo.

The restoration of the temple buildings implies also a revival of the old ritual, the *cura et caerimonia*. As to this we are very imperfectly informed,—we have no correspondence of this age, as of the last, and the details of life in the Augustan city are not preserved in abundance. But Ovid comes to the rescue here, as in secular matters, and on the whole the evidence in his *Fasti* suggests that the old sacrificing priesthoods, the Rex and the flamines, were set to their work again. He tells us, for example, how he himself, as he was returning to Rome from Nomentum,[17] had seen the flamen Quirinalis carrying out the *exta* of a dog and a sheep which had been sacrificed in the morning in the city, to be laid on the altar in the grove of Robigus. In spite of all its disabling restrictions, it was possible once more to fill the ancient priesthood of Jupiter ; and of the Rex sacrorum and the other flamines we hear in the early Empire.[18] They were in the *potestas* of the pontifex maximus, and as after 12 B.C. that position was always held by the Princeps himself, it was not likely that they would be allowed to neglect their duties. Other ancient colleges were also revived or confirmed by the inclusion of the Emperor himself among their members (a fact which Augustus was careful to record in his own words), *e.g.* the Fetiales, of whom he had made use when declaring war with Antony and Cleopatra ;[19] the Sodales Titienses, an institution of which we have lost the origin and meaning ; the Salii, Luperci, and above all the Fratres Arvales, the brotherhood whose duty it had once been to lead a procession round the crops in May, and so to ensure the *pax deorum* for the most vital material of human subsistence. The corn-supply now came almost entirely from Africa and Egypt ; the inner meaning of this old ritual could not be revived, and we must own that all this restoration of the old *caerimonia* must have appealed rather to the eye than the mind of the beholder. It was necessary to put some new element into it to give it life.   Here we come upon a most important fact in the work of Augustus, which will become apparent if we take a rapid glance at the work and history of the Fratres, and then go on to find further illustration of the curious mixture of old and new which the Roman religion was henceforward to be.

The fortunate survival of large fragments of the records of the Brotherhood, dating from shortly after the battle of Actium, show that it continued to work and to flourish down to the reign of Gordian (A.D. 241), and from other sources we know that it was still in existence in the fourth century.[20]   These records have been found on the site of the sacred grove, at the fifth milestone on the via Campana between Rome and Ostia, which from the time of this revival onwards was the centre of the activity of the Fratres.

The brethren were twelve in number, with a *magister* at their head and a flamen to assist him ; they were chosen from distinguished families by co-optation, the reigning Emperor being always a member.[21]   Their duties fell into two divisions, which most aptly illustrate respectively the old and the new ingredients in the religious prescriptions of Augustus, as they were carried out by his successors.   The first of these is the performance of the yearly rites in honour of the Dea Dia, the goddess or *numen* without a substantival name (a form perhaps of Ceres and Tellus), whose home was in the sacred grove, and who was the special object of this venerable cult. Secondly, the care of vows, prayers, and sacrifices for the Emperors and other members of the imperial house.   I must say a few words about each of these divisions of duty.

The worship of the Dea Dia took place in May on three days, with an interval always of one day between the first and second, according to the old custom of the calendar.[22]   On the first, preliminary rites were performed at Rome, in the house of the magister ; on the second was the most important part of the whole ceremony, which took place at the sacred grove.   These rites will give a good idea of the old Roman worship, and of the exactness with which Augustus sought to restore it.   At dawn the magister sacrificed two *porcae piaculares* 'to the Dea, and then a *vacca honoraria*, after which he laid aside the *toga praetexta* or sacrificial vestment, and rested till noon, when all the brethren partook of a common meal, of which the *porcae* formed the chief part.   Then resuming the *praetexta*, and crowned with wreaths of corn-ears, they proceeded to the altar in the grove, where they sacrificed the *agna opima*, which was the principal victim in the whole ceremonial.[23]   Other rites followed, *e.g.* the passing round, from one to another of the brethren, fruits gathered and consecrated on the previous day, each brother receiving them in his left, *i.e.* lucky hand, and passing them on with his right ; and the singing of the famous Arval hymn to Mars and the Lares to a rhythmic dance-tune.   Then after another meal and chariot-racing in the neighbouring circus, they returned to Rome and finished the day with further feasting.[24]   A cynical reader of these Acta might suggest that the appetites of the good brethren were made more of than their *pietas* ; but the feasting may be just as much a part of the ancient practice as any of the other curiosities of ritual.

The utensils employed were of the primitive sun-baked clay (*ollae*), and seem to have been regarded with a veneration almost amounting to worship.[25]   Long ago I had occasion to note how the old form of piacular sacrifice was used and recorded whenever iron was taken into the grove, or any damage done to the trees by lightning or other accident.   Once, when a tiny fig-tree sprouted on the roof of the temple, piacula of all suitable kinds had to be offered to Mars, Dea Dia, Janus, Jupiter, Juno, Virgines divae, Famuli divi, Lares, Mater Larum, sive deus sive dea in cuius tutela hic lucus locusque est, Fons, Hora, Vesta Mater, Vesta deorum dearumque, Adolenda

Commolenda Deferunda,—and sixteen *divi* of the imperial families![26] As the date of this extraordinary perform-ance is A.D. 183, nothing can better show the extent to which the revival of elaborate ritual had been carried by Augustus, and the amazing tenacity with which it held its ground.

The second part of the activity of the brethren well illustrates the new element which Augustus adroitly insinuated into the old religious forms : but I shall not dwell upon it, for the worship of the Caesars in its developed form is not of either Roman or Italian origin, any more than the other kinds of cult which were now pressing in from the East ; and it thus lies outside the range of my subject. The revival of this old priesthood, and doubtless of others, the Salii for example, was turned to account to mark the sacred character and political and social predominance of the imperial family. All events of importance in the life of the Emperor himself and his family were the occasion of vows, prayers, or thanks-givings on the part of the Fratres ; births, marriages, successions to the throne, journeys and safe return, and the assumption of the consulship and other offices or priesthoods. These rites all took place at various temples or altars in Rome, or at the Ara Pacis, recently exca-vated, which Augustus had built in the Campus Martius. Here, by way of example of them, is a " votum susceptum pro salute novi principis," on his accession.[27]

" Imperatore M. Othone Caesare Augusto, L. Salvio Othone Titiano iterum consulibus, III kalendas Febru-arias magistro Imperatore M. Othone Caesare Augusto, promagistro L. Salvio Othone Titiano : collegi fratrum Arvalium nomine immolavit in Capitolio ob vota nuncu-pata pro salute imperatoris M. Othonis Caesaris Augusti in annum proximum in III nonas Ianuarias Iovi bovem marem, Iunoni vaccam : Minervae vaccam : Saluti publicae populi Romani vaccam : divo Augusto bovem marem, divae Augustae vaccam : divo Claudio bovem marem : in collegio adfuerunt, etc."

This record, which belongs to the year 69 and the accession of Otho, shows the *divi, i.e.* the deified emperors Augustus and Claudius, together with the deified Livia, associated with the *trias* of the Capitoline temple and the *Salus publica* in the sacrificial rites. But under the Flavian dynasty which followed this association was judiciously dropped.[28] It may serve for the moment to illustrate what was to come of this new element so subtly introduced into the old worship; how it led to practices which are utterly repulsive to us, and repulsive too to an honest man even in that day. The noble words of Tiberius, declining to have temples erected to him in Spain, have been preserved by Tacitus from the senatorial records:[29] "Ego me, patres conscripti, mortalem esse fateor"; and he added that his only claim to immortality lay in the due performance of duty. Tiberius, whatever else he may have been, was beyond doubt an honest man; and so too was Seneca, the author of the famous skit on the deification of Claudius. But the extravagances of Caesar-worship are not to be met with in Augustus' time; for him the new element may be defined, as in Rome (and in Italy too, so far as his own wish could limit it) nothing more than *the encouragement of the belief in him, and loyalty to him as the restorer of the pax deorum.* To this end he sought to magnify his own achievements as avenger of the crime of the murder of Julius, by which the *pax* had been grievously disturbed. I propose to finish this lecture by giving some account of the way in which he attained this object. Let us briefly examine the famous ritual of the *Ludi saeculares*, of which we have more detailed knowledge than of any other Roman rite of any period; it marks the zenith of his prosperity and religious activity, and belongs to the year 17 B.C., two years after the death of Virgil,—a date which may be said to divide the long power of Augustus into two nearly equal halves.

This famous celebration is an epoch in the history of the Roman religion, if not in the history of Rome herself.

It stands on the very verge of an old and a new régime.
It was the outward or ritualistic expression of the idea,
already suggested by Virgil in the fourth *Eclogue* and the
Aeneid, that a regeneration is at hand of Rome and Italy,
in religion, morals, agriculture, government ; old things are
put away, new sap is to run in the half-withered trunk
and branches of a noble tree.   The experience of the past,
as with Aeneas after the descent into Hades, is to lead to
new effort and a new type of character, of which *pietas*
in its broadest sense is the inspiring motive.   Henceforward the Roman is to look ahead of him in hope
and confidence, *virtutem extendere factis*.   Augustus, the
Aeneas of the actual State, was firmly established in a
prestige which extended beyond Italy even to the far
East ; his faithful and capable coadjutor Agrippa was by
his side to take his part in the ritual, and no cloud in that
year 17 seemed to be visible on the horizon.

The *Ludi saeculares* are also unique in respect of the
records we have of them.   By wonderful good fortune we
can construct an almost complete picture of what was
done in that year on the last days of May and the first
three of June.   We have the text of the Sibylline oracle,
—how manufactured we do not know, nor does it much
matter,—which prescribed the ritual, preserved by Zosimus,
a Greek historian of the fifth century A.D., together with
his own account.[80]   Thus the outline of the ritual has been
known all along, together with many details ; and to help
it out we have also the perfect text of the hymn written
by Horace for the occasion, and sung by two choirs of
boys and girls respectively.   But great was the delight
of the learned world when, in September 1890, workmen
employed on the Tiber embankment, close, as it turned
out, to the spot where the nightly rites of the *ludi* took
place, came upon a mediaeval wall partly made of ancient
material, in which some marbles were found covered with
inscriptions relating to this same celebration.[81]   This
treasure was badly mutilated, but the inscription was
easily decipherable ; it contains a letter from Augustus

giving instructions, two decrees of the Senate, and a series of records of the Quindecemviri, who were of course in charge of a ritual which had been ordered by a Sibylline oracle. Some few points were at first puzzling, but have been cleared up since the discovery. Mommsen, of course, took the work in hand, and his exposition is still, and always will be, the starting-point for students. Wissowa has an excellent popular account of it, and recently, in the fifth volume of his *Greatness and Decline of Rome*, Ferrero has utilised it to give an animated account of the whole ceremony.[32]

The *Ludi saeculares* take their name from the word *saeculum* ; and the old Italian idea of a *saeculum* seems to have been a period stretching from any given moment to the death of the oldest person born at that moment,— a hundred years being the natural period so conceived.[33] Thus a new saeculum might begin at any time, and might be endowed with special religious significance by certain solemn ceremonies ; in this way the people might be persuaded that a new leaf, so to speak, had been turned over in their history : that all past evil, material or moral, had been put away and done with (*saeculum condere*), and a new period entered on of innocence and prosperity. There are faint traces of three early celebrations of this kind, beginning in 463 B.C., traditionally a disastrous year, and renewed in 363 and 263. But in 249, another year of distress and peril, a new saeculum was entered on with a new and a Greek ritual, ordered by a Sibylline oracle. A subterranean altar in a spot by the Tiber, near the present Ponte St. Angelo, and called Tarentum (possibly to mark the original home of the rite), was dedicated to Dis and Proserpina, Greek deities of the nether world ; and here for three successive nights black victims were offered to them. The subterranean altar and the use of the word *condere* (to put away), might suggest that this rite may have had something in common with those well-known quasi-dramatic ones in which objects are *buried* or thrown into the water, to represent the cessation of one period of vegetation and the beginning of another.[34] Or we may look on it in the light of one of those *rites de passage* in which a transition is made from one state of things to another, without any definite religious idea being attached to it.   There is no doubt some mystical element in the primitive idea of the beginning and ending of periods of time, which has not as yet been thoroughly investigated.[35]

Now it is easy to see how exactly a rite of this kind, with suitable modifications, would fit in with Augustus' purposes as we have explained them. Fortunately too Varro had in 42 B.C. published a book in which the mystic or Pythagorean doctrine was set forth of the palingenesis of All Souls after four saecula of 110 years each; the fourth *Eclogue* of Virgil may have been influenced by this, among other mystical ideas, as it was written only three years later; and in any case the doctrine was well known.[36] But Augustus had to wait a while, until peace and confidence were restored. Why eventually he chose the year 17 is quite uncertain; it does not exactly fit in with any calculation of four saecula of 110 years starting from any known date. But a saeculum, as we have seen, might begin at any moment; and in any case it was easy to manufacture a calculation, which was now duly accomplished by trusty persons, chief among them being the great lawyer, Ateius Capito, an ardent adherent of Augustus and his projects.[37] Probably too it was necessary to take advantage of the popular feeling of the moment, that a better time had come, and that it should be started on its way in some fitting outward form.

So an elaborate programme was drawn up, the main features of which I must now explain. On 26th May and the two following days (for the mystic numbers three, nine, and twenty-seven are noticeable throughout the ritual)[38] the means of purification (*suffimenta*)—torches, sulphur, bitumen[39]—were distributed by the priests to all free persons, whether citizens or not; for this once, all in

Rome at the time, with the exception of slaves, were to give an imperial meaning to the ceremony by their share in it.   Even bachelors, though forbidden to attend public shows under a recent law *de maritandis ordinibus*, were allowed to do so on this occasion.   No doubt the idea was that the whole people were to be purified from all pollution of the past ; it is what M. van Gennep calls a *rite de séparation*, the first step in a *rite de passage*.   The next three days all the people came to the Quindecemviri at certain stated places, and made offerings of *fruges*, the products of the earth, as we do at our harvest festivals ; these were the firstfruits of the coming harvest.[40]   It may be worth while to recall the facts that it was on these same days that the procession of the Ambarvalia used to go round the ripening crops, and that in the early days of June the symbolic *penus* of Vesta was being cleansed to receive the new grain.[41]   That Augustus wished to emphasise the importance of Italian agriculture is beyond doubt, and is apparent also in the hymn of Horace, *Fertilis frugum pecorisque Tellus spicea donet Cererem corona*, etc.

When the *suffimenta* had been distributed and the offerings made, all was ready for the putting away or burying of the old *saeculum*.   On the night before 1st June Augustus himself, together with Agrippa, sacrificed to the Greek Moirae, the Parcae of Horace's hymn, perhaps in some sense the Fata of the *Aeneid* ; on the second night to Eilithyia, the Greek deity of childbirth ; and on the third to Mother Tellus.   The form of prayer accompanying the sacrifice is preserved in the inscription ; it is Latin in language and form, as dry and concise as any we examined in my lectures on ritual, and contains the *macte esto* which I was then at pains to explain.   Augustus prayed for the safety and prosperity of the State in every way, and also for himself, his house, and his *familia*.[42]   The scene on the bank of the Tiber, illuminated by torches, must have been most impressive.

These were the nightly ceremonies.   But each day also

had its ritual, in which the Roman deities of the heaven were the objects of worship, not, as by the Tiber bank, Greek deities of the earth and the nether world.   On the first two days Augustus and Agrippa offered the proper victims to Jupiter and Juno respectively on the Capitol ; Minerva is omitted, and probably the other two are reckoned in Greek fashion as a married pair.   The form of prayer was the same as that used by night, with the necessary modifications.   Thus the great Capitoline temple and its deities have a full share of attention, and they go too far who think that Augustus was so wanting in tact as to put them in the shade.[43]   But on the third and last day the scene changes from the Capitol to the Palatine, the residence of Augustus, where he had built his great temple of Apollo ; here for the first time in the ceremony Horace's hymn was sung.   On all the days and nights there had been shows and amusements, and a hundred and ten chosen matrons had taken solemn part in the services.[44]   But I must pass these over and turn in the last place to the question, as interesting as it is old and difficult, as to how and where Horace's hymn was sung, and how we are to understand it.

The instructions given to the poet by Augustus are obvious as we read the Carmen in the light of the ceremonial of which it was to mark the conclusion.   He was to bring into it, as we have already seen, the ideas which were to be revived and made resonant, of religion, morality, and the fertility of man, beast, and crop ; and they are all there.   He was also to include all the deities who had been addressed in prayer both by day and night, by Tiber bank and on the Capitol, and to give the most prominent place to those who on this last day were worshipped on the Palatine ; to Apollo, for whom Augustus had built a great temple close to his own house (*in privato solo* [45]), as his own specially protecting deity since Actium, and Diana, who as equivalent to Artemis, could not but be associated with Apollo.   Thus the deities of the hymn are both Latin and Greek,[46] and this expresses the undoubted fact that the religion of the Romans was henceforward to be even in outward expression a cosmopolitan or Romano-Hellenic one, in keeping with the fact that all free men of every race might take part in this great festival. But it cannot fail to strike every careful reader that the great trias of the Capitol is hardly visible in the poem, though Jupiter and Juno had been the chief objects of worship on the two previous days. Jupiter is twice incidentally named, but in no connection with the Capitol ;[47] and it is only when we read between the lines of the fourteenth stanza that we discover Jupiter and Juno as the recipients of the white oxen which had been sacrificed to them there. I have already said that we must not make too much of the neglect of Jupiter and Juno by Augustus ; but it is plain that he directed Horace not to make them too prominent in this hymn, and I think it is quite possible that Horace a little overdid his obedience.

The result of all this is that the hymn, in spite of its neatness and adequacy, is wanting in spontaneity, and presents the casual reader with an apparently unmeaning jumble of Greek and Roman gods and goddesses. The only way to clear it up is by taking it in immediate relation with what we know about the places in which it was sung. To me at last it has become clear enough in all its main points ; and I will give here my own results, which do not altogether coincide with those of other recent inquirers.

Before the discovery of the great inscription we knew that this hymn was sung before the new temple of Apollo on the Palatine ; we now know that it was also sung on the Capitol,[48] thus uniting in one performance the old religion of republican Rome with the new imperial cult of Apollo. But this new fact has, in my opinion, led to misapprehensions both of the manner of singing and the order of subjects in the hymn. Mommsen thought that the first part was sung on the Palatine, the middle part on the Capitol, and the last again on the Palatine, and he is followed by Wissowa ; and both seem to think it possible that there may have been singing too during the procession from the one hill to the other.[49] I think we need not trouble ourselves about the latter point, for the Via Sacra, by which the procession must have gone, was far too narrow and irregular to allow fifty-four singers, with the *tibicines* who must have been accompanying them, to walk and perform at the same time.[50] The inscription, too, says plainly that the hymn was sung on the Palatine and then on the Capitol, and by that plain statement of fact we had better abide.

Now let us note that these two stations on the two hills were the best possible positions for Augustus' purpose, not only because of their religious importance, but because they afforded the most spacious views of the city, now everywhere adorned with new or restored buildings. The temple of Apollo was built upon a large and lofty area at the north-east end of the Palatine.[51] Recent excavations have shown it to be some hundred yards broad by a hundred and fifty in length, and Ovid, in a passage of his *Tristia*,[52] gives us an idea of its height :

> inde tenore pari gradibus sublimia celsis
>   ducor ad intonsi candida templa dei.

On this area the choirs of boys and girls took their station, facing the marble temple, on the *fastigium* of which was represented the Sun driving his four-horse chariot.[53] After singing, probably together, the first two stanzas or exordium of the hymn, they addressed this Sol :

> alme Sol, curru nitido diem qui
> promis et celas, aliusque et idem
> nasceris, possis nihil urbe Roma
>   visere maius.

As they sang these last words, they would turn towards the city that lay behind them, and look over it to the Tiber and the scene of the nightly sacrifices of the Tarentum ; and with the deities of these rites, who must of course be taken before those of day and light, as in the order of the festival, the next five stanzas are occupied :[54]

Eilithyia, the Moirae (Parcae), and Tellus or Ceres.   When that duty is over they turn once more to the temple, and the Greek deities of the Tarentum are mentioned no more. Three stanzas are devoted to Apollo and Diana (Luna), with a happy allusion to the *Aeneid*, and then once more the choirs turn, and this time they face the Capitol ; the hymn is long, and these changes of movement would be at once a relief to the singers and a pleasant sight to the spectators.   They address the deities of the Capitol in appropriate language :

> di probos mores docili iuventae,
> di, senectuti placidae quietem,
> Romulae genti date remque prolemque
>   et decus omne.

The allusion to Jupiter and Juno is thus veiled :

> quaeque vos bobus veneratur albis
> clarus Anchisae Venerisque sanguis,
> impetret, bellante prior, iacentem
>   lenis in hostem.

Horace has cleverly made Augustus himself the leading figure in this and the following stanza, and the listeners forget the Capitoline gods as they note the allusion to Venus, the ancestress of the Julii, the prestige of Augustus that has brought envoys to him from Scythia, Media, and India, and in the next stanza the public virtues, presented here as deities—Fides, Pax, Honos, Pudor, Virtus—on whose aid and worship the new régime is based.[55]

At the sixteenth stanza the choirs again face about to the temple of Apollo, and with him and Diana again the next two stanzas have to do.   Only one remains, in which as an *exodos* we may be sure the two choirs of boys and girls joined ; it sums up the whole body of deities, but with Apollo and Diana as the special objects of the day's worship :

> haec Iovem sentire deosque cunctos
> spem bonam certamque domum reporto,
> doctus et Phoebi chorus et Dianae
>   dicere laudes.

The performance on the Palatine was now over, and the procession streamed down the hill to join the Via Sacra near the Regia and the Vesta temple, and so to make its way up to the Capitol, where the performance was repeated.[56] Taking station at this noble point of view, he who will can again follow its movement with the hymn in his hand.   The area in front of the Capitoline temple looked across to the Palatine, and the image of Sol and his *quadriga* must have been in full view ; thus the *exordium* and the next stanza (alme Sol) would be sung looking in that direction.   Equally well in view, if they turned to the right, would be the scene of the midnight sacrifices across the Campus Martius ; and so on throughout the singing the changes of position would be easy and graceful, here as on the Palatine.

Here I prefer to make an end of the performance, following the text of the inscription, which tells us nothing of a return to the Palatine.   It would be far more in keeping with Roman practice that the Capitol should be the scene of the conclusion of the processional ceremony, even on a day when Apollo was, with Augustus himself, the principal figure.   From the musical point of view, too, a third performance is improbable, for the singers were young and tender.

And here, too, with this impressive scene, which can hardly fail to move the imagination of any one who has stood on Palatine and Capitol, I will close my account of the religious experience of the Romans.   A few remarks only remain for me to make about its contribution, such as it was, to the Latin form of Christianity.

NOTES TO LECTURE XIX

1. A summary of the relations between Virgil and Augustus may be found in Mr. Glover's *Studies in Virgil*, p. 144 foll.

2. Tiberius added to his Augustan inheritance a curious and possibly morbid anxiety about religious matters and details of cult, of which examples may be found in Tac. *Ann.* iii. 58, vi. 12, among

other passages. Perhaps, however, the most interesting is that connected with the famous story of "the Great Pan is dead," told by Plutarch in the *de Defectu Oraculorum*, ch. xvii. The news of this strange story reached the ears of Tiberius, who at once set the learned men about him to inquire into it; and they came to the no less strange conclusion that "this was the Pan who was born of Hermes and Penelope." S. Reinach has recently offered an explanation of this story, which is at least better than previous ones, in *Cultes, mythes, et religions*, vol. iii. p. 1 foll.

3. *C.I.L.* vi. 1001.

4. Jul. Capitolinus, 13.

5. Symmachus, *Rel.* 3.

6. *Cod. Theod.* xvi. 10. 2. On this subject generally consult Dill's *Roman Society in the Last Century of the Western Empire*, bk. i. chs. i. and iv.

7. This idea is exactly expressed by Horace in *Odes* iii. 23, perhaps addressed to the *vilica* of his own farm. Cp. Cato, *R.R.* 143, where the *vilica* is to pray to the *Lar familiaris pro copia*. Horace mentions only the Kalends for this rite; Cato adds Nones and Ides. Cp. Tibull. i. 3. 34; i. 10. 15 foll.

8. See above, Lectures iv. and v.

9. *Greatness and Decline of Rome* (E.T.), v. 93.

10. See especially lines 45 foll. and 56 foll.

11. *C.I.L.* vi. 32,323, or Dessau, *Inscriptiones selectae*, vol. ii. part i. p. 284.

12. For this reason the veiled figure in one of the fine sculptures on the Ara Pacis frieze, which used to be taken as Augustus Pont. Max., cannot be so identified (see Domaszewski, *Abhandlungen zur römischen Religion*, p. 90 foll.), for the date of the Ara Pacis is 13 B.C., the year before Lepidus died. The figure can be most conveniently seen by English students in Mrs. Strong's *Roman Sculpture*, plate xi. p. 46. It may be Agrippa acting as Pont. Max. for Lepidus.

13. *Monumentum Ancyranum*, ed. Mommsen (Lat.), iv. 17.

14. See above, p. 129.

15. Livy iv. 20. 7.

16. Valerius Maximus, *Epit.* 3, 4.

17. Ovid, *Fasti*, iv. 901 foll.

18. See Marquardt, 326 foll.

19. Dio Cassius, l. 4, 5.

20. Henzen, *Acta Fratrum Arvalium*, p. xxv. of the exordium.

21. Henzen, p. 154.

22. See above, p. 98.

23. Henzen, pp. 24, 28.

24. For the hymn, Henzen, p. 26; Dessau, *Inscr. select.* ii. pt. i. p. 276. See also above, p. 186.

25. Wissowa, *R.K.* p. 487, note 5.

26. Henzen, 142 foll. ; Dessau, p. 279 ; see above, p. 162.

27. Henzen, p. 105.

28. *Ib.* p. 107.

29. Tac. *Ann.* iii.

30. Zosimus, ii. 5 and 6.   The oracle and the extract from Zosimus are printed in Dr. Wickham's introduction to the *Carmen saeculare*, and in Diels, *Sibyllinische Blätter*, p. 131 foll.

31. *C.I.L.* vi. 32,323.   *Ephemeris epigraphica*, viii. 255 foll., contains the text and Mommsen's exposition.   Dessau, *Inscr. selectae*, ii. pt. i. 282, does not give the whole document.

32. Wissowa, *Gesammelte Abhandlungen*, p. 192 foll. ; Ferrero, vol. v. 85 foll.

33. The word was first explained by Mommsen, *Röm. Chronologie*, ed. 2, p. 172.

34. See, *e.g.*, *Golden Bough*, ed. 2, vol. ii. p. 70 foll.

35. The religious or mystical conception of time is the subject of an interesting discussion by Hubert et Mauss, *Mélanges d'histoire et de religion*, p. 189 foll. ; but the *saeculum* does not seem to have attracted their attention.

36. The actual words of Varro, from his work *ωe gente Populi Romani*, are quoted by St. Augustine, *de Civ. Dei*, xxii. 28 : "Gene-thliaci quidam scripserunt esse in renascendis hominibus quam appellant παλιγγενεσίαν Graeci ; hac scripserunt confici in annis numero quadringentis quadraginta, ut idem corpus et eadem anima, quae fuerint coniuncta in homine aliquando, eadem rursus redeant in coniunctionem."   The passage well illustrates the mystical tendency of which I was speaking in the last lecture.

37. For attempts to explain the difficulty see Wissowa, *op. cit.* p. 204.

38. The cakes offered to Eilithyia, and again to Apollo, are nine in number ; see the inscription lines 117 and 143.   The choirs of boys and girls were each twenty-seven.

39. The *suffimenta* are described by Zosimus, *l.c.*   There is a coin of Domitian, who also celebrated *Ludi saeculares*, in which he appears seated and distributing the *suffimenta*, as the inscription shows.

40. So Zosimus, who says they consisted of wheat, barley, and beans.

41. *R.F.* p. 148 foll.

42. See the inscription, line 92 foll.   Ferrero assumes that these words were to be taken as representing the families of all worshippers present, who would repeat the words "mihi domo familiae."   But this is arbitrary ; the prayer follows the old form as we have it, *e.g.*, in Cato, *R.R.* (see above, p. 182), and as Cato or any landowner would represent the rest of the human beings on the estate, so did Augustus represent the whole community.

43. So J. B. Carter, *Religion of Numa*, p. 160.

2 G

44. The matrons, equal in number to the years of the *saeculum*, first appear on 2nd June in the worship of Juno.

45. *Mon. Ancyr.* (Lat.), iv. 21.

46. Zosimus, *l.c.*, says that "hymns" were sung in Greek as well as Latin ; but this is not borne out by any other authority.

47. Line 31 (*et Iovis aurae*), where Jupiter simply stands for the heaven and its influence on the earth ; and line 73 (*haec Iovem sentire*, etc.), where he is introduced in the most general way as head of all deities.

48. Line 147 of the inscription : "Sacrificioque perfecto puer[i X] XVII quibus denuntiatum erat patrimi et matrimi et puellae totidem carmen cecinerunt : *eodemque modo in Capitolio*. Carmen composuit Q. Horatius Flaccus."

49. *Eph. epigr.* viii. 256. Wissowa, *Gesamm. Abhandl.* p. 206, note, who refers to Vahlen and Christ as differing from Mommsen, in papers which I have not seen. Wissowa says that the threefold division of the hymn "springt in die Augen" ; but this has never been my experience.

50. Apart from the awkwardness for singers of the descent from the Palatine and the steep ascent to the Capitol, we may remember that they would have to pass under the fornix Fabianus, which was not much more than nine feet broad (Lanciani, *Ruins and Excavations*, p. 217).

51. See Hülsen-Jordan, *Topographie*, iii. 72 and note. See also map at the end of the volume, No. 1 of the series. There is, however, some doubt as to whether the site was not on the side of the Palatine looking towards the Tiber over the Circus maximus. See my paper in the *Classical Quarterly*, 1910, p. 145 foll. If so, my explanation of the performance of the hymn seems rather to be confirmed than weakened.

52. Ovid, *Tristia*, iii. 1, 59 foll.

53. Propertius, iii. 28 (31): "In quo Solis erat supra fastigia currus." No one seems to have noticed the connection between this and Horace's allusion to Sol, which is otherwise not easy to explain.

54. I will not enter on the insoluble question as to what stanzas or parts of stanzas were sung by the boys and girls respectively. That the hymn was so sung in double chorus is intrinsically probable, and stated in the oracle, lines 20, 21. Some of the schemes which have been propounded are given in Wickham's *Horace*. I imagine that the stanzas may have been sung alternately except in the case of the first two and the last, but the ninth looks as though it might have been divided between the two choirs. Ferrero has a scheme of his own, p. 91 foll. ; and if he had taken a little more pains might have worked out the whole problem satisfactorily.

55. Of these quasi-deities Fides is the oldest, and was associated with Jupiter on the Capitol ; Wissowa, *R.K.* 103 foll. Thus we may find a *callida iunctura* between the thirteenth, fourteenth, and

fifteenth stanzas, for Fides and Pax would fit in well with the *responsa petunt* of the fourteenth.   Whether Pax was recognised as a deity at this time is not quite certain ; but a few years later, in 9 B.C., an altar of Pax Augusta was dedicated.   The Ara Pacis was begun in 13 B.C.   See Axtell, *Deification of Abstract Ideas* (Chicago, 1907), p. 37, who may also be consulted for the other deities here mentioned.   See also above, p. 285.   In Tibull. i. 10. 45 foll., Pax seems to be on the verge of deification, but not to have attained it except in the poet's fancy.

56. The route may be followed in the map of the Via Sacra in Lanciani's *Ruins and Excavations*, and in his chapter entitled, " A Walk through the Sacra Via," or more shortly in my *Social Life in the Age of Cicero*, p. 18 foll.

Note.—The whole question of the singing of the *Carmen saeculare* in its relation to the two principal sites and to the topography of the festival generally, is fully discussed by the author in *Classical Review* for 1910, p. 145 foll.

LECTURE XX

CONCLUSION

" A TIME of spiritual awakening, of a calling to higher destinies, came upon the world, the civilised world which lay around the Mediterranean Sea, at the beginning of our era. The calling was concentrated in the life and death of the Founder of Christianity." [1] The writer of these words goes on to point out that the beginning of our era was "a time of general stirring in all the higher fields of human activity," and that all such stirring, all that brings higher ideals before the minds of men of action, of imagination, or of reflection, if not itself religion, is in some sense religious, and in that age must be taken into account as having some bearing on the origin of Christianity, the greatest of all religious movements. And inasmuch as the new spirit of the age seems to have put new life into the old religious systems, with the help of philosophy and poetry, as well as of a purer and more effective conception of Man's relation to the Power manifesting itself in the universe, he finds it useful and legitimate to show how the ideas and characteristics of the leading types of religion in the civilised world of which he speaks were absorbed or "baptized" into the spirit of Christianity. In other words, we may ask what was the contribution of each of these religious types to the formation of the Christian type of religion ; for however new was the inspiration which was the essential living germ of our religion, yet that germ was of necessity planted in soil full of other religious ingredients,

452

which found their way into the sap of the plant as it grew towards maturity.

I have all along wished to bring our subject, the religious experience of the Roman people, into touch with Christianity, whether by marking points of contact, or of contrast, or both. In the last few lectures I have laid stress on certain points likely to be useful to us in this last stage of our studies, and these will, I hope, furnish us with some amount of material. But I confess that I have approached this subject with great hesitation. What I shall have to say will be tentative and suggestive only ; but I hope that the account that I have given in these lectures of Roman religious experience may be of use in helping a better qualified student to carry on the work more adequately.

Let us glance back for a moment at the results of the last four lectures, in which I have been dealing with Roman religious experience after the paralysis or hyp-notism of the old religion of the State. We saw, in the first place, that the educated part of Roman society had been brought to the very threshold of a new and more elevating type of religion, by Greek philosophy trans-planted to Roman soil, and chiefly by Stoicism. True, one great Epicurean genius had had his share in this process, by denouncing the weakness and wickedness of the Roman society, and the futility of all the religious forms and fancies with which they still dallied ; but Lucretius had nothing to offer in the place of these forms and fancies—nothing, that is, which could grip the con-science and act as a real force upon conduct. The Roman was in a religious sense destitute, both of a real sense of duty to his fellow-men of all grades, and in regard to God ; and for this destitution Lucretius' remedy, the accurate knowledge of a philosophical theory of the universe, was wholly inadequate. The first real appeal to the conscience of the Roman came from Stoicism, the reasonable and less austere type of Stoicism which Panaetius preached to the Scipionic circle. From this the Roman learnt that as a part of the divine universe Man himself is divine : that as endowed with a portion of that Reason which itself is God, he has a sacred duty to perform in using it.   Thus, as the Universal was revealed, so the Individual was ennobled ; and the only thing wanting to make of this a real religion was a bond that might unite the two more effectually in conduct as well as in thought.   Though a later development of Stoicism did indeed all but achieve this union, that of the later Republic failed to do so, because it inherited the old Stoic neglect of the emotional side of man's nature, and could take little advantage from a strong current of mystical feeling that was running side by side with it. The Stoic ingredient in the soil which was being prepared for Christianity was rich and valuable, but in this one respect it was poor.   It was intellectually beautiful, but it stirred as yet no " enthusiasm of humanity." [2]

Another ingredient in the soil was that imaginative transcendentalism which we discussed under the name of Mysticism, in which the soul becomes of greater interest than the body, and a strange yearning possesses the mind to speculate on the nature of the soul, its existence before this life, and its lot in another world.   These imaginative yearnings were not native to the Roman, who had never had any very definite idea of a future life, nor had ever troubled himself about a previous one ; they filtered through the Pythagorean and Platonic philosophy into that type of later Stoicism which attracted him.   They were hardly treated in Roman society with real religious earnestness, except perhaps in some few moments of sorrow and emotion such as I dwelt on in the experience of Cicero.   But the mere fact that they were in the air at Rome is of importance for us.   They *stimulated the imaginative faculty in religious thought* ; they kept alive in the minds at least of some men the questions why we are here, what we are, and what becomes of us after death.   They prepared the Roman mind for Christian eschatology ; and this, though never so important in the

Latin Church as in the Greek, was yet an important part of the teaching of the early Church. St. Paul exactly expresses the yearning thus dimly foreshadowed in the mystical movement of which I am speaking : " We that are in this tabernacle do groan, being burdened ; not for that we would be unclothed, but that we would be clothed upon, that what is mortal may be swallowed up of life " (2 Cor. v. 4). It was essential that the Roman should be able to understand words like these, and to associate them with a religion which, though in its most vital points one mainly affecting this life, was also, like those of Isis and Mithras, strongly tinged with mysticism. " All religions of that time," it has lately been said, " were religions of hope. Stress was laid on the future : the present time was but for preparation. So in the mysterious cults of Hellenism, whose highest aim is to offer guarantees for other worldly happiness ; so too in Judaism, whose legacy has but the aim of furnishing the happy life in the kingdom of the future. But Christianity is a religion of faith, the gospel not only giving guarantees for the future life, but bringing confidence, peace, joy, salvation, forgiveness, righteousness—whatever man's heart yearns after." [3]

Yet another ingredient was that kindly, charitable, sympathetic outlook on the world which we found in the poems of Virgil, and which is associated throughout them with the idea of duty and honourable service. The husbandman toiling cheerfully and doing his simple acts of worship, among the patient animals that he loves, and the scenes of natural beauty that inspire him with pure and tender thoughts ; and then again in the *Aeneid* the warrior kept true to his goal by a sense of duty stimulated by supernatural influence : both these sides of the Virgilian spirit show well how the soil is being prepared for another and a richer crop. Love and Duty are the essentials of Christian ethics ; they are both to be found in this poet, and through him made their way into the ideas of the better Romans of the next generation, and so into the philosophy of Seneca and

Marcus Aurelius. " To minds touched with the same sense of life's problems which pervades the poetry of Virgil, the ideas that came from Galilee brought the rest and peace which they could not find elsewhere." [4]   The early Christian writers loved the " vates Gentilium," and St. Augustine in particular is for ever quoting him ; but I should be going beyond the limits of my subject if I were to follow his gentle influence farther down the stream of time.

In my last lecture we discussed the revival of the old religious forms by Augustus, and the consummation of this work of his in the splendid ritual of the *Ludi saecu- lares.* Can it be said that such an astute and worldly policy as this had any value in the way of preparation for Christianity ?   Only, I think, in one way ; it renewed the idea of the connection between religion and the State, and of the religious duties of the individual citizen towards the State.   It preserved the outward features of the old State religion, such as the calendar, the ritual, and the terminology or vocabulary, and handed these down to a time when they could be of service to a Latin Christian church.[5]   Had the old forms been allowed to go utterly to rack and ruin, as they had been already doing for the last two centuries, the Roman State would have been as such without religion, or the worship of the Caesars would have become disastrously powerful and prominent, or maybe the State would have adopted the religion of Isis or Mithras or some other Oriental cult and belief, before Christianity could lay a firm grasp on it.   I think it might be shown that the continuity of the old religion in its connection with the State was really of value in keeping these growths from occupying too much ground : of value in checking too rapid a growth of individualism :[6] of value too in cherishing certain really precious religious char- acteristics, orderliness and decency in ritual, for example, which, as we have seen, were very early developed in the Roman religious system, and which owed their continued vitality to the overwhelming influence of the Roman State over all her citizens and their ideas. Thus when at last, after a period of anxious conflict between rival religions, the State proclaimed itself Christian, and henceforward for good or ill extended its protection to the Church, its religious tradition was still one of decency and order, still free from almost all that the old Roman State knew and dreaded as *superstitio*. There was, in fact, a legacy, not indeed a spiritual one, but yet one of some small value, left by the old Roman religion to the Latin Church : and this I will turn for a few minutes to examine.

As an example of the orderly, sane, and decent character which the Church inherited from the Roman religion, I might recall what I said in Lecture IX. about *lustratio*, that slow and orderly processional movement in which the old Romans delighted, and which is familiar still to all travellers in Italy.[7] Another is the tender and reverential care for the resting-places of departed relatives. I am not sure that Prof. Gardner is right in asserting that the prayers for the dead of the Catholic Church took the place of the worship of the dead in the Roman family ;[8] for it is not easy to say how far it is true that the dead were ever really worshipped at Rome, and the idea of prayer for the dead, if it can be traced to Roman sources at all, may be rather due to those tendencies which we discussed under Mysticism, than to anything inherent in the old Roman attitude to the departed. None the less there is in the *sacra privata* of the Parentalia, and especially of the Caristia which concluded it—a kind of love-feast of all members of the family, where all quarrels and differences were to be laid aside,[9]—something that suggests the Christian attitude towards the dead, and in some dim way too the doctrine of the Communion of Saints. And we may also notice how closely in regard to externals the great events of family life,—those critical moments when the aid of the *numina* was most needed—the first days of infancy, the eras of puberty and of marriage, passed on in their sober and orderly ritual into the baptism, confirmation, and sacramental wedding of the Christian Church.   In such ways the private religion of the Roman family had doubtless a real continuity in the new era, though the line of connection is difficult to trace.   This, and many other examples of survival, the worship of local saints which took the place of that of local deities, the use of holy water and of incense as symbolic elements in worship, and the general resemblance of the arrangement of festivals in the Calendars, Roman and Christian, might be interesting matter for a complete course of lectures, but must be omitted here.

Another point of interest, which might also be widely expanded, is the influence of the Roman religious *spirit*, as distinct from the outward form, on Christian thought and literature in the Western half of the Empire.   The subtle transcendentalism of the Greek fathers was foreign to Latin Christianity ; the characteristics of Roman life as reflected in Roman worship are plainly visible in the Latin fathers.   From Minucius Felix onwards, the Christians who wrote in Latin, so far from being imaginative and dreamy, are one and all matter-of-fact ; historical, abounding in illustration of life and conduct ; ethical rather than speculative ; legal in their cast of thought rather than philosophical ; rhetorical in their manner of expression rather than fervent or poetical.   They were well versed in the great literature of Rome, but most of them, and especially the African school (which carried Roman tendencies to an extreme), knew comparatively little of Greek.   St. Augustine, for example, could not bring himself to work at Greek with ardour, nor could he explain why this was so.[10]   Of Augustine, as the type of the literature of Latin Christianity, Bishop Westcott wrote with something of an exaggerated criticism, lamenting that he had not the Greek which had so large a place in the Bishop's own training.   " He looked " (more particularly in the *de Civitate Dei*) " at everything from the side of law and not of freedom : from the side of God, as an irresponsible sovereign, and not of man, as a loving servant.

In spite of his admiration for Plato, he was driven by a passion for system " (how this reminds us of the old Roman religious lawyers !) " to fix, to externalise, to freeze every idea into a rigid shape. In spite of his genius he could not shake off the influence of a legal and rhetorical training, which controversy called into active exercise." [11] The lecture from which I am quoting is an interesting one, on the work and character of Origen, the great Alexandrian of the third century A.D., with whom Augustine is contrasted, as in an earlier age we might contrast Seneca with Philo ; the Latin writers rhetorical, practical, realistic ; the Greek authors idealistic and fervent, apt to see deep moral significance in all human life. And this is really the manner and mental attitude of all the famous Latin fathers : of Lactantius, the clear, precise Ciceronian, whose every page shows the perennial value of the Latin tongue ; of Tertullian, the subtle and acute rhetorician, more gifted with imagination than his fellows ; of Arnobius, another Roman African, the reputed teacher of Lactantius.

One of the characteristics of these Latin fathers is their fondness for using the famous words of the old Roman religion, but in new senses. They inherit that Roman love for a strong technical word of pregnant meaning which has left us so many imperishable legacies in terminology. *Municipium, colonia, imperium, collegium,* rise in one's mind the moment the subject is mentioned ; and a few minutes' thought will reveal another score of words which in various forms pervade all our modern European terminology. So, too, with the language of religion. These Latin advocates of Christian doctrine took the old words which we have so often dwelt on in the course of these lectures, and gave them new but almost equally clear and pregnant meanings. Let us glance at three or four of these ; for such a legacy as this is no mean property of the Christian religion of the West.

Let us take, to begin with, the greatest of all these words—*religio*. I have maintained throughout these lectures that the original sense of this word was the natural feeling of man in the presence of the supernatural; and though this has actually been questioned since I began them,[12] I see no good reason to alter my conviction. But in the age of Cicero and Lucretius the word begins to take on a different meaning, of great importance for the future. Though Cicero as a young man had defined *religio* as "the feeling of the presence of a higher or divine nature, which prompts man to worship,—to *cura et caerimonia*,"[13] yet later on in life he uses it with much freedom of that *cura et caerimonia* apart from the feeling. To take a single example among many : in a passage in his *de Legibus* he says that to worship private or strange or foreign gods, "confusionem habet religionum";[14] and again he calls his own imaginary *ius divinum* in that treatise a *constitutio religionum*, a system of religious duties.[15] In many other passages, on the other hand, we find both the feeling which prompts and the cult-acts which follow on it equally connoted by the word ; for example, the phrase *religio sepulcrorum* suggests quite as much the feeling as the ritual. So it would seem that *religio* is already beginning to pass into the sense in which we still use it—*i.e., the feeling which suggests worship, and the forms under which we perform that worship.* In this broad sense it is also used by Lucretius, who included under it all that was for him the world's evil and folly, both the feeling of awe which he believed to be degrading, and the organised worship of the family and the State, which he no less firmly believed to be futile. "Tantum *religio* potuit suadere malorum."[16] The fact is that in that age, when the old local character of the cults was disappearing, and when men like Posidonius, Varro, and Cicero were thinking and writing about the nature of the gods and kindred subjects, a word was wanted to gather up and express all this religious side of human life and experience : it must be a word without a definite technical meaning, and such a word was *religio*.

Thus while *religio* continues to express the feeling only or the cult only, if called on to do so, it gains in the age of Cicero a more comprehensive connotation, as the result of the contemplation of religion by philosophy as a thing apart from itself; and this enabled the early Christian writers, who knew their Cicero well, to give it a meaning in which it is still in use among all European nations.

But there was yet to be a real change in the meaning of the word, one that was inevitable, as the contrast between Christianity and other religions called for emphasis. The second century A.D. was that in which the competition was keenest between various religious creeds and forms, each with its own vitality, and each clearly marked off from the others. It is no longer a question of religion as a whole, contemplated by a critical or a sympathetic philosophy; the question is, which creed or form is to be the true and the victorious religion. Our wonderful word again adapts itself to the situation. Each separate religious system can now be called a *religio*. The old polytheistic system can now be called *religio Deorum* by the Christian, while his own creed is *religio Dei*. In the *Octavius* of Minucius Felix, written about the end of the second century, the word is already used in this sense. *Nostra religio, vera religio*,[17] is for him the whole Christian faith and practice as it stood then—the depth of feeling and the acts which gave it outward form. The one true religion can thus be now expressed by the word. In Lactantius, Arnobius, Tertullian, in the third century A.D., this new sense is to be found on almost every page, but a single noble passage of Lactantius must suffice to illustrate it. " The heathen sacrifice," he says, " and leave all their religion in the temple; thus it is that such *religiones* cannot make men good or firm in their faith. But ' nostra *religio* eo firma est et solida et immutabilis, quia mentem ipsam pro sacrificio habet, quia tota in animo colentis est.' "[18]

Here at last we come upon a force of meaning which the word had never before attained. *Religio* here is not awe only or cult only, but *a mental devotion capable of building up character.* " The kingdom of God is within you." Surely this is a valuable legacy to the Christian faith from our hard, dry, old Roman religion.

Another legacy in words is that of *pius.* Our English word " pious " has suffered some damage from the sanctimoniousness of a certain type of Puritanism ; but *piety* still remains sweet and wholesome, and, like its Latin original in the middle ages it seems to express one beautiful aspect of the Christian life better than any other word. In the old Roman religion *pius* meant the man who strictly conforms his life to the *ius divinum* ; this we know from the very definite ancient explanations of its contrary, *impius.* The *impius* is the man who *wilfully* breaks the *ius divinum* and the *pax deorum* ; for him no *piaculum* was of avail.[19] Such a crime is the nearest approach in Roman antiquity to our idea of sin. *Pius* is therefore, as we saw in discussing Aeneas, the man who knows the will of the gods, and so far as in him lies adjusts his conduct thereto, whether in the life of the family or as a citizen of the State. As applied to things, to a war for example, the word *pium* is almost equivalent to *iustum* or *purum, i.e., pium bellum* is a war declared and conducted in accordance with the principles of the *ius divinum.*[20] *Pietas* is therefore a virtue, that of obedience to the will of God as shown in private and public life, and it herein differs from *religio,* which is not a virtue, but a feeling. But we need not be surprised to find that in Lactantius *pietas* can be used to explain *religio* ; for *religio* is no longer a feeling only or a cult only, but, as we saw just now, a mental devotion capable of building up character. In one passage he says that it is no true philosophy which " veram religionem, id est summam pietatem, non habet." [21] In another interesting chapter he shows plainly enough that he uses *pietas* just as he uses *religio,* to express the whole Christian mental furniture.[22] He begins by scornfully pointing to Aeneas as the typical *pius,* and asking what we are to think of the *pietas* of a man who could bind the hands of prisoners in order to slaughter them as a sacrifice to the shade of Pallas [23] (little dreaming, indeed, that Christian piety should ever be guilty of such slaughter in the cause of the faith); and ends by asking, " What, then, is *pietas*? Surely it is with those who know not war ; who keep at peace with all men ; who love their enemies and count all men their brethren ; who can control their anger and curb all mental wilfulness." And once again, *pietas* is the main ingredient in *iustitia*, that is, in Christian right- eousness, for " pietas nihil aliud est quam Dei notio." Even here it is not so far removed from its old meaning ; but in a Christian writer it can mean conformity to the will of God, based on a real knowledge of Him, in a sense which shows us by a sudden illuminating flash the deep gulf set between the old religion and the new.

Another word, bequeathed in this case rather by the Latin language than the Roman religion, in which it held no strictly technical meaning, is *sanctus*, which has played so large a part in the terminology of the Catholic Church, and passed thence into the language of Puritanism for the living Christian, as in Baxter's famous book, *The Saints' Rest*. The exact meaning of *sanctus* is extremely difficult to fix, and this may be why it was found to be a convenient word for a type of character negative rather than positive. The lawyers defined it as meaning what is *sancitum* by the State,[24] without tracing it back to a time when the State was a religious as well as a civil entity. But there was beyond doubt a religious flavour in it from the beginning, as in other old Italian words connected with it ; and thus it seems to be able to express a certain conjunction of religious and moral purity which finally brought it into the hands of the Christian writers. A single verse of Virgil will serve to explain what I mean. Turnus, before he rushes forth to meet his death at Aeneas' hand, and knowing that he is to meet it, asks the Manes to be good to him, " quoniam superis aversa voluntas," for—

sancta ad vos *anima* atque istius nescia culpae
descendam magnorum haud unquam indignus avorum.[25]

He goes to the shades with a conscience clear of guilt
or of *impietas* ; as the ancient scholiast interprets the
word, it is equivalent to *incorrupta*.[26]   In this sense it
became one of the favourite superlatives to describe in
sepulchral inscriptions, pagan or Christian, the purity of
departed women and children.[27]

Lastly, we have the great word *sacer*, with its com-
pounds *sacrificium* and *sacramentum*.   The adjective
itself has no new or special significance, I think, in the
language of the early Christians, and in our Teutonic
languages the Roman sense of it, " that which is made
over to God," is expressed by the word *holy*, *sacred*
being retained in a general sense for that which is not
" common."   But *sacrificium*, the act of making a thing,
animate or inanimate, or yourself, as in *devotio*, over to
the gods, is indeed a great legacy on which I do not
need to dwell.   *Sacramentum*, on the other hand, needs
a word of explanation.

Sacramentum in Roman public law meant (1) a legal
formula (*legis actio*), under which a sum of money was
deposited, originally in a temple,[28] to be forfeited by
the loser in a suit.   The deposition *in loco sacro* gives
the word to the process, and helps us to see that it
must mean some act which has a religious sanction.
So with (2) its other meaning, *i.e.* the oath of obedience
taken by the soldier, who was *iuratus in verba*, that is,
sworn under a formula with a religious sanction attached.[29]
It is tempting to suppose that it is through this channel
that it found its way into the Christian vocabulary—the
soldier of Christ affirming his allegiance in the solemn
rites of baptism, marriage, or the Eucharist.   It is a
curious fact that it seems to be used in this way in the
religion of Mithras,[30] which was especially powerful among
the Roman legions of the Empire, and in which there
was a grade of the faithful with the title of *milites*.
Sacramentum was here the word for the initiatory rites

of a grade. In the earliest Christian writers of Latin
it usually means a mystery; thus Arnobius writes of the
Christian religion as revealing the "veritatis absconditae
sacramenta";[31] but in another passage the idea in his
mind seems to be that of military service. It is better,
he says, for Christians to break their worldly contracts,
even of marriage, than to break the *fides Christiana*, "*et
salutaris militiae sacramenta deponere*;"[32] and Tertullian
more than once attaches the same military meaning to
it: "Vocati sumus ad militiam Dei vivi iam tunc *cum
in verba sacramenti spopondimus*."[33] Perhaps we may
take it that the word, though of general significance for
a religiously binding force produced by certain mysterious
rites, had a special attraction for writers of the painful
third century A.D., as reflecting into the Christian life
from old Roman times something of the spirit of the
duty and self-sacrifice of the loyal legionary. In any
case we have once more a verbal legacy of priceless
value.[34]

To sum up what I have been saying, there were certain
ingredients in the Roman soil, deposits of the Roman
religious experience, which were in their several ways
favourable to the growth of a new plant. There were
also certain direct legacies from the old Roman religion,
of which Christianity could dispose with profit, in the
shape of forms of ritual, and, what was even of greater
value, words of real significance in the old religion, which
were destined to become of permanent and priceless value
in the Christian speech of the western nations. There
were also other points in the society and organisation of
the Roman Empire which were of great importance for
the growth of the new creed; but these lie outside my
proper subject, and have been dealt with by Professor
Gardner in the lecture to which I alluded at the beginning of this lecture, and most instructively by Sir W. M.
Ramsay in more than one of his books, and especially
in *St. Paul, the Traveller and Roman Citizen*.

And yet, all this taken together, so far from explaining

Christianity, does not help us much in getting to understand even the conditions under which it grew into men's
minds as a new power in the life of the world.   The
plant, though grown in soil which had borne other crops,
was wholly new in structure and vital principle.   I say
this deliberately, after spending so many years on the
study of the religion of the Romans, and making myself
acquainted in some measure with the religions of other
peoples.   The essential difference, as it appears to me
as a student of the history of religion, is this, that
whereas the connection between religion and morality
has so far been a loose one,—at Rome, indeed, so loose,
that many have refused to believe in its existence,—the
new religion was itself morality,[35] but morality consecrated
and raised to a higher power than it had ever yet reached.
It becomes active instead of passive ; mere good nature
is replaced by a doctrine of universal love ; *pietas*, the
sense of duty in outward things, becomes an enthusiasm
embracing all humanity, consecrated by such an appeal
to the conscience as there never had been in the world
before—the appeal to the life and death of the divine
Master.

This is what is meant, if I am not mistaken, by the
great contrast so often and so vividly drawn by St. Paul
between the spirit and the flesh, between the children of
light and the children of darkness, between the sleep or
the death of the world and the waking to life in Christ,
between the blameless and the harmless sons of God
and the crooked and perverse generation among whom
they shine as lights in the world.   I confess that I never
realised this contrast fully or intelligently until I read
through the Pauline Epistles from beginning to end with
a special historical object in view.   It is useful to be
familiar with the life and literature of the two preceding
centuries, if only to be able the better to realise, in
passing to St. Paul, a Roman citizen, a man of education
and experience, the great gulf fixed between the old and
the new as he himself saw it.

But historical knowledge, knowledge of the Roman society of the day, study of the Roman religious experience, cannot do more than give us a little help ; they cannot reveal the secret. History can explain the progress of morality, but it cannot explain its consecration. With St. Paul the contrast is not merely one of good and bad, but of the spirit and the flesh, of life and death. No mere contemplation of the world around him could have kindled the fervency of spirit with which this contrast is by him conceived and expressed. Absolute devotion to the life and death of the Master, apart even from His work and teaching (of which, indeed, St. Paul says little), this alone can explain it. The love of Christ is the entirely new power that has come into the world ; [36] not merely as a new type of morality, but as "*a Divine influence transfiguring human nature in a universal love.*" The passion of St. Paul's appeal lies in the consecration of every detail of it by reference to the life and death of his Master ; and the great contrast is for him not as with the Stoics, between the universal law of Nature and those who rebel against it ; not as with Lucretius, between the blind victims of *religio* and the indefatigable student of the *rerum natura* ; not, as in the *Aeneid*, between the man who bows to the decrees of fate, destiny, God, or whatever we choose to call it, and the wilful rebel, victim of his own passions ; not, as in the Roman State and family, between the man who performs religious duties and the man who wilfully neglects them—between *pius* and *impius* ; but between the universal law of love, focussed and concentrated in the love of Christ, and the sleep, the darkness, the death of a world that will not recognise it.

I will conclude these lectures with one practical illustration of this great contrast, which will carry us back for a moment to the ritual of the old Roman *ius divinum*. That ritual, we saw, consisted mainly of sacrifice and prayer, the two apparently inseparable from each other. I pointed out that though the efficacy of the whole process was believed to depend on the strictest adherence to prescribed forms, whether of actions or words, the prayers, when we first meet with them, have got beyond the region of charm or spell, and are cast in the language of petition; they show clearly a sense of the dependence of man on the Power manifesting itself in the universe. There was here, perhaps, a germ of religious development; but it was arrested in its growth by the formalisation of the whole Roman religious system, and no substitute was to be found for it either in the imported Greek ritual, or in the more enlightening doctrines of exotic Greek philosophy. The prayers used in the ritual of Augustus' great festival, which was almost as much Greek as Roman in character, seem to us as hard and formal as the most ancient Roman prayers that have come down to us. In the most emotional moments of the life of a Roman of enlightenment like Cicero, when we can truly say of him that he was touched by true religious feeling, as well as by the spiritual aspirations of the nobler Greek philosophers, prayers find no place at all.

But for St. Paul and the members of the early Christian brotherhood the whole of life was a continuous worship, and the one great feature of that worship was prayer. It has been said by a great Christian writer of recent times that "when the attention of a thinking heathen was directed to the new religion spreading in the Roman Empire, the first thing to strike him as extraordinary would be that a religion of prayer was superseding the religion of ceremonies and invocation of gods; that it encouraged all, even the most uneducated, to pray, or, in other words, to meditate and exercise the mind in self-scrutiny and contemplation of God." [37] And, as the same writer says, prayer thus became a motive power of moral renewal and *inward civilisation*, to which nothing else could be compared for efficacy. And more than this, it was the chief inward and spiritual means of maintaining that universal law of love, which, so far as this life was concerned, was the great secret of the new religion.

NOTES TO LECTURE XX

1. P. Gardner, *The Growth of Christianity*, 1907, p. 2. Cp. some remarks of Prof. Conway in *Virgil's Messianic Eclogue*, p. 39 foll.

2. The phrase "enthusiasm of humanity" is, of course, that of the author of *Ecce Homo*, a most inspiring book for all students of religious history, as indeed for all other readers.

3. Dobschütz on "Early Christian Eschatology," in *Transactions of the Third Congress for the History of Religions*, vol. ii. (Oxford, 1908), p. 320.

4. The words are those of Mr. Glover in the last page of his *Studies in Virgil*.

5. It should be understood that these legacies, with the exception of the last (the vocabulary), were only taken up by the Church after the first two centuries of its existence. And even the vocabulary of the early Roman Church was mainly Greek (Gwatkin, *Early Church History*, ii. 213, and it was not till the rise of the African school of writers (Tertullian, Arnobius, Augustine) that the Latin vocabulary really established itself. Any real assimilation of Christian and pagan forms of worship was not possible until the latter were growing meaningless ; then "the assimilation of Christianity to heathenism from the third century is matter of history" (Gwatkin, i. 269).

6. Caird, *Gifford Lectures*, vol. ii. p. 353, has some interesting remarks on this point.

7. See above, p. 211.

8. *Growth of Christianity*, p. 144.

9. See *Roman Festivals*, p. 308.

10. *Confessions*, i. 14.

11. Westcott, *Religious Thought in the West*, p. 246. Gwatkin writes (vol. ii. 236) that all Augustine's conceptions are shaped by law and Stoicism. Cp. p. 237. So, too, of Tertullian.

12. By W. Otto, in the *Archiv für Religionswissenschaft*, vol. xii. (1909) p. 533 foll.

13. *De Inventione*, ii. 161.

14. *De Legibus*, ii. 10. 25.

15. *Ib.* 10. 23.

16. Lucretius i. 101.

17. *E.g.* Octavius 38. 2 ; and again at the end of that chapter.

18. Lactantius, bk. v. (*de Iustitia*) ch. 19. I may note here that the paragraph in the text where this is quoted was first published in the *Transactions of the Congress for the History of Religions*

(Oxford, 1908), vol. ii. p. 174. I may also add that the restricted sense of the word *religio* as meaning the monastic life is, of course, comparatively late. This restrictive use of heathen words, from the third century onwards, is the subject of some valuable remarks by Prof. Gwatkin in his *Early Church History*, vol. i. p. 268 foll.

19. See *Roman Festivals*, p. 299, and the references there given.

20. Livy i. 32, ix. 8. 6; Wissowa, *R.K.* p. 476; Greenidge, *Roman Public Life*, p. 56.

21. Lactantius iv. 3 (*de vera sapientia*).

22. *Ib.* v. (*de Iustitia*) ch. 10.

23. *Aen.* xi. 81.

24. Marquardt, 145, note 5.

25. *Aen.* xii. 648.

26. Servius, *ad Aen.* xii. 648.

27. The original meaning of *sanctus* as applied to things, *e.g.* walls and tombs, was probably "inviolable"; Nettleship, *Contributions to Latin Lexicography, s.v.* "sanctus," who also suggests a connection between the word and the attitude of the Roman towards his dead: thus Cicero in *Topica* 90 writes of *aequitas* as consisting of three parts,—*pietas, sanctitas*, and *iustitia*,—meaning man's relation to the gods, the Manes, and his fellow-men. Nettleship also quotes *Aen.* v. 80 (*salve sancte parens*), Tibull. ii. 2. 6, and other passages, which show that the word was specially used of the dead and their belongings. But when used of persons living, as frequently in the last century B.C., it expresses a certain purity of life, not without a religious tincture, which could not so well be expressed by any other word, owing to the original meaning being that of religious inviolability. Thus Cicero uses it in the 9th Philippic of his old friend Sulpicius, one of the best and purest men of his time; and long before Cicero, Cato had used it of an obligation at once ethical and religious: "Maiores *sanctius* habuere defendi pupillos quam clientem non fallere." It is interesting to notice that it was used later on of Mithras and other oriental deities (Cumont, *Mon. myst. Mithra*, i. p. 533; *Les Religions orientales*, p. 289, note 45); in the case of Mithras, at least, this meant that his life was pure, and that he wished his worshippers to be pure also.

28. Marquardt, p. 318, note 4; Mommsen, *Strafrecht*, pp. 902, 1026. See also Greenidge, *Roman Public Life*, p. 56; Festus, p. 347.

29. Greenidge, *op. cit.* p. 154.

30. Cumont, *Mysterien von Mithras*, p. 116 of the German edition. See also De Marchi, *La Religione nella vita privata*, vol. ii. 114. It may be worth noting that the idea of life as the service of a soldier bound to obedience by his oath is found also in Stoicism; see Epictetus (*Arrian*), *Discourses*, i. 14, iii. 24, 99-101, ii. 26, 28-30; (Crossley's *Golden Sayings of Epictetus*, Nos. 37, 125, 132, 134).

31. Arnobius, *adv. Nationes*, i. 3.

32. *Ib*. ii. 6.

33. Tertull., *ad Martyr.* c. 3.   Cp. *de Corona Militiae*, c. 11.

34. It is curious that the word *sacerdos* did not find its way into the Christian vocabulary. Apparently it had its chance; for Tertullian uses it in several ways, *e.g.*, "summus sacerdos" for a bishop (*de Bapt.* 17; "disciplina sacerdotalis," *de Monog.* 7. 12; and for other examples see Harnack, *Entstehung und Entwickelung der Kirchenverfassung und des Kirchenrechts in den zwei ersten Jahrhunderten*, 1910, p. 85). But the words finally adopted for the grades of the priesthood were Greek: bishop, priest, and deacon. Nevertheless, the general word for the priesthood, as distinguished from the laity, is Latin (*ordo*); hence "ordination" and holy "orders." It is not of religious origin, but taken from the language of municipal life, *ordo et plebs* being contrasted just as they were contrasted in *municipia* as senate (*decuriones*) and all non-official persons. See Harnack, *op. cit.* p. 82.

35. This is, of course, in one light, the legitimate development of the union of religion and morality in the Hebrew mind. "For the Israelite morality, righteousness, is simply doing the will of God, which from the earliest age is assumed to be ascertainable, and indeed ascertained. The Law in its simplest form was at once the rule of morality and the revealed will of God." "The central feature of O.T. morality is its religious character" (Alexander, *Ethics of St. Paul*, p. 34). In the religious system we have been occupied with, religion can only be reckoned as one of the factors in the growth of morality; it supplied the sanction for some acts of righteousness, but (in historical times at least) by no means for all.

Prof. Gwatkin, in his *Early Church History*, vol. i. p. 54, states the relation of early Christianity to morality thus: "Christ's person, not His teaching, is the message of the Gospel. If we know anything for certain about Jesus of Nazareth, it is that He steadily claimed to be the Son of God, the Redeemer of mankind, and the ruler of the world to come, and by that claim the Gospel stands or falls. Therefore, the Lord's disciples went not forth as preachers of morality, but as witnesses of his life, and of the historic resurrection which proved his mightiest claims. Their morality is always an inference from these, never the forefront of their teaching. They seem to think that if they can only fill men with true thankfulness for the gift of life in Christ, morality will take care of itself." I cannot but think that this is expressed too strongly, or baldly; but it is in the main in keeping with the impression left on my mind by a study of St. Paul. It must, however, be remembered that the Pauline spirit is not exactly that of early Christianity in general: see Gwatkin, vol. i. p. 98. In the *Didache*, *e.g.*, there is no trace of St. Paul's influence (104).

36. In a book which had just been published when I was delivering

these lectures at Edinburgh (*The Ethics of St. Paul*, by Archibald Alexander), I found a very interesting chapter on "The Dynamic of the New Life," p. 126 foll. The word which for the author best expresses that dynamic is *faith*, which is "the spring of all endeavour, the inspiration of all heroism" (p. 150). "It brings the whole life into the domain of spiritual freedom, and is the animating and energising principle of all moral purpose." What exactly is here understood by faith is explained on p. 151 to the end of the chapter, of which I may quote the concluding words: "Faith in Christ means life in Christ. And this complete yielding of self and vital union with the Saviour, this dying and rising again, is at once man's supreme ideal and the source of all moral greatness."

37. Döllinger, *The First Age of Christianity and the Church* (Oxenham's translation), p. 344 foll.

APPENDIX I

On the Use of Huts or Booths in Religious Ritual

THIS may be taken as an addendum to Lecture II. on taboo at Rome; but owing to the uncertainty of the explanation given in it, I reserved it for an Appendix. The custom here dealt with is found both in the public and private worship of the Romans, and also in Greece and elsewhere, but has never, so far as I know, been investigated by anthropologists.

On the Ides of March, at the festival of Anna Perenna, a deity explained as representing "the ring of the year," whose cult is not recognised in the ancient religious calendar, the lower population came out of the city, and lay about all day in the Campus Martius, near the Tiber. Ovid, fortunately, took the trouble to describe the scene in the third book of his *Fasti*, as he had witnessed it himself. Some of them, he says, lay in the open, *some constructed tents, and some made rude huts of stakes and branches, stretching their togas over them to make a shelter.*

> plebs venit ac virides passim disiecta per herbas
>   potat, et accumbit cum pare quisque sua.
> sub Iove pars durat, pauci tentoria ponunt,
>   sunt quibus e ramis frondea facta casa est,
> pars, ubi pro rigidis calamos statuere columnis,
>   desuper extentas imposuere togas.
> sole tamen vinoque calent, annosque precantur,
>   quot sumant cyathos, ad numerumque bibunt.[1]

It appears also from Ovid's account that there was much drunkenness and obscene language; this was, in fact, a *festa* very different in character from those of the Numan calendar; and that there was a magical element in the cult of the deity seems proved by the mysterious allusion to "virgineus cruor" in connection with her grove not far from this scene of revelry, in Martial iv. 64. 17 (cp. Pliny, *N.H.* xxviii. 78, and Columella

---

[1] *Fasti*, iii. 525 foll. See *R.F.* p. 50 foll.

473

x. 558). Tibullus describes something of the same kind at a rustic festival,[1] though he does not make it clear what time of year he is speaking of; a few lines before he had mentioned the drinking and leaping over the fire at the Parilia, the shepherd's festival in April, though I cannot feel sure that the following lines are also meant to refer to it :—

> tunc operata deo pubes discumbet in herba,
>   arboris antiquae qua levis umbra cadit,
> aut e veste sua tendent umbracula sertis
>   vincta, coronatus stabit et ipse calix.

Here it is too much to suppose that the *umbracula* were contrived to make up for the want of shade in a country so covered with woodland as Italy was then; and the words "*sertis vincta*" show that there was some special meaning in the practice. I think we may guess that in both instances the extemporised huts had some forgotten religious meaning. Yet another passage of Tibullus, which also describes a rural festival, alludes to a similar custom.[2] I have given reasons in the *Classical Review* for thinking that this was a summer festival, accompanied as it was, like many midsummer rites all over Europe, by bonfires and revelry, though the usual interpretation ascribes it to the winter.[3]

> tunc nitidus plenis confisus rusticus agris
>   ingeret ardenti grandia ligna foco,
> turbaque vernarum, saturi bona signa coloni,
>   ludet et ex virgis exstruet ante casas.

The slaves can here hardly be playing at building houses of twigs, like the children in Horace's *Satire*,[4] unless we are to suppose that Tibullus is thinking of slave children only, which is indeed possible; but even if that were so, how are we to account for the popularity of this curious form of sport?

There was, however, at Rome a public summer festival, included in the calendar, in which we find this same custom. At the Neptunalia, on July 23, huts or booths were erected, made of the foliage of trees. "Umbrae vocantur Neptunalibus *casae frondeae pro tabernaculis*," says Festus[5] (following Verrius Flaccus), where the last word is one in regular use for military tents. This is the only thing that is told us about this festival,

---

[1] Tibull. ii. 5. 89 foll. Mr. Mackail has pointed out to me a passage in the *Pervigilium Veneris*, line 5, which seems to contain a hint of the same practice (cp. line 43).

[2] Tibull. ii. 1. 1-24.

[3] *Classical Review*, 1908, p. 36 foll. My conclusions were criticised by Dr. Postgate in the *Classical Quarterly* for 1909, p. 127.

[4] Hor. *Sat.* ii. 3, 247.

[5] Festus, ed. Müller, p. 377.

and we may assume that even this would not have come down to us if it had not been a survival rigidly adhered to, *i.e.* the construction of shelters from the foliage of trees, instead of using tents, which could easily have been procured in the city. As the festival was in the hot month of July, we might suppose that shelter from the sun was the real object here; but we do not hear of it at other summer festivals, and the parallel practices I shall now mention make the rationalising explanation very doubtful. It is unlucky that we know hardly anything about the older and un-Graecised Neptunus, and nothing about his festival except this one fact; the comparative method is here our only hope.

The Jewish feast of tabernacles will, of course, occur at once to every one; this was in the heat of the summer, and the booths were here, as at the Neptunalia, made of the branches of trees;[1] the explanation given to the Israelites was not that they were thus to shelter themselves from the heat, but to be reminded of their homeless wanderings in the wilderness, plainly an aetiological account, as in the case of the passover. There are distinct examples in Greece of the same practice, *e.g.* the σκιάδες at the Spartan Carneia,[2] and tents (σκηναί) in several cases, as at the mysteries of Andania, where the peculiar regulations for the construction of the tents points to a ritualistic origin almost unmistakably.[3] But perhaps the most striking parallel is to be found in the famous letter of Gregory the Great, preserved by Bede, about the British converts to Christianity, who were to be allowed to use their heathen temples as churches:

"Et quia boves solent in sacrificio daemonum multos occidere, debet iis etiam hac in re aliqua solemnitas immutari: ut die dedicationis, vel natalicii sanctorum martyrum quorum illic reliquiae ponuntur, *tabernacula sibi circa easdem ecclesias quae ex fanis commutatae sunt, de ramis arborum faciant,* et religiosis conviviis sollemnitatem celebrent: nec diabolo iam animalia immolent, et ad laudem Dei in esu suo animalia occident," etc.[4]

Why should Gregory here take the trouble to describe the material out of which these huts were to be made? Surely

---

[1] Leviticus xxiii. 40-42. Cp. Plutarch, *Quaest. conviv.* 4. 2. This was a feast of harvest and first-fruits (Exodus xxiii. 16). Nehemiah viii. 13 foll. gives a graphic account of the revival of this festival after the captivity.

[2] Athenaeus iv. 41. 8 F. Cp. Farnell, *Cults of the Greek States*, vol. iv., p. 260.

[3] Dittenberger, *Sylloge inscript.* (ed. 2), 653, lines 34 foll. Cp. p. 200 (Teos).

[4] Baeda, *Hist. eccl.* i. 30 (ed. Plummer). There is a curious case of isolation in a hut in a process by which the sacrificer of the *soma* in the Vedic religion becomes divine, quoted by Hubert et Mauss, *Mélanges*, p. 34. This may possibly afford a clue to the mystery.

because the custom was one which had been described to him by Augustine or Mellitus as part of the heathen practice, and one which he was willing to condone as harmless (possibly with a recollection of the Jewish feast), since the Britons set great store by it.

If these examples from Europe and Palestine are sufficient to suggest that there was originally a religious or mystic meaning in the custom, we must look for its explanation in anthropological research. Robertson Smith was,[1] I think, the first to suggest a possible explanation of the Feast of Tabernacles, by comparing with it the rule, stated in Numbers xxxi. 19, that men might not enter their houses after bloodshed: "Do ye abide without the camp seven days: whosoever hath killed any person, and whosoever hath touched any slain, purify both yourselves and your captives on the third day and on the seventh day." He also pointed out that pilgrims are subject to the same rule, or taboo, in Syria and elsewhere. Since then an immense mass of evidence has been collected showing that all the world over persons in a holy or unclean state are placed under this or some similar restriction;[2] and if this be the case with pilgrims and warriors after a battle, it may also have been so with worshippers at some particular festival, even if we are quite unable to recover the special character of the worship which produced the restriction.[3] In the Feast of Tabernacles, which was a harvest festival, the cause seems to have been the great sanctity of the first-fruits, which are regarded with extreme veneration in many parts of the world. In the now famous festival of the first-fruits among the Natchez Indians of Louisiana, of which the details have been recorded with singular care and obvious accuracy,[4] we find that the chief, the Great Sun, and all the celebrators, have to live in huts two miles from their village, while the corn, grown for the purpose in a particular spot, is sacramentally eaten. It is quite impossible, without further evidence, which is not likely ever to be forthcoming, to explain either the Greek, Roman, or British customs in this way; we must be content with the general principle that the holiness of human beings at particular times is liable to carry with it the practice of renouncing your

---

[1] *Religion of the Semites*, notes K and N at the end of the volume.

[2] See *e.g.* Frazer, *G.B.* ed. 2, index, *s.v.* "Seclusion."

[3] It has occurred to me that the shedding of blood in animal sacrifice may possibly be the reason in some of these rites. The last words of the passage quoted above from Baeda suggest this explanation in the case of the Britons. In the first-fruits festivals the "killing of the corn" may be a parallel cause of taboo. See *G.B.* i. 372.

[4] Du Pratz, translated in *G.B.* ii. 332 foll.

own dwelling and living in an extemporised hut or booth. The tents that we hear of in the Greek rites I look upon as late developments of this primitive practice. The inscription of Andania, which is the best Greek evidence we possess, dates only from 91 B.C.; and by that time there would have been every opportunity for the rude huts to become civilised tents. The *casae* made by the *vernae* in Tibullus' poem were, I would suggest, a kind of unconscious survival of the same feeling and practice, the real religious meaning being almost entirely lost.

Lastly, I will venture to suggest that the *casae* of the Roman custom, made of branches at the Neptunalia and the feast of Anna Perenna, and of *virgae* by the slaves on the farm, are a reminiscence of the earliest form of Italian dwelling, which survived to historical times in the round temple of Vesta, and of which we have examples in the hut-urns discovered in the necropolis at Alba.[1] The earliest form of all was probably a round structure made of branches of trees stuck into the ground, bent inwards at the top and tied together.[2] Just as bronze instruments survived from an earlier stage of culture in some religious rites at Rome, so, I imagine, did this ancient form of dwelling, which really belongs to an age previous to that of permanent settlement and agricultural routine. The hut circles of the neolithic age, such as are abundant on Dartmoor, were probably roofed with branches supported by a central pole.[3]

---

[1] See *e.g.* Helbig, *Die Italiker in der Poebene*, p. 50 foll. Lanciani, *Ruins and Excavations of Ancient Rome*, p. 132. It is worth noting that in a passage quoted by Helbig, Plutarch (*Numa* 8) uses for some of the most ancient Roman attempts at temple building the same word by which he describes the booths at the feast of tabernacles (καλιάδες).

[2] Whether there was in later days any special religious signification in the use of green foliage and branches I will not undertake to say, but I have been struck by the constant use of them in cases of religious seclusion, even where the person is secluded in some part of the house, and not outside it. See *e.g. G.B.* ii. pp. 205-214.

[3] Prof. Anwyl, *Celtic Religion* (Constable's series), p. 10. Mr. Baring-Gould told Mr. Anwyl that he had seen in some of the Dartmoor circles central holes which seemed meant for the fixing of this pole. I will add here that it has occurred to me that these huts must, in one sense at least, be a survival (like other points of ritual), from the days of pastoral life, and of the migration of the Aryans. Temporary huts are characteristic of pastoral as contrasted with agricultural life, and must have been used during the wanderings, as by the Israelites. See Schrader, *Prehistoric Antiquities of the Aryan Peoples* (Eng. Trans., London, 1890), p. 404.

APPENDIX II

Prof. Deubner's Theory of the Lupercalia
(See pp. 34 and 106)

In the *Archiv für Religionswissenschaft*, 1910, p. 481 foll., Prof. Deubner has published an interesting study of this puzzling festival, to which I wish to invite attention, though it has reached me too late for use in my earlier lectures.

It has long been clear to me that any attempt to explain the details of the Lupercalia on a single hypothesis must be a failure. If all the details belong to the same age and the same original festival, we cannot recover the key to the whole ceremonial, though we may succeed in interpreting certain features of it with some success. Is it, however, possible that these details belong to *different* periods,—that the whole rite, as we know it, with all the details put together from different sources of knowledge, was the result of an accretion of various features upon an original simple basis of ceremonial? Prof. Deubner answers this question in the affirmative, and works out his answer with much skill and learning.

He begins by explaining the word *lupercus* as derived from *lupus* and *arceo*, and meaning a "keeper off of wolves." The *luperci* were originally men chosen from two gentes or families to keep the wolves from the sheepfolds, in the days when the Palatine was a shepherd's settlement, and they did it by running round the base of the hill in a magical circle (if I understand him rightly). If that be so, we need not assume a deity Lupercus, nor in fact any deity at all, nor need we see in the runners a quasi-dramatic representation of wolves as vegetation-spirits, as Mannhardt proposed (see my *Roman Festivals*, p. 316 foll.). This view has the advantage of making the rite a simple and practical one, such as would be natural to primitive Latins ; and the etymology is apparently unexceptionable, though it will doubtless be criticised, as in fact it has been long ago.

478

But in course of time, Prof. Deubner goes on, there came to be engrafted on this simple rite of circumambulation without reference to a deity, a festival of the rustic god Faunus; and now there was added a sacrifice of goats, which seem to have been his favourite victims (kids in Hor. *Odes*, iii. 18). The *luperci*, who had formerly run round the hill quite naked, as in many rites of the kind (see p. 491), now girt themselves with the skins of the goats, in order to increase their "religious force" in keeping away the wolves, with strength derived from the victims.

But the *luperci* also carried in their hands, in the festival as we know it, strips of the skins of the victims, with which they struck at women who offered themselves to the blows, in order to make them fertile. This, Prof. Deubner thinks, was a still later accretion. Life in a city had obliterated the original meaning of the rite—the keeping off wolves; but a new meaning becomes attached to it, presumably growing out of the use of the skins as magical instruments of additional force. Here, too, Juno first appears on the scene as the deity of women, for the strips were known as *amicula Iunonis* (*R.F.* 321 and note). The strips may have been substituted for something carried in the hand to drive away the wolves; the goat, it should be noted, is prominent in the cult of Juno, *e.g.* at Lanuvium. The mystical meaning of striking or flogging has been sufficiently explained in this instance by Mannhardt (*R.F.* p. 320), and is now familiar to anthropologists in other contexts.

In the period when the fertilisation of women became the leading feature of the rite, the State took up the popular festival, and it gained admittance to the religious calendar, which was drawn up for the city of the four regions (see above, Lect. IV., p. 106). The State was represented, as we learn from Ovid, by the Flamen Dialis (*Fasti*, ii. 282).

But we still have to account for some strange detail, which has never been satisfactorily explained in connection with the rest of the ceremony. The runners had their foreheads smeared with the blood of the victims, which was then wiped off with wool dipped in milk; after which, says Plutarch (*Romulus*, 21), they were obliged to laugh. These details, as Prof. Deubner remarks, seem very un-Roman; we have no parallel to them in Roman ritual, and I have remarked more than once in these lectures on the absence of the use of blood in Roman ceremonial. I have suggested that they were allowed to survive in the religion of the city-state, though actually belonging to that of a primitive population living on the site of Rome. Prof.

Deubner's explanation is very different, and at first sight startling. These, he thinks, are Greek cathartic details added by Augustus when he re-organised the Lupercalia, as we may guess that he did from Suet. *Aug.* 31. They can all be paralleled from Greek religion. We know of them only from Plutarch, who quotes a certain Butas as writing Greek elegiacs in which they were mentioned; but of the date of this poet we know nothing. Ovid does not mention these details, nor hint at them in the stories he tells about the festival. (It is certainly possible that Augustus's revision may have been made after Ovid wrote the second book of the *Fasti*; it could not have been done until he became Pont. Max. in 12 B.C., and perhaps not till long after that, and the *Fasti* was written some time before Ovid's banishment in A.D. 9.) That Augustus should insert Greek cathartic details in the old Roman festival is certainly surprising, but not impossible. We know that in the *ludi saeculares* he took great pains to combine Greek with Roman ritual.

The above is a mere outline of Prof. Deubner's article, but enough, I hope, to attract the attention of English scholars to it. Whether or no it be accepted in whole or part by learned opinion, it will at least have the credit of suggesting a way in which not only the Lupercalia, but possibly other obscure rites, may be compelled ultimately to yield up their secrets.

APPENDIX III

THE first paired deity mentioned by Gellius is *Lua Saturni*, also known as *Lua Mater*, of whom Dr. Frazer writes (p. 412), "In regard to Lua we know that she was spoken of as a mother, which makes it not improbable that she was also a wife." We are not surprised to find him claiming that because Vesta is addressed as Mater in the *Acta Fratr. Arv.* (Henzen, p. 147), that virgin deity was also married. This he does in his lectures on Kingship (p. 222), quoting Ennius and Lactantius as making Vesta mother of Saturnus and Titan. No comment on this is needed for any one conversant with Graeco-Roman religion and literature from Ennius onward. The title Mater here means simply that Vesta was to her worshippers in a maternal position : "quamvis virginem, ındole tamen quadam materna praeditam fuisse nuper exposuit Preunerus," says Henzen, quoting Preuner's *Hestia-Vesta*, an old book but a good one (p. 333). But to return to Lua : I freely confess that I cannot explain why she was styled Mater. We only know of her, apart from the list in Gellius and one passage of Servius, from the two passages of Livy quoted without comment by Dr. Frazer. The first of these (viii. 1), which may be taken from the pontifical books, seems to let in a ray of light on her nature and function. In 338 B.C. the Volscians had been beaten, and "armorum magna vis" was found in their camp. "Ea Luae Matri se dare consul dixit, finesque hostium usque ad maritimam oram depopulatus est." That is, as I understand the words, he dedicated the enemy's spoils to the *numen* who was the enemy of his own crops.[1] For if Lua be connected etymologically with *lues*, she may be the hurtful aspect of Saturnus, like *Tursa Cerfia Cerfii Martii* as Buecheler explains it (*Umbrica*, p. 98).

---

[1] For the taboo on such spoils, and their destruction, see M. S. Reinach's interesting paper "Tarpeia," in *Cultes, mythes, et religions*, iii. 221 foll.

A curious passage of Servius may be quoted in support of this view, in which Luae is an almost certain correction for Lunae (see Jordan's edition of Preller's *Rom. Mythol.* vol. ii. p. 22). Commenting on Virgil's "Arboribusque satisque lues" (*Aen.* iii. 139), he writes: "quidam dicunt, diversis numinibus vel bene vel male faciendi potestatem dicatam, ut Veneri coniugia, Cereri divortia, Iunoni procreationem liberorum: sterilitatem horum tam Saturno quam Luae, hanc enim sicut Saturnum orbandi potestatem habere." Whatever Lua may originally have been, she seems to have been regarded as a power capable of working for evil in the crops and in women; if you could get her to work on your enemy's crops (cp. the *excantatio*, above p. 58), so much the better, and the better would her claim be to the title of Mater (but Dr. Frazer supplies us with examples of a *hostile* spirit being called by a family name, *e.g.*, Grandfather Smallpox, *G.B.* iii. p. 98). When the consul had dedicated the spoils to her he proceeded to assist her in her functions by ravaging the crops of the enemy; thus she became later on a deity of spoils. In the Macedonian triumph of B.C. 167 we find her in company with Mars and Minerva as one of the deities to whom "spolia hostium dicare ius fasque est" (Livy xlv. 33).

I may add here that Dr. Frazer has another arrow in his quiver to prove that Saturnus was married: if Lua was not his wife (which no Roman asserts) certainly (he says) Ops was. He quotes a few words from Macrobius (i. 13. 19) in which these two are mentioned as husband and wife. If he had quoted the whole passage, his reader would have been better able to judge of the value of the writers of whom Macrobius says that they "crediderunt" that Ops was wife of Saturn. For it appears that some of them fancied that Saturnus was "a satu dictus *cuius causa de caelo est*"—(a desperate attempt to make the old spirit of the seed into a heaven-god), while Ops, whose name speaks for itself, was the earth. But the real companion deity to Ops was not Saturnus, but Consus. This has been placed beyond all reasonable doubt by Wissowa in his *de Feriis* (reprinted in *Gesammelte Abhandlungen*, p. 154 foll.). See also my *R.F.* p. 212. The names Ops and Consus obviously refer to stored corn, and everything in their cult points the same way. Saturnus' connection with Ops is a late and a mistaken one, derived from the Graecising tendency, which brought Cronos and Rhea to bear on them.

Next a word about Hora Quirini. As this coupling of names is followed by Virites Quirini, in the characteristic method explained in the text (cp. Cic. *Nat. Deor.* ii. 27 of Vesta, "*vis* eius ad aras et focos pertinet "), it is hardly necessary to comment on it. Hora is perhaps connected with Umbrian Heris (cp. Buecheler, *Umbrica*, index), which with kindred forms means will, willingness. Thus in " Nerienem Mavortis et Herem" (Ennius, fragm. 70, in Baehrens, *Fragm. Poet. Lat.*) we may see the strength and the will of Mars (cp. Herie Iunonis). Hora is also connected in legend with Hersilia (Ov. *Met.* 14. 829), and this helps to show how the Alexandrian erotic legend-making faculty got hold of her. But, says Dr. Frazer, Ennius regarded her as wife of Quirinus : " Teque Quirine pater veneror, Horamque Quirini " (fragm. 71 of the *Annales*). This is Dr. Frazer's interpretation of the words, but Ennius says nothing of conjugal relations ; and even if he had, his evidence as to ancient Roman conceptions would be worthless. Ennius was not a Roman ; he came from Magna Graecia ; and if Dr. Frazer will read *all* that is said about him, *e.g.* in Schanz's history of Roman literature, he will allow that every statement of such a man about old Roman ideas of the divine must be regarded with suspicion and subjected to careful criticism.

Next we come to Salacia Neptuni. Of this couple Dr. Frazer says that Varro plainly implies that they were husband and wife, and that this is affirmed by Augustine, Seneca, and Servius. The accumulation of evidence seems strong ; but Varro implies nothing of the kind (*L.L.* v. 72). He is indulging in fancy etymologies, and derives Neptunus from *nubere*, "quod mare terras obnubit ut nubes caelum, ab nuptu id est opertione ut antiqui, a quo nuptiae, nuptus dictus." If he had meant to make Salacia wife of Neptunus, this last sentence would surely have suggested it ; but he goes on after a full stop, "Salacia Neptuni a salo." It is only the later writers, ignorant of the real nature of Roman religious ideas, who make Salacia into a wife. It is worth noting that Varro adds another feminine deity in his next sentence, Venilia, whom Virgil makes the mother of Turnus (*Aen.* x. 76) ; and Servius, commenting on this line, goes one better, and says she was identical with Salacia. Perhaps both were sea or water spirits, connected with Neptunus as *famulae* or *anculae* (see Wissowa, *R.K.* p. 19), but they are lost to us, and speculation is useless. In *R.F.* p. 186, I suggested an explanation of Salacia which I am disposed to withdraw. But for anyone wishing to study the treatment of old Roman *numina* by the mythologists and philosophers of the Graeco-Roman period, I would recommend an attentive reading of the whole chapter of Augustine from which Dr. Frazer quotes a few words (*C.D.* vii. 22) ; and further a careful study of the Graeco-

Roman methods of fabricating myths about Roman divine names, for which he will do well to read the passages referred to by Wissowa in *R.K.* pp. 250 and 251, and notes.

Lastly, comes Maia Volcani.   Here for once we get a fact of cult, which is a relief, after the loose and reckless statements of non-Roman and Christian writers.   The flamen Volcanalis sacrificed to Maia on May 1st, which proves that there was a real and not a fancied connection between Volcanus and Maia, but certainly not that they were husband and wife.   Dr. Frazer, however, quotes Cincius " on the *Fasti* " as (ap. Macrob. i. 12. 18) stating this, and refers us to Schanz's *Gesch. der röm. Lit.* for information about him.   In the second edition of that work he will find a discussion of the very doubtful question as to whether the Cincius he quotes is the person whom he asserts him to be, viz., the annalist of the second Punic War.   The writer of the article " Cincius " in Pauly-Wissowa *Real-Encycl.* is very confident that the one who wrote on the *Fasti* lived as late as the age of Augustus.   But putting that aside, what are we to make of the fact that another annalist, L. Calpurnius Piso (famous as the author of the first lex de repetundis, 149 B.C.), said that the wife of Volcanus was not Maia, but Maiestas ?   Piso was not a good authority (see above, p. 51), but he seems here to bring the "consort" of the fire-god into line with such expressions of activity as Moles, Virites, and so on ; and it seems that as early as the second century B.C., sport and speculation with these names were beginning.   I have quoted the whole pedantic passage from Macrobius in my *Roman Festivals*, p. 98, where the reader may enjoy it at leisure.   I shall not be surprised if he comes to the conclusion that neither Macrobius nor his learned informers knew anything about Maia.   When he reads that she was the mother of Mercurius, he will recollect that Mercurius was not a Roman deity of the earliest period, and did not belong to the *di indigetes* ; and when he finds that that she is identified with Bona Dea, he must not forget that that deity, as scholars are now pretty well agreed, was introduced at Rome from Tarentum in the age of the Punic Wars.   The one fact we know is the sacrifice by the flamen Volcanalis on May 1.   Someone went to work to explain this and another, viz. that the Ides of the month was the dedication day of the first temple of Mercurius (B.C. 495), and also the fact that the temple of the Bona Dea on the Aventine was dedicated on the Kalends.   The result was an extraordinary jumble of fancy and myth, which has been recognised as such by those who have studied closely the methods of Graeco-Roman scholarship.   The unwary, of course, are taken in. A student of these methods might do well to take as an exercise in criticism the three "specimens of Roman mythology" which Dr. Frazer says (p. 413) have "survived the wreck of antiquity"—the loves of Vertumnus and Pomona, of Jupiter and Juturna, of Janus and Cardea. In the last of these especially he will find one of the most audacious pieces of charming and wilful invention that a Latin poet could perpetrate, in imitation of Hellenistic love tales, and to suit the taste of a public whose education was mainly Greek.

The above lengthy note was written before I had seen von Domaszewski's paper on this subject ("Festschrift für O. Hirschfeld") reprinted in *Abhandlungen zur röm. Religion*, p. 104 foll. cp. p. 162.) His explanations are different in detail from mine, but rest on the same general principle that the names Salacia, etc., indicate functions or attributes of the male deity to whom they are attached.

APPENDIX IV

(Lecture VIII., page 169 foll.) Ius and Fas

In historical times the two kinds of *ius*, *divinum* and *humanum*, were strongly distinguished (see Wissowa, *R.K.* p. 318, who quotes Gaius ii. 2 : " summa itaque rerum divisio in duos articulos diducitur, nam aliae sunt divini iuris, aliae humani "). But it is almost certain that there was originally no such clear distinction. The general opinion of historians of Roman law is thus expressed by Cuq (*Institutions juridiques des Romains*, p. 54) : " Le droit civil n'a eu d'abord qu'une portée fort restreinte. Peu à peu il a gagné du terrain, il a entrepris de réglementer des rapports qui autrefois étaient du domaine de la religion. Pendant longtemps à Rome le droit théocratique a coexisté avec le droit civil." (See also Muirhead, *Introduction to Roman Law*, ed. Goudy, p. 15.) Possibly the formation of an organised calendar, marking off the days belonging to the deities from those which were not so made over to them, first gave the opportunity for the gradual realisation of the thought that the set of rules under which the citizen was responsible to the divine beings was not exactly the same as that under which he was responsible to the civil authorities. The distinction took many ages to realise in all its aspects, and is not complete even under the XII. Tables or later, because the sanction for civil offences remained in great part a divine one; on this point Jhering is certainly wrong (*Geist des röm. Rechts*, i. 267 foll.). As Cuq remarks (p. 54, note 1), one institution of the *ius divinum* kept its force after the complete secularisation of law, and retains it to this day, viz. the oath.

If there was originally no distinction between religious and civil rules of law, it follows that there were originally no two distinguishing terms for them. The earliest passage in which they are distinguished as *ius divinum* and *humanum* (so far as I know) is Cicero's speech for Sestius (B.C. 56), sec. 91, quoted by

Wissowa, p. 319 : " domicilia coniuncta quas urbes dicimus, *invento et divino iure et humano*, moenibus cinxerunt." But by all British writers on Roman law, and by many foreign ones, the word *fas* is used as equivalent to the ius divinum, and sharply distinguished from *ius*. Thus the late Dr. Greenidge, in his useful work on Roman public life (p. 52 and elsewhere), makes this distinction ; he writes of the *rex* as the chief expounder of the divine law (*fas*), and of the control exercised by *fas* over the citizen's life. Cp. Muirhead, ed. Goudy, p. 15 foll., where Mommsen is quoted thus : "Mommsen is probably near the mark when he describes the *leges regiae* as mostly rules of the *fas*." But Mommsen, like Wissowa in his *Religion und Kultus*, does not use the word *fas*, but speaks of "Sakralrecht." Sohm, on the other hand (*Roman Law*, trans. Ledlie, p. 15, note), compares *fas* with Sanscrit *dharma* and Greek *themis*, as meaning unwritten rules of divine origin, which eventually gave way before *ius*, as in Greece before δίκαιον. (Cp. Binder, *Die Plebs*, p. 501.) But it is safer in this case to leave etymology alone, and to try to discover what the Romans themselves understood by *fas*, which is indeed a peculiar and puzzling word. (For its possible connection with *fari*, *effari* (ager effatus), *fanum*, and *profanum*, etc., see H. Nettleship's *Contributions to Latin Lexicography*, s.v. " Fas.")

Fas was at all times indeclinable, and is rarely found even as an accusative, as in Virg. *Aen*. ix. 96 :

> mortaline manu factae immortale carinae
> fas habeant ?

In the oldest examples of its use, *i.e.* in the ancient calendar QRCF, on March 24 and May 24, *i.e.* " quando rex comitiavit fas" (Varro, *L.L.* vi. 31), and QStDF on June 15, *i.e.* " Quando stercus delatum fas " (Varro, *L.L.* vi. 32), it is hard to say whether it is a substantive at all, and not rather an adverb like *satis*. So, too, in the antique language of the *lex templi* of Furfo (58 B.C.) we read, " Utii tangere sarcire tegere devehere defigere mandare ferro oeti promovere referre *fasque esto* " (*liceat* should probably be inserted before *fasque esto*). See *CIL*. i. 603, line 7 ; Dessau, *Inscript. Lat. selectae*, ii. 1. 4906, p. 246. In these examples *fas* simply means that you may do certain acts without breaking religious law; it does not stand for the religious law itself. To me it looks like a technical word of the *ius divinum*, meaning that which it is lawful to do under it ; thus a *dies fastus* is one on which it is lawful under that *ius* to perform certain acts of civil government, "sine piaculo " (Varro, *L.L.* vi. 29). *Nefas* is, therefore, in the same way a word which conveys a prohibition under the divine law.   By constant juxtaposition with *ius, fas* came in course of time to take on the character of a substantive, and so too did its opposite *nefas*.   The dictionaries supply many examples of its use as a substantive and as paralleled with *ius*, but the only one I can find that is earlier than Cicero is Terence, *Hecyra*, iii. 3. 27, *i.e.* in the work of a non-Roman.

I cannot find that it is so used by Varro, where we might naturally have expected it.   Cicero does not call his imaginary ius divinum a *fas*, but iura religionum, constitutio religionum (*de Legibus* ii. 10-23, 17-32).   *Ius* is the word always used technically of particular departments of the religious law, *e.g.* ius pontificium, ius augurale, and ius fetiale (*CIL.* i. p. 202, is preimus ius fetiale paravit).   The notion that *fas* could mean a kind of code of religious law is probably due to Virgil's use of the word in "Quippe etiam festis quaeddam exercere diebus Fas et iura sinunt," *Georg.* i. 269, and to the comment of Servius, "id est, divina humanaque iura permittunt: nam ad religionem fas, ad homines iura pertinent."

It is strange to find it personified as a kind of deity in the formula of the fetiales, used when they announced the Roman demands at an enemy's frontier (Livy i. 32): "Audi Iuppiter, inquit, audite Fines (cuiuscunque gentis sunt nominat), *audiat Fas.*"   Whence did Livy get this formula ?   We have no record of a book of the fetiales ; if this came from those of the pontifices, as is probable, the formula need not be of ancient date, and the personification of Fines also suggests a doubt as to the genuineness of the whole formula.

APPENDIX V

THE WORSHIP OF SACRED UTENSILS (page 436)

THERE can be no doubt that some kind of worship was paid by the Arval Brethren to certain *ollae*, or primitive vessels of sun-baked clay used in their most ancient rites. This is attested by two inscriptions of different ages which are printed on pp. 26 and 27 of Henzen's *Acta Fratrum Arvalium*. After leaving their grove and entering the temple "in mensa *sacrum fecerunt ollis*"; and shortly afterwards, "in aedem intraverunt et *ollas precati sunt.*" Then, to our astonishment, we read that the door of the temple was opened, and the *ollae* thrown down the slope in front of it. This last act seems inexplicable; but the worship finds a singular parallel in the dairy ritual of the Todas of the Nilghiri hills.

Dr. Rivers, in his work on the Todas (Macmillan, 1906, p. 453), in summing up his impressions of their worship, observes that "the attitude of worship which is undoubtedly present in the Toda mind is becoming transferred from the gods themselves to the material objects used in the service of the gods." "The religious attitude of worship is being transferred from the gods themselves *to the objects round which centres the ritual of the dairy.*" These objects are mainly the bells of the buffaloes and the dairy vessels; and an explicit account of them, the reverence in which they are held, and the prayers in which they are mentioned, will be found in the fifth, sixth, and eighth chapters of Dr. Rivers' work, which, as an account of what seems to be a religion atrophied by over-development of ritual, is in many ways of great interest to the student of Roman religious experience. The following sentence will appeal to the readers of these Lectures :—

"The Todas seem to show us how the over-development of the ritual aspect of religion may lead to atrophy of those ideas and beliefs through which the religion has been built up; and then how, in its turn, the ritual may suffer, and acts which are performed mechanically, with no living ideas behind them, may come to be performed carelessly and incompletely, while religious observances which involve trouble and discomfort may be evaded or completely neglected."

Whether the worship of the *ollae* was a part of the original ritual of the Brethren, or grew up after its revival by Augustus, it is impossible to determine. But if we can allow the dairy ritual of the Todas to help us in the matter, we may conclude that in any case it was not really primitive, and that it was a result of that process of over-ritualisation to which must also be ascribed the *piacula* caused by the growth of a fig-tree on the roof of the temple, and the three Sondergötter Adolenda Commolenda Deferunda. (See above p. 161 foll., and Henzen, *Acta Fratr. Arv.* p. 147.)

INDEX

Acca Larentia, 67
Acolytes, 177
Adolenda, 162
Adolenda Commolenda Deferunda, 162, 490
Aedes Vestae : see Vesta
Aediles, plebeian, 255
Aemilius Paulus, 340, 362, 433
Aeneid, the, 119, 206, 230, 250, 251 ; as a means of understanding the spirit of the Roman religion, 254 ; a poem of religion and morals, 409-425
Aesculapius, 260
Ager paganus : lustration, 80, 213
  Romanus : lustration, 78, 100
Agriculture, the economic basis of Roman life, 99 ; festivals, *see* Festivals
Agrippa, 442, 443
Alba Longa, 109, 128
Alban Mount : Latin festival, 172 ; temple of Jupiter Latiaris, 237, 238, 245
Alexander, Archibald, on faith, 472
Ambarvalia, procession of the, 214, 218, 442
Amburbium, 214, 218, 332
Amulets, 42, 59, 60, 74, 84
Ancilia, 97 ; lustration, 96, 217 ; moving, 36
Angerona, 117
Animism, 65, 122, 148, 164, 287
Anna Perenna : festival, 65, 105, 346 ; Ovid's account of, 473
Antoninus Pius, 429
Apollo, 257, 449 ; cult of, 268 ; associated with Diana, 443, 446 ; with Latona, 262 ; the Pythian, 323 ; temple, 443-445 ; institution of Apolline games, 326
Appius Claudius, 300
Aquaelicium, ceremony of the, 50, 52

Ara, meaning of, 146
Ara Maxima in the Forum Boarium, 29, 230
Ara Pacis of Augustus, 177, 437, 448
Argei : festival, 36, 65 ; puppets thrown into the Tiber, 54, 105, 321, 322 ; chapels called, 321, 322
Armilustrium, 97
Army : lustration of, 96, 100, 215, 217
Arnobius, 51, 52, 459, 461, 465
Artemis, 235, 443
Arval Brethren : see Fratres Arvales
Asclepios, 260
Astrology, 396-398, 401
Ateius Capito, 441
Athene Polias, 234
Attalus, king of Pergamus, 330
Atticus, Cicero's letters to, 385
Attus Navius, soothsayer, 297
Augurium canarium, 310
Augurs, 174-176, 193, 271, 276 ; and the art of divination, 292-309 ; in relation to the Rex, 301 ; art strictly secret, 301 ; compared with pontifices, 303 ; lore preserved in books 303 ; political importance, 305
Augustus, 35, 133, 213, 344 ; revival of religion, 428-447 ; his connection with Virgil, 428 ; pontifex maximus, 433 ; restoration of temples, 433 - 434 ; revival of ancient ritual, 434-436 ; restorer of the *pax deorum*, 438
Aurelius, Marcus, 456
Auspicia, 175, 214 ; in life of family, 299 ; in State operations, 300 ; indissolubly connected with *imperium*, 301
Aust, on religion of the family, 68 ; on Roman deities, 157 ; on prayer,

THE END

Printed in Great Britain by R. & R. CLARK, LIMITED, *Edinburgh.*